The Golden Age of

WIDER

Studies in Development Economics embody the output of the research programmes of the World Institute for Development Economics Research (WIDER), which was established by the United Nations University as its first research and training centre in 1984 and started work in Helsinki in 1985. The principal purpose of the Institute is to help identify and meet the need for policy-oriented socio-economic research on pressing global and development problems, as well as common domestic problems and their interrelationships.

The Golden Age of Capitalism

Reinterpreting the Postwar Experience

Edited by
Stephen A. Marglin
and
Juliet B. Schor

Clarendon Press · Oxford

Oxford University Press, Walton Street, Oxford OX2 6DP
Oxford New York Toronto
Delhi Bombay Calcutta Madras Karachi
Petaling Jaya Singapore Hong Kong Tokyo
Nairobi Dar es Salaam Cape Town
Melbourne Auckland
and associated companies in
Berlin Ibadan

Oxford is a trade mark of Oxford University Press

Published in the United States
by Oxford University Press, New York

First published 1990
Hardback reprinted 1991
First issued in Clarendon Paperbacks 1991

British Library Cataloguing in Publication Data
The Golden age of capitalism.—(WIDER studies in
development economics).
1. Economic development. Role of capitalism, history
I. Marglin, Stephen A. (Stephen Alan), 1983–   II. Schor,
Juliet B.   III. Series
330.12'2'09
ISBN 0–19–828677–5
ISBN 0–19–828741–0 (Pbk)

Library of Congress Cataloging in Publication Data
The Golden age of capitalism/edited by Stephen A. Marglin and Juliet
B. Schor.
p.   cm. — (WIDER studies in development economics)
Includes bibliographical references.
1. Capitalism.   2. Economic policy.   3. Economic development.
4. Economic history — 1984–   I. Marglin, Stephen A.   II. Schor,
Juliet.   III. Series.
HB501.G584   1990   330.12'2—dc20   90–23055
ISBN 0–19–828677–5
ISBN 0–19–828741–0 (Pbk)

Printed in Great Britain
by Biddles Ltd.
Guildford and King's Lynn

Preface

Whenever we try to predict or shape the future, it is invariably in the image of our understanding of the past. This is especially so in areas as complex as economic policy-making at a national level, and policy coordination at an international level. In trying to indicate the directions in which economic policies need to proceed both nationally and internationally during the 1990s, this volume draws inspiration from an analysis of the 'golden age' of the post-war economic boom, and tries to blend historical analysis with economic theory. It marks, I believe, an important stage in the continuing development of economics.

It would be foolish to imagine that we can somehow reproduce in the 1990s the conditions which gave rise to the rapid growth of the 1950s and 1960s. It would be even more foolish, however, to ignore the experience of those years. At least we have one advantage over the policy-makers and economists who struggled to understand the post-World War II system at the time, which is, that we know that the system broke down. But why it collapsed remains a controversial yet highly relevant issue.

Was the fundamental cause of the breakdown the structure of the international economic order itself? Did the system collapse through its 'internal contradictions', as some economists predicted at the time? Or was the international system itself made possible only by a unique set of conditions at the national level, the weakening of which undermined its foundations? Was the collapse of the 1970s the result of accidental nominal and real 'shocks' (a concept that only entered the economic vocabulary during that decade), or was it rather due to the inevitable working-out of long-term systemic, forces? The answer suggested by the research presented in this volume is that both domestic and international conditions were required to sustain the 'golden age'; and that it broke down when these forces ceased reinforcing one another, and began instead to undermine one other.

Chapter 1, by Stephen Marglin, introduces the volume by providing an overview of the historical and theoretical arguments of the book. The lesson I would urge upon readers is the distinction drawn between what I would call *causes* and *triggers*. Conventional wisdom dates the end of the 'golden age' by the first oil shock, OPEC I, in 1973. The second oil shock, OPEC II in 1979, in turn is conventionally argued to have ushered in the current phase of neo-liberalism, monetarism, and the return to the market. In Marglin's argument, by contrast, OPEC I and OPEC II are not fundamental causes but triggers which set off forces that had deep roots in the internal economies of the industrial countries and in the relationships among them and between them and the Third World. OPEC I triggered reactions to a full employment profit squeeze which was well under way before OPEC appeared as an actor on the world stage. OPEC II triggered the retreat from growth-oriented policies. But the climate in which growth could continue had already been destroyed by the demise of US hegemony, a process which also was well under way by the end of the 1960s and was signalled by the suspension of gold convertibility and the breakdown of the Bretton Woods system between 1969 and 1973. We may summarize in tabular form the relationship between the underlying reasons why different periods of postwar capitalism ended ('causes') and the events that sparked off these ends ('triggers').

The periods of postwar capitalism, why they ended and the triggering events

Period	Cause of period's end	Triggers
Golden age (1950s and 1960s)	Full employment profit squeeze (late 1960s and early 1970s)	OPEC I
Transition—golden age policies without golden age structures (1970s)	Demise of American hegemony (late 1960s and 1970s)	OPEC II
Neo-liberalism (1980s)	?	?

The historically oriented analysis by Andrew Glyn, Alan Hughes, Alain Lipietz, and Ajit Singh in Chapter 2 is concerned with the six major OECD countries (France, Germany, Italy, Japan, United Kingdom and United States) during the 'golden age' and its aftermath. The chapter follows the 'regulation' approach invented by French economists such as Michel Aglietta, Robert Boyer, and Alain Lipietz, and developed as well by Americans such as David Gordon and Michael Piore. The important innovation developed in this volume is the emphasis on the *interaction* of internal and external forces, forces operating within each country and forces operating in the international arena. By developing this interplay of domestic and international forces, this chapter tells the story of how once mutually reinforcing institutional structures became mutually destructive.

Chapter 2 is supplemented, in Chapter 3, by a more systematic analysis of the nature of demand management. Gerald Epstein and Juliet Schor show that monetary policy in particular was very important, first in accommodating the post-war boom and later, in restricting demand during the phase of stagnation. The central contribution of the chapter lies in its attention to the institutional requirements for policy-making, especially the implications of the degree of independence enjoyed by central banks in formulating national monetary policies. Epstein and Schor find that the UK and the US, two countries with independent central banks, pursued significantly more restrictive monetary policies during the 'golden age'. By contrast, the continental countries and Japan had much more accommodating policies. Given contemporary enthusiasm for monetarist-type approaches and increased central bank independence, it is worth remembering that during the 'golden age' these more accommodating countries posted significantly higher growth rates than the US and the UK.

These analyses of post-war economic history and policy provide a rich background for theorizing. Chapter 4 by Stephen Marglin and Amit Bhaduri and Chapter 5 by Samuel Bowles and Robert Boyer take up this challenge, and provide a sharper theoretical formulation to selected aspects of the historical analysis.

Marglin and Bhaduri explain the importance of the macroeconomic 'climate', especially the investment climate, in generating different economic regimes according to differences in the relationship between real wages and investment and hence employment. The empirical investigation of this issue has been inconclusive so far, and, for any econometric study indicating a positive relationship between these variables, one can find another study indicating a negative relationship, or indeed no relationship at all. Yet a resolution of the issue remains important as policy-makers in developed countries invariably act as if they believed that higher real wages always lead to higher unemployment.

The impact of a wage change on economic growth and employment is complex. There are two effects on demand. Consider the impact of a fall in wages. A wage reduction will lower consumption demand. Whether there is an offsetting rise in investment demand depends on the responsiveness of the individual firm to a higher profit margin as wage costs fall. What happens to *aggregate* demand and employment, therefore, depends crucially on how vigourous the 'animal spirits' (in Keynes's phrase) of entrepreneurs are. Corresponding to whether 'animal spirits' are weak or strong, the analysis distinguishes between a 'stagnationist' and an 'exhilarationist' Keynesian regime. In the former, a fall in wages always lowers aggregate demand through the effect on consumption. In the latter, it raises aggregate demand by stimulating investment.

This work defines the relationship between real wages and unemployment in a manner which sheds light on the crucial policy issue. Consider a wage increase. In the 'stagnationist' regime higher real wages do *not* lead to higher unemployment; the adverse effects on incentives to invest resulting from lower profit margins do *not* offset the beneficial effects of higher wages on demand. By contrast, in the 'exhilarationist' case investment effects dominate, and higher real wages *do* lead to higher unemployment. In the 'stagnationist' case higher real wages are indeed necessary to promote a process of wage-led growth; in the 'exhilarationist' case higher real wages interfere with investment-led growth, so that wage restraint becomes the preferred policy stance.

In Chapter 5, Bowles and Boyer focus on the theoretical implications of another aspect of the institutional arrangements that went into the making and unmaking of the 'golden age', namely the relations between capital and labour and the organization of the labour process. They arrive at theoretical results complementary in many ways to those obtained by Marglin and Bhaduri. Their paper integrates the Marxian insight of the importance of the labour process with modern-day macroeconomic analysis, and the 'labour extraction function' in their scheme has a role analogous to the 'investment function' in more traditional Keynesian analysis (e.g. that of Marglin and Bhaduri in Chapter 4). In particular, close analogues of 'exhilarationist' and 'stagnationist' regimes emerge from an analysis of the incentive effects of wages and unemployment on effort and productivity.

The two final chapters of the book by Rowthorn and Glyn and by Aoki draw out more explicitly the lessons of the past for formulating future policies. In my view, they reinforce the basic thrust of this book, namely that the formulation of future economic policies must proceed from an intelligent understanding of previous experience. The first analyses the experience of various countries in coping with unemployment after the 'golden age' of capitalism began to tarnish in the 1970s. This chapter shows that while the slowdown in growth has had adverse effects everywhere, the capacity of a country to maintain high levels of employment depended crucially on the existence of appropriate social, economic and political institutions, along with the ability to mobilize effective coalitions to act through these institutions. This, in the view of Rowthorn and Glyn, is the key to the superior performance of small countries—Austria, Sweden, and Norway—that are often seen as exemplars of the virtues of 'social corporatism'. This chapter has indeed stimulated a separate WIDER research project on the social corporatist model of economic management whose distinctive feature is the negotiation of a centralized wage bargain between employers and workers. This is being undertaken jointly with the Finnish Labour Research Institute and will include an assessment of Finnish experience in the 1980s along with that of countries where social corporatism has had more mixed results.

Aoki's contribution, which concludes the volume, addresses the question of how Japan has been able to maintain a rate of growth of labour productivity consistently at the forefront of the OECD countries. Aoki analyses the organization of production in the Japanese firm and contrasts it with the organization of production in the Western firm. In his view, superior flexibility, the ability to respond to local 'shocks', such as interruption in the supply of parts or the breakdown of a machine, results from the larger scope for workers to exercise initiative and is the key to the Japanese success story.

Aoki thus makes us question the bias in Western management theory and practice towards hierarchy and centralized control. The challenge Aoki presents to this bias may be important in unlearning the prejudices that clog our brains, which as Keynes taught long ago, is perhaps the single most important step in the formulation of solutions adequate to the magnitude of our economic problems. One of the important lessons of this volume is the necessity to restructure the relationship between labour and capital, and while no one may have either the wish or the ability to copy the Japanese system of production, everyone can learn from the Japanese experience.

My own recent preoccupations tempt me to apply some of the arguments of this volume to the problem of the persistent imbalances in international trade that plague the world economy today. It seems to me that the situation of the surplus countries, namely Germany and Japan, which are conventionally called upon to expand their economies in the interest of improved global macroeconomic co-ordination, can be understood in terms of the distinction drawn between 'stagnationist' and 'exhilarationist' regimes. Germany and Japan would, in terms of what we know about their entrepreneurial behaviour patterns, belong in the 'exhilarationist' category, where any slackening of consumption demand due to a policy of wage restraint is more than offset by the increased investment demand of dynamic entrepreneurs, so that *aggregate* demand also increases. *Per contra*, these are economies where higher real wages would mean lower *aggregate* demand because of the disproportionate fall in investment. The fears of policy-makers in these countries concerning higher real wages cannot simply be dismissed as illogical.

What is also important for Germany and Japan is the fact that aggregate demand stems, in their case, substantially from their export sectors as well, and from a significant build-up of export surpluses which triggers a foreign trade multiplier impact on their domestic economies. A higher real wage would thus, in all probability, *reduce* their international competitiveness and slacken the growth of effective demand at home. From this point of view also, wage restraint does indeed make sense as a national policy, as does its corollary, namely extreme caution in adopting expansionary domestic policies in the interests of improving the international balance of payments adjustment process..

But it remains an open question in what sense, and to what degree, this behaviour can be sustainable over time because, definitionally, the persistent Japanese and German export surpluses that result are the counterpart of deficits elsewhere in the world economy which must sooner or later be corrected. The problem is to ensure that the correction occurs while maintaining global economic activity at a high enough level. Leaving this to the discipline of the market alone would risk reducing activity unnecessarily, and perhaps disrupting global financial arrangements. Specifically, the problem is that of ensuring that the deflationary impact of the required turn-around in the US deficit is matched by corresponding expansion elsewhere, the conventional candidates for which are the surplus economies. Put another way, the positive contribution of the US deficit must be given its due amidst the hand-wringing about the US economy. Unless some substitute is found for this stimulus to world production, putting the American house in order may bring the world house down.

Yet there is today an alternative to surplus countries pursuing too far the expansionary policies that they are understandably reluctant to adopt, if their characterization as 'exhilarationist' regimes makes sense. This is that of their continuing to run moderate surpluses, and of seizing the extraordinary opportunity for global cooperation impli-cit in this. If some substantial part of Japan's and Germany's export surpluses could be diverted from financing the US deficit, towards supporting Third World development through long-term loans, this would enhance developing-country import capacity, currently being threatened by the 'double squeeze' of low primary commodity prices and a heavy debt servicing burden. In particular, the US payments deficit would benefit from larger exports to the Third World and a growth impulse restored thereby to the US economy. More gen-erally, it would help counter the deflationary bias implicit in the required correction of the US deficit placed by many analysts at between $150 to $200 billion and equivalent to 8 to 10 per cent of world exports, in a situation where the offsetting expansion in surplus economies seems both unlikely and unwarranted.

Any such switching of surpluses away from financing the US deficit towards financing Third World development raises complex issues of phasing, coordination and domestic policy reform in both the US and the developing countries. Recycling need not always be a euphemism for taking from the prudent to give to the profligate, for transfer in turn to the irresponsible, an accusation levelled against the private banking community who lent so boldly to developing countries in the 1970s. In a WIDER Study Group design for recycl-ing, the profligate would be appropriately disciplined, and the irres-ponsible penalized to a degree. The design involves an international debt reconstruction facility, which passes on the discounts on debt in secondary markets to developing countries in exchange for domestic policy reform packages. It looks to Japan to take an initiative and has attracted widespread international attention;[1] as the debt crisis worsens and Japan continues to run surpluses, the tide may well run in favour of solutions of this kind.

I must of course, leave it to the reader to decide how much this book improves our understanding of post-war economic history. But I do not hesitate to suggest that it has a particular value in the provocative blend of history and theory that it provides. There can be little doubt that this mode of analysis has continuing relevance. The book will serve its purpose if it acts as an antidote to ahistorical and vacuous, 'pure theory' exercises in economic analysis on the one hand, and unfocused historical description on the other.

Lal Jayawardena
Director, WIDER

NOTE

1. Saburo Okita, Lal Jayawardena and Arjun Sengupta, *Mobilizing International Surpluses for World Development, A WIDER Plan for a Japanese Initiative,* WIDER Study Group Series No. 2, May 1987. See, e.g., *London Financial Times,* 8 and 11 May 1987, *International Herald Tribune,* 29 May 1987, *The London Economist Financial Report,* 19 May 1987, *The Hindu,* International Edition, 16 May 1987.

Acknowledgements

The authors of this volume received help from a variety of sources. The members of WIDER's Macroeconomics Research Project contributed in two ways: by formulating the context of this research, and by offering constructive criticism of drafts of the chapters that follow.

The authors would also like to express their collective appreciation to guests at two meetings held in Helsinki in 1985 and 1986, particularly to Stephen Marris, and to A. J. Brown, Wendy Carlin, Richard Cooper, Robin Matthews, and Thomas Weisskopf.

Contents

WIDER Macroeconomics
Research Project

1
Lessons of the Golden Age:
An Overview

STEPHEN A. MARGLIN

This book, though directed towards the future, is largely about the past. Its premiss is that any attempt to restore economic performance in the OECD countries to the levels achieved in the 1950s and 1960s, the 'golden age' of twentieth-century capitalism, must be based on an understanding of the key economic arrangements of those years. How did these arrangements mutually interact to produce consistently high rates of growth—averaging over 4 per cent annually in the 1950s and near 5 per cent in the 1960s, compared with 3 per cent in the 1970s and 2 per cent in the 1980s? Equally important is an understanding of how these arrangements disintegrated. Were the problems essentially domestic ones, problems internal to the functioning of each national economy, or were the problems rather in the international sphere, in the political and economic relationships that linked national economies with one another? Only after answering basic questions such as these can one proceed to think constructively about economic reform and restructuring.

None of this is to be read as a suggestion that policy should be directed to reproducing the economic arrangements of the 1960s in the 1990s. Such an attempt runs counter to another premiss of this book, namely that economic arrangements are changed over time by their very functioning, by the actions conscious and unconscious of economic agents who modify the framework within which they operate, with the result that this framework continually evolves and to that extent is beyond the control of policy-makers. Policy-makers' freedom, to paraphrase Hegel, presupposes insight into the necessities which constrain their choices. To apply the lessons of the golden age, we must understand not only what allowed capitalism to deliver the goods for a reasonably long period of time, and where things went wrong, but also the ways in which the very success of the system in the 1950s and 1960s undermined it and eventually led to the drift of the 1970s and the stagnation of the 1980s. We must understand in what ways the givens of today's arrangements are different from those of yesterday's.

It is not necessarily for the worst that policy-makers do not have as free a hand as is sometimes imagined—especially given the present political mood and climate. It is all too easy to lose sight of the positive side of the changes which were instrumental in undoing the golden age. For instance, it will be argued that increasing labour militancy contributed importantly to the profit squeeze which in the late 1960s altered the economic climate to the detriment of capital accumulation and growth. But the other side of the coin to labour militancy was a real and substantial gain with respect both to working conditions and remuneration. The growth of the welfare state and the persistence of low unemployment may have made workers less responsive to pressures from their employers to increase productivity and maintain profits, but these features of the golden age also gave a new security and confidence to people whose lives had previously been characterized by all too little of both.

On the international side, it will be argued that the decline of American hegemony (the Greek *hegemon* means leader, but the English suggests an *imposed* leadership) not only contributed to the profit squeeze by making important raw materials—chiefly oil—more expensive, but more importantly ultimately crippled the use of fiscal and monetary policies to manage aggregate demand by the major players. But the end of American hegemony also reflected both the economic and political recovery of those belligerents—winners as well as losers—that had emerged from World War II with severely demaged economies and polities, and the emergence of new forces out of the wreck of the colonial empires that fell in the aftermath of war. Prosperity at the price of the dignity of individuals or nations would not be much of a bargain even if it were on the policy menu.

This book, then, seeks to understand the making and the unmaking of capitalism's golden age in terms of the arrangements which fostered sustained growth and high employment after World War II and the forces which undermined the effectiveness of these arrangements in the 1960s and, increasingly, in the 1970s. We make two passes at this target, one historical (Chapters 2 and 3) and one theoretical (Chapters 4 and 5). Chapter 2 discusses the historical evolution of the key arrangements, which together provided the historical framework of the post-war regime. First are the arrangements which shaped the macroeconomic climate internally, what we term the 'macroeconomic structure'. Second are the arrangements which framed the international economy, the 'international order'. Third are the institutions within which capital–labour relations evolved, here termed the 'system of production'. And finally the mechanisms for eliciting the requisite behaviour on the part of individual agents, the 'rules of co-ordination'. This four-part schema is in the first instance simply a classificatory device, a beginning of theory, and these four components appear one way or another in many descriptions of capitalist development (for example, Aglietta 1976; Bowles *et al.* 1983; Piore and Sabel 1984). But more than mere classification is at issue: our analysis focuses on the interactions between the macroeconomic structure and international order, the system of production, and the rules of co-ordination.

Chapter 3 has a narrower focus: it analyses the evolution of a particularly important aspect of the macroeconomic structure, namely demand management. Once again the focus is on the interaction of this part of the puzzle with other parts—a key question is how monetary policy related to other forms of government intervention in the management of aggregate demand—fiscal policy, trade policy, and policies dealing with capital flows.

The two chapters that follow analyse features of the historical narrative, the investment climate, and its impact on accumulation and growth (Chapter 4), and capital–labour relations (Chapter 5). These chapters are intended to serve two purposes: first, to spell out more precisely our view of the relationship between key features of the macroeconomic structure and the system of production, and, second, to elaborate the discussion of how the evolution of the investment climate and labour–capital relations is affected, and was affected by, the evolution of other features of the post-war regime. Thus the historical chapters set the stage for and frame the theoretical chapters, and the theory illuminates and focuses the history.

Finally a first cut is made at applying the lessons of the past to the future. Chapter 6 analyses the characteristics of those countries which have maintained high employment levels after the golden age and focuses on four countries—Austria, Japan, Norway, and Sweden—which have been particularly successful in this regard. It should be noted at the outset that these 'star performers' have been less stellar in maintaining high rates of growth. Nevertheless the experience of these countries is important in indicating both common features and differences in ways in which the system of production and the rules of co-ordination can successfully cope with economic adversity. Chapter 7 speaks to the question of restructuring labour–capital relations; an important implication of the historical and theoretical analysis of Chapters 2–5 is that fundamental reorganization of the system of production is a precondition for the resumption of growth on a sustainable, long-term basis. Recognizing this necessity we, like legions of social scientists before us, have been drawn to Japanese labour–capital relations as an alternative to the model that has dominated in the West. We share the widespread view that the West has much to learn from Japan, but, as Chapter 7 shows, we believe the proper lessons are generally obscured by the extensive use of 'made in Japan' as a cover for one sort or another of special pleading. A concluding section of this chapter poses the question of the 'exportability' of the Japanese system of production: to what extent can specific techniques that have proved successful in Japan be transplanted to Western soil?

I. THEME AND VARIATIONS

A central theme of this book is that the golden age of capitalism, like other historical epochs, must be understood as a set of interlocking institutions, and that the interactions between the institutions that operate in different spheres are crucial.

I.1 The Historical Background

As background to how these institutions functioned during the golden age, the historical record of Depression and War is essential. The first legacy of the Depression was the commitment to the welfare state. The trauma of unemployment on a scale too wide to be plausibly blamed on the shortcomings and failures of the individual worker permanently changed the way people throughout Europe and North America would think about the role of the government. What conservatives—except for the fringe of the New Right—and liberals argue about today are the margins of the welfare state, not its principles.

Changes in both law and customs that enhanced the power of organized labour were another legacy of the Depression, particularly in the United States. In other countries the position of trade unions improved in the aftermath of World War II rather than during the Great Depression. However, except in the United Kingdom and in the Scandinavian countries, organized labour did not achieve the power it won in the United States. An initial eruption of grassroots radicalism, which for a time threatened to convulse Europe and Japan, was repulsed soon after the war ended; by and large, trade-union leaders worked to contain more radical workers (Armstrong *et al.* 1984, ch. 2).

Nowhere did the trade unions mount a coherent and sustained challenge to capitalists' prerogatives to organize work, control production, or determine investment. Trade-union leaders, for the most part, accepted a bargain in which managing was left to the bosses. In so far as union demands went beyond the division of the pie, the focus was on one or another issue of employment security, such as respect for seniority in deciding who would be promoted or laid off.

The institutionalization of aggregate demand management is generally thought to date from the publication of Keynes's *General Theory* in 1936. But whereas the *General Theory* was important in providing a justification for aggregate demand management, the commitment came only in the wake of war. That was no accident. The Soviet Union, along with Germany, was generally conceded to have abolished unemployment while the capitalist democracies were wallowing in Depression. Germany's economic success was widely attributed to the militarism and rearmament that culminated in World War II. Early military successes may have enhanced the prestige that Germany enjoyed in circles in the West that had earlier chosen to ignore or play down the political concomitants of Nazi economic successes. But with the turning of the tables came a growing prestige for the Soviet Union; one aspect of this was the contrast between the dismal employment record of pre-war capitalism with the performance of Soviet socialism. In consequence, the Western democracies were put under considerable political pressure to prevent output and employment from being regulated by swings in private confidence. This political demand took on special urgency as victory approached: it seemed unfair to the larger part of the population of the Western allies, even to people otherwise little sympathetic to the Left, that young men should be asked to give up their lives for their country while their country was willing to consign their livelihoods to the vicissitudes of the market.

Another important legacy of war was the emergence of the United

States as the dominant power internationally, both politically and economically. On the political side, the United States assumed the role of international policeman from the British after the inter-regnum of the inter-war years, and regularly intervened covertly and occasionally overtly to prevent hostile elements from coming to power. Iran in 1953, Guatemala in 1954 are well-known instances of covert intervention. In Lebanon in 1957 and in the Dominican Republic in 1965, the marines actually landed.

The war also made the United States the dominant power economically, as the only major belligerent to emerge with its productive power enhanced. For many years after the cessation of hostilities, there was a range of goods which only the United States could produce competitively at any reasonable exchange rate, and certain goods which only the United States could produce at all.

In short, as the dominant power both politically and economically, the United States faced little effective opposition to its attempts to carve out a new international order, one responsive to its interests and its perceptions of the larger interests of the world economy—America was not the first hegemonic power in world history to confuse the two.

It was, then, in the context of the welfare state, a trade-union movement that was tame even where it was powerful, the commitment to demand management, and American international leadership, that the regime of post-war capitalism—the macroeconomic structure and international order, the system of production, and the rules of co-ordination—had to operate. Let us see how these circumstances conditioned the functioning of each.

I.2 The Macroeconomic Structure

A macroeconomic structure is a set of mechanisms for managing the overall level of economic performance—output, employment, and growth. To be successful, macroeconomic management must meet two requirements. On the one hand, the level of aggregate demand must be set at a level adequate to utilize fully the available productive resources, both capital and labour. On the other hand, the share of output devoted to capital formation must be sufficient to achieve a high rate of growth of the capital stock, and over time the demand for investment and the supply of saving must grow in balance with each other.

A critical element of the post-war macroeconomic structure was investment demand. Most views of investment demand (Kalecki 1971; Malinvaud 1980; Tobin 1969) take the expected rate of profit relative to the cost of capital as the crucial determinant, but most economists have taken profit expectations as playing a distinct role only in the short period. Capital markets are conventionally assumed to eliminate any gap between profits and capital costs in the long period, at least at the margin. Indeed mainstream economists might even *define* the long period as one in which the returns to capital and capital costs are equalized. In the analysis of the long period it is only neo-Keynesians like Joan Robinson (1956, 1962) who have emphasized the centrality of profit expectations as an independent variable. The expected rate of profit, in turn, can be related to three components of the current rate of profit—the output per unit of capital at some standard rate of capacity utilization, the rate of capacity utilization relative to that standard rate, and the share of profit in value added. The first of these components, which we may identify with the ratio of potential GNP to the capital stock, need not detain us until much later in the story, when it begins to decline markedly. Nor was the profit share problematic, at least at the outset of the golden age. As we shall see, one consequence of the war was to temper wage demands for a long time. Profits in the early post-war period reflected the substantial decline in real wages (continental Europe) and the substantial growth in productivity (the United States). In the United States even the intense wave of strike activity in the immediate aftermath of the war did not significantly undermine profit margins. Japan, where war damage was most extensive and production in total disarray, was an exception to the general pattern of profits in excess of pre-war shares of GNP (Armstrong *et al.* 1984, Chart 6.4).

Once the political challenge to capitalism from the Left was contained, the problem for investment demand lay in the prospects for selling the additional goods that new capacity would generate. Here is where the new role of trade unions and the commitment to government intervention to maintain aggregate demand proved essential to fostering a successful macroeconomic structure. The gospel of 'co-operative capitalism' was that high and growing wages and high and growing government expenditure would guarantee a stable expansion of demand and utilization of newly installed capacity. This gospel may have initially been received with considerable scepticism, clashing as it did with vivid memories of the dismal demand performance of the Great Depression. But investor confidence responded in time to the evidence that demand expansion could and would be maintained, so that low capacity utilization would not undermine profitability.

On the saving side of the problem of business capital accumulation, the post-war macroeconomic structure depended heavily on corporate profits. In the United States, for example, household saving was directed in large part to investment in owner-occupied housing, and business relied primarily on earnings and depreciation allowances and, increasingly, on the saving of pension funds (Marglin 1984, ch. 17).

Thus profits played a double role in the post-war regime. On the one hand, profits today increased investor confidence in profits tomorrow and thereby spurred investment demand. On the other hand, profits provided a substantial part of the saving required for investment.

I.3 The International Order

It has been noted that the United States emerged from the war politically and economically dominant, with a new ability to influence the international order. American political dominance enters the story at several points. First, the 'Pax Americana' facilitated an orderly flow of goods between the so-called less developed and the advanced countries. An orderly flow of goods at 'reasonable' prices: those were the days when oil sold for two dollars per barrel. Second, American political dominance contributed to the political dominance of the Centre-Right in Western Europe. The splintering of the trade-union movement virtually everywhere in Europe but the United Kingdom and Scandinavia, at once cause and consequence of the ascendance of the political centre, played an important role in maintaining and enhancing profit margins. The containment of trade-union militancy postponed for a considerable period of time the threat that high employment inherently poses to profitability under capitalism, about which we shall have more to say presently. Third, political dominance gave the United States a stake in the economic well-being of Western Europe and Japan that allowed the traditional isolationism of important segments of the American polity to be overcome. The first fruit of the new internationalism was the Marshall Plan, which certainly contributed enormously to the recovery of Western Europe, and perhaps was an essential economic and political foundation of that recovery.

Finally, American political dominance provided the context for the post-war regime of international trade and finance, usually called the 'Bretton Woods system', even though the Bretton Woods agreement covered a limited range of issues and many of the subsequent steps envisioned by the signatories of Bretton Woods never came to pass. The new international order was to be one in which restrictions on the flow of goods would gradually be eliminated; trade would invigorate the world economy as a whole. The founders of Bretton Woods envisioned an international order that would contrast sharply with both the pre-war tendency to protect domestic production by means of trade barriers and the post-war reality, outside the United States at least, of a world economy largely in shambles. As the first step, the Bretton Woods agreement itself put into practice a system of fixed parities among the currencies of the major economic powers, parities which were to be adjusted only periodically and with the consent of the international body set up under Bretton Woods, the International Monetary Fund. The idea was to steer a middle course between the excessive rigidity of gold and a gold-exchange standard and the excessive uncertainty of a floating-rate regime.

American political dominance was necessary but hardly sufficient to make the Bretton Woods system function smoothly. For any fixed-rate system has inherent economic problems. In a celebrated series of papers that he began to publish as early as 1947, Robert Triffin outlined the internal contradiction of a fixed-rate system, in which the reserve currency is convertible to gold. In Triffin's view, the main problem is that the steady expansion of international liquidity in line with the volume of trade requires chronic deficits on the part of the key currency country or countries, but these very deficits can only undermine confidence in the key currency and ultimately force suspension of gold convertibility.

Accordingly, Triffin predicted the demise of the Bretton Woods system. Triffin was better as prophet of the end-result than as prophet of the mechanism. Deficits turned out to be less crucial than Triffin, working out his position in the late 1940s and the 1950s, could have imagined. The introduction of Eurodollars made US trade deficits unnecessary for system liquidity. With Eurodollars, the international banking system had a way to meet liquidity requirements by money created out of whole cloth. Even as American surpluses decreased in the 1960s—or rather despite the decreases in American surpluses—credit money came to play an ever more important role in providing liquidity through the Eurodollar market.

In actual fact, a fixed-rate regime requires the opposite of what Triffin supposed, namely an excess demand for the reserve currency. Without persistent excess demand, the vagaries of supply and demand will result in periodic pressure on the reserve currency; when the key currency is in excess supply, it is obviously difficult to maintain the fixed-rate system.

For some period of time, political dominance may be sufficient to create and maintain an excess demand for the hegemon's currency. To the extent military might and political power made the United States a safe haven for *rentiers* grown fearful for the prospects for private wealth in their own countries, the result would be a strong demand for dollars irrespective of the economic position of the United States. But excess demand is unlikely to persist for a long period of time unless the hegemon is economically dominant as well, so that its *goods* are in short supply in world markets.

In the event, World War II made the United States the dominant power economically as well as politically. It has been observed that for many years after the cessation of hostilities, there was a wide range of goods which only the United States could produce competitively. In consequence of the importance of these goods to production and particularly to capital formation, the dollar was in effect undervalued in economic terms, as evidence by large US current account surpluses in the 1950s.

The importance of the Bretton Woods arrangements to the success of the post-war capitalist regime is controversial, but there were undoubted advantages. Indeed one of the supposed disadvantages of the fixed-rate system, the lack of a mechanism for correcting surpluses and deficits, was very likely a positive factor in the growth of the capitalist world economy in the early post-war period. As has been noted, the United States enjoyed considerable surpluses. Not only would a floating-rate system have failed to eliminate these surpluses 'automatically', as recent experience shows, but the *quality* of capital flows would likely have been much less beneficial if a floating-rate system had been in operation. Exchange rate uncertainty would have put a great premium on liquidity, so that the foreign investment which is the necessary concomitant of a trade surplus would very likely have taken the form of accumulation of financial assets. The assurance (or illusion) of stability that the fixed-rate system provided undoubtedly facilitated the recycling of the US surpluses into fixed capital formation. Direct foreign investment, concentrated most heavily in Western Europe, was doubtless a boon to American profits, but it also contributed to capital formation and productivity growth abroad, particularly as it was a vehicle for other countries to plug into more advanced American technologies.

A floating-rate system is supposed to allow individual countries more autonomy in managing domestic demand; exchange rate flexibility is supposed to unbind the foreign-balance constraint. In fact, fluctuating exchange rates have not decreased the importance of the foreign-balance constraint. In a fixed-rate system, at least one country can manage aggregate demand without too much heed to a balance-of-payments constraint, provided its currency is undervalued. Pursuing expansionary policies, a country with the economic weight of the United States would not only stimulate its own economy, but would through its imports stimulate production and income abroad. All countries would benefit from such 'international Keynesianism'.

The United States did not in fact play its Keynesian card internationally until the mid 1960s, and then more in response to the exigencies of President Johnson's policy of guns and butter than in response to a sense of responsibility for the international economy. And, ironically, by this time the days of American economic and political hegemony were numbered. The late 1960s were the time when trade surpluses shrank and American political power came increasingly under attack. But, partly because of the expansionary fiscal stance of the United States at this time, the 1960s were a period of general prosperity, the brightest years of the golden age.

For a long time, the United States willingly accepted the costs as well as the benefits of its political and economic hegemony. For instance, the United States was prepared to incur short-run costs to promote European recovery and, beyond recovery, development and integration. The long-run interests of the world capitalist economy as a whole were served by improved productivity in Europe and Japan even though the relative position of American exports would suffer as European countries looked increasingly to one another.

There were of course substantial benefits to leadership. In the first place, prosperity is a non-zero-sum game, and America, as the biggest player in the game, stood to profit the most. There were also more immediate and tangible benefits. Because of the widespread use of the dollar as an international means of payment, the United States could earn a banker's profit in exchanging short-term liabilities for long-term assets. In the extreme version the reserve currency country can finance direct foreign investment by merely printing banknotes, an accusation levelled at the United States, particularly by the French, in the late 1960s, when the US current account was more or less in balance, but its foreign direct investment continued as if it were the 1950s and early 1960s, when the US current account was in surplus.

I.4 The System of Production

Capital–labour relations, summarized in the term 'system of production', exhibited much more continuity with the past than did the macroeconomic and international order. The organization of work in factories, the use of machinery, the organization of firms as large corporations—all this had a long history. While these forms of production developed after World War II, it could hardly be said that they represented a new departure.

More dramatic was the extension of what Richard Edwards (1979) has called 'technical' and 'bureaucratic' systems of control, machine-paced and rule-directed systems which share a common aim of replacing the direct and personal knowledge, authority, and responsibility of the worker by their impersonal counterparts in the machine and the rule-book. Chapter 2 uses the term 'Taylorization' to describe this process, after the father of 'scientific management', Frederick W. Taylor. Even here innovation in the system of production was largely confined to Europe. The United States had been experimenting with Taylorism since before World War I, although it must be said that Taylorism had always been more of a capitalist project than an achievement: workers consistently resisted being Taylorized. And Japan never travelled very far down the road of Taylorization. Although early on Japan experimented with a variety of systems of production, and there was considerable enthusiasm for this system, which could lay claim to being not only Western and modern but also scientific, Taylorism never meshed very well with Japanese cultural models or political exigencies. Even before World

War II, the worker as family member—rather than the worker as interchangeable part—became established as the dominant metaphor (Nakagawa 1979).

It was not coincidental that expansion of Taylorist production in Europe took place against the background of war. The war pressed home the conclusion on allies and enemies alike that the torch had passed from the Old World to the New, and this realization made Europe more open to American methods and systems. Productivity missions, under the aegis of the Marshall Plan, spread the word (Brown and Opie, 1953).

I.5 The Rules of Co-ordination

The term 'rules of co-ordination' describes the methods by which the actions of agents, individuals, firms, and states are brought into line with one another as well as with the exigencies of the macrostructure and the systems of production. Capitalist economies have always relied to a great extent on the price mechanism as a mode of co-ordination, profits guiding the allocation of capital as well as stimulating its accumulation, and wages guiding the allocation of labour as well as stimulating effort. Of course the price system has never functioned in the moral, cultural, and political vacuum which mainstream economic theory assumes. Political compulsion and cultural values have always played an important role in every set of rules for co-ordinating economic activity.

In particular, capitalists have never been entirely comfortable with the price mechanism as a means of extracting labour from workers, or to use the Marxian terminology (which is only reasonable since Karl Marx pioneered the analysis of the problem), as a means of converting labour power into labour. Typically what the worker sells is not a definite amount of corn delivered to the capitalist's barn but a quantity of time spent in the capitalist's field. The capitalist is left with the problem of transforming the worker's labour power into corn. Nor is the capitalist in general free to make the most productive use possible of the time he has purchased. The length of the working day, its intensity, the organization of work—which is to say, the system of production—remain objects of struggle.

Piece-rate wages represent one attempt to induce the worker to become the agent of the extraction of labour from his own labour power, but piece-rates have historically been at best a partial success. For one thing, piece-rates can be used only when the individual worker produces an identifiable product which can be directly attributed to his or her efforts. Equally important, even where there is an identifiable and attributable product, piece-rates themselves are the object of dispute and struggle, particularly in an environment in which technology and effort are rapidly and continuously changing. How the gains of productivity growth are to be shared in the revision of piece-rates is the dynamic counterpart of the original problem: how to extract labour from labour power. In the struggle over piece-rates it is evidently in the interest of the worker to minimize effort and apparent productive capacity: his best effort has a way of becoming the norm by which he and his mates are subsequently calibrated. Management is obviously at a disadvantage in monitoring a worker's performance if the workers possess the greater part of knowledge about the production process.

Taylorism may be seen as an attempt to solve this problem. By recombining and reconstituting workers' knowledge into a new system in which the capitalist (or in practice his agents—engineers, planners, and time-and-motion specialists) monopolizes the knowledge of production, management intends to circumvent a major obstacle to the extraction of labour (Marglin, forthcoming). Here the system of production joins up with the rules of co-ordination—or rather the solution to inherent problems of co-ordination is sought in the system of production. But Taylorism has proved only a partially effective solution to the labour–labour power problem: when they are able, workers consistently resist Taylorization. No wonder that the capitalist rules for co-ordinating production have—before and since Taylor—provided other solutions to this problem.

One solution is the use of the wage mechanism itself, what has come in the economic literature to be called 'efficiency wages' (Bowles 1985; Calvo 1979; Salop 1979, Shapiro and Stiglitz 1984; Yellen 1984). The basic idea is an old one. Over a century and a half ago Andrew Ure, the early apologist for the factory system and later *bête noire* of Marx, asked 'how with ... surplus hands the wages of fine spinners can be maintained at their present high pitch' (Ure 1835, p. 336), why in other words the wage rate failed to respond to demand–supply conditions and to clear the labour market. His answer contained the central idea behind efficiency wages:

one of the best informed manufacturers made me this reply: 'We find a moderate saving in the wages to be of little consequence in comparison of contentment and we therefore keep them as high as we can possibly afford, in order to be entitled to the best quality of work. A spinner reckons the charge of a pair of mules in our factory a fortune for life, he will therefore do his utmost to retain his situation, and to uphold the high character of our yarn.

Long before economists invented the term 'efficiency wages', capitalists were using the wage mechanism to purchase the commitment, loyalty, and effort of their workers along with their labour power.

But for at least an equally long period the carrot of efficiency wages has been complemented by the stick of direct supervision and control of the production process. Indeed, supervision and control are arguably the key to the emergence of the factory as a central feature of the capitalist system of production in the late eighteenth and early nineteenth century (Marglin 1974). Supervision and control—monitoring of the production process—have been key elements of the rules of co-ordination ever since.

How effective efficiency wages and supervision are in extracting labour from labour power depends critically on the economic arrangements in force, for these arrangements determine the cost of job-loss to the worker if he or she fails to respond to the carrot or the stick—and is found out. The chief determinants of the cost of job-loss are the rate and duration of unemployment and the level of unemployment insurance (Schor 1985a).

The essential point about the role of unemployment was made by Michal Kalecki (1943). Kalecki argued that high employment would eventually undermine worker discipline and adversely affect productivity. Ultimately, profits would have to suffer even though the day of reckoning would be postponed because the impact on profits would be disguised for a time by the beneficial effects of high capacity utilization that generally goes along with high employment. Kalecki drew the conclusion that sustained full employment was not in the interest of capitalists and would therefore be unlikely under capitalism. Even earlier, Wesley Clair Mitchell (1913) had observed that the general rate of unemployment affects productivity through its effect on discipline. In short, when alternative jobs are plentiful, the cost of job-loss is relatively low. When alternative jobs become scarce, the cost of job-loss rises.

II. EVOLUTION OF THE INSTITUTIONS

Innovations with respect to the welfare state and the management of aggregate demand after World War II had a significant impact on the rules of co-ordination. Over time, as we shall see, the cost of job-loss fell dramatically, which reduced the effectiveness of efficiency wages and supervision as co-ordinating rules. In due course, this had important repercussions on both the supply of saving and the demand for investment, that is, on the macroeconomic structure.

These developments played themselves out in the relationship between productivity growth and wage growth. Over the 1950s, the OECD countries in general maintained a neat balance between productivity and wage growth, so that profits remained a roughly constant share of output. Japan was able to contain wage growth more successfully, so that the Japanese profit share actually grew substantially over the 1950s. The overall stability of the profit share reflected the stability of the growth process, and this, it has been suggested, would in the circumstances of the times translate into improved profit rate expectations: the actual performance of demand did much to dispel the fears of depression and excess capacity. At the same time, high rates of growth very likely added to the resources which corporate retentions of earnings and depreciation allowances made available for accumulation; households found themselves with incomes rising more or less continuously and consequently found it relatively easy to save while learning how to spend their new riches. Thus both the demand for investment and the supply of saving grew at an even faster rate than output, and by the end of the 1950s the share of GDP devoted to gross business fixed investment in the OECD countries as a whole was 20 per cent higher than at the beginning. (In Japan and Europe the increase was even more striking; it was the United States, where the growth process was less smooth, which held the average down.) During this period, the rules of co-ordination and the macroeconomic structure reinforced each other, both resting on a system of production that generated a high rate of productivity growth and continued wage growth.

Thus the new economic arrangements of the post-war period initially worked smoothly. Internally, the welfare state, the power of trade unions to raise wages, and demand management combined to maintain high capacity utilization and stable profits. Internationally, American hegemony maintained a smooth flow of raw materials from the less developed countries at stable and low prices (the commodity price shocks of the Korean War years were a flash in the pan). Within the OECD countries, the excess demand for the dollar and the disposition of the United States to recycle trade surpluses initially allowed growth to proceed unconstrained by problems of external balance.

To be sure, there were clouds on the horizon. The cost of job-loss fell, in line with the new arrangements for demand management (which kept unemployment low) and with the growth of the welfare state (which increased both the coverage and levels of unemployment insurance). But the memories of the Depression made workers and trade-union leaders alike hesitate to act in terms of the new realities, to take actions that would threaten the steady march of productivity and profits. On the international side, although the difference in rates of productivity growth—the United States consistently lagged Europe and Japan—undermined the dollar, the initial undervaluation perpetuated excess demand for the dollar for a considerable period of time, and even allowed the international order to survive for a time with the key currency country clearly headed for deficit.

Things began to unravel in the 1960s. Increasingly as the decade wore on and even more so in the early 1970s, the balance between productivity growth and wage growth was upset. However the process was not the same everywhere. As Table 1.1 shows, productivity growth fell in the United States while wages maintained a roughly steady growth rate. In Europe and Japan, by contrast, productivity growth fell less dramatically, but wage growth accelerated.

There are many reasons why productivity growth fell. Some favour the mature economy thesis, which explains the slow-down in terms of the exhaustion of the possibilities of technologies and the saturation of markets. Others lean towards an explanation in terms of the limits of Taylorization, in which the key problem is that capitalists ran out of workers to Taylorize. Still others emphasize labour militancy and its effects on resistance to Taylorization. In this view the key element is the fall in the cost of job-loss, which reduces the responsiveness of workers to the carrot of efficiency wages and the stick of supervision, while increasing the pressure on real wages.

The wage acceleration of the late 1960s and the early 1970s has been widely commented upon; suffice it to say that in our perception the fall in the cost of job-loss once again looms large. The importance of the fall in the cost of job-loss both to the slow-down in productiv-

Table 1.1. Productivity and wage growth, 1964–1973

		Average annual productivity growth	Average annual wage growth	Difference (1)−(2)
		(1)	(2)	(3)
US	1964–8	2.4	2.5	−0.1
	1969–73	1.0	2.0	−1.0
Europe	1964–8	4.5	4.3	+0.2
	1969–73	4.2	5.0	−0.8
Japan	1964–8	8.7	7.6	+1.1
	1969–73	7.8	10.6	−2.8

Note: The series in columns (1) and (2) are not strictly comparable so column (3) is only an approximation to the change in the wage share. 'Average annual productivity growth' is the growth rate of GDP per person in civil employment, whereas 'average annual wage growth' is the growth rate of the product wage in the business sector. 'Europe' is an unweighted average of France, Germany, Italy, and the UK.

Source: Armstrong and Glyn (1986).

ity growth and to the acceleration of wage growth raises an obvious question: why did the cost of job-loss fall?

The answer lies in the behaviour of two components of the cost of job-loss; the ease or difficulty of finding another job, and the loss of earnings between jobs.

Although memories of the Depression and fears of another kept workers in line for a time, the threat of being fired progressively lost its sting as low levels of unemployment persisted through the 1950s and into the 1960s. Memories fade, and if Ford was hiring down the street, a GM worker did not need to be so concerned about losing her job. At the same time the welfare state increasingly cushioned the blow and reinforced the effects of low rates of unemployment. The result was that by the end of the 1960s, the cost of job-loss, and more important the perception of this cost, had fallen; productivity growth began to suffer and pressure on wages increased. The existing rules of co-ordination, operating in a system of production in which the interests of capital and labour were fundamentally at odds, lost their effectiveness in extracting labour from labour power. (The fall in the cost of job-loss was only one among many complementary causes of the fall in productivity growth and wage acceleration. As Chapter 2 makes clear, the data do not permit us to sort out the relative importance of different problems, but we do not believe that we mislead by emphasizing the cost of job-loss.)

II.1 Full-employment profit squeeze

Whatever the sources of the productivity growth slow-down and the wage acceleration, together they had a strong impact on the macro-economic structure. Profits fell markedly since the decline in productivity growth in no way impeded the power of workers to impose wage demands on their employers; in Europe especially, it has been observed, this power was enhanced by the fall in the cost of job-loss. But the pressure on wages had deeper underpinnings. Steady growth in real wages was a tacit part of post-war economic arrangements, and none the less real for being tacit. Indeed, having renounced any real say in the organization of production, trade-union leaders were under all the more pressure to deliver the goods in the form of real wage increases, regardless of productivity growth. In consequence the profit share fell almost everywhere. In Europe the decline was from a high of 25 per cent in the mid 1950s to 20 per cent at the end of the 1960s, in the United States, from 20 per cent to 15 per cent. Only in Japan, where the system of production and the rules of co-ordination were substantially different, were profits higher in 1970s than in the mid 1950s, but soon (before the first oil shock) Japanese profits too were substantially reduced, from an average of about 35 per cent of corporate output in the mid 1960s to 30 per cent in 1973. There was, in short, well before the oil shock, a general 'full-employment profit squeeze' throughout the OECD countries. This was not a phenomenon associated with business 'cycles'—that is with swings of a few years' duration—but the result of a long period of sustained growth, rising wages, high employment, and increasing economic security for working people.

This full-employment profit squeeze had a direct effect on accumulation. The rate of growth of the capital stock fell in the wake of the profit squeeze; for the OECD countries as a group the decline was from a rate of over 5 per cent p.a. in the late 1960s to about 4 per cent in the late 1970s. But this decline was the result of a fall in the output/capital ratio rather than a fall in the investment share. Indeed, the share of GDP devoted to business investment proved remarkably resilient in all countries except Japan!

How can the resilience of the investment share be accounted for in terms of a logic of accumulation based on the centrality of profits? The arguments developed in Chapter 4 lead to an answer along the following lines: investment remained strong because until the very end of the golden age and possibly beyond, profit expectations declined by much less than profit realizations. The paradox is explained by the gradual erosion of fears of Depression; profit expectations improved as these fears dissipated despite static and even declining profits. Indeed, profit expectations only caught up to actual profits as the tide began to recede markedly in the late 1960s, and even then actual profits fell by more than expected profits. This relative resilience of profit expectations was reinforced by declining real interest rates as inflation accelerated and was accommodated by relatively passive monetary policy.

If this explanation is correct, then time-series data obscure rather than illuminate the connection between profit and investment shares. Had the profit share remained constant, the investment share would have risen, which would have offset the fall in the capital/output ratio and allowed the capital stock to continue to grow in the 1970s at more or less its accustomed rate.

The view that profits strongly influence investment is supported by the cross-country data. For example, until very recently the Japanese profit share has exceeded the British share by roughly the same margin—50 per cent—by which the Japanese investment share has exceeded the British. And overall the cross-country correlation between the two shares, while not as striking as these two extreme figures, is impressive.

II.2 Bretton Woods and Pax Americana

The harm done to accumulation by the profit squeeze was compounded by international developments. Bretton Woods was undermined by slower productivity growth relative to real wage growth in the United States than elsewhere. The productivity growth differential was presumably due primarily to the difference in initial conditions—the United States was way out in front at the end of the war. The recycling of United States' trade surpluses into foreign direct investment helped to improve productivity and competitiveness abroad, and ultimately helped to turn the dollar problem of the 1950s—too few dollars—into the problem of the late 1960s—too many dollars. The requirements of international liquidity made the reduction in the US surplus not only tolerable but functional for a time, but the development of the Eurodollar market soon rendered the US balance of payments superfluous as a source of liquidity. During the 1960s the dollar was transformed from an undervalued to an overvalued currency, and as the 1960s wore on the United States, increasingly torn by strife over the Vietnam War, looked less and less like a safe haven, despite the return of political unrest to Europe after an interlude of 20 years.

The first symptom of change was that European countries were able to remove exchange controls that had been imposed to cope with the dollar shortage of the immediate post-war period. More ominous signs appeared as the 1960s wore on: the decline in the US balance-of-payments surplus persisted and deepened, and the United States pulled back from full convertibility of the dollar into gold. Finally, Bretton Woods could no longer function and in 1971 was definitively and unilaterally abandoned by the United States. The consequences were momentous, if somewhat delayed: faced with an external constraint for the first time since the war, the United States could no longer play a leadership role in the management of aggregate demand internationally. In the late 1970s when the United States attempted to induce a global expansion by stimulating aggregate demand, the rest of the world was no longer willing to accept a flood of US dollars, except at a price which sent shudders through the financial community from New York to Zurich and from London to Tokyo. Though modest in terms of more recent experience, the fall in the dollar appeared to threaten the stability of the international financial system. The United States did not persist in expanding aggregate demand, and the stage was set for a new head of the US central bank, Paul Volcker, to introduce a restrictive thrust into Federal Reserve management of monetary policy.

The retreat from Keynesian policies of demand management, it should be said, was based on internal as well as an external considerations. From the vantage-point of capital, expanding output and employment would only exacerbate the problem of work-force discipline and motivation which had already cut deeply into productivity growth and profits.

Moreover, gains in production and employment would come at the cost of higher rates of inflation. Now reasons for disliking inflation are many and varied, and the deepest reasons are probably psychological rather than economic, at least if we confine our attention to rates of inflation characteristic of the industrial economies in the post-war period. In a world where all values—ethical, moral, and social as well as economic—are in flux, price stability serves the important symbolic value of connecting the older generation to its past, to a world which seems, in retrospect at least, simpler, safer, and surer.

Speculative as this explanation might be, there is no reason to be apologetic. It is the worst-kept secret in the economics profession that no one has a convincing story about why inflation, even at the highest rates that prevailed in the OECD countries in the 1970s and early 1980s, should be regarded as such an evil that all economic policy had to be directed to its containment. (For the United States alone, the costs of containing inflation—in terms of output forgone since 1980—have been estimated in hundreds of billions and even in trillions.) The best story mainstream economists can offer is that inflation is like pregnancy: there is no such thing as a little bit. Single-digit inflation, if allowed to continue, will inexorably develop into double digits, and double digits into triple digits. The next thing we know the advanced capitalist countries will be in the position of Germany in the 1920s, when money finally lost all its value.

In contrast with psychological costs of inflation, which are widely felt if only dimly perceived, its economic costs (and gains) are infinitely complicated to work out. But it is worth reflecting on the fact that the sure losers from inflations of the kind that prevailed in the industrial countries are the very rich who constitute the bulk of the holders of assets denominated in nominal terms. Unlike common stocks or houses or other assets whose returns rise more or less in line with the underlying income streams, bond income and principal are generally fixed in nominal terms. Now according to a recent *Survey of Consumer Finances* (Federal Reserve Board 1984, pp. 679–792) in the United States, 40 per cent of federal government and corporate bonds and 70 per cent of non-taxable holdings, chiefly municipal bonds, are held by the wealthiest 2 per cent of American families. Even without introducing psychological considerations, it is easy to see why the rich would oppose inflation.

In short, while there may be adequate reasons for a retreat from Keynesian policies rooted in international considerations, these were at the very least reinforced by domestic considerations of both capital–labour conflict and the acceleration of inflation. Once again internal and external problems became intertwined, perhaps inextricably so.

Other international developments also had an immediate bearing on the macroeconomic structure. The defeat of American forces in Vietnam formally signalled the end of the Pax Americana. OPEC was quick to take advantage of the changes in America's world position; there was nothing accidental in the timing of its dramatic entry into prominence in 1973. If instead of in 1973 OPEC had tried to raise oil prices and restrict production in 1953 or in 1963, American marines would almost certainly have been dispatched to teach the lessons that were taught to the Lebanese in 1957 and the Dominicans in 1965.

It seems clear that the increase in the price of energy contributed to the reduction in the output/capital ratio in the 1970s, which accounts in large part for the slow-down in the rate of accumulation. Outside the energy sector, value added per unit of capital would surely have fallen as a larger share of output was required to pay for energy. But, as Chapter 2 shows, it is difficult to sort out the contribution of energy price increases from other changes that occurred almost simultaneously, particularly the sharp decreases in the rate of capacity utilization.

III. THE END OF THE GOLDEN AGE:
AN ASSESSMENT

We now have the ingredients at hand to essay a preliminary answer to one of the key questions that has motivated this study: are we to understand the demise of the golden age, and hence to conduct the search for new institutions, in terms of problems internal to each of the economies of Western Europe and the United States or in terms of the relations among the OECD countries and between these countries and the rest of the world? Evidently the historical account can be read two ways, first, that the essential problem was an internal one, the full-employment profit squeeze that resulted from the failure of the system of production and the rules of co-ordination to accommodate the basic conflict between labour and capital; second, that the essential problem lay on the international side, in the erosion of profits that resulted from the energy shock(s), traceable to the erosion of American hegemony, and the demise of international arrangements that effectively suppressed the constraint of external balance for the United States as hegemonic power and allowed relatively expansionary demand management policies both in the United States and elsewhere—without the disorder and uncertainty of floating exchange rates. In the first reading, the end to the golden age comes about 1970, when productivity growth began to decline markedly throughout the OECD countries. In the second reading, the real end comes in 1979 when OPEC II triggered a new round of inflation, which in turn catalysed doubts about the international order into fears of a total collapse of the dollar-based financial system. In this climate, the United States proved unwilling to continue to expand the world economy by stimulating the American economy and US imports, for fear of a fall in the value of the dollar of unprecedented proportions. (Subsequently, the United States has run enormous deficits and the dollar has gyrated on international exchanges—without the dire consequences that were generally anticipated from such behaviour. But that is another story.) In this reading, the post-war regime foundered on the shoals of pluralism.

The part of wisdom is probably to reject both of these single-cause explanations. Having emphasized the interaction of complementary institutions as the key to understanding both success and failure, it makes relatively little sense to search for a single essence. The internal problems which produced a profit squeeze are adequate to explain why the growth in the investment share achieved in the 1950s and 1960s did not continue into the 1970s, though even here international problems (OPEC I in particular) contributed to the profit squeeze. But it is the perception (if not the reality) of an external constraint in the late 1970s that explains why the United States, and hence other countries, were no longer disposed to use Keynesian policies to maintain the high levels of employment and capacity utilization as in the earlier period. Thus there are different explanations for the decline in growth rates (where internal issues come to the fore) and the rise in unemployment rates (where the emphasis is on the international side).

The preceding discussion is not intended as a summary of the chapters that follow, even though it draws extensively on these chapters. Each chapter is a distillation of a larger work, and summaries of summaries are unlikely to illuminate. Even then we do not pretend to a complete account. Our research thus far gives relatively little attention to the increasing importance of managerial capitalism; transnational corporations; the rise of competition from the newly industrialized countries like Brazil and South Korea; the direct impact on accumulation of the increase, relative to the pre-war period, in government spending on civil and military account—to mention only some of the considerations without which the story of the golden age and its demise is incomplete.

The purpose of this introduction rather is to connect the various chapters, to indicate why the general historical narrative of Chapter 2 is followed by discussion of monetary policy and its role in aggregate demand management (Chapter 3), and why these two historical discussions are followed by theoretical discussion of the investment function and its role in determining macroeconomic outcomes (Chapter 4), and of the theory of labour extraction and its role in shaping macroeconomic equilibrium (Chapter 5). It also should be clear why we find it important to investigate how some countries have managed, in the face of adversity, to adapt the system of production and the rules of co-ordination to the end of high employment (Chapter 6). Finally, our perspective on the Japanese alternative to Taylorism and carrot/stick regulation should now be apparent, as should the context in which Chapter 7 is intended to be read.

IV. LESSONS OF THE GOLDEN AGE: METHODOLOGICAL, ANALYTICAL, AND POLITICAL

A final purpose of this introduction is to suggest the lessons which emerge from the study as a whole. We believe there are methodological, analytical, and policy lessons to be drawn. The main methodological point is the need to integrate history and theory. In our view the failure of most economic analysis, particularly neoclassically inspired analysis, to provide any useful insight into the successes and failures of post-war capitalism lies in excessive abstraction.

The key word is 'excessive'. All theory is abstraction and we have nothing against abstraction in principle. The problem of theorizing is to trade off the potential generality of the theory, which leads one to institutional sparseness, against the need to say something specific about specific problems in specific historical circumstances. The balance is obviously a delicate one, but it seems clear enough that the kind of theory which dominates in the economics profession has erred in the direction of too much abstraction. In pursuing generality, neoclassical theory has become so sparse in its institutional specification that it has next to nothing to say about concrete problems. The *ad hoc* assumptions that are then added to make the theory operational are, to say the least, far from compelling.

By contrast, the theory of growth that underlies the present volume is firmly rooted in capitalist institutions. We draw heavily on Marxian and Keynesian traditions to make up for what we perceive to be the deficiencies of mainstream theory: the Marxian tradition for the discussion of the system of production, particularly the analysis of labour extraction, and the Keynesian tradition for the discussion of macroeconomic structure, particularly the analysis of saving and investment. Each tradition makes assumptions that tie the analysis closely to the conditions of a developed capitalist society.

Both of these traditions make the rate of profit central to the growth of the capitalist economy. In part this is because both traditions, drawing on classical economics, place considerable emphasis on profits as a source of saving. In our view, the distribution of income, particularly between corporations and households, is central to the determination of the overall propensity to save, in sharp contrast with the mainstream insistence on a uniform propensity to save that is independent of distribution. Observe that the Kalecki-Robinson–Kaldor 'neo-Keynesian' tradition, in which we would situate our own view of saving and investment, has in some respects parted company not only with the mainstream but, arguably, with Keynes himself.

Our view of saving differs from the mainstream of the profession for two reasons. First, when we speak of 'saving' we have something very different in mind from what the mainstream intends by this term. In the mainstream view, saving consists of additions to the stocks of *all* durable goods, although empirical work which uses national income accounts excludes durables other than housing. By contrast, our interest focuses on plant, equipment, and related 'productive' capital.

Second, we mean something very different by the term 'household'. In accordance with the logic of their theory, purists in the mainstream attribute virtually all private saving to households by reason of the beneficial ownership that one way or another is attributable to households. In our view, saving by organizations like corporations and pension funds is not reducible to households, at least not behaviourally, whatever the legal situation might be.

At issue here is an important difference with neoclassical theory as to how saving behaviour is to be viewed. Neoclassical theory assumes that saving behaviour, like all economic behaviour, is purposefully calculated: the preferred models, Franco Modigliani's life-cycle hypothesis (Modigliani and Brumberg 1954) and Milton Friedman's permanent-income hypothesis (1957), are concocted in terms of household utility maximization over a long period of time. It obviously fits such a framework to assume that households take account of the saving done by the corporation or pension funds of which households are beneficial owners. The corporation or pension fund is in effect simply an extension of the household.

We see households as more reactive than reflective, for the most part responding to the stimulus of income by the action of spending, with some saving taking place as incomes rise simply because there is a lag in the adjustment process. There are, to be sure, exceptions: the salaried professional whose life prospects are reasonably certain and whose life experience reinforces the notion that he or she is 'in control'—a necessary precondition for the utility-maximization framework to make psychological sense. (A colleague once observed that the life-cycle hypothesis is exactly the theory of saving behaviour one might except of a middle-aged college professor!) And then there are the rich and super-rich—about whose saving behaviour we must admit we know next to nothing.

Since we regard long-period utility maximization as an exceptional basis for household saving behaviour rather than the normal basis, we consider corporations and pension funds to be distinct behavioural entities, which cannot be assimilated to households. Unlike the 'assimilationists' (for example, Feldstein 1973), we regard the relatively high observed rate of corporate profit retention as indicative of a structural relationship between profit and saving—not the mere substitution of one kind of household saving for another.

For all these reasons, we put relatively little emphasis on the household as a source of saving in the modern capitalist economy (Japan, and to a lesser extent Italy, being exceptions to the general pattern). Our working hypothesis is that the more income stays in the hands of organizations like the corporation and the pension fund, the higher will be the community's propensity to save.

But the role of profits in determining the propensity to save is only part of the story, and the other parts of the Marxian and Keynesian theories are very different, indeed diametrically opposed to each other, despite the fact that the rate of profit is central to both. The

Marxian theory focuses on a chain of causality running from real wages and productivity to the rate of profit, whereas the Keynesian theory emphasizes the interconnections between profit and investment *demand*.

Marx begins from the notion of a 'subsistence wage' inherited from Smith and Ricardo. Although Marx went to great lengths to emphasize the historical, social, and moral elements that enter into wage determination, 'subsistence' still suggests to many a biologically determined standard of living bordering on malnutrition or even starvation. In our view, it is not biology but community standards which play the central role in determining real wages.

Community standards depend in some part on the course of class struggle and the balance of class power between capitalists and workers. In part, the norms that govern real wages come out of a shared cultural tradition about what constitutes a fair day's pay. Wages are thus a matter of *convention* in two senses of the term, one being the idea of custom, the other the idea of an agreement, accord, or contract. Indeed, 'conventional wage' better fits our understanding of the Marxian view of wage determination than does the older terminology of subsistence, with its misplaced connotation of a biologically determined wage rate.

Over a period of time like the one this book covers, the conventional wage cannot be conceived of as an unchanging norm: productivity growth must be reckoned in. However, it is not primarily through the demand for labour, as mainstream theory would have it, that productivity has affected wages. Rather, it is through the cultural assumption, common to the advanced capitalist countries, that workers may, by right, lay claim to a share of productivity growth. Community standards combine with the power of the working class to dictate that real wages should rise roughly in line with productivity. As time goes on, the presumption of wage growth takes on a life of its own, in the form that collective bargaining agreements assume and in the general expectations of workers and capitalists. It was partly the persistence of the momentum of wage growth as productivity growth declined in the late 1960s which led to profit squeeze in most of the industrialized capitalist world.

It will immediately occur to many to ask how a conventional wage can suspend the laws of supply and demand. The Marxian answer is that, in the long run, demand and supply operate quite asymmetrically in the labour market. Over the long period the supply of labour is highly elastic at the conventional wage because of the 'reserve army' of labour. The reserve army is not a static concept, not a number of bodies to be counted, but a force which expands (and contracts, albeit with greater difficulty and a considerable lag, hence the complex relationships analysed in Chapter 6 between population growth, participation rates, output growth, and unemployment in the period of slow-down after the early 1970s) to fit the needs of capitalist growth.

Students of economic development will recognize a strong connection between this conception of the labour market and W. Arthur Lewis's 'unlimited supplies of labour' (1954). Lewis took the Marxian notions of conventional wages and the reserve army and applied these ideas to poor, densely populated countries with large rural populations and correspondingly large agricultural sectors, particularly in Asia. But this conception, in our view, remains applicable to the capitalist economies of Western Europe, North America, and Japan.

The post-war reserve army was constituted out of a variety of sources. In virtually all the capitalist countries, workers were drawn from the farm and the kitchen: the agricultural labour force shrank to insignificance and women entered into capitalist production in increasing numbers. Europe (and Canada) also relied heavily on immigration, as the United States had done in an earlier epoch of expansion.

With the long-run labour supply highly elastic at the conventional wage, the wage rate is in the first instance a supply-side issue. The demand for labour operates on the wage only indirectly, through its impact on the conditions of class struggle and accommodation. It took a quarter century of golden age growth to produce the confrontational conditions in which wage growth began to diverge sharply from productivity growth.

Productivity, like wages, is treated very differently in a Marxian account of profit determination from the way it is treated in the mainstream story. Mainstream views emphasize technology to the virtual exclusion of other considerations. In the Marxian perspective, technology is an important, but not the sole, determinant of productivity. Productivity also depends upon the system of production which, under capitalism, reflects both the underlying antagonism of the interests of bosses and workers and the accommodations made to allow the two classes to get on with the business of production in spite of their fundamental differences. Once again, naked power and cultural norms both play a role; together they determine what is acceptable as a 'fair day's work', the other side of the coin of a 'fair day's pay'. Mechanisms of labour extraction, ranging from close supervision and monitoring to the payment of high wages, *à la* Ure (see Section I.5), are ways by which the capitalist seeks to enhance labour productivity. 'Stints' and 'pacing' are ways by which workers defend themselves. The important point for present purposes is not the specific accommodation through which the conflict is resolved, but the idea that conflict and accommodation take place, are central to the determination of productivity, and change over time as economic, political, and social conditions change. Since productivity is central to profitability, the rate of profit cannot be reduced to the operation of technological parameters mediated by impersonal markets.

The Marxian theory of growth, to summarize, starts from the conventional wage and the system of production to determine the rate of profit. The propensity to save out of profits determines the rate of growth of the capital stock. In the long run at least, saving determines investment—as it does in neoclassical theory.

This is of course not the only possible interpretation of Marx. The labour-extraction model of Chapter 5 is firmly grounded in the Marxian distinction between labour and labour power and on this basis argues for a positive relationship between labour productivity and unemployment and a negative relationship between the wage rate and unemployment. In this model, the reserve army fails to adjust the supply of labour in time; it reacts to an increase in labour demand by increasing the supply of labour, but too late to avoid a squeeze on profits. This profit squeeze reflects the fall in the cost of job-loss, which both induces workers to produce less and requires capitalists to pay them more.

Although the labour-extraction view of the labour market is different from one that emphasizes the endogeneity of the labour supply, the two views can be reconciled: the labour supply can be taken as endogenous in the long run but fixed in the short run. This would make the dependence of labour extraction on the unemployment rate a phenomenon of the short run of the business cycle, and open the door to a different explanation of profit squeeze in the long period. Labour extraction would remain an issue in the long period, but be tied less strongly to the *unemployment rate* and more strongly to long period changes in the realities of *class relations* and perceptions of those relations on the part of both capitalists and workers. These long period changes would replace the unemployment rate as the central explanation of the change in the relationship between wage growth and productivity growth that occurred in the late 1960s and early 1970s.

Formally, the difference between the two explanations is that the 'class-relations' model interprets profit squeeze as a shift in the aggregate supply schedule relative to a fixed aggregate demand schedule, whereas the 'unemployment' model interprets profit squeeze as a shift in the aggregate demand schedule along a fixed aggregate supply schedule. Of course, this puts the difference between the two models in the starkest possible way. In fact, the two chapters which attempt to apply formal models to the question of profit squeeze (Chapters 4 and 5) tell more nuanced stories, in which both aggregate demand and aggregate supply schedules shift.

Neo-Keynesian theory, it has been observed, shares the Marxian view of saving as a function of the distribution of income. Where it offers a novel and distinctive interpretation of growth is in its emphasis on the capitalist as investor, and particularly on his psychological state as a determinant of the propensity to invest. In the neo-Keynesian view, businessmen as a class, if not individually, have the power of self-fulfilling prophecy. Suppose businessmen are optimistic about the future and therefore about the prospects for profit, and that they are consequently disposed to take a chance in committing their capital to specific physical forms, as *investment* requires but *saving* does not. Then investment demand will be high and the rate of profit will have to be high in order that the requisite saving be forthcoming; that is, in order that the demand for investment and the supply of saving be equal, as macroeconomic equilibrium requires. By the same token, if investors are pessimistic and little investment demand is forthcoming, the rate of profit required to equate desired investment with desired saving is relatively low. In short, the 'animal spirits' of businessmen, their state of confidence, rather than rational calculation, brings about a corresponding state of affairs. As Keynes put it in the preface to *Essays in Persuasion*, 'There is a subtle reason drawn from economic analysis why...faith may work. For if we act consistently on the optimistic hypothesis, this hypothesis will tend to be realized; whilst by acting on the pessimistic hypothesis, we can keep ourselves forever in the pit of want.'

This is not the place to elaborate a neo-Keynesian theory of investment in any detail. That ground is partially covered in Chapter 4 and more extensively in Marglin (1984, 1987). Suffice it to say here that a variety of auxiliary assumptions enter into the neo-Keynesian view. These range from endogenous, or at least passive, money to the assumption of slack resources, in the manner of a Marxian reserve army. Here we shall focus on only one of these assumptions, namely that adjustments in the real wage accommodate propensities to invest and save. The essential point is the sluggishness of money wages compared to prices: prices respond to demand with greater alacrity than do money wages. In the *General Theory*, this process accompanies changes in the level of capacity utilization and output, or rather drives producers to change the level of capacity utilization, which adjusts in accordance with the dictates of profit maximization. But from the point of view of growth, it is changes in the distribution of income between wages and profits which are primary, since profits affect both saving and investment. In the long run, distributional changes can take place whether or not capacity utilization changes.

In short, in the neo-Keynesian view, it is investment and saving which jointly determine rates of profit and growth, even as each is separately determined by the rate of profit. Productivity is determined by technology, and the real wage is a residual, determined by the output that remains after businessmen's appetites for accumulation have been satisfied.

Evidently this is a very different point of view from the Marxian (not to mention the mainstream) view. In contrast with Marxian theory, the rate of profit and the rate of growth are determined within the macroeconomic structure, rather than within the system of production. The system of production plays a role only in so far as it influences investors' animal spirits.

An obvious question at this point is whether two such diametrically opposed interpretations of the basic mechanisms of capitalist growth can be harnessed together into a single, coherent theory—one, it may be hoped, which does not rely on empirically doubtful propositions like the relative rigidity of money wages as compared with prices. There are at least three alternative tacks that might be followed. First, we might treat inflation as a safety-valve which resolves the tension between the pressure of conventional wages and productivity and the pressure of aggregate demand on profits. Inflation can erode both the real wage *and* investment, as well as the real value of government spending, and thus 'harmonize' the conflicting claims on a limited economic pie. In this hybrid of Keynes and Marx, conventional wages and productivity on the one hand and investment and saving on the other jointly determine the profit rate and the growth rate—each of these elements operates with diminished force relative to a pure strain of Marxian or Keynesian model. This is the tack followed in Rowthorn (1977, 1980) and Marglin (1984).

An alternative is to treat the conventional wage, aggregate demand, and aggregate supply as constraints which may or may not be binding. That is, the space of possible outcomes is partitioned into distinct sub-spaces, each associated with a regime in which the conventional wage *or* aggregate demand *or* aggregate supply drops out of the picture. This 'regime' approach is followed by Edmond Malinvaud (1980) in a somewhat different context.

A third possibility is to drop the assumption that producers determine output by profit maximization but retain the notion that capacity utilization responds to aggregate demand. In this model, aggregate demand affects the profit rate through its effect on capacity utilization, whereas the real wage is not, in contrast with the *General Theory*, determined by capacity utilization alone. This model, unlike the pure Keynesian one, has room for a Marxian conventional wage. Kalecki (1971, chs. 1–8) is the intellectual father of this approach; although in Kalecki the conventional wage is transformed into a mark-up determined by what he calls the 'degree of monopoly'. Chapters 4 and 5 of this book can be interpreted as Kaleckian hybrids, Keynesian models with an admixture of Marx. The difference between the two is that Chapter 4 emphasizes the investment function and Chapter 5 the labour-extraction function. In this sense, the two chapters tell complementary stories about the golden age and its demise.

None of these theories, however they might be combined with one another, offers more than a bare-bones analytic structure, an *approach* to understanding growth in the post-war capitalist economy rather than a detailed blueprint or econometric model of how the post-war regime functioned. In particular, these theories do not have much, if anything, to say about the international economy, nor do they have much to offer on the relationship of the state to other actors in the economy.

The basic premiss of this book in respect to both the state and the international economy is more Marxian than Keynesian: the state and the international economy are each regarded fundamentally as arenas of conflict. This fundamental conflict does not however prevent at least some of the contending players from mutually benefiting from compromise and agreement, explicit or tacit, which may endure for substantial periods of time. This was the case, at least until the golden age began to tarnish, both as regards the internal class compromise that governed the intervention of the state in the domestic economy and the international understandings that underlay American hegemony.

V.1 Beyond Keynes and Marx

A major innovation of this book is the attempt to situate the theory of growth within an institutional framework, and to explain the successes and failures of the post-war regime in terms of the mutual interaction of these institutions. One virtue of this approach is that it allows us to transcend the reductionism inherent in separating the analysis of the internal and external aspects of the golden age. Not only does the emphasis shift from 'external shocks' like OPEC I and II (which became effects of the erosion of American hegemony rather than independent causes) to more fundamental issues, but individual causes are seen in their relation to the whole. The question no longer is whether the demise of the golden age was the result of the breakdown of internal cohesion of the productive system or the result of the breakdown of international arrangements. It becomes instead how the internal and international institutions played upon one another and how these institutions stopped reinforcing and began to undermine one another—in short, how the successes of individual parts of the system bred failure of the system as a whole.

Major policy conclusions follow from this way of looking at things. Take the economic policies produced by right-wing governments in the United States and the United Kingdom during the 1980s. In terms of the perspective developed in this book, both 'Reaganomics' and 'Thatcherism' may be understood as an attempt to construct new institutional arrangements to foster a resumption of growth. Reaganomics, in this view, aims to create conditions under which an essentially Keynesian macroeconomic structure can once again function.

Of course, this has not been the rhetoric. For Reagan and his ilk of supply-siders, Keynes was the demon of profligacy incarnate. But like Molière's Monsieur Jourdain, who spoke prose for 40 years without knowing it, Reagan—whatever he calls his macroeconomic policy—could not have followed the fiscal precepts of Keynes better if he had studied at the feet of the master. To be sure, Reagan's brand of fiscal stimulus was highly skewed towards the rich: the regressiveness of the tax breaks and 'reforms' that have been enacted over the last few years would have been unthinkable in an earlier era. But this difference should not obscure the logic of budget deficits. Nor is this aspect of Reaganomics in itself unappealing. In a world awash with saving, the budget deficits of the Reagan years have had a positive impact on our own and on the world economy.

It is the other planks of the Reagan platform that are distressing from the point of view of this book. First, Reagan's peculiar vision of a new international order has led to a vast expenditure of money and rhetoric on restoring American political hegemony. Grenada seems to be all there is to show for this expenditure, unless destabilization in Nicaragua and counterterror in Libya are counted as successes. The odd thing is that no serious attempt has been made to play a leadership role in forging new international economic arrangements. A charming if rather naïve faith in the market has substituted for real efforts at leadership.

The main focus of Reaganomics, macro-stimulus apart, has been to resurrect the system of production and rules of co-ordination of the early post-war period, in which primary reliance was placed on unemployment, or rather the fear of unemployment, to discipline labour, raise productivity, hold wages in check—all to restore profits as the engine of investment, saving, and growth. (This too has been the goal of Thatcherism. Indeed, Thatcherism might be characterized as Reaganomics without macro-stimulus.)

Thus the containment and even the roll-back of the welfare state. Thus the assault on organized labour. Thus the deepest recession since the Great Depression.

How well has all this succeeded? Better, it must be admitted, than many of us would have expected. But the costs have been staggering. As has been noted, estimates put the costs to the American economy in terms of forgone output in trillions of dollars.

And if the recession of the 1980s imposed significant costs on the people of the United States and other countries of the First World, the advanced capitalist countries, the results have been nothing short of disastrous in the poor countries of the Third World, particularly

in Latin America. Estimates of unemployment run from 30 per cent
in Peru to 20 per cent in Mexico; real wages in Latin America are
estimated to have fallen by as much as one-third in the wake of the
debt crisis triggered by the Volcker–Reagan recession. For the first
time in living memory, perhaps for the first time since the era of the
conquistadores, net capital flows from the First to the Third World are
negative: they are aiding us!

Costs and equity apart, the Reagan–Thatcher solution is problematic on its own terms. It is a quick fix rather than the basis for
renewal. The problem is not the massive US budget deficits. The
problem is rather that under Reaganomics and Thatcherism prosperity
relies on labour rolling over and playing dead, a posture workers are
unlikely to acquiesce in once jobs are, and are widely perceived to
be, plentiful, and the perceived cost of job-loss accordingly returns
to pre-1980s levels. Once prosperity becomes sustained and general,
the internal problems that undid the arrangements of the golden age
are likely to undo the Reagan–Thatcher-era arrangements, despite
the undoubted weakening of trade unions in both the United States
and the United Kingdom—unless the lack of a stable international
order produces a global recession first.

There is a further problem. Even if the Reagan restoration has
finally succeeded in bringing unemployment below its level when
Reagan took office, the recovery is incomplete in an important respect, namely the behaviour of business investment. Although the
initial recovery from the trough of 1983 was strong, non-residential
fixed investment has since declined relative to gross national product,
so that by 1987 the ratio had fallen below 10 per cent to its lowest
level since 1964 (Council of Economic Advisers, 1988, Table B-1).
Conventional wisdom blames the dismal performance of business
investment on high interest rates associated with the US budget
deficit—crowding out and all that—but a more basic problem lies
elsewhere, in the international arena.

Austerity, attacks on the welfare state, union bashing, which along
with deregulation are the conventional wisdom practically everywhere in the capitalist world today, at best address only part of the
problem. Even on the most optimistic assumptions about the effects
on worker motivation and in turn on labour productivity, it is
unlikely that capitalists will respond to higher profit margins with a
higher rate of accumulation—the uncertainties of the international
economic order are likely to dampen investor enthusiasm as fears of
major depression did earlier.

By the same token, any 'solution' which deals with only one aspect of the problem—the internal *or* the international—is likely to be a temporary stop-gap at best. For example, co-ordination of fiscal and monetary policies, the liberal answer to Reagan and Thatcher, and not a bad one at that, aims to reproduce the international Keynesianism that characterized the last phase of American hegemony in the 1960s. It is quite likely that such a measure, permitting a simultaneous expansion of the major industrial economies, would provide substantial relief on the employment front. But since co-ordination fails utterly to address the problem of profit squeeze, it could hardly make much of a contribution to restoring the growth rates of the golden age.

VI. CONCLUSION

Full employment and high growth *can* be restored, but only on condition that policy-makers face up to the need for a profound restructuring of the system of production, and along with it the rules of co-ordination, the macroeconomic structure, and the international order.

We do not question the need for arrangements geared to a high rate of growth of the capital stock, although we are more disposed to argue the case for growth in terms of the need to provide employment than in terms of the need for more goods and services. But if we are persuaded of the need for a high rate of investment, and the need for a macroeconomic structure and an international order conducive to investment and saving, we are less sure of the ramifications for the system of production and the rules of co-ordination.

The first problem is that there are various ways of restructuring the accumulation process. At one end of the spectrum one can imagine totally new mechanisms that do away with the need for profit as a catalyst to investment and a source of saving. More modestly, one can imagine retaining profit as the motive for investment or the means for saving, and formulate the problem instead as one of how to restore profitability.

The implications of these two strategies for the system of production and the rules of co-ordination are obviously different. The first alternative presupposes drastic revision of the institutions that govern labour and capital relations. The second requires revision of the bargain between labour and capital, but this revision of the bargain could take place more or less within existing institutions. In this case the question becomes: what is a satisfactory quid pro quo if labour is to acquiesce in pressure to increase productivity without compensation in the form of higher wages? The problem is not how to roll back wages under conditions of labour weakness such as have characterized the 1980s in the aftermath of the recession of the early 1980s. Roll-backs of one kind or another are fairly easily achieved in these circumstances. The problem is how to lay a foundation that endures even during a period of sustained prosperity, when labour historically becomes much stronger.

We could approach the problem from the other direction and ask what the implications are for the macroeconomic structure and the international order of changes in the system of production or the rules of co-ordination. For example, consider a strategy of eliciting the loyalty and commitment of workers by democratizing the workplace. How would a project of giving workers a greater voice in the workplace affect the prospects for a high rate of investment and saving? Could a reasonable start on the project of democratizing work relations be made within present institutions, with workplace democracy the quid pro quo for wage restraint? Or would it be necessary to do away altogether with an institutional framework based on profits in order to advance the project of democracy? In this case, how would the compatibility of accumulation and democracy be fostered? In particular, what institutions would ensure that democratically controlled enterprises ploughed enough income back into expanding the means of production?

Finally, it must be recognized that however necessary, no reform of the internal institutions of individual capitalist economies will be sufficient for a renewal of prosperity. There must as well be a restructuring of capitalist economic relations internationally. A central issue here is whether there are alternatives to hegemony. If no single country any longer has the political and economic clout to impose its leadership on to the others, is there nevertheless a set of practices, a system of behaviour, which one or more major powers can follow in order to induce co-operative behaviour on the part of the others?

In the answers to these questions may lie the future of capitalism.

2

The Rise and Fall of the Golden Age

ANDREW GLYN, ALAN HUGHES,
ALAIN LIPIETZ, AND AJIT SINGH

I. INTRODUCTION

In 1972 after two decades of what has been termed a golden age of economic performance it could be confidently written that

there is no special reason to doubt that the underlying trends of growth in the early and middle 1970s will continue much as in the 1960s . . . the growth objectives and the capacity of governments broadly to achieve them, have not altered significantly and no special influence can now be foreseen which would at all drastically change the external environment of the European economies (United Nations 1972, p. 125).

Similar optimism could be found in forecasts and comments about the prospects for the OECD as a whole at that time. Whereas in the early 1960s OECD real GNP growth potential was forecast to grow by 4.1 per cent p.a. in the medium term, this had been revised upwards to 4.6 per cent by the mid 1960s and to 5.1 per cent by the early 1970s (McCracken *et al.*, 1977, p. 38).

Now after a decade and a half of stagnation and policy confusion the growth objectives of governments and their capacity to achieve them are viewed in a much more circumspect way. In contrast to earlier real growth rates of around 5 per cent OECD output growth in the medium term is currently forecast to grow at less than 3 per cent p.a., with no significant changes in unemployment rates by the end of the decade. A key question facing policy-makers in the advanced and developing economies is whether this represents a permanent or long-term decline in the growth prospects in the industrial countries, for on their rates of progress hinge prospects for the world economy as a whole.

We attempt in this chapter to throw some light on this vitally important question by adopting a historical approach to the pattern of post-war development across the advanced capitalist countries

(ACCs). This approach is designed to examine the factors which lay behind the emergence of the period of rapid and sustained post-war advance in economic performance in these countries, as well as the factors that lay behind the erosion of the 'golden age' and which account for the uneven and erratic progress since the early 1970s. We hope to isolate those factors which may be expected to persist as a permanent influence on progress in the longer term, as compared to those which are more transitory, as well as to reveal the fundamental characteristics of the golden age itself.

Our analysis ends in 1979. The appointment of Paul Volcker as Chairman of the Federal Reserve in that year symbolized the triumph of monetarist policies and ushered in a period of deliberate, heavy deflation, widely imitated abroad, especially in the UK. This effectively put paid to any prospect of overcoming the second oil price increase by conventional demand management. It finally ended attempts to breathe life back into the golden age economic regime.

The chapter begins with a short outline of the principal macro-economic characteristics of the golden age in the biggest six ACCs, (the US, the UK, Japan, Germany, Italy, and France).[1] The length, steadiness, speed, and spread of the post-war boom are revealed to be so exceptional in the history of capitalism as to suggest that an explanation for its occurrence must be found in a unique *economic regime* rather than in a chance set of particularly favourable economic circumstances. We have thus organized our analysis of the functioning and emergence of the golden age in Section III in terms of a fourfold division of the principal characteristics of this pattern.

We discuss first the *macroeconomic structure*, which summarizes the macroeconomic relations which ensure the perpetuation of the growth path. Under this heading come the relations between wages and productivity, between profits and capital employed, and between investment and consumption. In this connection we place special emphasis on the profits–investment–productivity–wages–profits chain.

The key relationship between investment and productivity growth rests on far more than a technical relationship between machines and output. It is important to isolate the *system of production*, or general principles governing the techniques of production and the organization of work, most typical of a particular period. Such an excursion beyond what is conventionally regarded as economics into the spheres of industrial organization and sociology is, we believe, essential to a rounded account of patterns of growth.

Our third area of analysis is of the *rules of co-ordination* which produce compatibility between individual behaviour and the macro-economic pattern. This includes the systems of wage-setting and pricing which generate the path of distribution between wages and profits, the state fiscal and credit policies which guarantee incomes or maintain demand and so forth.

Finally, individual countries combine to form an international system, with a particular configuration of trade and capital flows reflecting a hierarchy of competitiveness, and function according to certain implicit or explicit rules. This is the fourth element in the pattern of development—the *international order*.

We believe that a particular pattern of development has to exhibit a coherence not just within these spheres, but between them as well. The macroeconomic structure of individual countries during the golden age was founded on and reproduced by a particular system of production, was regulated by a set of co-ordinating rules, and functioned within a particular international order. Such a structure could be undermined by problems originating in one or more of these spheres which then threw the others out of synchronization. The way in which this occurred is analysed in Section IV, which deals with the erosion of the golden age. This is followed by a final section in which we present our principal conclusions.

We trust that the account of the golden age and its erosion that we give in the course of this chapter will demonstrate that our approach is a valuable way of interpreting economic history.[2] We hope that it helps to create a clearer understanding of the constraints and challenges facing policy-makers in their pursuit of a return to a more stable, full-employment growth path.

II. THE GOLDEN AGE IN HISTORICAL PERSPECTIVE

There is little doubt that the quarter century following post-World War II reconstruction was a period of unprecedented prosperity and expansion for the world economy.[3] Between 1950 and 1975 income per person in the developing countries increased on average by 3 per cent p.a., accelerating from 2 per cent in the 1950s to 3.4 per cent in the 1960s. This rate of growth was historically unprecedented for these countries and in excess of that achieved by the developed countries in their period of industralization (World Bank 1978). In

Table 2.1. Growth characteristics of different phases, 1820–1979 (arithmetic average of figures for 16 individual countries)

Phases	Annual average compound growth rates			
	GDP	GDP per head of population	Tangible reproducible non-residential fixed capital stock	Volume of exports
I 1820–70	2.2[a]	1.0[a]	(na)	4.0[b]
1870–1913	2.5	1.4	2.9	3.9
II 1913–50	1.9	1.2	1.7	1.0
III 1950–73	4.9	3.8	5.5	8.6
IV 1973–9	2.5	2.0	4.4[c]	4.8

[a] Average for 13 ACC's.
[b] Average for 10 ACC's.
[c] 1973–8.

Source: Maddison (1982).

the developed countries themselves Table 2.1 shows that GDP and GDP per head grew almost twice as fast as in any previous period since 1820. Labour productivity grew twice as fast as ever before, and there was a massive acceleration in the rate of growth of the capital stock. The increase in capital stock represented an investment boom of historically unprecedented length and vigour.

Rapid though the rate of growth of GDP was, it was outstripped by the growth in the volume of trade which was eight times faster than in the period 1913–50 and twice as great as in the century from 1820 (Table 2.1). Trade among the Western industrial economies was the most dynamic element in this,[4] with trade and output growth especially marked in manufactures. For the world as a whole output of manufactures more than quadrupled between the early 1950s and the early 1970s, and world trade in manufactures grew eightfold (Batchelor *et al.* 1980; United Nations 1972). The major industrial countries began the golden age with an inheritance from the inter-war Depression of a historically low proportion of manufactures exported and a low level of trade in manufactures (Table 2.2*b*). They ended it with the position radically transformed.

There were also major structural changes in the sectoral composition of total output and in the sectoral distribution of the labour force. These represented the continuation of the long-term structural

Table 2.2. Export shares of GDP 1950–1984 and proportion of production of manufactures exported, 1899–1959

(*a*) Export shares

	1950	1955	1960	1965	1973	1979	1984
OECD Total							
Current prices	10.3	11.8	13.1	13.1	16.1	19.0	21.2
Constant prices[a]	9.0	9.8	11.6	12.4	16.8	19.3	21.3
OECD Europe							
Current prices	22.3	20.9	21.8	21.0	25.4	28.3	31.7
Constant prices	12.7	14.8	16.7	18.1	25.6	28.3	32.0
Japan							
Current prices	12.7	10.7	10.8	10.5	10.0	11.6	15.2
Constant prices	4.7	3.9	5.6	6.9	9.0	12.2	17.1
US							
Current prices	4.3	4.4	5.1	5.1	6.9	9.1	7.5
Constant prices	4.3	4.6	5.6	5.8	7.9	9.4	8.2

Note: Constant prices are 1980 prices and exchange rates linked to 1963 prices and exchange rates.

Source: OECD National Accounts 1950–68 and 1960–84.

(*b*) Proportion of manufactures exported (%)

	1899	1913	1929	1937	1950	1955	1959
France	33	26	25	12	23	18	18
Germany	31	31	27	15	—	—	—
West Germany	—	—	—	17	13	19	23
UK	42	45	37	21	23	19	19
Other Western Europe	17	18	23	21	17	18	21
US	5	5	6	5	5	4	4
Japan	25	40	29	40	29	26	23
TOTAL	19	18	15	12	10	10	11

Note: 1955 constant prices.

Source: Maizels (1963), p. 223.

transformation in employment away from agriculture towards industry and then services (Rowthorn and Wells 1987; Singh 1977, 1987). In this period the principal employment shift was towards services, with the industrial share peaking and then falling between 1960 and 1981 (Table 2.3). Since productivity growth in industry was substantially higher than in services between 1950 and 1973, the output share of industry did not shift to the same extent as employment.

Table 2.3. Productivity growth and employment structure: Employment by sector as a percentage of total employment and growth of output per employee, 1870–1981

		Employment Shares (%)				Output growth per employee (% p.a.)		
		1870	1960	1973	1981	1870–1950	1950–73	1973–81
France	A	49.2	21.4	11.0	8.3	1.4	5.6	3.5
	I	27.8	36.2	38.6	34.3	1.4	5.2	3.2
	S	23.0	42.4	50.3	57.4	0.7	3.0	1.6
Germany	A	49.5	13.8	7.3	5.8	0.2	6.3	3.9
	I	28.7	48.2	46.6	43.4	1.3	5.6	2.6
	S	21.8	38.0	46.1	50.8	0.7	3.0	1.6
Japan	A	72.6	30.2	13.4	10.0	0.7	7.3	1.1
	I	—	28.5	37.2	35.3	1.7	9.5	4.7
	S	—	41.3	49.3	54.7	0.5	3.6	1.9
United Kingdom	A	22.7	4.1	2.9	2.8	1.4	4.7	2.8
	I	42.3	47.8	42.0	35.8	1.2	2.9	1.8
	S	35.0	48.1	55.1	61.4	0.2	1.6	0.7
United States	A	50.0	8.0	4.1	3.4	1.3	5.5	1.6
	I	24.4	32.3	32.3	29.5	1.6	2.4	−0.2
	S	25.6	59.7	62.4	67.1	1.1	1.8	0.1

Key: A = Agriculture; I = Industry; S = Services.

Source: Maddison (1984).

Table 2.4. Cyclical characteristics of different phases (ACC's) , 1820–1979 (arithmetic average of figures for individual countries)

Phases	Maximum peak-to-trough fall (or smallest rise) annual	Maximum peak-to-trough fall in export volume	Average unemployment rate (% of labour force)	Average annual rise in consumer prices
I 1820–73	−6.7[a]	−21.7[b]	(na)	0.2[b]
1970–1913	−6.1	−18.2	4.5[c]	0.4
II 1920–38	−11.9	−36.5	7.3	−0.7[d]
III 1950–73	+0.4	−7.0	3.0	4.1
IV 1973–9	−1.3	−6.4	4.1	9.5

[a] Denmark, France, and UK, only.
[b] France, Germany, Sweden, UK, and US only.
[c] UK and US, 1900–13.
[d] 1924–38 for Austria and Germany, 1921–38 for Belgium.

Source: Maddison (1982).

The years 1950–73 were also characterized by a marked improvement in stability. Table 2.4 shows that fluctuations in GDP and in export growth were substantially lower than ever before, with unemployment rates one-third lower than in the period 1870–1913 and less than one-half of those during 1928–30. Consumer prices, however, drifted upwards at an average of 4 per cent p.a., faster than in the previous periods analysed.

After 1973 there was a deterioration in the performance of the world economy and the industrial countries within it. Whilst investment in capital stock held up reasonably well to 1979 (Tables 2.1 and 2.4), output, productivity, and export growth all fell sharply, instability in export volumes and GDP increased, and unemployment and inflation both rose. Even so performance during the period 1973–79 still looks comparatively good in long-term historical perspective. The position deteriorated radically after 1979.

Whilst all the major industrial countries shared in this period of prosperity and stability to some degree, there were significant differences between them (Table 2.6). Thus the US experienced a more modest acceleration in output and capital stock growth than its principal industrial competitors and experienced levels of unemployment quite comparable with long-term historical experience (except for the worst Depression years). Equally marked was the failure of

Table 2.5. Productivity levels per man-hour relative to US (US=100)

	1870	1913	1950	1973	1979
US	100	100	100	100	100
UK	114	81	56	64	66
France	60	54	44	76	86
Germany	61	57	33	71	84
Italy	63	43	32	66	70
Japan	24	22	14	46	53

Sources: Maddison (1982).

the rate of productivity growth in the US to match the acceleration experienced elsewhere. The growth of output per hour worked in the US remained around 2.5 per cent from the turn of the century to the 1970s (before collapsing dramatically in the period 1973–81) (Maddison 1982). This was in stark contrast to the experience of the other major industrial countries, and has been consistently related by commentators to the technological leadership role of the US in the golden age (Maddison 1982; Freeman *et al.* 1982). As Table 2.5 shows, between 1870 and 1913 technical leadership, as proxied by relative levels of output per hour worked, passed from the UK to the US. In 1950 only the UK of the major industrial countries had a productivity level over half that of the US. By 1973 productivity levels ranged between one-half and three-quarters of the US level and the gap continued to narrow thereafter.

These differential productivity performances were, as Table 2.6 also shows, paralleled by export and trade performance, output and capital stock growth, the rate at which capital intensity changed, and in inflation and unemployment. Against this background of the long-term statistical record we can now turn to the first of our tasks, an account of the genesis of the golden age, and the nature of the economic regime on which it was based.

III. THE GOLDEN AGE AND HOW IT EMERGED

In this section we outline the main features of the golden age and indicate briefly how they emerged from post-war reconstruction.

III.1 The Macroeconomic Structure

The central features of the macroeconomic pattern during the golden age were: (i) rapid and parallel growth of productivity and capital

Table 2.6. Post-war economic performance in six major industrial countries (average annual percentage growth rates)

	Average unemployment (% rates)				Consumer prices			Real GDP			Real GDP per Man-Hour	
	1952–64	1965–73	1973–79	1980–83	1950–73	1973–79	1979–83	1950–73	1973–79	1979–83	1950–73	1973–81
US	5.0	4.5	6.5	8.4	2.7	8.2	8.2	2.2	1.9	0.7	2.6	1.1
UK	2.5	3.2	4.6	9.0	4.6	15.4	10.7	2.5	1.3	0.4	3.1	2.9
France	1.7	2.4	4.2	7.6	5.0	10.7	12.1	4.1	2.6	1.1	5.1	3.0
Germany	2.7	0.8	3.1	5.7	2.7	4.7	5.1	5.0	2.6	0.5	6.0	3.7
Italy	5.9	3.4	6.0	8.6	3.9	16.3	17.5	4.8	2.0	0.6	5.8	2.5[a]
Japan	1.9	1.3	1.8	2.3	5.2	10.0	4.3	8.4	3.0	3.9	8.0	3.1

	Non-residential fixed capital stock[b]		Non-residential fixed capital stock per man-hour		Volume of exports		
	1950–73	1973–9	1950–73	1973–78	1950–73	1973–9	1979–83
US	4.0	3.0	2.9	1.8	6.3	4.9	−1.6
UK	3.9	3.2	4.0	4.3	3.9	4.7	−0.1
France	4.5	4.5	4.5	5.3	8.2	6.1	2.3
Germany	6.1	4.1	6.1	6.3	12.4	4.7	4.1
Italy	5.1[b]	4.2[c]	5.4	6.3	11.7	7.1	1.2
Japan	9.2[d]	6.2[d]	7.6	6.8	15.4	7.6	10.2

[a] 1973–9.
[b] Averaged gross and net except where stated.
[c] Gross stock only.
[d] Average of gross stock for whole economy and net stock for private sector only.

Sources: Maddison (1982, 1984); OECD (1985g); Matthews *et al.* (1982).

stock per worker; and (ii) parallel growth of real wages and productivity. The significance of these two relations is that they guaranteed both a roughly constant profit rate and roughly equal growth rates of consumption and production, thus perpetuating the initial rate of accumulation.

Of course such golden age growth took place at very different rates in different countries (fastest in Japan, slowest in the US and UK with continental European countries somewhere between). Growth was mainly centred on the domestic market. Although international trade grew rapidly, it began from a very low base so that for individual countries (other than the very small ones) the domestic market dominated the overall growth of demand. Moreover, an increasing proportion of international trade took place between the advanced countries. Thus it was the internal market of the advanced countries as a group that provided the demand necessary to justify the investment.

As already emphasized the golden age saw an unprecedented growth rate of labour productivity along with a similarly high rate of capital accumulation (growth rate of the capital stock) (Fig. 2.1). Based on the generalization of mass-production systems (see Section III.2 below) it was this high rate of capital accumulation per worker employed that permitted the acceleration of productivity growth as compared to previous periods. Simple econometric estimates based on the experience of capitalist countries over the last 100 years suggest that for every 1 per cent growth of capital stock per worker employed, hourly labour productivity increases by 0.75 per cent. Given that on average capital per worker grew around 2.5 per cent p.a. faster over the period 1950–73 than during 1870–1913, this would account for about two-thirds of the 3 percentage points increase (from about 1.5 per cent p.a. to almost 4.5 per cent p.a.) in productivity growth actually observed. This point deserves emphasis because of the continued popularity of neoclassical growth accounting which typically attributes much less weight to capital stock growth.[5]

The rough parallelism between the growth rate of capital per worker and productivity growth in turn ensured that the output/capital ratio remained roughly constant. This is an over-simplification inasmuch as other factors such as hours of work and relative rates of productivity growth in consumption and capital goods sectors are involved; nevertheless, taking the average of the ACCs, the

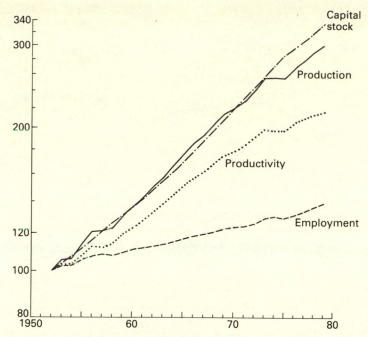

FIG. 2.1 ACC production, capital stock, productivity, and employment, 1955–1980. *Source*: Armstrong and Glyn (1986)

ratio of net output to net business capital stock hardly varied between the early 1950s and the late 1960s (Fig. 2.2).

The profit rate depends on profit share.[6] This in turn depends on the growth rate of product wages (that is, measured in terms of business product rather than workers' consumption) rising in line with the growth rate of labour productivity. Fig. 2.3 shows that these constituents of the profit share grew in parallel. Together with a stable capital/output ratio this contributed to the rough constancy in the profit rate (Fig. 2.4).

The balance between the growth of real wages and productivity does not simply ensure that the profit rate is maintained; it also allows consumption to grow roughly in line with production. Between 1952 and 1970 the private consumption of the ACCs rose by 4.2 per cent p.a. whilst production rose by 4.5 per cent. A fundamentally new development of the post-war period was that the massive growth in production was counterbalanced by an equal growth of consumption—a growth of consumption which, as a result of the institutional and policy innovations discussed below (Section

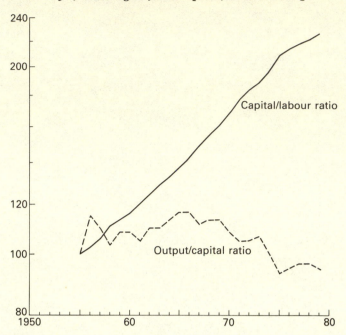

FIG. 2.2 ACC business mechanization and output/capital ratio, 1955–80. *Source*: Armstrong and Glyn (1986)

III.2) came to be more or less universally forecast and anticipated, extending to all sectors of the population but first and foremost to wage-earners.

The significance of the growth of consumption lay not only in the impact on mass living standards but on the assurance it gave to those taking investment decisions of a steadily growing market. This together with the maintenance of what was frequently an already very high profit rate, in relatively tranquil political conditions, provided the essential conditions for the perpetuation of the very high accumulation rates which had seemed likely to fade with the accomplishment of the tasks of post-war reconstruction.

These high rates of accumulation were certainly also bolstered by the rapid growth of international trade which permitted the most successful individual companies to invest at rates which could not have been justified simply by the growth of their national markets. The ratio of exports to GDP at constant prices increased from 9 per cent to 12.4 per cent between 1950 and 1965 and then accelerated to reach 16.8 per cent in 1973. Exports of manufactures also grew faster

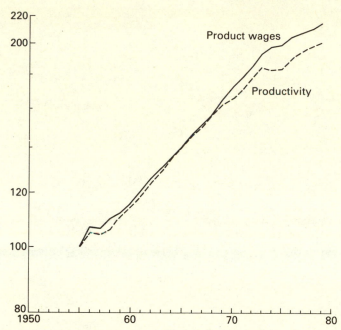

FIG. 2.3 ACC business productivity and product wages, 1955–80. *Source*: Armstrong and Glyn (1986)

in volume terms than production, though for countries other than Germany this trend did not emerge strongly until the 1960s, and in part the overall figures reflected the relatively rapid growth of Europe and Japan where much larger proportions of manufactured output were exported. Despite this strong growth of the volume of exports, the proportion of resources devoted to exports (measured by the current price ratio of exports to GDP) actually declined in Europe and Japan up to the mid 1960s as productivity growth in the export sectors was relatively fast (see Table 2.2*a*). Moreover, whilst the proportions of imports in supplies of manufactures rose steadily in the European countries, by the early 1960s they were still below the levels of 1913 (Maizels 1963; Batchelor *et al*. 1980). So the stress placed on the growth of trade must be a nuanced one; whilst certainly important for individual sectors it was not until the end of the 1960s that production for international trade absorbed an increasing proportion of labour within the advanced countries—in this sense the golden age growth could be regarded as primarily domestically based.

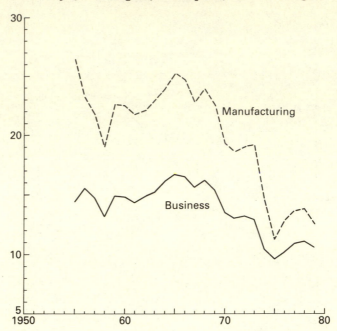

FIG. 2.4 ACC profit rates, 1955–80. *Source*: Armstrong and Glyn (1986)

Under the golden age pattern of development the inflation rate was not determined prior to the growth process and in principle could take on a range of values. The actual rate reflected the 'real' macroeconomic pattern of productivity and income distribution determination. Unlike an (idealized) gold standard, where the determination of the price level reflects relative productivity growth in gold-mining as compared to production as a whole, the post-war structure of macroeconomic relations could have taken place in principle at any rate of inflation (positive or negative). The actual rate reflected the patterns of wage-bargaining, price-setting, credit creation, and international economic relations outlined in Sections III.3 and III.4 below. Here we note that inflation was moderate at around 4 per cent p.a. between 1952 and 1968 in the advanced countries, slower in sectors where productivity growth was particularly rapid (exports, manufactures).

Our description of the macroeconomic structure of the golden age has left aside the question of how it was established within the various countries. It should not be assumed that it emerged relatively unproblematically from the exigencies of post-war recovery; quite a complex and differentiated process was involved.

In the US the business capital stock grew at around 4 per cent p.a. from the end of the war up to the mid 1950s (this was double the average inter-war rate but no higher than before 1914). The end of the war saw exceptionally high profits, even after tax the profit rate was similar in 1945 to the 1929 peak. Demand was kept high initially by pent-up post-war demand (including net exports to countries reconstructing after war damage) and then by Korean War spending and rearmament. Indeed as the latter burst of spending fell away, so did the accumulation rate. It fell to 2.5 per cent at the end of the 1950s until it was revived by the Kennedy–Johnson fiscal expansion, associated with social programmes and then Vietnam War spending. Post-war institutional and policy development did not generate the level of investor confidence required to push up the corporate propensity to invest to a level sufficient to drive demand up to full utilization of capacity (and thus realize the potential full-employment profit rate). The US only experienced a brief period of exceptional accumulation (growth rate of the capital stock of nearly 5 per cent) in the latter part of the 1960s. To adapt Joan Robinson's colourful phrase, the US experience of the golden age was rather a limping one (giving rise to under-consumptionist analyses of the US of which Baran and Sweezy's (1968) was the most famous).

In the other major countries, by contrast, the rate of accumulation edged up more or less steadily to reach peak rates in the early 1960s (mid 1950s in Germany). The 1950s, therefore, saw an enormous investment boom. In Europe the rate of accumulation doubled after the late 1940s to reach some 5.5 per cent in the early 1960s; in Japan the acceleration was even more spectacular, a quadrupling of the growth rate of the capital stock to 12 per cent. This levered up productivity growth and allowed output to continue to grow rapidly after the reserves of spare capacity and unemployed labour had been used up. The other side of this investment boom was that business investment was also the most dynamic element of demand. As a percentage of GDP it rose from 10 per cent to 13 per cent in Europe between 1952 and 1961 and from 13 per cent to 24 per cent in Japan over the same period. Over the same period total government spending on goods, services, and transfers (at current prices) stayed rather steady at around 27 per cent of GDP in Europe and 16 per cent in Japan (Armstrong and Glyn 1986).

What role did high or rising profits play in this process of accelerated accumulation? After the war the balance between productivity
and wages allowed the profit share to be at least at comparable levels
to pre-war (even in Germany and Italy where pre-war meant the
fascist system). These high rates of profit were generally maintained
until the end of the 1950s, before the slow downward trend set
in (see Section IV.1). Japan was the exception where profitability
climbed from far below the pre-war figure to a level probably exceeding it by the end of the 1950s (Armstrong et al. 1984, Chart 6.4;
Armstrong and Glyn 1986).

This high level of profitability was a necessary condition for the
investment boom of the 1950s (and in Japan in particular was further
increased by that boom—(Armstrong et al. 1984, ch. 8). But it would
be wrong to see that investment boom as simply flowing mechanically from the high profit rate. All these countries, with only the UK a
partial exception, underwent periods of severe deflation during the
period 1947–50. Conservative governments bolstered by Marshall
aid, a potent symbol of US support, sought successfully to restore
the 'social and financial discipline' which had been disrupted by the
turbulence of the immediate post-war years (Armstrong et al. 1984,
chs. 4 and 6).

Whilst successful, these deflationary policies did not immediately
restore confidence in the vision of a smooth progression of the
economy towards US productivity and consumption standards. In
1951 stock markets in Europe registered share prices, adjusted for
inflation, well below the pre-war level. The UN Economic Commission for Europe reported 'The general impression was that, after the
Korean boom, Western Europe—with the notable exception of W.
Germany—had entered a period, not of outright downturn, but
rather of protracted stagnation' (UNECE 1955, p. 3). In the same
report the UN noted that such expectations had been disproved and
that 'one of the notable features of the present upswing in Europe is
the great increase in purchases of consumer durable goods' (p. 21).
This underlines the fact that whilst investment, underpinned by high
profits, was the most dynamic factor the growth of consumption
expenditure was an essential part of the process of expansion.

In Japan the pattern was rather different; between 1955 and 1961
production of investment goods trebled, whilst consumption (public
and private) rose by less than 50 per cent. This extraordinary burst
of investment, probably unparalleled in the history of advanced

capitalist countries, defies any simple explanation; with hindsight it is clear that all the preconditions—high profits, abundant and now docile labour supply, access to new technologies, an active industrial policy, and a state committed to rebuilding positions in world markets—were there, but that hardly accounts for the virulence of the upswing. It was not till the 1960s that Japan exhibited the macroeconomic pattern of more balanced growth typical of the golden age.

The golden age structure was reached at different times, by different routes, and corresponding to different rates of expansion in the various ACCs. It should be seen as a way of comprehending the most important trends and interrelationships, rather than as a precise description of the course of development within individual countries.

III.2 The System of Production

The golden age saw the consolidation and extension of the Taylorist principles of work organization (Braverman 1974; Coriat 1978):

(i) Rigorous standardization of work practices through analysis of the 'one best way', covering both the manual operations themselves and the time taken to carry them out.

(ii) A corresponding separation between the conception of work (design, engineering) and its execution.

Taylorism was aimed at increasing productivity in its strict sense (output per unit of effort) by the generalization of the most efficient methods of production, themselves the product of a collective process of 'learning by doing'. But Taylorism was also aimed at control of the intensity of work (effort per hour worked) through the standard procedures with which the worker was obliged to comply.

The expansion of Taylorism was partly extensive. The proportion of those at work who were self-employed, and therefore not directly subject to Taylorist methods of control in the workplace, fell from 34 per cent of total employment in 1954 to 17 per cent in 1973. The most important reason for this was the run-down of numbers working in agriculture. Industrial employment (the traditional heartland of Taylorism) rose more slowly than services, but Taylorist principles were extended into many service sectors as well (supermarkets, typing-pools) (Lipietz 1978).

But the most important expansion of Taylorism was intensive—the incorporation of work norms into the machinery itself. The classic example, and the symbol of post-war mass production, is the car assembly line where the operations required of workers and the time allowed to carry them out are dictated, mechanically, by the machinery. The separation of conception and execution is thereby deepened because the design of new machinery, as well as associated work practices, is entirely divorced from those who work the machines. Mechanization was not of course a new phenomenon, but the unprecedented rate at which it occurred during the post-war period justifies singling out the golden age system of production as a qualitatively distinct combination of Taylorism and mechanization.

The spread of best-practice American technologies and systems of work organization throughout Western Europe and Japan was reflected at the macroeconomic level in the slow process of 'catch-up' of average productivity levels. In the immediate post-war years employers in some countries (notably Japan and Italy) faced the strong and organized opposition of workers to rationalization which was the precondition for the introduction of such technologies. It was not until the late 1940s that the employers' hands were sufficiently strengthened to move ahead as they wished. In other countries (Sweden) a more or less explicit bargain was made whereby labour traded off growing wages against managerial freedom to reorganize production. Common to all were productivity missions sent to the US to bring back the message as to how American prosperity could be emulated. Thus the delegation sent from the UK by the TUC to study the role of US trade unions in promoting productivity emphasized the need to come to terms with 'scientific management'.[7] The various joint industry teams from the UK were unanimous in recommending 'more standardization, more research; the use of more effective managerial techniques (e.g. time study and budget control), more mechanization (especially of, handling operations), and the better layout of existing factories (Leyland 1952, p. 395).

III.3 Rules of Co-ordination

Our interpretation of the golden age has emphasized a macroeconomic structure which was characterized by: profit shares roughly stabilized as a result of roughly parallel growth in productivity and earnings; an unprecedented investment boom; persistent but by later standards moderate inflation; and an overall balance between the rate of growth of productive potential and the demand for output. However, capturing the essence of the golden age requires more than defining arithmetically the macroeconomic conditions for balanced growth. It also requires a discussion of the rules of coordination which led decisions by economic agents—firms, groups of workers—into paths consistent with those macroeconomic conditions. It is, thus, a question of the social acceptance of these conditions and of the institutions seen as guaranteeing them.

Two aspects are of central importance: first the interrelationships between price and wage formation, productivity growth and profits; and second the role of the state in macro-and micro-economic policy formation (e.g. demand management, competition policy, and the provision of social welfare).

Prices, Wages, Productivity, and Profits

In the golden age prices of industrial goods were much as before determined by adding a mark-up to costs in a way which was relatively insensitive to short-term variations in demand. Primary products, however, remained more sensitive to short-term fluctuations in the balance of market forces.[8] By contrast there were important developments in the pattern of wage formation. Wages were determined by a bargaining procedure that was increasingly collective and centralized in nature. In wage and price determination the state took an increasingly active role via incomes and prices policies, welfare state provisions, and its role as a major employer and producer.

Wage Determination

Increasing concentration was associated with increased insensitivity of mark-up-based pricing to short-run variations in demand and with concentrated industries having more stable mark-ups over the cycle (Blair 1972; Hultgren 1965; Means 1935; Boyer and Mistral 1978).

Given the system of fixed exchange rates which characterized the international order in this period, the ability to maintain margins in the face of international competition depended essentially on control over input costs. Since raw material costs were largely set on international markets, control of unit wage costs, through superior productivity growth and the ability to strike a keener wage bargain was crucial. It was a primary characteristic of the golden age that the money wage bargains produced nevertheless a rapid rise in real wages, linked more or less closely to productivity growth.

This link did not emerge on the same terms, or in the same way, in the individual ACCs. Once established, however, its more or less explicit recognition became embedded in the particular institutions of the wage-determination process, so that a general law could be said to have emerged, in which the rate of money wage increases corresponded to the rate of change of prices plus the rate of change of productivity. Institutionally this involved elements of the following processes (Eatwell, *et al.* 1974; Turner and Jackson 1970; OEEC 1961; OECD 1979; Tylecote 1981):

- Leading companies in the most dynamic sectors reached collective agreements with their workers, incorporating a cost-of-living element and an annual improvement factor. These agreements then spread across companies in those sectors, either spontaneously, or under union pressure, by the authority of employers' associations or as a result of state action.
- Similar wage increases spread out to the non-leading sectors through the pressure of labour-market collective bargaining and/or indexed minimum-wage regulations.

Depending on the relative strength of these mechanisms (leading sectors, plus comparability and wage drift), the money wage rises were more or less general and the labour markets more or less 'dual'. This implied an upward drift in prices but also that the general rise in productivity would be reflected in a general rise in consumer purchasing power. Since business expectations came to reflect this, the overall effect was a general encouragement to capacity-expanding investment. There was also a particular encouragement for leading firms because the most efficient producers were able to squeeze the margins of their less efficient competitors by forcing up their wage costs. They were also encouraged by rising wages to scrap their own least efficient plant (Salter 1959).

All of this is not to suggest that individual wage bargains were made explicitly on the basis of anticipated macroeconomic outcomes. Rather it was the mechanisms of wage-bargaining and competitive rivalry in fix-price markets for manufactured goods that tended to produce that effect.

Market Structure and Price Determination in Industrial Goods

The increase in centralization and collective bargaining in the labour market was matched by structural changes in product markets. The period between the 1930s and the early 1950s saw slight downward movements in aggregate concentration in the US, Japan, and the UK, and there were initially concerted efforts to deconcentrate and restructure German and Japanese industry during the US occupation. But outside the US the golden age was marked in all the major industrial economies by an upward drift in the concentration of domestic production especially in the mid and late 1960s. The technical basis of this, in terms of capital intensity and scale economies, was reflected in a parallel but much less marked tendency for average plant sizes to increase and in the emergence of similar industrial patterns of concentration, across countries. These trends were reinforced at the beginning of the period in France, Italy, and the UK by a substantial programme of public ownership and nationalization, and later by extensive merger activity. This was predominantly horizontal in character in Europe and Japan, and conglomerate in the US (Hughes and Singh 1980; Lieberman 1977; Caves and Uekusa 1976).

The renewed tendency for domestic production to be concentrated in fewer hands was not associated with a general increase in the degree of monopoly power. In fact the period was marked by an increasingly widespread anti-trust attack on restrictive trade practices, and cartelization (Edwards 1967). More significantly, the increasing concentration of domestic production was the outcome of a competitive process that was increasingly international in character. The enormous expansion of manufactured exports and intra-European trade, coupled with substantial direct investment flows as the period wore on, was associated with an increase rather than a diminution in the intensity of competition. Whereas domestic concentration rose, world market concentration was stable or fell in a wide range of primary and manufacturing industries (e.g. automobiles) and US and UK multinational dominance was challenged by the growth of European and especially Japanese corporations operating and trading on a world scale (Vernon 1977; UN 1978; Franko 1978).

Welfare State Transfer Payments and the Growth of the Public Sector

Collective agreements, minimum-wage legislation, and the competitive process provided the essential framework within which the incomes of active wage-earners rose with productivity. A similar outcome for the economically inactive emerged with the growth of welfare state transfer payments.

The social conflicts of the first half of the century (and the rivalry between fascist, communist, and social democratic systems) led to the successive introduction of collective provision for those rendered inactive by industrial accidents, sickness, and age, and to a limited degree by involuntary unemployment. The golden age was characterized by a great expansion in the coverage and level of support for those made unemployed (including those formerly self-employed); the introduction of family allowances; the indexation of pensions to cost-of-living changes; and the introduction of earnings-related benefits and pension schemes. There was also a significant convergence in levels of support between countries[9] (Flora and Heidenheimer 1981; Shonfield 1968).

In Europe the share in current price GDP of transfer payments and subsidies to households as a whole rose from around 8 per cent in 1955–7 to around 12 per cent by the late 1960s and around 16 per cent by the mid 1970s whilst the share of income maintenance expenditures rose from 8.3 per cent in 1962 to 11.4 per cent in 1972 (Sawyer 1982).[10]

To the extent that these transfer and benefit incomes were themselves indexed to prices, and to earnings growth amongst the active population, then the tendency was reinforced for positive anticipations to develop of an upward general trend in purchasing power. Moreover, these payments contributed to an increase in the short-term stability of demand and of income. This eased the ability of wage-earners to raise loans, thus facilitating the expansion of consumer credit arrangements.

The combination of public sector income maintenance and the high wage–high investment pattern was so successful in maintaining effective demand that the policy problem for much of the golden age appeared to be how to damp down excess demand rather than how to boost it to maintain full employment.

There seem to have been two broadly defined routes to the implementation of welfare state policies. In some countries the golden age saw the emergence of a social democratic consensus in favour of full employment, the welfare state, modernization, and Keynesianism. In others a liberal capitalist restoration based on a more or less explicit suppression of radical elements in the labour movement was associated in time with the granting of similar reforms (Keohane 1984; Katzenstein 1978; Goldthorpe 1984).

The most obviously social democratic consensual systems have been those of the Nordic countries, especially Sweden, whose post-war system has its roots in the pre-war period. There collective bargaining was centralized between strongly organized employer and trade-union federations, and based on an explicit recognition of the twin constraints of international competition and of the macro-economic accumulation pattern. It included a conscious diffusion of settlements across different sectors of the economy and different classes of income recipient (Edgren *et al.* 1973).

In Germany a solution along the liberal capitalist restoration route emerged. Its elements included decentralized wage-bargaining, and pattern-making settlements in key sectors; the use of its occupational power status by the US to prevent the emergence of socialist indus-trial initiatives; a union movement organized on US initiative on sectoral lines, concerned more with co-determination and recovery rather than short-term money wage gains; and the use of Marshall aid to restore, via the banking system, the essentially pre-war corpo-rate structure. The result was the development of a virtuous circle of high profit, high investment-led growth cycles (Kindleberger 1967; Shonfield 1968; Esping-Andersen and Korpi 1984; Hennings 1980; Faxen 1980; Markovits 1986).

Fiscal Policy and the Expansion of the Public Sector

A second important aspect of public sector activity was state civilian expenditures (e.g. on health, education, and other public-good and service provision), which (with Japan as a notable exception) rose half as fast again as output in the OECD economies in the period 1950–70. This growth along with the even faster expansion of trans-fer payments meant a substantial increase in the share of overall public sector expenditure in GNP, notwithstanding a relatively stable share of government investment expenditure and a declining share in GNP for expenditure on defence (Delorme and André 1982). Where-as public expenditure was around 28 per cent of GNP in the OECD economies in the mid 1950s, it was around 34 per cent by the late 1960s and 41 per cent by the mid 1970s (OECD 1979).

This increase was largely but not entirely financed by taxation. The increased fiscal leverage meant an increase in automatic stabi-lization over the cycle. The balanced budget multiplier and when not balanced the tendency for the average fiscal stance to be expansion-ary ensured that private sector effective demand was reinforced and sustained by public expenditure patterns (see Fig. 2.5). Whether based on explicitly Keynesian commitments to full-employment de-

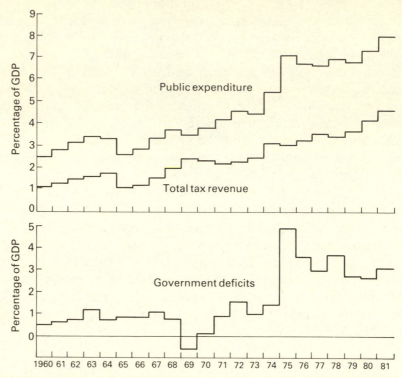

FIG. 2.5 Public expenditure, total tax revenue, and government deficits as a percentage of GDP, 1960–1981. *Source*: OECD (1985b) (unweighted average for seven major OECD countries); averages for 1960–4 exclude Japan.

mand management or not, public expenditures directly fostered and reinforced expectations of high and stable demand. Thus whilst private consumption and investment demand played the crucial dynamic role in the golden age without recourse to systematic public sector deficit financing, the fact that there was a growing perception that governments would run deficits if necessary was an essential complement to that role. By the 1960s policy-makers everywhere were claiming to be Keynesian, most significantly perhaps in the United States which until the 1960s had alone among the industrial nations persistently run its economy at below full capacity (Cornwall 1977; Maddison 1982).

Credit Supply and Inflation

In the macroeconomic pattern which we have described, the growth in the volume of transactions is determined by capital accumulation and productivity. Nominal prices and incomes are the outcomes of more or less formalized price and wage-determination procedures. Given the velocity of circulation credit must be available to finance the resulting nominal value of total transactions. Credit creation to achieve this was possible in the golden age without the constraints imposed by adherence to national metallic currency standards, which proved so restrictive in earlier periods. This development of a pure credit money system at the national level was matched by the emergence at the international level of a dollar standard (see Section III.4 below). Adherence to fixed parities relative to the dollar in the Bretton Woods fixed exchange rate system obviously imposed limitations on the extent to which individual countries could vary their money supply for internal policy purposes. Nevertheless monetary policy operating under a typically hierarchical central bank–commercial bank system (Aglietta and Orléan 1982; Lipietz 1983) was sufficiently malleable to form an important element in macroeconomic demand management (e.g. in the US and Germany in the 1960s); and the ability to create credit at the national level was an important facilitating condition for sustained growth of real incomes. The question remains however of the extent to which real growth was accompanied by a particular inflation rate.

The process of price and wage determination described earlier is consistent with any overall rate of price change. The macroeconomic pattern of the golden age involved a sharing out of the gains of productivity between firms and wage-earners, the latter being the majority of customers. In principle this could be achieved by a stability in nominal wages, and a diffusion of the benefits of productivity in lower prices direct to customers. However, with productivity bargaining in leading sectors this is not possible. Moreover, to the extent that these bargains diffuse to other sectors an upward bias is imparted to prices elsewhere as they are marked up on wage costs. This effect can only be offset by reduced margins or improved productivity in the affected sectors. Without these forces leading to fully offsetting price and productivity changes, the net effect is that relative price changes were brought about at the cost of a chronic upward drift in the overall price level (Lipietz 1986; Morgan 1966; Streeten 1962).

Given that in these circumstanaces some upward drift in inflation is inevitable what forces if any set an upper limit? What constrained firms from improving margins, and unions in their claims for higher nominal wages?

As we have seen, the possibility of a profit push exerting an independent upward pressure on prices through rising monopoly power was not a feature of this period. Mark-ups were therefore maintained rather than increased. Price responded instead to the pressures of cost changes via the mark-up, though the cost changes of course embodied the effects of demand changes in the domestic and international economies (Brown 1984). In a fixed exchange rate system, with the dollar as a reserve currency pegged to gold, inflation in the US fixed the average rate around which the inflation rates of the other industrial countries had to move if they were to avoid international payments imbalance, pressure on their currencies, and pressure to use domestic credit and fiscal policy management to deflate their economies. As long as US inflation, as determined by internal demand pressure and the upward drift required by relative price changes and productivity bargaining, was relatively low, the system as a whole was stable at low inflation rates. Endogenous credit creation to validate changes in nominal values was correspondingly limited. Currency and credit expansions much below or above this range introduced as an aspect of domestic policy would be constrained by corresponding pressures on the exchange rate via the reserves and capital movements. Thus the fixed exchange rate system effectively constrained the extent to which countries could, in the medium to long term, pursue credit creation policies much different from those necessary to validate the real growth of output and a rate of price change of the same order of magnitude as that experienced in the USA.

III.4 International Order

The rules of co-ordination in each national economy functioned within and interacted with the international order. This comprised a coherent set of international monetary, financial, and trading arrangements under which economic interchange, particularly between the industrial capitalist countries, could take place in a more orderly and mutually beneficial manner than in the inter-war period.

The Evolution of the Post-War International Economic Order

The 'new' international economic order which came into being after the war was not a spontaneous development. It was carefully planned, mainly by the governments of the US and the UK, while World

War II was still in progress. It rested on the view that an expansion in the volume of international trade would be essential to the attainment of full employment in the US and elsewhere, to the preservation of private enterprise, and to the development of an international security system.

Moreover, the international economic system would need effective leadership by the US if a liberal international economic order along these lines were to be established (Penrose 1953; Gardner 1969; Maier 1978; Scammel 1983). Action required would include the following:

1. An international organization for the maintenance of exchange stability and to deal with balance-of-payments problems.
2. An international organization to deal with long-term international investment.
3. An international agreement on primary-commodity price control.
4. International measures for the reduction of trade barriers.
5. The international organization of relief and reconstruction
6. International measures to maintain full employment.

This comprehensive programme of international economic planning was the basis of numerous initiatives following the end of the war (Scammel 1983; Milward 1984). In the event the entire plan was never fulfilled. In particular items (3) and (6) were not embodied in a new institution, although some efforts in these directions were made. The first two points of the programme were implemented by the establishment of the International Monetary Fund (IMF) and the International Bank for Reconstruction and Development (IBRD).

There is a voluminous literature on the negotiations and considerations leading to the Bretton Woods agreement and the setting-up of the IMF (see Gardner 1969; Van Dormael 1978; Horsefield 1969; Harrod 1951; Milward 1984). As is well known, there were basically two plans for the proposed new monetary authority: the more expansionist Keynes plan put forward by the British side and the more orthodox White plan submitted by the United States. In the end, the US plan carried the day and the result is an international monetary authority which has inherent in it a deflationary bias in that it imposed most of the burden of adjustment on the deficit countries and relatively little or none on the surplus countries. The original Keynes plan envisaged a more equitable sharing of the burden of adjustment between the surplus and deficit countries;

Keynes's conception of the IMF also involved an automatic mechanism for increasing international liquidity in accordance with the needs of world trade and world economic growth. These shortcomings in the actual institutional arrangements of the IMF became highly significant in the 1960s and 1970s as we shall see later.

The institution of an international trade organization proved much more difficult. The Havana Charter and the International Trade Organization, negotiated in 1947, were stillborn. Instead, a less ambitious General Agreement on Tariffs and Trade (GATT) became the central vehicle for the promotion of free trade. The central principle of GATT was non-discrimination, as embodied in the concept of the most favoured nation. This stipulated that any advantage, favour, privilege or immunity granted by any contracting party to any product originating in or destined for any other country shall be accorded immediately and unconditionally to the like product originating in or destined for the territories of all other contracting parties.[11]

Over the years, the GATT has provided the main forum for multilateral negotiations to reduce trade barriers and tariffs between countries.

The international regulatory framework which emerged from the Anglo-US plans was the result of the interaction of domestic and foreign policy in both the economic and political spheres. In this process the US held the upper hand. It had emerged from the war with its relative economic power greatly enhanced. The US also owned nearly 60 per cent of the world's gold reserves and the other main rival economic power (the UK) was heavily in its debt. In 1946, the European countries had a balance-of-payments deficit of $5.8bn. with the rest of the world; in 1947, the deficit rose to $7.6bn., in part as a result of rising US prices in the aftermath of the abolition of price controls (Fodor 1986). West European reserves in 1948 amounted to only $6.7 bn. In contrast, the US surplus on goods and services was more than $7bn. in 1946 and $11bn. in 1947. These were the years of the dollar shortages.

The Dollar Shortage and the Marshall Plan

From the point of view of countries other than the United States a US surplus on current account and an accompanying dollar shortage became a serious problem when it implied either a restriction of their imports, unemployment in order to avoid a continual loss of reserves to the USA, or borrowing on terms that were either financially or politically expensive (Kahn 1950).

The dollar shortage also implied difficulties for the US since import restrictions by, or recession in, her trading partners threatened her own activity levels. Hence the policy conclusion was drawn that maintenance of US export levels would require a large foreign aid programme since neither the infant IMF or IBRD were politically or financially up to the task of maintaining activity levels both in the US and Europe.

This perspective provided one basis for the Marshall Plan. However, as Block (1977) notes, the Marshall Plan was far more than an effort to finance the US export surplus for a few more years. It simultaneously attacked all the forces which were moving Western Europe away from the liberal, capitalist, multilateral, international economic order desired by the US: the strength of the European Left, the relative weakness of the European economies, and the pull from the Soviet Union. These political factors and the Cold War were decisive in the passage of the Marshall Plan legislation through the US Congress.

As Milward (1984, p. 466) puts it, the US objective in facilitating the recovery programme in Europe (ERP) was 'the total political reconstruction of Western Europe, not just its economic recovery'. The goal was the integration of Western Europe into one common economic area before the end of ERP', an immediate US political interest in this process being the foreign policy objective of binding West Germany firmly into a Western alliance. Marshall aid thus was part of a more general policy of isolating communist parties and trade unions as adversaries of production, and of ameliorating social conflict over distribution in favour of a consensus on growth (Maier 1978; Scammel 1983). As we have seen in our discussion of national aspects of the transition from reconstruction to the long boom, this side of the Marshall aid programme played a critical part in the way the subsequent national rules of co-ordination were to develop.[12]

Marshall aid was massive, amounting to around 1 per cent of US GNP in each of the years 1948 to 1952 (OEEC 1958, pp. 22–3). It also involved a high degree of conditionality.[13] The most important economic objectives of the Marshall Plan were: the restoration of multilateralism, price stability, and recovery of production. In pursuit of these goals, under US encouragement and pressure, the European countries carried out major realignments of their currencies. In September 1949, sterling was devalued by nearly 30 per cent against the US dollar. This was followed by similar changes in the exchange rate in thirty other countries. These events were combined with deflationary policies between 1947 and 1949 in Italy, France, Germany, and other countries. Wage increases were to be prevented from cutting into profits and expenditure on social services to be curtailed in order to promote industrial investment. The upshot in economic terms in the immediate period of Marshall aid was to allow the continuation of the domestic programmes of recovery in the European economies with an income distribution tilted towards profits and investment (Armstrong *et al.* 1984).

In the event the successful pursuit of a national recovery programme in individual countries (itself facilitated by Marshall aid) and the foreign policy objectives of Britain and France thwarted rapid movement towards a widely based supra-national Western European union. Increased integration of a different kind did however emerge after 1950 via the European Payments Union and the European Coal and Steel Community (ECSC). The formation of the latter was strongly supported by the United States and served the purpose of bringing about closer relations between West Germany and France by resolving the historical conflict over the Saar. It also provided an answer to the politically emotive issue of German rearmament (Block 1977; Camps 1966; Milward 1984). In the circumstances US ambitions for a greater European union were ultimately transformed into support for a 'little' Europe of the six which was seen as a more practical alternative (Camps 1966).

The US interest in Little Europe's unity coincided with the aims of the Christian Democratic Parties in the leading European countries as well as those of certain European technocrats and intellectuals who had in various forms long pursued these objectives. The EEC was established with the signing of the Treaty of Rome on 24 March 1957.

The International Economy under US Leadership 1945–1968

In contrast to the post World War I period, a coherent institutional framework for international trade, finance, and payments came into being under US leadership after 1945. By the end of the 1950s, most European countries had made their currencies convertible and the Bretton Woods system had come into its own. The European Community had been established. Under the auspices of GATT but with active US leadership, a number of so-called 'rounds' of multilateral tariff reductions took place in the 1950s and 1960s. By the mid 1960s, after the Kennedy Round reductions, tariffs on dutiable non-agricultural products were reduced to an average of 9.9 per cent in the US, 8.6 per cent in the six EEC countries, 10.8 per cent in the UK, and 10.7 per cent in Japan. The establishment of this post-war international trading and financial system generated the enormous increase in world trade which we underlined in Section II.

The crucial leadership function of the US in guiding the capitalist international economy and in managing the imbalances in the system in the two decades following the war cannot be overestimated. Apart from promoting currency realignments and monetary stability and other measures noted earlier, the US took several steps to facilitate adjustment. In the short term, foreign aid and military expenditures helped to offset the huge trade surpluses with Europe and Japan; the Bretton Woods goal of convertibility was abandoned; and trade discrimination by Europe and Japan against the United States accepted. The US supported the European Payments Union which also discriminated against the dollar. In the longer term, aid to Europe and Japan, and the abolition of occupation controls in the defeated Axis countries, were aimed at rebuilding productive and export capacity in the expectation that this would ultimately widen the market for American exports. (Spero 1977, p. 37)

As a consequence of these measures, and of the European and Japanese economic recoveries, and also in part as a result of government spending overseas especially on the Korean War, after 1950 the US surplus on goods and services fell sharply and the country started to run overall deficits. The US balance on goods and services fell from an average of over $6bn. in 1948–9 to an average of less than $2bn. per annum in the four years 1952 to 1955. The US overall balance excluding net military expenditure but including government grants and capital transactions as well as private capital transactions was $1.0bn. in 1948, $0.2bn. in 1949, −$2.1bn. in 1953, and −$1.5bn. in 1954. (See Argy (1981) for full details of the US balance of payments during this period.) European governments were encouraged to use their corresponding surpluses to build up reserves. The resulting redistribution was considered to be highly desirable. Further, the US deficits were financed almost entirely by the creation of liabilities against herself. As Argy (1981) notes, between 1950 and 1958 the foreign exchange component of world reserves increased by nearly $7bn.; all of this took the form of US dollars. Thus during this period, the dollar was the world's reserve currency and the US was the world's central bank. The overall outcome was an international trade and payments system that facilitated an unprecedented boom in the growth of trade and of national output and productivity. For the greater part of the period, the US authorities followed conservative economic policies, and the US, and hence the world rate of inflation—given relatively stable commodity prices—remained relatively low by later standards.

However, as early as the beginning of the 1960s, the weaknesses of this international economic system were becoming manifest. The root cause of these difficulties was the continuing deterioration of the US balance-of-payments position. The US-led international financial system was not truly multilateral and was not therefore capable of dealing with the imbalances caused by the US itself. By the 1960s the European countries were no longer willing to accept this situation without appropriate constraints on US economic policy. Thus the system of international order which complemented the national systems of production, macroeconomic structure, and rules of co-ordination was put under stress by the patterns of relative national performance to which they gave rise.

Comments on the Logic of the Whole

The interdependence of the system of production, the macroeconomic structure, the rules of co-ordination, and the international order make it very difficult to identify *the* driving-force behind growth. Explanations focusing on one aspect of the pattern of development such as export-led growth (Beckerman 1962), dynamic economies of scale (Kaldor 1967), reserves of surplus labour (Kindleberger 1967), or Keynesian demand management (Boltho 1982) tend to neglect these interrelationships. The system of production and rules of co-ordination underpins a certain macroeconomic structure. This in turn justifies the extension of the system of production and reinforcement of the institutional mechanisms. In fact, it is the right balance between these three factors and, more especially, a social consensus on the value of this pattern of development in its various forms which account for its success.

Thus in the golden age pattern of development the extension of Taylorist systems of working organization, combined with rapidly deepening mechanization, generated enormous productivity gains.

These were particularly important in the mass-production consumer goods industries, especially durables. Problems of 'under-consumptionism' or inadequate demand were avoided by the persistent increase in real wages, fast enough to provide a market but not fast enough to jeopardize the profit share. The extension of collective bargaining and of welfare state spending ensured this growth of demand and in turn reflected a degree of social consensus and secured the necessary degree of 'informal involvement' of workers at work. Anticipation of high profits and expanded markets justified the high rate of investment. The system appeared to operate in a stable fashion against the background of a coherent world trade and payments system and with relatively marginal domestic regulation in terms of wages and credit policy. This stability however could obviously be threatened by difficulties in the system of production, the rules of co-ordination, the macroeconomic structure, or international order. For instance:

1. If productivity growth falters because of problems in the system of production, and is not sufficiently matched by a corresponding moderation of real wage growth or offset by revised systems of management and production, then pressures on profit margins and output capital ratios may threaten the macroeconomic structure.
2. Similar pressures arising from changed bargaining strengths or aspirations may threaten the rules of the co-ordination framework within which the existing margins and distribution of income are accepted. These pressures could arise both from tightening labour markets as well as from increasing recognition by employees of international differences in living standards.
3. Raw material cost pressures in the international system (which for most of the golden age were slight because of stable or improving terms of trade with primary producers) could threaten real wage growth unless offset by higher productivity growth or squeezed margins, thus creating difficulties in the macroeconomic structure.
4. A weakening of US economic performance—higher inflation and cost or production problems—coupled with unwillingness in other industrial countries to accept a US deficit at fixed parities, could undermine the international order.
5. Historical cost-based mark-up pricing behaviour, and incorrect

anticipation of the pace and magnitude of wage increases in conditions of increasing inflationary pressure,[14] may lead to a squeeze on margins, and threaten the macroeconomic pattern.

As we shall see elements of each of these possibilities appear in the period of erosion of the golden age.

IV. THE EROSION OF THE GOLDEN AGE 1968–1979

It is clear in retrospect that 1973 marked the watershed between the golden age years of rapid growth and the stagnation which followed. What is more contentious is whether the golden age pattern of development was undermined by its own internal tensions or alternatively was derailed by relatively exogenous factors such as the OPEC oil price increases. We seek in this section to justify the former view.

Nineteen sixty-eight marks a symbolic starting-point for the erosion of the golden age both internally, being for instance the year of the May events in France, and internationally as it marked the break up of the gold pool. Although the major decline in growth rates can be dated from 1973, we must carry the story on into the late 1970s. For it was during the years after 1973 that it became obvious that the basis for a return to rapid growth would not be restored by a temporary recession and that the institutional and behavioural framework of the golden age proved incapable of containing the pressures deriving from deteriorating economic performance. The appointment of Volcker as Chairman of the US Federal Reserve indicated commitment to pre-World War II financial orthodoxy. Thus 1979 can be taken as symbolic of a much broader recognition that the post-war economic regime had come to an end.

IV.1 The Macroeconomic Structure

The first part of this section seeks to demonstrate that there was a rather general and widespread deterioration in key macroeconomic relations *prior* to 1974 which makes it quite implausible to attribute to OPEC I the main responsibility for the subsequent stagnation. We discuss the growth of labour productivity first, both in absolute terms and in relation to the increase in capital intensity (the 'productivity slow-down'). Then we discuss the relationship between the growth rates of real wages, real materials costs, and labour productivity (the 'profits squeeze'). These two relations in turn determine the trend in the profit rate and we assess the implications of the decline in the profit rate for capital accumulation.

The Productivity Slow-down

Conventional wisdom dates the productivity slow-down from 1973.[15] This is an over-simplification, as there are signs of labour productivity problems in some important countries well before 1973. And of equal significance, there is widespread evidence of a deterioration of the trend of the output/capital ratio indicating a tendency towards a decreasing effectiveness of investment in maintaining productivity growth.

Table 2.7 shows that in the three most important capitalist countries—the US, Germany, and Japan—there was a slippage in the growth rate of hourly labour productivity in business as a whole in the late 1960s or early 1970s. The same pattern shows up in manufacturing, except that in the USA productivity growth rebounded in the early 1970s after a sharp decline in the late 1960s. The slow-down is not universal—in the UK productivity growth rates were at their peak in the early 1970s. Nevertheless the fact that productivity growth rates had slipped back in both the 'leader' country, and its two key followers, must be regarded as of significance.

The pattern for the output/capital ratio (Table 2.8) complements these conclusions in an important way. In none of the three major countries (and French manufacturing) where the trend of labour productivity deteriorated in the late 1960s, or early 1970s, was this offset by an improvement in the trend of the output/capital ratio (such as would be implied by a neoclassical explanation of declining productivity growth reflecting a slowing of capital intensification). Indeed, the trend of the output/capital ratio was at best maintained (German business), typically deteriorated (US, Japanese, and German manufacturing), and sometimes deteriorated to record a value unprecedented in post-war experience (Japanese business, French manufacturing). It is striking that in both Germany and Japan output/capital ratios were falling by 2–3 per cent p.a. in the early 1970s. A similar pattern of, at best, maintenance of the trend of the output/capital ratio is observable in the other European countries, but in most cases (UK, French business, Italian manufacturing) any deterioration was at least partly counterbalanced by some improvement in labour productivity growth (see Sargent (1982) for a neoclassical interpretation).

A way of summarizing these comments is to compare the experi-

Table 2.7. Hourly productivity growth
(average annual percentage growth rates)

	1950s		Early 1960s	Late 1960s	Early 1970s
US[a]					
Business	4.1	2.9	3.9	2.1	2.3
Manufacturing	3.3	1.8	3.9	1.6	4.2
Japan[b]					
Business		7.7	9.9	10.7	7.8
Manufacturing		9.0	8.6	11.4	9.5
Germany[c]					
Business		(6.6)	5.8	6.3	5.4
Manufacturing		6.8	6.8	6.2	5.0
UK[d]					
Business		1.9	2.4	3.0	3.3
Manufacturing		2.9	3.4	4.1	5.1
France[e]					
Business		4.9	5.5	5.6	6.3
Manufacturing		5.5	6.5	7.6	6.1
Italy[f]					
Business		5.8	7.3	6.9	7.0
Manufacturing		5.8	8.1	7.3	8.6

[a] 1948–53, 1953–60, 1960–6, 1966–9, 1969–73: Kendrick and Grossman (1980).
[b] 1954–61, 1961–4, 1964–70, 1970–3: Dennison and Chung (1976).
[c] 1952–61, 1961–5, 1965–69, 1969–73: Volkswirtschaftliche Gesamtrechnungen.
[d] 1950–60, 1960–6, 1965–9, 1969–73: National Income and Expenditure.
[e] 1951–60, 1960–6, 1966–70, 1970–3: DMS disaggregated data-set.
[f] 1951–61, 1961–6, 1966–70, 1970–3: Annuario di Contabilita.

Sources: Manufacturing data adjusted and updated from US *Bureau of Labor Statistics*, Underlying Data for Indices of Output per Hour' (1984). Business data main sources as indicated above. Dating is cyclical peaks.

ence in the early 1970s with what would have been expected on the basis of the achieved growth of fixed capital per worker. As compared to the early 1960s, the capital/labour ratio grew faster in the biggest six countries over the early 1970s. This 'should', according to the relationship obtaining in the golden age already described, have led to hourly productivity growth increasing by around 0.5 per cent p.a. in business and manufacturing. In actual fact it declined by on average 0.5 per cent p.a. in business and by 0.1 per cent p.a. in manufacturing. So, relative to accumulation, there was a distinct decline in labour productivity growth. The trend of the output/capital ratio should have also deteriorated a little[16] but the failure to get the 'expected' labour productivity improvement, means that the

Table 2.8. Output/capital ratios
(average annual percentage growth rates)

	1950s	Early 1960s	Late 1960s	Early 1970s
US				
Business	0.4	2.6	0.4	0.9
Manufacturing	−1.5	4.5	−1.6	1.3
(adj. cap. ut.)	0.4	1.6	−0.1	1.4
(adj. hrs.)	—	—	—	—
Japan				
Business	4.6	−0.3	0.2	−3.4
Manufacturing	5.0	−3.4	0.5	−2.4
(adj. cap. ut.)	3.5	−1.1	−0.4	0.1
(adj. hrs.)	4.5	−2.4	1.5	−1.4
Germany				
Business	0.4	−2.6	−1.8	−2.3
Manufacturing	0.3	−1.6	−0.3	−2.1
(adj. cap. ut.)	0.3	−1.6	−0.3	−1.5
(adj. hrs.)	1.3	−0.8	−0.3	−1.2
UK				
Business	−0.2	0.4	−1.5	−0.7
Manufacturing	−1.3	−0.1	−0.4	−0.7
(adj. cap. ut.)	−1.2	0.4	−0.2	−1.1
(adj. hrs.)	−1.2	0.6	0.1	0.3
France				
Business	(2.0)	1.6	0.2	0.1
Manufacturing	—	2.3	1.7	0.0
(adj. cap. ut.)	—	1.7	1.3	0.8
(adj. hrs.)	—	1.7	2.1	0.3
Italy				
Business	1.8	−0.1	2.4	−1.2
Manufacturing	0.3	−0.2	4.1	0.3
(adj. cap. ut.)	0.4	0.7	2.5	0.3
(adj. hrs.)	0.4	1.3	5.2	3.6

Note: For each country line (3) adjusts for estimated changes in capacity utilization. Line (4) adjusts for hours of work.

Sources: As Table 2.7 plus Artus (1977) for capacity utilization.

deterioration in the trend of the output/capital ratio was that much worse.

Our conclusion is that there is some evidence of productivity problems in a number of the major countries prior to 1973. After 1973 the decline in productivity growth is not in contention. Table 2.9 shows a further deterioration over the period 1973–79 in the

Table 2.9. Productivity and output/capital ratios manufacturing 1965–1985 (% change per annum)

	Late 1960s	1973–9	1979–85
US			
Hourly/labour productivity	4.2	1.3	3.4
Output/capital ratio	1.3	−1.6	−0.7
Japan			
Hourly labour productivity	9.5	5.6	6.2
Output/capital ratio	−2.4	−0.8	2.8
Germany			
Hourly labour productivity	5.0	4.3	3.1
Output/capital ratio	−2.1	−0.4	−0.3
France			
Hourly labour productivity	6.1	4.9	3.5
Output/capital ratio	0.0	−1.1	−3.8
UK			
Hourly labour productivity	5.1	1.2	3.9
Output/capital ratio	−0.7	−3.1	−1.7
Italy			
Hourly labour productivity	8.6	3.3	3.3
Output/capital ratio	0.3	0.0	−1.0

Sources: Table 2.7 plus OECD *Economic Outlook*, Dec. 1985, Table 18; December 1987, Table 20.

growth rates of hourly manufacturing labour productivity, which was very marked except in Germany and France. The pattern for the output/capital ratio is more mixed with both Japan and Germany showing an improvement despite the slower growth of output. By 1973–9 the growth of labour productivity was unprecedentedly low by golden age standards in all countries other than the US and France. The trend of the output/capital ratio was unprecedentedly bad in France and the UK. Only the US escaped having one or other indicators exceptionally unfavourable. The precedents for the US pattern (late 1950s, late 1960s) does not make the 1.3 per cent growth of manufacturing productivity (and similar decline in output per unit of capital) any less feeble.

The Profit Squeeze

As summarized in Table 2.10 the share of profits in net value added had, by 1973, declined by about one-quarter in each of the three main blocs—US, Japan, and Europe, as compared to peak shares.

Table 2.10. Profitability, 1960–1973 (%)

	ACC[a]	US	Europe	Japan
PROFIT RATES				
Business				
Peak year[b]	16.2	19.8	16.5	32.0
1973	12.9	13.1	11.3	19.6
1973 ÷ peak year	0.80	0.66	0.68	0.61
Manufacturing				
Peak year[b]	24.1	35.5	20.7	46.8
1973	19.4	21.8	12.9	33.5
1973 ÷ peak year	0.80	0.61	0.62	0.72
PROFIT SHARES				
Business				
Peak year[b]	23.5	22.5	25.2	38.4
1973	20.0	16.7	18.9	30.4
1973 ÷ peak year	0.85	0.74	0.75	0.79
Manufacturing				
Peak year[b]	23.7	23.0	25.0	40.7
1973	20.4	17.4	17.9	32.9
1973 ÷ peak year	0.86	0.76	0.72	0.81
OUTPUT/CAPITAL RATIOS				
Business				
Peak year[b]	0.69	0.88	0.66	0.83
1973	0.64	0.78	0.60	0.64
1973 ÷ peak year	0.93	0.89	0.91	0.77
Manufacturing				
Peak year[b]	1.01	1.54	0.83	1.15
1973	0.95	1.26	0.72	1.02
1973 ÷ peak year	0.94	0.82	0.87	0.89

[a] ACC refers to average of the largest seven OECD countries.
[b] Year before sustained decline in profitability, which is ACC—1968; US—1966; Europe—1960; Japan—1970.
Source: Armstrong and Glyn (1986).

This decline, whilst of remarkably common extent once the four major European countries are averaged, varied in intensity, being extended over three cycles in Europe, two in the US, and one in Japan.

Some indication of the factors underlying the profit squeeze can be gleaned from the analysis of manufacturing profitability shown in Tables 2.11 and 2.12. These tables present decompositions of the trend in the profit rate in manufacturing for the average of the

Table 2.11. ACC's Manufacturing (unweighted) profit shares and rates (% change per annum)

	Late 1950s	Early 1960s	Late 1960s	Early 1970s	1973–5	1975–9
(1) Hourly productivity		6.2	6.4	6.4	2.3	4.5
(2) Effect of input costs		0.4	0.4	-0.2	-3.3	-0.2
(3) Real factor incomes = (1)+(2)		6.6	6.8	6.2	-1.0	4.3
(4) Product wages		7.0	7.1	7.3	4.2	3.4
(5) Wage share = (4)−(3)		0.4	0.3	1.1	5.2	-0.8
(6) Profit share		-1.1	-1.0	-3.9	-24.4	6.0
(7) Real output/capital ratio		0.2	0.6	-0.6	-7.2	1.9
(8) Effect of capital costs		0.0	0.1	-1.6	-1.2	-0.9
(9) Current price O/K = (7)+(8)		0.2	0.7	-2.2	-8.3	1.0
(10) Profit rate = (6)+(9)		-1.0	-0.4	-6.1	-30.5	7.5

Memorandum items

(c) Weekly hours worked		−0.7	−0.6	−1.2	−2.6	0.4
(d) Relative consumer price		2.4	1.3	0.3	−1.1	1.0
(a) Real weekly wages = (4)+(a)−(b)		3.9	5.2	5.8	2.6	2.8
(b) Real direct costs		4.1	3.9	4.5	3.8	2.4
(e) Relative prices of capital goods		0.8	0.8	0.9	0.4	0.2
(f) Output prices		1.4	2.5	6.2	15.5	8.4

End of period levels

(g) Profit share (%)	25.8	24.2	23.1	20.1	11.5	14.5
(h) Profit rate (%)	23.4	22.2	21.8	17.6	8.5	11.2

Notes: ACCs are the biggest six OECD countries, unweighted averages, and averaged over cycles covering periods shown in Table 2.7.

( ) Real value added per hour worked.

( ) Effect of relative price of inputs (materials etc.) and of weight of capital consumption in reducing the growth rate of wages and profit measured in terms of manufacturing output (see Appendix).

(—) Employee compensation per hour deflated by gross output prices.

(—) Employee compensation adjusted for self-employment as % of net value added.

(g) Net operating surplus (adjusted for self-employment) as % of NVA.

( ) Real value added divided by real gross fixed capital stock.

( ) Effect of relative prices of capital stock and output and other factors (see Appendix).

( ) Net value added divided by net capital stock (current prices).

(10),(h) Net operating surplus divided by net capital stock.

(b) Relative price of consumer goods and manufacturing output.

(d) Weighted average (60%, 40%) of product wages and real input prices—the latter calculated from output prices and real input prices—the latter calculated from output prices and value added prices assuming output is 2/3 value added, 1/3 inputs.

(e) Relative prices of capital stock and manufacturing output.

(f) Manufacturing output prices (wholesale prices)

The addition of the growth rates of the profit-share (line 6) and the output/capital ratio (line 9) to reach the growth rate of the profit-rate (line 10) is very approximate when the growth rates are large.

Sources: Armstrong and Glyn (1986) and national sources.

Table 2.12. ACC's Manufacturing (weighted) profit shares and rates (% change per annum)

	Late 1950s	Early 1960s	Late 1960s	Early 1970s	1973–5	1975–9
(1) Hourly productivity		5.4	4.7	5.6	1.6	3.7
(2) Effect of input costs		0.3	0.3	-1.3	-3.4	-0.3
(3) Real factor incomes = (1)+(2)		5.7	5.1	4.3	-1.7	3.4
(4) Product wages		5.5	5.7	5.2	2.0	3.0
(5) Wage share = (4)-(3)		-0.2	0.6	0.9	3.7	-0.4
(6) Profit share		0.7	-2.1	-3.4	-16.4	2.1
(7) Real output/capital ratio		1.7	-0.4	0.0	-8.1	2.1
(8) Effect of capital costs		0.3	-1.0	-2.1	-0.1	-1.5
(9) Current price O/K = (7)+(8)		2.0	-1.4	-2.1	-8.2	0.6
(10) Profit rate = (6)+(9)		2.6	-3.4	-5.3	-23.6	2.6
(a) Weekly hours worked		-0.2	-0.6	-0.7	-2.1	0.4
(b) Relative consumer price		1.9	1.6	0.4	-1.6	0.9
(c) Real weekly wages = (4)+(a)-(b)		3.6	3.5	4.1	1.5	2.6
(d) Real direct costs		3.3	3.2	4.1	2.7	2.0
(e) Relative prices of capital goods		1.0	1.4	0.7	-0.1	0.1
(f) Output prices		1.1	2.4	5.4	14.2	7.4
End of period levels						
(g) Profit share (%)	23.7	24.7	22.5	19.9	13.9	15.1
(h) Profit rate (%)	24.7	28.8	24.7	20.4	11.9	13.2

Notes: ACCs are the biggest six OECD countries, weighted (by 1965 GDPs), and averaged over cycles covering the periods shown in Table 2.7. See notes to Table 2.11.

Sources: Armstrong and Glyn (1986) and national sources.

biggest six countries (unweighted in Table 2.11, weighted in Table 2.12). Line (3) shows the real growth rate of wage and profit income combined which is permitted by the growth of hourly productivity after allowing for changes in the real cost of non-labour inputs. The wage share in value added rises or falls (line (5)), depending on whether the growth of product wages (wages deflated by the price of manufacturing output, line (4)) rises faster or slower than the growth of total factor incomes. Line (6) translates this growth rate of the wage share into a growth rate for the profit share (opposite in sign and greater in magnitude in proportion to the ratio of wages to profits). Also relevant to the interpretation are the memorandum items (a)–(c) which show the impact of changes in hours of work and of the price of consumer goods (relative to manufactured goods) on the growth rate of workers' real wages.[17]

Already in the early 1960s the share of wages in value added was rising by 0.4 per cent p.a. as hourly product wages rose faster than what was available for distribution as real factor incomes (wages plus profits). The falling real cost of inputs of materials (and depreciation) halved the impact on the wage share of the excess of product wages growth over productivity growth.

The more severe profit squeeze of the early 1970s reflected a reversal of the favourable input cost trend (reducing the growth rate of real factor incomes by 0.6 per cent p.a.) whilst product wages growth increased a little. Whilst hours of work were declining faster in the early 1970s, consumer prices grew hardly faster than manufacturing prices. This was in contrast to much faster relative growth of consumer prices in the early 1960s and allowed real weekly wages (in terms of what workers could buy) to rise by 1.5 per cent faster in the period.[18]

These unweighted results show the 'typical' position amongst the major countries. Developments in the USA dominate the differences between them and the weighted estimates (Table 2.12). The weighted pattern is for profit squeeze to develop in the late 1960s due to a slow-down in productivity, and to intensify in the early 1970s due to the sharp increase in real input costs despite the recovery in productivity and a slight slow-down in product wage growth.

Any such 'accounting' for the profit squeeze does not establish causation. For example, a slowing down of productivity growth, or adverse trend in real materials costs, only leads to profit squeeze if product wages do not absorb the deterioration. Maintenance of real mark-ups would automatically offload on to workers a share of this reduction in the growth of real factor incomes and allow the profit share (of a more slowly growing total) to be maintained. That this did not happen suggests a combination of pressures on profit margins— first, workers' bargaining position had been somehow strengthened which allowed them to maintain, and actually increase, the growth rate of the real wages they bargained for, despite the adverse movements in input costs and on occasions productivity; second, some forces inhibited a full passing on of these cost pressures in the form of higher prices. Prices did accelerate—in the early 1970s manufacturing prices were rising at around 5 per cent p.a. as compared to 1 per cent p.a. in the early 1960s—but not sufficiently to prevent the continuing and intensifying profit squeeze.

So in addition to the underlying factors of productivity and input costs the situation in both labour and product markets has to be considered. The tight labour markets established in the early 1960s in Europe, mid 1960s in the US, and early 1970s in Japan, undoubtedly strengthened labour's bargaining position as reserves of unemployed and underemployed labour were eroded.[19] The extent to which a regular growth of real wages had become etched into workers' expectations was most dramatically manifested in the wage explosions of the late 1960s. The behavioural and institutional background to these changes is discussed in Section IV.3 below.

The failure of product wages to slow in line with real factor incomes had a positive effect on productivity. It forced the earlier scrapping of the less productive vintages of equipment. But such a pattern also reflected pressures preventing prices accelerating in line with money wages. A Keynesian explanation of such a peak-to-peak profit squeeze, in terms of lack of aggregate demand, could hardly be convincing since demand was very high at the cyclical peaks in the late 1960s and early 1970s. The lags in the application of mark-up rules could of themselves lead to reduced real profits as cost increases accelerated. No doubt an important role in inhibiting faster adjustment of mark-ups was played by competition from new vintages of equipment, and especially international competition as tariff barriers fell and international trade between the advanced countries expanded rapidly (see Section IV.3 below).[20]

Our eclectic summary of influences on the profit squeeze prior to 1973 would emphasize productivity slow-down, rising real input costs, tighter labour markets which had lead to a secular increase in workers' bargaining position, and intensified competition, especially across national boundaries, as contributory factors. Attempting to attribute relative importance to these would be a very tricky counter-factual exercise. It is one we can side-step by noting that the dominant forces in this process were clearly not of a temporary character.

In the years up to 1979 the profit squeeze continued at a rather similar rate to that of the early 1970s (Tables 2.11 and 2.12). Productivity growth slowed markedly and there was a much faster rise in the real cost of inputs (both materials and depreciation) than in the early 1970s. So despite a halving of the growth rate of product wages they were still increasing by more than 1 per cent faster than real factor incomes. The squeeze on profits was at its most intensive over the recession years of 1974 and 1975—the profit share in manufacturing halving in Japan and nearly halving in Europe (the falls in business were much less dramatic—Armstrong and Glyn (1986)). The growth of productivity was slowest, and the rise in materials costs steepest, in those two years of recession induced by the oil crisis. But the recovery after 1975 neither returned the growth of productivity to its pre-1973 rate nor wholly relaxed the continuing pressure from materials costs. So although product wages continued to grow much more moderately than prior to 1973 the recovery in the profit share only made up for part of the ground lost during 1973–5. By 1979 the profit share was typically around two-thirds of its peak level (half for Japanese manufacturing, see Table 2.13).

The Profit rate and Investment

As shown earlier the movement of the profit rate can be decomposed into movements in the profit share and in the output/capital ratio. Whilst the fall in the profit share dominates the pre-1974 pattern (Table 2.10), declines in the output/capital ratio of the order of one-tenth contributed to the fall in the profit rate in each of the major blocs.[21]

By 1973 the profit rate had declined by about one-third in North America, Western Europe, and Japan, in both manufacturing and business. The output/capital ratio declined sharply in 1974–5, reflecting mainly excess capacity. Although there was some recovery by 1979, the ratio was still below the 1973 level and so contributed, along with the fall in the profit share after 1973, to the further decline in the rate. By 1979 the profit rate in both business and manufacturing was around half or less of the peak rate in each of the major blocs (Table 2.13).

Such a substantial fall in the profit rate, even before 1974, estab-

Table 2.13. Profitability, 1973–1979 (%)

	ACC[a]	US	Europe	Japan
PROFIT RATES				
Business				
1973	12.9	13.1	11.3	19.6
1979	10.6	10.7	9.4	14.7
1979 ÷ peak year[b]	0.63	0.54	0.57	0.46
Manufacturing				
1973	19.2	21.8	12.9	33.5
1979	12.7	15.5	9.6	14.2
1979 ÷ peak year[b]	0.53	0.44	0.46	0.36
PROFIT SHARES				
Business				
1973	20.0	16.7	18.9	30.4
1979	18.4	15.7	16.7	26.6
1979 ÷ peak year[b]	0.78	0.7	0.67	0.66
Manufacturing				
1973	20.4	17.4	17.9	32.9
1979	15.6	15.1	13.3	19.2
1979 ÷ peak year[b]	0.66	0.66	0.53	0.47
OUTPUT/CAPITAL RATIOS				
Business				
1973	0.64	0.78	0.59	0.64
1979	0.57	0.68	0.56	0.55
1979 ÷ peak year[b]	0.83	0.77	0.85	0.66
Manufacturing				
1973	0.95	1.26	0.71	1.02
1979	0.81	1.03	0.72	0.74
1979 ÷ peak year[b]	0.80	0.67	0.87	0.64

[a] ACC refers to average of the biggest seven OECD countries.
[b] Year before sustained decline in profitability, which is ACC—1968; US—1966; Europe—1960; Japan—1970.
Source: Armstrong and Glyn (1986).

lishes rather clearly that the golden age pattern was being eroded. But just what were the implications of this fall in profitability, in particular for the rate of accumulation which was the motor of the whole process?

Contrary to earlier work (see, for example, Helliwell 1976) recent econometric analysis has supported the importance of profitability in explaining investment trends (see Lindbeck 1983; Weisskopf 1985; Bruno 1986). Following this approach we explored the relationship between the growth rate of the capital stock and profitability using

Table 2.14. Accumulation and profit share regressions, 1952–82 (dependent variabale—growth rate of gross stock of fixed capital (K))

	Const	K(−1)	PS(−1)	$\bar{R}2$	Durbin's *t*-stat	Chow's F-stat
Japan						
Business	−3.54	0.67	0.2	0.84	0.5	1.2
	(2.0)	(6.6)	(2.9)			
Manufacturing	−2.28	0.36	0.29	0.73	1.3	0.6
	(1.2)	(1.7)	(2.6)			
Germany						
Business	−1.65	0.54	0.17	0.92	1.6	2.1
	(3.3)	(5.6)	(5.0)			
Manufacturing	−2.74	0.57	0.22	0.96	3.3	2.6
	(5.2)	(6.6)	(5.7)			
US						
Business	−0.41	0.71	0.08	0.53	1.0	2.2
	(0.5)	(5.5)	(2.1)			
Manufacturing	−1.31	0.72	0.12	0.58	1.7	11.8
	(1.4)	(6.0)	(2.6)			
France						
Business	−0.19	0.88	0.04	0.87	2.9	12.7
	(0.3)	(14.1)	(1.4)			
Manufacturing	−0.08	0.9	0.03	0.83	0.5	6.1
	(0.2)	(12.1)	(1.4)			
UK						
Business	0.09	0.81	0.03	0.72	0.4	0.2
	(0.2)	(8.4)	(1.8)			
Manufacturing	0.87	0.27	0.07	0.46	0.4	0.5
	(1.8)	(1.5)	(3.2)			
Italy						
Business	−0.5	0.71	0.11	0.85	1.2	4.6
	(1.1)	(7.5)	(3.7)			
Manufacturing	−1.17	0.84	0.12	0.75	1.4	6.0
	(1.3)	(8.3)	(2.1)			

Notes: *t* values in brackets (5% confidence interval *t* = 1.7, 1% *t* = 2.5) K(−1) is lagged growth rate of the capital stock. PS(−1) is the lagged net profit share. Durbin's *t*: autocorrelation (with lagged dependent variable). Chow's F: structural break at 1973 (2.7, 5% confidence).

data on business and manufacturing for the ACCs (see Armstrong and Glyn 1986). We report the results in Table 2.14 using the lagged profit share as our profitability indicator (see Chapter 4). With lagged capital stock growth also included the profit share is significant everywhere except France (where it is not far from significant). Whilst we have not carried out fully specified tests of alternative

Table 2.15. Pooled regressions, 1952–82 (dependent variable—growth rate of gross stock of fixed capital (K))

	Const.	PR(−1)	$\bar{R}2$
Business			
1952–82	0.71	0.33	0.60
	(2.6)	(17.7)	
1952–73	0.13	0.36	0.59
	(0.3)	(14.1)	
Manufacturing			
1952–82	0.7	0.24	0.49
	(2.0)	(14.2)	
1952–73	0.73	0.24	0.42
	(1.3)	(10.1)	

Notes: t values in brackets (5% confidence interval $t = 1.7$, 1% $t = 2.3$). PR(−1) is the lagged net profit rate. Countries covered: as Table 2.14 plus Canada.

hypotheses it is noteworthy that experiments with other specifications including the addition of lagged output growth left profitability significant more often than not, and more often than lagged output. These experiments (not reported here) suggest that profitability is not just proxying for accelerator terms.[22]

Table 2.15 presents some pooled regressions for the seven countries, using the profit rate rather than the profit share. For the period up to 1973 the lagged profit rate explains 42 per cent of the variance (across countries and time) of the manufacturing accumulation rate and 59 per cent of the variance of the business accumulation rate. Applying the estimated coefficients to the fall in profit rates would imply a fall in the rate of accumulation in business of about 1.5 per in Europe, 2 per cent in the US, and 4 per cent in Japan between the years after peak profit rates (1960, 1966, and 1970 respectively) and 1974. The actual outcomes were very close to the predictions for Europe and Japan (1.25 per cent and 4 per cent respectively), but with very little fall in the US. The patterns for manufacturing are similar, except that there was a larger actual decline in the accumulation rate in Europe and a small decline in the US.[23]

In the absence of a more fully articulated explanation of the determinants of profitability and accumulation, and the links between the two, these results are suggestive. They indicate that by 1974 the pressures which had driven profit rates down had made a definite dent in the accumulation rate, especially in Japan and Europe. Of course causality need not run from a decline in profits to a decline in investment. It is quite possible, as Chapter 4 argues, that it was the decline in the output/capital ratio which drove the rate of growth of the capital stock downward. Had profit margins been maintained the increase in investment per unit of profit might have offset the decrease in the output/capital ratio. In the event, the failure of profitability to recover in Europe and Japan in the years up to 1979 was reflected in a further slippage in the accumulation rate. By 1980 the growth rate of the capital stock in European business was 3.8 per cent, as compared to peak rates of 5.8 per cent in the early 1960s; in Japan the fall was to 6.7 per cent, just under half the peak reached in 1970. In manufacturing accumulation rates were about one-third of peak rates in Europe and Japan. Only in the US was the decline in profitability without a strong impact on investment; accumulation maintained its rather limping path.

Internationalization

We have characterized the golden age structure of growth as being primarily focused on the internal market. International trade grew rapidly, but from a very low starting-point. Although the volume of exports grew more rapidly than GDP or manufacturing production the faster productivity growth of exporting sectors prevented the share of exports in the value of production rising. The end of the 1960s saw an important change. Between 1965 and 1973 the increase in the volume of exports was so strong in both Europe and the US (rising by more than one-third as a ratio to GDP) that the current price ratio increased as well (see Table 2.2a). It was only Japan, where output growth as a whole was so enormous over this period, that the ratio rose in neither current or constant price terms. Japan was also unique in having a share of imported manufactures in manufacturing supply far below its pre-World War I level (5 per cent in 1971 as against 34 per cent in 1913) whereas the UK and Germany regained historical levels of import penetration rates and the US was for the first time importing substantial volumes of manufactures.

This growing internationalization was paralleled by capital flows—direct, portfolio, and banking. As already noted it played a role in cementing the pressure on wages from tight labour markets and militant unions into a decisive squeeze on profits. The most important sense in which this contributed to the erosion of the golden age, however, was that it weakened the ability of individual countries to regulate their macroeconomies through demand and exchange rate management.

Inflation

The modest inflation rates of the golden age reflected the pattern of wage-bargaining, price-setting, credit creation, and international relations as described earlier. The real pressures on the golden age macroeconomic structure which we have identified—tendency to declining productivity growth, increasing cost of imported inputs—put pressure on inflation rates as well, as did the erosion of the reserves of labour and the consolidation of trade union organization. Increasing real costs of production coincided with increased capacity for organized labour to press its claims. Whilst increased international competition acted as a constraint on price increases the incapacity of the international monetary system to absorb the strains resulting from this increased competition led to the breakdown of fixed exchange rates, and the limitation that imposed on inflation rates. The combination of these pressures, and in particular the oil price increase of 1973, had pushed the inflation rate up from 3 per cent in 1965 to over 15 per cent by 1974. Slower growth thereafter only provided some remission, with the inflation rate stuck at around 8 per cent throughout the rest of the 1970s.

IV.2 The System of Production

The writing was already on the wall for the Fordist system of production in the 1970s. As three Harvard Business School Professors commented of the US automobile industry: 'Having in the most deliberate manner possible committed themselves to standardization, managers usually believed they had no alternative to sticking with it to the bitter end. As events have shown the end has been bitter indeed' (Abernathy *et al.* 1983, p. 18).

By the early 1980s it was 'officially' pronounced outmoded in an authoritative article in the *Harvard Business Review*:

At the heart of this traditional model is the wish to establish order, exercise control and achieve efficiency in the application of the workforce...the model's real father is F. W. Taylor...Recently, however, changing expectations among workers have prompted a growing disillusionment with the apparatus of control. At the same time of course, an intensified challenge from abroad has made the competitive obsolescence of this strategy clear...

Especially in a high wage country like the United States, market success depends on a superior level of performance, a level that, in return requires the deep commitment, not merely the obedience—if you could obtain it—of workers. And as painful experience shows, this commitment cannot flourish in a workplace dominated by the familiar model of control (Walton 1985, pp. 77–8).

The search for a way out of productivity problems seems to express a fundamental weakness in the golden age system of production. On the one hand the mass of unskilled workers are systematically and *in principle* excluded from the search for new technologies. The design of these, and the work patterns required to implement them, is carried out exclusively by specialist departments (research and development, industrial relations, and so forth). And yet the effective functioning of the new machinery does require workers' involvement in the process of production. This is in order to guarantee the smooth running of the process in the face of hiccups in the supply of components, mechanical malfunctioning, or breakdowns.[24]

That such *informal involvement* (Linhart and Linhart 1985) is assumed by management is demonstrated most clearly by the fact that the 'work-to-rule' is a weapon in the hands of workers rather than representing their ultimate compliance with Taylorist norms. Workers' experience and ingenuity was systematically disregarded in the design of new technologies but implicitly relied on in their implementation. Drawing on workers' experience could become increasingly necessary if the possibilities of generalizing existing techniques of production began to slacken and/or if returns from specialized research and development activity began to weaken. Equally, implementation of new technologies might become problematic if increasingly sophisticated processes and products began to rely more on the informal involvement of workers, thus cutting against the grain of formal organization of work and incentive structures. Similar tensions could arise if improved security and bargaining position on the shop-floor reduced the pressure on workers to display such an unrecognized commitment to what they were doing. Some combination of these pressures seems the most plausible way of understanding the factors underlying the slow-down in productivity growth and the search for a new system of production which emerged in the 1970s.

What further light can be shed on this through examination of productivity patterns in more detail? Mainstream accounting for the

Table 2.16. Cars and mining labour productivity[a] (annual average percentage increases)

	1950s	Early 1960s	Late 1960s	Early 1970s
Transport equipment				
US (hrly)	3.7	4.4	0.9	3.8
Japan	12.4	14.0	10.3	2.3
Germany (hrly)	—	6.1	5.3	3.9
UK (hrly)	6.1	2.9	2.6	0.5
Italy	10.0	7.5	4.0	−0.2
France	—	6.7	4.5	5.5
Mining				
US (hrly)	3.5	4.8	3.2	−1.0
Japan	8.8	15.2	6.8	3.3
Germany	4.3	6.3	6.3	3.9
UK	0.4	3.7	4.6	1.6
Italy	9.7	2.3	8.4	2.4

[a] Output per working or per hour worked (hrly).

Sources: as Table 2.7.

slow-down of productivity growth after 1973 centres on the slower increase in the capital/labour ratio, resource allocation effects, and the observed positive relationship between manufacturing output growth and productivity growth—the Verdoorn effect. According to Maddison's survey (1984), quite substantial unexplained residual slow-downs remain, though these would be much smaller if more weight were placed on capital accumulation.[25] However, the much slower overall growth makes it especially difficult to disentangle the source of productivity problems after 1973. Thus the period prior to 1973 is particularly interesting. We assembled as comprehensive as possible a disaggregated industrial data-set on productivity to examine pre-1973 trends.

The automobile industry is generally seen as epitomizing the golden age system of production. The US industry did suffer a disastrous period during 1966–9, with labour productivity growth declining to 1 per cent p.a., and the output/capital ratio falling. However, in common with the rest of manufacturing, the 1969–73 cycle saw a rebound in both variables, with productivity growing at nearly 4 per cent p.a. Table 2.16 also shows very sharp declines in labour productivity growth in the transport equipment sectors in all the other major countries except France (the Japanese case may be affected by the inclusion of shipbuilding). In Italy and Japan there

Table 2.17. Comparative productivity levels in 1967
(Output per worker; US level = 100)

	France	Germany	UK	Japan
Construction materials	45	50	30	50
Metal manufacture	45	60	40	55
Textiles	45	60	40	55
Wood/Paper	40	55	40	35
Mechanical engineering	45	55	25	45
Electrical engineering	40	40	35	45
Transport equipment	25	35	20	30
Chemicals	65	55	45	35
Food	50	45	50	35
Total Manufacturing	45	50	35	45

Note: Figures are heavily rounded to emphasize the necessarily very approximate nature of calculations.

Source: Calculated from Guinchard (1984), Tables 1 and 2.

were sharp deteriorations in the output/capital ratio trend in the early 1970s, and this was also true in France. The *level* of labour productivity in transport equipment varied from around one-fifth the US level in the UK (Table 2.17) to one-third in Germany; this strongly suggests that the difficulties in maintaining the momentum of productivity *growth* must stem more from social rather than technical limits.

The pattern in other industries (not shown in the table for reasons of space) varies. Non-electrical machinery sometimes shares the slow-downs detected in transport equipment (Japan, Italy, and France) but not elsewhere. The 'heavy' sectors—chemicals and metal manufacture—showed exceptionally poor productivity growth only in Germany (a world leader in chemicals and the most important European steel producer). Textile productivity growth was exceptionally poor only in the US. Indeed it is striking that in the US, which has the highest level of productivity in all these sectors (Table 2.17), and thus is presumably more susceptible to any impending exhaustion of existing technologies, several important industries show productivity growth as fast (chemicals, non-electrical machinery) or faster (clothing, paper, wood) in the early 1970s as over any previous cycle.

Construction productivity declines in the US, and does poorly in Japan and the UK, but not elsewhere. Mining—a barometer industry for industrial relations—shows productivity slowing typically to half its previous rate (Table 2.16); by contrast agriculture and energy show peak productivity growth rates.

Hours of work typically fell around 0.5 per cent p.a. faster in the early 1970s than in the late 1960s; in some countries (France and Italy) this was an unprecedented reduction by post-war standards, whilst in Japan and Germany it was rather a reversion to previous trends (OECD 1985*e*). This might suggest a stronger position for workers on the shop-floor which could extend to work practices as well; there seems outside Japan, however, to have been a trend towards increasing shift work typically covering an additional 0.25–0.5 per cent of manufacturing employment each year (Prais 1981; Barou 1979; Cette and Jolly 1984).

This brief survey of our disaggregated productivity data falls short of a definitive conclusion. In the great majority of cases either labour productivity or output per unit of capital decelerate in the early 1970s (or late 1960s) whilst the trend in the other variable is at best maintained. The more adverse cases include Japanese business, French manufacturing, and a large number of transport equipment and machinery sectors.

As far as the US is concerned, the deterioration in productivity performance generally pushed growth rates back down to the level of the 1950s. In the main industries typical of the golden age model productivity rebounded in the early 1970s (the problem industries were mining and construction). There was still a very wide productivity gap in the mid 1960s between other countries and the US (at least according to some of the available estimates—see note to Table 2.17). This makes it hard to credit 'catch-up' with the US (or limits to the further generalization of existing technologies) as the main explanation for slow-downs outside the US. On the other hand the fact that the trends in the early 1970s were generally less unfavourable in Italy, France, and the UK, where class conflict was of exceptional severity from the mid 1960s, suggests that traditional systems of production could be effectively strengthened and tightened under some circumstances. Whilst the widespread nature of productivity problems is confirmed, the lack of a clear pattern leads us back to the rejection by employers of the golden age system of organizing work as the strongest confirmation that these problems reflected fundamental difficulties in obtaining the necessary degree of labour commitment.

IV.3 The Rules of Co-ordination in the Period of Erosion

That costs and prices rose steadily during the golden age reflected the interaction of the system of wage settlements with mark-up pricing behaviour. The persistence of inflation had some important feedbacks on government policy which affected the nature of this interaction. Moreover, the tendency of the system to produce a drift of income share away from profits towards wages led management to take bargaining initiatives.

Pressures on the Growth of Real Wages

Where governments were committed to maintaining a fixed international parity, inflation much out of line with international trends implied a weakening balance of payments. Attempts to control inflation in these circumstances took the form of deflation and/or controls over wages and prices.[26] Both of these developments threatened the steady expansion of real wages. Increasing government involvement also led to some shift in those countries with decentralized systems of collective bargaining towards a more centralized approach. This pressure on grass-roots autonomy was reinforced by developments in management strategies. The growth of divisionalized management structures and the associated imposition of company-wide bargaining procedures in diversified conglomerate firms threatened the independence of plant- and enterprise-level bargaining.[27] At the same time there was, as we have seen, a general tendency for the intensification of job evaluation and measurement systems. The incorporation of work norms into the machines themselves further challenged plant-level control of the labour process. There was a growing perception of the costs in terms of autonomy and control of Taylorist scientific management and productivity bargaining (McKersie and Hunter 1973; OECD 1979).

In the tightening European labour market of the late 1960s the response to interrupted real wage growth, and the erosion of locally based negotiating procedures and work practices was a wave of predominantly unofficial, plant-led strikes, and an acceleration of money wage growth. A similar but more drawn-out process of growing labour unrest occurred in the United States. Only Japan with less severe labour-market pressures escaped relatively unscathed (Crouch and Pizzorno 1978; Sabel 1982).

In the 1970s in the aftermath of these developments, and in the light of the steady rise in inflation, the explicit indexation of money wages to cost-of-living changes became much more widespread. There was also a tendency everywhere for collective bargaining to include industry- or company-specific schemes covering such issues as job protection, pension provision, and working hours.

The growth of indexation, in conjunction with historical cost mark-up pricing, meant that the potential for profit squeeze was significantly increased. The impact was particularly noticeable in the early 1970s as major raw material and primary commodity price changes fed into the system. These reflected high pressure of demand, natural crop failures, and diminished US raw material and agricultural stockpiles (which were deliberately run down in the 1960s) as well as the erosion of the colonial and semi-colonial status of oil and other primary commodity producers (Maddison 1982).

In the 1970s, then, the increasing pace of input cost and money wage pressures combined with mark-up pricing contributed to a squeeze on profits as firms failed to anticipate inflation correctly and were unable to recoup lost ground (Flemming *et al.* 1976; Martin 1981; Lipietz 1983). This compounded the problems arising from competitive pressures which were being maintained or intensified in the 1970s.

The Pressure of Competition

In this period slower economic growth was associated with a reversal of the upward shift in the concentration of domestic production which had characterized the golden age. The major wave of mergers which marked the turn of the decade served to maintain rather than further increase aggregate concentration levels, at least in the UK and US. In both of these economies, as well as in Japan and Germany, concentration in aggregate was stable or fell over the 1970s (OECD 1984*b*). Further, a study of over 200 European product markets in the period 1970–9 showed that there was a tendency for single-firm dominance to weaken and be replaced by more oligopolistic structures. Part of this was undoubtedly the result of international integration (EEC 1982).

Between 1969 and 1978 the ratio of manufactured imports to GNP continued to rise in each of the major industrial economies.[28] The rate of growth of direct investment, although slackening from the early 1970s, also held up much better than domestic capital formation, and was increasingly multidirectional, both into and out of the US and the major European economies as well as outward from

Japan (OECD 1981). It is not surprising therefore that competitive pressures limited attempts by firms to recoup margins by raising prices more frequently or by greater amounts than cost changes could justify. Prices rose but by not enough to match costs. So inflation was combined with a profit squeeze.

Income Maintenance and the Welfare State

Meanwhile, state provision for income maintenance and employment protection was steadily advancing. As Table 2.18 shows the share of household transfers in OECD current price GDP, which averaged 7.5 per cent in the period 1955–7, and 10.5 per cent in the period 1967–9, rose to 13.9 per cent by 1974–6.

In Europe in particular these financial developments were associated with extended arrangements guaranteeing higher levels of job protection, safeguards against unfair dismissal, and provision for greater degrees of consultation prior to, and compensation after, redundancy (OECD 1979). This, along with the company-based non-wage elements in collective bargaining discussed earlier, led to the emergence of an increasingly dual labour market. Employers sought to maintain a flexible margin of workers whose length and terms of employment left them unable to qualify for state and company benefits open to those in more permanent jobs (Doeringer and Piore 1971). Whilst the income-maintenance expenditures helped maintain demand, the emergence of a fringe of workers outside the central safety-net threatened the comprehensiveness of the system which had been a hallmark of the golden age. Moreover, as the problem of unemployment worsened, the long-term unemployed posed problems for systems designed for relatively short periods of interrupted employment.[29]

Nevertheless the overall impact of public expenditure patterns was supportive of demand maintenance. As Fig. 2.5 shows, the steady progress of public expenditure as a percentage of GDP was accelerated in the mid 1970s. With tax revenues lagging there were big increases in government deficits.

In this sense the fiscal and public expenditure patterns of the period of erosion were similar to the period of the golden age itself. Thus the main feature of the period of explicit erosion of the golden age (roughly speaking, the inter-oil-shock period 1974–9) is the *stability* of the rules of co-ordination. President Nixon was right in stating in 1971 'we are all Keynesians now'.

There was an explicit attempt to manage effective demand so as to

Table 2.18. Unweighted average shares of public expenditure in GDP in current prices by economic category in the OECD economies 1955–76 (%)

	Total public expenditure	Final consumption	of which to Defence	Transfers and subsidies	of which to		Interest on public debt	Investment
					Households	Producers		
1955–7	28.5	13.0	4.0	8.8	7.5	1.3	1.7	4.0
1967–9	34.5	15.3	3.4	12.2	10.5	1.6	1.8	4.7
1974–6	41.4	18.0	2.7	16.1	13.9	2.1	2.3	4.5

Source: OECD (1978).

maintain growth and moderate inflation. This was both the result of the mainstream confidence in Keynesian anti-crisis devices, and of the pressure of the political left and trade unions.

Real wages increase slowed down in the 1970s and became more and more disconnected from gains in productivity. But there was generally no question that real wages should decrease. The indexation of wages to prices was explicitly or implicitly strengthened and dominated the movement of nominal incomes.

Keynesian policies of recovery, through deficit financing, became the general rule. The expansion of credit through the national banking systems was permitted by an easy-money policy by central banks. The real dollar rate of interest was close to zero in the inter-shock period, so that the international central banker too was playing its part.

Summary

This 'Keynesian' period in the crisis after 1973 had many positive aspects. The greater importance granted to the 'security-net' of the welfare state helped to prevent a spiral of depression in the mid 1970s. Credit creation and bank financing smoothed the difficulties of firms in the face of decreasing profitability, and of the worsening world trade and payments position.

All of this could not conceal underlying problems. Increased welfare state provision meant increased taxes and contributions. And if the real post-tax income of the active population was not to decrease, then the profit share had to bear the burden. Resistance by workers or employers to these forces exacerbated inflation. This problem was heightened by worsening productivity performance. Finally the rising indebtedness of nations, public sectors, and corporations gave rise to concerns about the quality of the debt held by creditors.

Thus the institutional and behavioural framework was fraying at the edges. These problems of inflation, the funding of rising public sector deficits and expenditures, and persistent unemployment were superimposed upon underlying problems in the organization of the system of production, and in the macroeconomic structures. The policies applied were not sufficient to reverse the increase in unemployment after the first oil shock; even so the growth of real wages did not sufficiently lag behind productivity growth to allow a recovery of profitability. Neither in terms of restored confidence in high and stable demand growth, nor in terms of restored profitability, were the conditions recreated in Europe and Japan for renewed accumulation at the rates achieved in the golden age. The second oil shock thus hit the system at a critical period and led to the final unhinging of the co-ordinating rules upon which the golden age had been based.

IV.4 The Collapse of Bretton Woods: And the Unravelling of the Post-War International Order

From Dollar Shortage to Dollar Glut: The Evolution of International Competitiveness among Industrial Countries

The dollar shortage of the early 1950s became a dollar glut in the following decade. By then, the European countries had started to shift the composition of their reserves towards gold. With the persistent US payments deficit, this became a serious systemic problem as gold outflows replaced official liability financing. The 'gold pool' was created, appeals were made to European countries not to change their official dollars into gold (and accepted by most countries except France), and other measures were taken. Nevertheless whereas US official liabilities in 1959 were only half the size of her gold reserves by 1967, they were one and half times larger than them.

Moreover, between 1960 and 1965 there was an enormous outflow of long-term capital from the US (mainly to Europe) and this more than offset improvements in the current account balance occurring in that period. Low-interest policies designed to combat recession at home encouraged large short-term capital outflows from the US into newly convertible overseas currencies. Expenditures on the government account (military expenditure and foreign aid) also contributed to the payments deficit. Finally, there was a sharp decline in the US *trade* balance by the late 1960s. From an average annual surplus of $5bn. during 1961–5 the US trade account deteriorated to a bare balance by 1968–9.

In view of the USA's strategic and military posture in the world as well as its commitment to currency convertibility and free capital markets, the sharp deterioration in the trade balance provided evidence of a 'fundamental disequilibrium' in the US economy. The principal symptoms of this were major declines in consumer goods and automobiles trade balances (not compensated for by a capital goods surplus benefiting from tied military aid). The US lead in high

technology goods was also shrinking. The time it took other countries to duplicate an American innovation became shorter with each
passing year (Block 1977).

More fundamentally, the main reason for the weakening trade
position of the US (and for that matter the UK over a similar period)
was the uneven development of the world economy which inevitably
meant an underlying adjustment problem in a fixed parity system.
Uneven development was reflected in the different rates of growth of
manufacturing production, productivity, and competitiveness of the
leading OECD countries. The relative rate of growth of manufacturing productivity is one of the best dynamic indicators of an economy's international competitiveness. As Table 2.19 shows, during
the second half of the 1960s the US and UK had the poorest record
on this criterion. Since these were also the two reserve currency
countries, this had serious systemic implications for payments imbalances in the international economy.

The implications for domestic policy of these developments and
the associated payments imbalances to which they gave rise were
equally serious. The feasibility of a persistent US deficit depended on
the ability to defend the parity against speculative capital flows. This
was only viable so long as other countries were willing to accumulate
dollars and resist the urge to convert them into gold. There were
other forces militating against this outcome.

US Multinational Investment and the European Reaction

After the post-war recovery and the restoration of currency convertibility there was an upsurge of private US long-term capital flows and
multinational investment in Europe. By 1966, there were nearly
9,000 American subsidiaries in Western Europe, over three times the
number in 1957 (Spero 1977).

As we have seen this US direct foreign investment contributed
significantly to the deterioration in the US balance of payments,
particularly in the first half of the 1960s. It also generated other
tensions, for the growth rate of American subsidiaries in Europe was
considerably greater than that of the European companies (although
because of the relatively slow post-war growth of the United States'
economy, the growth rates of the American parent companies were
in fact lower than those of their European counterparts (Rowthorn
and Hymer 1971).

The European response was to seek a reduction in the US

Table 2.19. Manufacturing production, productivity, and indicators of competitiveness in six leading industrial countries, 1964–70 (average annual % growth rates)

	US	Japan	Germany	France	Italy	UK
Output	4.6	14.6	6.1	6.1	6.9	2.5
Output per man-hour	3.4	12.3	4.9	6.9	3.8	3.5
Wage costs per unit of output in national currencies	1.4	1.9	2.9	1.6	4.2	4.8
In US$	1.4	2.2	4.5	−0.5	4.2	2.2
Export unit values of manufactures (in US$)	3.5	2.2	2.5	1.6	1.0	1.9
Shares in 'world' exports of manufactures (%)						
1964	21.5	8.1	19.3	8.7	6.3	14.4
1970	18.5	11.7	19.8	8.7	7.2	10.8

Source: See Singh (1981).

payments deficit so as to limit the perceived American take-over of European industry (Ball 1982). Hence the French decision to ignore the US appeals to not convert their surplus dollars into gold.

In response to European pressures, in 1963 and again in 1965, the US introduced certain measures to stem capital flows (Argy 1981). However, these restrictions did not seriously slow down the growth of US multinational investment abroad which was increasingly financed out of borrowings abroad and reinvested profits.

Increasing Interdependence of the Industrial Economies

The GATT rounds of tariff reductions, the enormous increase in international trade, and the growth of multinational investment led to increasing interdependence among the industrial countries. Moreover, one paradoxical consequence of the US restriction on capital flows in the middle 1960s was to encourage the development of the Euro-dollar market and thus greater financial integration in the world economy. Over the decade 1965 to 1975, the Eurocurrency market grew at a rate three to four times that of world money supply, adding enormously to international liquidity.

The growing economic and financial integration of the OECD countries meant that there was an increasingly large impact of economic policy changes in one country, particularly in the leading countries, on other economies. Deflationary (as well as reflationary) impulses arising from attempts to adjust imbalances at fixed parities were more pervasive and destabilizing in their effects. There was also an increasing synchronization of economic expansions. Thus in the late 1960s the US was reluctant to restrict demand, and Japan was in the middle of sustained expansion. In these circumstances Germany's first post-war use of deficit financing in 1967–8 and a similar shift in policy stance in France in 1968, produced (in terms of the size of the initial impact) one of the largest recorded swings in the stance of fiscal policy among the OECD countries (Llewellyn *et al.* 1985). Such episodes of simultaneous fiscal or monetary expansion, whether brought about by accident or design, had serious repercussions for commodity prices, inflation, and payment imbalances in the system as a whole.

The Bretton Woods system can be regarded as having broken down in August 1969 when President Nixon suspended the convertibility of dollars into gold.[30] The dollar remained however the key currency in the system. And in August 1971, when the US formally closed the gold window, the world moved to a fully fledged dollar standard. The US then also entered into negotiations which culminated in the Smithsonian Agreement of December 1971. In these negotiations, the US, until then still in favour of fixed exchange rates, demanded of its allies currency appreciation relative to the dollar.

This agreement did not last long. Under the pressure of massive capital flows, the UK floated its currency in 1972. Subsequently, other European countries floated their currencies and by 1973 all the major currencies were floating. The world had moved from a system of fixed exchange rates to that of managed floats. As a consequence of the floating rates the US announced the elimination of all capital controls in January 1974.

Was the breakdown of Bretton Woods inevitable? The mainstream view accepts its inevitability and is perhaps best embodied in the so-called 'Triffin Dilemma'. Triffin had argued that the system was flawed since it had no mechanism for automatic growth of international liquidity to meet the requirements of expanding world trade and economic activity. Under the Bretton Woods arrangements, as practised, the main source of such liquidity was the payments deficit of the US. Over the longer term, this had serious implications since it was bound to lead to a loss of confidence in the reserve currency. If, however, the US payments deficit was eliminated, this would reduce world liquidity and hence the world level of activity. To deal with this dilemma, many proposals for reform were mooted which culminated in the agreement to create SDRs in the mid 1960s. However, the so-called problem of international liquidity lost its urgency with the enormous growth of the Eurodollar market in the late 1960s and 1970s.

In our view the system was flawed for more fundamental reasons, namely the decline in US dominance due to the uneven development of the productive potential, and hence, the economic and political power of the leading industrial countries. As Block (1977) put it:

The fundamental contradiction was that the United States had created an international monetary order that worked only when American political and economic dominance in the capitalist world was absolute. That absolute dominance disappeared as a result of the reconstruction of Western Europe and Japan, on the one hand, and the accumulated domestic costs of the global extension of US power, on the other. With the fading of the absolute dominance, the international monetary order began to crumble. The US deficit was simply the most dramatic symptom of the terminal disease that plagued the postwar international monetary order (p. 163).

From early 1968 the US attitude to its balance-of-payments deficit and to other problems of the international system had noticeably changed. It became more unilateral and overtly nationalistic. A prominent view (see Kindleberger 1965; Krause 1970) argued for a passive US approach to its balance-of-payments problem, a policy of 'benign neglect'. In effect this analysis amounted to an argument for flexible exchange rates as a way of freeing US economic policy from international constraints.

The International Order with Floating Exchange Rates

The collapse of the Bretton Woods system, and its replacement by floating rates, had serious implications for economic activity, employment, and policy in the OECD countries. First, the abandonment of fixed parities and dollar–gold convertibility and the reduction in gold's role in the international monetary system, reduced the constraints on the US freedom of manœuvre over domestic and international policy. The US payments deficit and the position of the dollar remained, however, matters of concern to the US policy-makers. Some extreme proponents of the new regime had thought that with floating rates, the market would ensure balance-of-payments equilibria for all countries thus allowing each country autonomy in its monetary and fiscal policies.[31] The balance-of-payments disequilibria following the first oil shock soon proved this view to be incorrect. Since the dollar remained the major reserve currency, its standing on the international currency markets was clearly a matter of international concern.

Second, and more importantly, at the international level the floating system had serious shortcomings. Although the US is still the largest economy, the global economic system is no longer being controlled and supervised by a single all-powerful nation as it was in the 1950s. Thus the floating-rate system of international regulation lacks coherence. In particular, the post-Bretton Woods trading and payments system is no longer capable of dealing with imbalances in the system in such a way as to ensure a world level of aggregate demand, and its distribution among countries which would be compatible with full employment in the OECD economies. The international regime, under US hegemonic control, performed this task with outstanding success in the 1950s, and despite many difficulties with still considerable success for most of the 1960s. The inability or unwillingness of the US to provide the leadership necessary to re-establish an effective system of international regulation is central to the failure of the new regime. No effective collective or co-operative leadership among the OECD countries has been able to emerge to replace the former US role. Kindleberger (1985) is per-haps right in arguing that historically a collective leadership of the international economic system has been problematical; successful systems have invariably required leadership by a single hegemonic power.

As an example of the relative effectiveness of the pre- and post-1971 regimes we may analyse how successfully the floating exchange rate regime coped with the huge payments imbalances generated by the first oil shock. Table 2.20 shows the magnitude of the payments disequilibria which emanated from the oil shock of 1973. OPEC's current surplus rose fifteenfold to $60bn. from 1973 to 1974, whilst the OECD countries' current balance deteriorated to around $37bn. The 1975 recession, the sharpest until then in the post-war period, helped to restore the current balances in the OECD countries and to reduce the OPEC surplus. Over the next three years, with an enormous increase in OPEC imports, the OPEC surplus had more or less disappeared.

How efficient was this adjustment? There are several points which deserve attention in this connection. First, the OECD economies had to undergo a severe deflation in 1975 to reduce their current deficits. The floating exchange rates thus did not eliminate the balance-of-payments constraint for the industrial countries. As a proportion of world GDP, the OPEC surpluses were of much the same order of magnitude as the US surpluses during the immediate post-war years. The latter were gradually eliminated in the 1950s without impeding reconstruction and economic growth in Europe. This did not happen after 1973.

Suppose the world monetary system had been under similarly strong US hegemonic control in the 1970s as it was in the 1950s, what would have been the best way of dealing with the increase in the price of an essential raw material (oil) produced by only one group of countries (OPEC) in the system? It is not difficult to see that the optimal course would have been to maintain as far as

Table 2.20 Summary of payments balances on current account[a], 1973–79 (US $bn.)

	1973	1974	1975	1976	1977	1978	1979
Industrial countries	20.3	-10.8	19.8	0.5	-2.2	32.7	-5.6
Canada	—	-1.6	-4.7	-3.9	-4.0	-4.0	-4.3
US	9.1	7.6	21.2	7.5	-11.3	-11.6	3.1
Japan	0.1	-4.5	-0.4	3.9	11.1	16.8	-8.0
France	2.1	-2.8	3.8	-2.4	1.0	8.5	6.9
Germany	7.0	13.0	7.6	7.7	8.5	13.4	—
Italy	-2.2	-7.6	-0.1	-2.6	3.1	7.9	6.4
UK	-1.3	-6.9	-2.6	-0.2	1.9	5.2	2.6
Other industrial countries	5.5	-8.1	-5.1	-9.6	-12.6	-3.5	-12.3
Developing countries							
Oil-exporting countries	6.7	68.3	35.4	40.3	30.2	2.2	68.6
Non-oil developing countries[b]	-11.3	-37.0	-46.3	-32.6	-28.9	-41.3	-61.0

Table 2.20. (*Cont.*)

	1973	1974	1975	1976	1977	1978	1979
By analytical group							
Net oil exporters	−2.6	−5.1	−9.9	−7.7	−6.4	−7.9	−8.5
Net oil importers[c]	−8.8	−31.9	−36.4	−24.9	−23.6	−32.7	−51.0
Major exporters of manufactures	−3.6	−18.8	−19.1	−12.2	−7.9	−9.8	−21.7
Low-income countries[c]	−4.1	−7.5	−7.6	−4.3	−3.7	−8.2	−10.4
Other net oil importers[d]	−1.1	−5.6	−9.7	−8.3	−12.0	−14.7	−18.9
By area							
Africa[e]	−1.9	−3.2	−6.6	−6.1	−6.6	−9.4	−9.9
Asia[c]	−2.6	−9.9	−8.9	−2.7	−1.7	−6.5	−13.2
Europe	0.6	−4.4	−4.9	−4.7	−8.4	−6.7	−9.9
Middle East	−2.6	−4.5	−6.9	−5.4	−5.1	−6.2	−8.5
Western Hemisphere	−4.7	−13.5	−16.3	−11.8	−8.5	−13.3	−21.4
TOTAL[f]	15.7	20.5	8.9	8.2	−0.9	−6.4	2.0

[a] On goods, services, and private transfers.
[b] Figures are rounded to the nearest $0.5 bn.
[c] The People's Republic of China, which is classified as a low-income country but is also a net oil exporter, is included in the total (from 1977 onwards) but not in the subgroups.
[d] Middle-income countries that, in general, export mainly primary commodities.
[e] Excluding South Africa.
[f] Reflects errors, omissions, and asymmetries in reported balance-of-payments statistics on current account, plus balance of listed groups with other countries (mainly the USSR and other non-member countries of Eastern Europe and, for years prior to 1977, the People's Republic of China).

Source: IMF (1983).

possible the previous trend rate of growth of the world economy and to divert a somewhat greater proportion of this growing output to the OPEC countries without causing socially unacceptable rates of inflation in the non-OPEC economies. There would have been some adverse supply-side effects in the short-term because of the sharp changes in the relative prices of different kinds of fuels and of fuels and other commodities. However, as long as oil and other fuels were available in the necessary quantities, albeit at higher prices, and such prices were expected to prevail also in the future, there should have been a once-for-all supply-side impact of the oil price rise, with relatively little effect on the long-term trend rate of economic growth.[32] Second, the achievement of this optimal solution in terms of world economic growth and its distribution would only have been achieved if the following conditions had been satisfied (Corden 1977; Feinstein and Reddaway 1983):

1. The non-OPEC countries would need to run current account deficits for some years if world economic growth was to be maintained; and an outflow of OPEC capital would need to finance them.

2. To be able eventually to service the debt accumulated, and to offset the fall in the world propensity to consume arising from low OPEC absorptive capacity, it would have been desirable to increase non-OPEC investment (particularly in fuel saving and in the development of alternative sources of energy) and to offset the fall in the world propensity to consume arising from low OPEC absorptive capacity.

3. The national rules of co-ordination in the non-OPEC countries would have needed to ensure a reduction in the rate of growth of real wages and other incomes in line with the deterioration in the non-OPEC terms of trade. Feinstein and Reddaway (1983) argue that: 'This should not in principle have been a difficult operation. The loss of real incomes caused by the initial worsening of the terms of trade was a non-recurring phenomenon and was less than the normal gain from one year's rise in productivity. All that would have been required was thus a brief pause in the normal advance of real wages.'

In view of the erosion of the national regulatory regimes discussed earlier it was, however, extremely difficult for the industrial countries to fulfil the last condition. Moreover, in a world of nation states, of enormous short-term capital movements and widely fluctuating exchange rates, where no single state was in hegemonic control of the international trading and payments system, it was also far from easy to meet these first two conditions even *in principle*. This is because if each non-OPEC nation acted in its own national economic interest, rather than that of the world economy as a whole, it would be concerned not with the overall deficit between non-OPEC and OPEC, but with its own deficit with all other countries. Any single non-OPEC country could cover its deficit with OPEC by increasing its surpluses with the other non-OPEC countries. If all non-OPEC countries attempted to reduce their deficit in this manner (e.g. by deflation), the result would be a vicious circle of competitive deflation rather than economic expansion of the kind envisaged under condition (2) above.

At the beginning of the oil crisis, international organizations such as the OECD exhorted the non-OPEC countries to take a co-operative approach to reducing their deficit with the OPEC countries and to maintain their pace of economic activity. Not all countries acted on this advice and those who did so (e.g. the UK and some small European countries) soon found themselves with large current account deficits. Thus the problem of oil shock was not simply one of non-OPEC deficits with the OPEC, but it soon became one of large payments imbalances among the OECD countries themselves. As Table 2.20 shows, W. Germany and Japan ran sizeable surpluses in mid 1970s, Japan's surplus in 1978 was a huge $16.5bn., and that of W. Germany $13.4bn.

Moreover, although by 1978 the aggregate OPEC current account surplus was small, this was due to the deficits of the high absorbers (e.g. Nigeria) while the six main low absorbers (e.g. Saudi Arabia) were still running significant surpluses (see Table 2.21). The surpluses of the low absorbers were as much a source of disequilibrium in the international payments system as those of Japan and West Germany.

The difficulties facing the US under the new regime also became apparent in this period. In 1977 and 1978, the first two years of President Carter's new administration, the US economy grew quickly. This boosted employment and also provided a significant stimulus to the world economy. The US rate of unemployment fell from 8.3 per cent in 1975 to 5.9 per cent in 1978. The US economy was runing close to, if not faster than, its productive potential. However

Table 2.21. Oil-Exporting countries: Balance of payments on current account, 1973–83 (US$bn.)

	1973	1974	1975	1976
Exports (f.o.b.)	39.0	117.9	109.6	133.2
Oil exports	35.0	112.3	103.7	126.2
Other exports	4.0	5.6	5.9	7.1
Imports (f.o.b.)	−20.2	−35.8	−56.2	−68.1
Balance on merchandise trade	18.8	82.2	53.4	65.1
Net services and private transfers	−12.2	−13.9	−18.0	−24.8
Receipts	4.3	8.8	12.1	14.6
Payments	−16.4	−22.7	−30.1	−39.4
Balance on current account	6.7	68.3	35.4	40.3
of which:				
Six 'surplus' countries[a]	6.8	43.8	31.2	36.6
Other oil exporters[b]	−0.1	24.5	4.1	3.7

[a] Defined to include the six countries that had a current account surplus each year: Libyan Arab Jamahiriya, Qatar, Saudi Arabia, and the United Arab Emirates.
[b] Algeria, Indonesia, Iran, Nigeria, Oman, and Venezuela.
Source: IMF (1983).

in the rest of the OECD, the unemployment rates over this period either remained steady or rose as the rate of growth of demand and output was considerably below the productive potential (Oppenheimer and Posner 1983). Not surprisingly the net result of these policies was a huge deterioration in the US current balance: from a surplus of $21.2bn. in 1975, to a deficit of $11.6bn. in 1978 (Table 2.20). US inflation which had been falling in the mid 1970s rose to 7.4 per cent in 1978. The value of the dollar thus fell sharply on the financial markets. By November 1978, it had fallen by 20 per cent compared to its value a year earlier and had depreciated by 50 per cent against other major currencies compared with its value in 1973.

In view of the overwhelming significance of the dollar in world trade and capital flows, its continuing depreciation became a subject of wide international concern. Further, in the second half of 1978 foreign dollar balances in the US (excluding foreign holdings of liquid assets) exceeded $200bn.; there were similar amounts of dollar claims held by non-US residents in the Euro-banks (Oppenheimer and Posner 1983). The US authorities as well as the foreign finance ministries thus became seriously concerned by the prospect that with the perceived weakness of the dollar, many holders of it might wish to switch out at whatever the rate.

These developments led the US authorities to urge surplus countries (Japan and Germany) to expand their economies. At the Bonn economic summit in 1978 it was agreed that in order to restore payments equilibrium among the OECD countries, the US should deflate and that Japan and Germany should take reflationary measures. On the basis of the preparatory work for the summit by the OECD and IMF (the so-called locomotive and convoy theories), detailed economic measures were accepted by the summit countries. West Germany undertook to launch within six weeks fiscal expansion equivalent to about 1 per cent of GNP. Japan agreed to achieve a real growth target in fiscal 1978 1.5 per cent higher than in fiscal 1977; it also promised to keep the volume of Japanese exports for fiscal 1978 at or below the level of fiscal 1977 (Llewellyn *et al.* 1985).

The extent to which the pledges of the Bonn summit were actually implemented is controversial, but soon the summit decisions were overtaken by the second oil shock. To reduce inflation, to correct the current deficit, and to improve the exchange rate of the dollar (all interrelated objectives), the US authorities had already adopted restrictive monetary policies at the end of 1978. With the second oil price increase, these policies were reinforced in 1979 and the US moved to a close approximation to pure monetarism: adoption of money supply ranges and the quantitative targeting by the Federal Reserve of commercial bank reserves (Nordhaus 1982). The extremely restrictive monetary targets led to a sharp deflation of demand as well as high and widely fluctuating nominal and real interest rates. With similar immediate objectives of containing inflation and current account deficits emanating from the second oil shock, the other industrial countries also put into effect restrictive monetary and fiscal policies. Thus unlike measures taken after the first oil shock, there was not even any attempt by the industrial economies in 1979 to counteract the deflationary consequences of the oil price increase itself.

The Less Developed Economies and the Newly Industralizing Countries (NICs)

A significant feature of the inter-shock period was the much better growth performance of the less developed countries (LDCs) relative to the OECD. As Table 2.22 shows, the first oil shock appears to have had little impact on the long-term trend rate of growth of GDP

Table 2.22. A comparison of growth rates for GDP, manufacturing value added (MVA), and exports of manufactures[a], 1960–1980 (% change p.a.)

Indicator	1960–70	1970–74	1974–80	1970–80
Developing countries				
GDP, in current dollars	7.8	20.7	16.8	18.3
GDP, in constant dollars	5.6	6.9	5.4	6.0
Total exports in current dollars	7.1	40.4	16.4	26.2
Total exports; volume index/constant dollars	6.9/7.3	4.3/7.3	2.3/4.4	1.5/4.4
MVA, in current dollars	8.7	20.9	15.2	17.5
MVA, production index/constant dollars	5.9/7.1	9.1/8.8	6.0/6.0	6.9/6.9
Manufactured exports, in current dollars	13.7	36.3	23.0	26.6
Manufactured exports, quantum index	—	—	13.4[b]	—
Developed market economies				
GDP, in current dollars	8.4	14.4	13.2	13.7
GDP, in constant dollars	5.1	4.3	3.2	3.2
Total exports in current dollars	10.0	25.2	15.7	18.9
Total exports; volume index/constant dollars	8.5/8.0	9.6/8.6	5.3/5.6	6.1/6.2
MVA, in current dollars	8.1	15.1	12.2	12.5
MVA, production index/constant dollars	6.1/6.3	5.5/5.5	3.1/3.3	3.0/3.3
Manufactured exports, in current dollars	11.5	24.8	15.7	19.0
Manufactured exports, quantum index	10.0	9.6	5.3	6.5
Centrally planned economies				
NMP, in constant dollars	6.7	6.6	4.4	5.4
Total exports in current dollars	9.8	22.3	16.0	18.6
Index of industrial production	9.0	8.9	6.2	7.5
Manufactured exports, in current dollars	10.0	20.4	14.7	17.0

[a] SITC 5–8 less 68.
[b] 1975–80

Source: UNIDO (1985).

in the developing countries. Between 1960 and 1970, LDC rate of growth of GDP was 5.6 per cent p.a.; over the period 1974–80, it fell slightly to 5.4 per cent p.a. In contrast, in the OECD countries (the middle part of Table 2.22) there was a significant decline in the rate of growth of GDP from 5.2 per cent p.a. to 3.2 per cent p.a.

Similarly, manufacturing production in the LDCs rose at a rate of 5.9 per cent p.a. between 1960 and 1970 and at a slightly higher rate of 6 per cent p.a. during the inter-shock period 1974–80.[33] In the OECD countries, the trend rate of growth of manufacturing production was nearly halved between 1974 and 1980 relative to that recorded during 1960–70. Consequently, the Third World's share of world manufacturing production—which had remained more or less constant during the 1960s—increased appreciably during the inter-shock period: from 6.9 per cent in 1960 to 7.6 per cent in 1970; and to more than 10 per cent by 1980. Its share in world exports of manufactures also rose from 3.9 per cent in 1960 to just over 5.0 per cent in 1970; and to 9.0 per cent in 1980 (UNCTAD 1981). As Table 2.22 shows, during 1974–80, the volume of manufactured exports from the Third World countries increased at a phenomenal rate of 13 per cent p.a. whilst those from the OECD countries grew by 5 per cent p.a. During the 1970s, Third World imports into the OECD increased at about twice the rate of imports from other sources. These developments led to concern about de-industrialization in the OECD countries on account of cheap labour imports from the LDCs.[34]

The Third World's economic performance during the inter-shock period is particularly remarkable in view of the huge payments deficits which the oil price increase caused in the non-oil LDCs. As a percentage of GDP the current account deficit of the average middle-income oil-importing country increased from 1 per cent in 1973 to 5 per cent in 1975; for the average low-income economy, the deficit increased from 2.4 per cent in 1973 to 3.9 per cent in 1975. These deficits were mainly financed by an enormous increase in commercial loans, particularly in the case of middle-income countries (World Bank 1978).

The total outstanding public long-term debt of these countries increased threefold between 1973 to 1979. Although the rapid increase of Third World exports meant that the debt to exports ratio of LDCs changed very little during the 1970s, other debt indicators do show a deterioration in the debt situation.

The increased Third World indebtedness in the mid 1970s was in line with market signals. Between 1974 and 1978, the average real interest rate (measured as the difference between the London Inter-Bank Offer Rate (LIBOR) on three-month US dollar deposits and the US GDP deflator) was only 0.5 per cent, and was on occasion (e.g. 1978), negative. By and large the LDCs used these loans to increase domestic savings and investment (IMF 1983; Avramovitch 1982).

In conclusion, superficially the floating exchange rate regime had coped with the huge world imbalances generated by the first oil shock reasonably well. Owing to a large increase in imports by the 'high absorber' OPEC countries, as well as deterioration in their terms of trade, by 1978, the aggregate OPEC surplus had disappeared. Moreover, private banking systems managed to recycle funds to the balance-of-payments-constrained Third World economies thus enabling them to maintain their growth momentum. However, even before the second oil shock of 1979, the system was subject to serious financial and exchange rate disequilibria among the OECD countries themselves. Even to the extent that the financial disequilibria of the oil shock had been accommodated, a heavy price had been paid by the industrial countries. The peak-to-peak growth rate of the OECD countries in the period 1973–79 was only 1.9 per cent p.a. compared with the corresponding growth rates of 4.8 per cent between 1966 and 1969 and 4.6 per cent between 1969 and 1973 (Llewellyn *et al.* 1985). As far as the Third World countries were concerned, notwithstanding their good growth record during the inter-shock period, they had large current account deficits and many countries were fast approaching their borrowing limits. In terms of the overall performance of the world economy, the post-Smithsonian system of international regulation was significantly less efficient in coping with international imbalances during the period 1973–8 than was the post-war system of international regulation under Pax Americana in the decade following the end of the war.

V. CONCLUSION AND PROSPECTS FOR THE WORLD ECONOMY

This chapter has argued that the erosion of the golden age economic regime began well before 1973 and that even without the exogenous shocks it would have been difficult to sustain. Our account of the pre-1973 period thus differs significantly from the best-known mainstream writing on the subject. First of all we have emphasized the productivity problems prior to 1973, manifested in terms of slackening rates of labour productivity growth, faster reductions in hours of work, and declines in the underlying output/capital ratios. Neither Bruno and Sachs (1985), nor Lindbeck (1983), nor Maddison (1982) mention these latter two aspects in any detail. In relation to labour productivity, Maddison assumes that there was no significant deterioration before 1973, Lindbeck asserts that there was 'hardly any general slowdown of productivity among developed countries' before 'approximately 1972–74', and Bruno and Sachs play down the significance of pre-1973 productivity problems.

Second, we have placed strong emphasis on declines in profits prior to 1973. This is not mentioned in Maddison's account, and plays little or no role for Lindbeck (although he places great importance on the fall in profitability after 1973 in explaining the reduced rate of accumulation and productivity growth). Bruno and Sachs are rather the exception, pointing out that a 'soft landing' (after 1973) from the 'burden of inherited inflation and a growing profit squeeze' would have been difficult to manage even without the commodity and oil price explosion. They see 'real labour costs' manifested in their 'wage gap' (essentially a cyclically adjusted profit share) as a second supply factor of importance (in addition to commodity prices) affecting particularly Europe and Japan. They say 'even before the oil shocks, therefore, many OECD countries faced a major problem of declining profitability and slowing growth' (p. 167). They do not, however, examine this slowing growth (and particularly slackening of accumulation) in any detail. So in terms of the internal tensions there is more emphasis in our account on profitability and productivity.

Third, we have emphasized the inevitability of the breakdown of the post-war system of international regulation (the Bretton Woods regime) as a consequence of the differential development and the varied evolution of competitive capacities of the leading industrial economies. The new system of international regulation (the floating exchange rate regime) which came into force after 1973 was not subject to hegemonic control by a single powerful nation; nor had a co-operative leadership emerged to replace the former US role. In an increasingly interdependent world economy, the new system was therefore not capable of resolving global financial disequilibria in such a way as to ensure a full-employment level of world aggregate demand and its appropriate distribution among countries.

Fourth, in view of the close interconnections between balance of payment disequilibria, exchange rate changes, inflation, and the level of activity, we have stressed throughout the important interactions between national co-ordinating rules and the international order. The fragility of the world economy in 1973 is demonstrated by the deep and long-lasting stagnation triggered by the oil shocks.

During the period between the two oil shocks, the floating exchange rate system and national Keynesian policies led to a transitory period with some suggestion of stability between 1975 and 1979. However, the overall economic performance was much inferior to that of the golden age itself (see Table 2.6). Moreover, the erosion of the institutional and behavioural framework of the golden age interacting with the severe tensions (e.g. the payments imbalances and currency movements) of the international regulatory regime made the new system extremely vulnerable.

The second oil shock saw the final abandonment of what we have termed in section II the golden age regime. It is beyond the scope of this chapter to provide a proper discussion of such patterns as may be emerging in the post-1979 period. However, we briefly note that at the international level, as seen earlier, instead of attempting to compensate for the deflationary effects of the 1979 oil price rise, restrictive monetary and fiscal policies were strongly reinforced in the US and adopted by other major industrial countries. In an international economy, ever more closely linked by 'free' and gigantic capital movements, this resulted in the early 1980s in a beggar-my-neighbour competitive deflation and a prolonged recession. After 1983 the expansionary impacts of US policy benefited European, Japanese, and NIC export growth. But from 1985 onwards the combined impact of the US trade and public sector deficits meant that the US was less and less able to play the role of an independent engine of growth in the international system.

At the national level, the assault on the existing domestic rules of co-ordination within the individual countries has inevitably taken on a differentiated and uneven character. Nevertheless a number of common features can be discerned:

(*a*) The golden age presumption that workers should bargain collectively to protect wages against inflation and to collect a share of the fruits of productivity growth was challenged. Norms of indexation were repudiated (Italy), and attempts made to weaken trade unions by legislation (UK—secondary picketing, Germany

—social security payments for strikers). Increasingly, collective bargains involved the giving up of previously established gains.

(b) Demands for wage flexibility have been paralleled by demands for employment flexibility—the right to hire and fire through rolling back employment protection legislation (UK, France).

(c) Attempts to reduce the coverage and value of welfare state benefits have been general.

(d) There has been an explicit abandonment of full employment policy embodied in the adoption of rules about monetary growth and public sector deficits.

(e) There has been a general trend towards extending market pressures—privatization of nationalized industries (UK, France, Japan), cuts in government subsidies to loss-making firms and industries (Germany).

Viewed from the standpoint of governing economic circles in the leading OECD countries, this emerging new economic regime has already been 'successful' in some important directions. First, there has been a major change in the balance of power both internationally and internally. Internationally, the collapse of commodity prices, extremely high real interest rates, and the reduction of capital flows (all directly attributable to the economic policies of the advanced countries (Singh 1987; Lipietz 1985)) have greatly weakened the economic and political power of Third World countries. In the mid 1970s these countries were vociferously demanding a new international economic order, today most of them (particularly in Africa and Latin America) are severely constrained by adverse balance of payments, heavily in debt, and in the position of supplicants before the IMF and the World Bank. The latter two institutions are willing to provide the much needed foreign exchange only if these countries carry out so-called 'structural reforms', which usually follow the same pattern of denationalization, deregulation, and internal and external liberalization of markets which are the hallmark of changes in the advanced countries. Similarly in the latter, the bargaining position of the trade unions and of the working class in general has been weakened at both the workplace and macroeconomic level.

The second main success of the emerging new systems has been an improvement in inflationary performance compared with the mid 1970s. Instead of the stagflation (low growth and high inflation) of those years the 1980s have been characterized by low growth and low inflation. This of course has been directly related to the weakened bargaining power of the unions and the fall in commodity prices that accompanied the changing internal and international balance of power to which we have just referred.

There are, however, important weaknesses in the 1980s record. First, although unemployment rates may benefit in the mid 1990s as the rate of growth of the labour force declines due to demographic factors, they look set to remain exceptionally high in most OECD countries. Only a trend increase in the rate of growth of world economic activity can offer the prospect of substantial improvement.

Second, despite many years of IMF management by means such as austerity programmes and debt-rescheduling, there is still no solution to the Third World debt problem in sight. The debtor countries have suffered enormous economic losses during this period without being anywhere near to recovering their creditworthiness or their pre-1980 long-term growth rates. A wide range of observers believe that for many countries the debt problem is no longer one of 'liquidity' but is one of 'insolvency' (see Cline 1985; Singh 1986; Lipietz 1985).

Third, there are extremely large payments imbalances in the international economy which have become a source of major instability on the world's currency and stock-markets.

Nevertheless, as long as high unemployment rates in the advanced countries are politically acceptable, the balance of advantage (from the standpoint of conservative governments in the leading countries) lies in continuing with the current macroeconomic pattern of low growth and low inflation. For if expansionary policies were followed and the world rate of economic growth rose on a sustained basis to anywhere near its golden age level, it will again lead to an increase in the power of unions as well as a sharp rise in commodity prices, including oil. This in turn will rekindle a conflict over distribution threatening to push up inflation. For conservative policy-makers the only perceived benefit of a trend increase in the rate of growth of the world economy will be that it will greatly help towards a solution of the Third World debt problem. However, they fear that this will be at the expense of rising commodity prices, inflation, and adverse changes in economic and political balance of power. Since there are a variety of other ways of addressing the debt problem (some write-offs, interest-capping, etc.), it is unlikely that the leading OECD countries will seek to expand the world economy for this purpose alone. They may, however, respond to US pressure to boost activity as a way of softening the impact of reductions in its budget and trade deficits.

To be sure there is a great deal of discussion about policy co-ordination among the leading industrial countries to revive the world economy. However, it is important to note that the central objective of the policy co-ordination is not to bring about an overall increase in the rate of growth of world demand, but rather to redistribute the current level of demand among the leading countries in a way which will reduce their huge payments imbalances and thus help restore stability in the currency and financial markets.

The foreseeable prospect for the OECD countries (and hence for the world economy) must be at best one of continued slow growth. This perspective assumes that the policy co-ordination which is currently being pursued by the leading OECD countries is wholly successful; if it is not, the world economy is likely to grow at a still slower rate and even the possibility of a serious slump in the short term cannot be ruled out.

Finally, there are circumstances which could lead to much higher rates of growth in the OECD countries. For example, if the current high unemployment rates become politically unacceptable again in the leading countries, their governments will be obliged to seek a higher rate of growth of world demand. Second, if the reform programme in the Soviet Union shows spectacular success leading to a much higher rate of growth of productivity in that country, ideological and military reasons will compel the Western countries to improve their own economic performance. Growth rates approaching the golden age levels will only be feasible and sustainable with low inflation, on the basis of new domestic rules of co-ordination, and a rather different international order. However, this will require the abandonment of the fledgling economic regime of the 1980s.

APPENDIX

Decomposition of Changes in the Profit Rate

Tables 2.11 and 2.12 are based on the following decomposition:

1. *Profit Rate*

$$\text{Profit rate} = r = \frac{PROF}{NK} = \frac{PROF}{NY} \cdot \frac{NY}{NK},$$

where $PROF$ = net operating surplus after adjustment for self-employment;
NK = net capital stock at current prices;
NY = net value added at current prices.

Writing this expression in approximate proportionate rate-of-change-form, and using dots (for example, $\dot{x}$) for the proportionate rate-of-change variables ($\dot{x} = x^{-1}dx/dt$ = proportionate rate of change of x) we have:

$$\dot{r} = \left(\frac{\dot{PROF}}{NY}\right) + \left(\frac{\dot{NY}}{NK}\right).$$

Thus the rate of change of the profit rate is the sum of the rate of change of the profit share ($PROF/NY$) and the rate of change of the output/capital ratio (NY/NK).

2. Profit Share

$$\text{Profit share} = \frac{PROF}{NY} = 1 - \frac{W}{NY},$$

where W is employee compensation adjusted for self-employment.

$$\text{Wage share} = \frac{W}{NY} = \frac{W}{P_q \cdot H} \cdot \frac{P_y \cdot H}{NY} \cdot \frac{P_q}{P_y}$$

$$= w \cdot \frac{1}{LP} \cdot \frac{P_q}{P_y},$$

where P_q = price index of gross output,
H = total hours worked,
P_y = price index for value added,
w = hourly product wages (wages deflated by gross output prices),
LP = hourly labour productivity.

Writing this expression in approximate proportionate rate-of-change form:

$$\left(\frac{\dot{W}}{NY}\right) = \dot{w} - \left[\dot{LP} - \frac{\dot{P_q}}{P_y}\right].$$

Thus the rate of change of the wage share is the excess of the rate of change of product wages over the rate of change of 'real factor incomes' (the bracketed expression). The rate of change of real factor incomes is the rate of change of productivity, adjusted for the effect of changes in the ratio of output prices to value added prices, which in turn reflects the relative prices of inputs (including capital consumption) and net value added. In Tables 2.11 and 2.12 the rate of change of product wages is estimated as the rate of change of real factor incomes plus the rate of change of the wage share.

3. *Net Output/Capital Ratio*

$$\text{Net output/capital ratio} = \frac{NY}{NK} = \frac{Ny}{Nk} \cdot \frac{P_y}{P_k}$$

where Ny = net value added at constant prices,
$\quad Nk$ = net capital stock at constant prices,
$\quad P_k$ = price index for capital stock.

$$\frac{NY}{NK} = \frac{q}{k} \cdot \frac{y}{q} \cdot \frac{P_q}{P_k} \cdot \frac{P_y}{P_q} \cdot \frac{Ny}{y} \cdot \frac{k}{Nk},$$

where q = gross output at constant prices,
$\quad k$ = gross capital stock at constant prices,
$\quad y$ = gross value added at constant prices.

Writing this expression in approximate proportionate rate-of-change form:

$$\left(\frac{\dot{NY}}{NK}\right) = \left(\frac{\dot{q}}{k}\right) + \left(\frac{\dot{y}}{q}\right) + \left(\frac{\dot{P_q}}{P_k}\right) + \left(\frac{\dot{P_y}}{P_q}\right) + \left(\frac{\dot{Ny}}{y}\right) + \left(\frac{\dot{k}}{Nk}\right)$$

Thus the rate of change of the net output/capital ratio at current prices is the rate of change of the gross output/capital ratio at constant prices plus the rate of change of real value added relative to gross output and the 'effect of capital costs' (the last four terms). The effect of capital costs includes relative price effects (capital goods to gross output and gross output to value added), the changing real weight of capital consumption (reflecting the output/capital ratio and its asset structure), and the ratio of gross to net capital stock (reflecting its average age). In Tables 2.11 and 2.12 the second term is ignored (materials productivity has to be assumed unchanged for want of data), and the effect of capital costs is estimated *en bloc* as the difference between the rates of change of the net value added/capital ratio at current prices and the gross value added/capital ratio at constant prices. Data for relative prices of the capital stock and output (the third term in the expression above) is shown as a memorandum item.

NOTES

1. For compatibility with OECD series our data-set for profitability, capital accumulation, and state spending covers the 'Big Seven' (i.e. including Canada, see Armstrong and Glyn (1986)). We refer to this data as covering the ACCs. In the text we also on occasion refer to data for the OECD as a whole.
2. This general approach has been developed by the so-called Regulation School of French economists (see Aglietta 1976; Boyer and Mistral 1978; Lipietz 1979, 1983, 1985; Boyer 1986). What we have termed macroeconomic structure and rules of co-ordination correspond to what is sometimes translated literally as

regime of accumulation and mode of regulation. The golden age pattern as a whole is described by these writers as 'Fordism'. The details of, and emphasis within, our analysis of the golden age differ in many respects from this work (which in turn contains many nuances of interpretation); we draw also on other analyses in a broadly comparable tradition (Armstrong *et al.* 1984; Bowles *et al.* 1983; and Rowthorn 1980 in particular).

3. This section draws on a background of industrial country experience based on Angus Maddison's seminal contribution (Maddison 1982).

4. For the 'Big Seven' exports of manufactures between them rose as a percentage of total exports from 41% in 1950 to 62% in 1971 (Batchelor *et al.* 1980, Table 2.4).

5. This estimate was derived from a pooled regression of the growth of hourly labour productivity on the growth rate of the fixed stock of capital per worker for the big seven capitalist countries (excluding France) for three periods 1870–1913, 1913–50, and 1950–73, using data from Appendices C and D of Maddison (1982). A pooled regression for growth rates of the two variables over successive cycles during the years 1950–73 for the big seven countries yields an almost identical coefficient. Lindbeck (1983) reports similar regression co-efficients. Such regression results could be interpreted within the 'growth accounting' framework as suggesting that differences in rates of technical progress across countries and time-periods generated nearly proportional differences in rates of capital accumulation. The kernel of truth in the growth accounting approach is that the impact of capital accumulation on productivity cannot be understood independently of the technology and work organization which accompanies it; its basic weakness lies in the implication that new technology and work organization can be incorporated in the production process *without* investment.

6. This is based on the simple decomposition of the profit rate (P/K) into $P/K = P/Y \times Y/K$, where P is profits, Y is output, and K is the capital stock. We present a fuller decomposition in Section IV.1 below.

7. The history of the spread of Taylorism throughout Europe and Japan during the inter-war period, and its implicit or explicit acceptance by much of the labour movement at that time has been extensively studied. In the US, Germany, France, and Italy the main battles over these principles began just before or after World War I. Reformist elements in the trade-union movement had accepted the 'bargain' as early as the 1920s. The pro-communist 'red international' of trade unions did so in the 1930s. None of this of course put an end to resistance at the shop-floor level. (See e.g. De Montmollin and Pastre 1984.) It is worth emphasizing that a prominent role has been claimed for the importation of scientific management technique as part of the Japanese strategy of importing advanced technology in the post-World War II period (see for example Caves and Uekusa (1976) and the references therein).

8. The original behavioural evidence behind the theory of the kinked demand curve—suggesting that producers try to avoid destabilizing short-term price warfare (especially in capital intensive industries), prefer to maintain stable long-term supplier–customer relationships, and more readily accept as 'fair' price changes based on actual or anticipated common cost increases—all pre-

dates the post-war golden age period (Hall and Hitch 1939; Sweezy 1939; Means 1940). The structural basis for this behaviour, in markets where rivalry takes place between relatively few interdependent producers, was as we document below reinforced in these years.

9. The pace of these developments and the levels of cover provided varied between countries with the US lagging behind Europe, and Japan providing the least social protection of all (Flora and Alber 1981; Kudrle and Marmor 1981; Boltho 1975).

10. In Japan the growth in transfer payments was by contrast very small from 3.7% of GNP in the mid 1950s to 4.5% by the early 1970s (Boltho 1975).

11. Future customs unions and free trade associations were, however, under Article 24 of GATT specifically excluded from this general rule of equal treatment provided that they did not involve any overall increase in trade barriers against countries outside the union.

12. A number of US scholars (e.g. Kindleberger 1987) emphasize the altruism of the Marshall Plan. That may well have been the main motivation of some of the economic architects of the Plan in the State Department, but as noted above, it was not that of others. However, by the time the Plan was approved by the US Congress, the US interest and the broader aims of US foreign economic policy were squarely in the forefront.

13. Recipient countries were required to sign pledges promising a range of economic actions, including the stabilization of currency and reduction of trade barriers, which were in many respects more stringent than under IMF conditions for developing countries. See Block (1977).

14. Full cost pricing does not guarantee fixed income shares unless firms can vary the timing of their price increases to account for unanticipated wage increases and include in their mark-up an element to cover the gap between price increases and expected wage increases which otherwise will have to be met (at the going cost of finance) by borrowing (see e.g. Tarling and Wilkinson 1985; Godley and Cripps 1983).

15. E.g. Lindbeck (1983) and Matthews (1982). The fact that Bruno and Sachs (1985) play down the suggestion of a slow-down in productivity growth before 1974 is the more surprising since they actually find that in half the countries they examine the most significant break in the manufacturing productivity trend occurs before 1973 and they do not test whether in other cases (e.g. Japan) there was a break before 1973 though less severe than after 1973.

16. This is because the golden age relationship shows every 1% faster growth in the capital/labour ratio increasing labour productivity by around 0.7% (and thus increasing the growth of the output/capital ratio by 0.3%). The regression coefficients are 0.76 for business and 0.68 for manufacturing. The smaller (unweighted) average decline in manufacturing productivity growth than business is largely accounted for by the United States where manufacturing productivity rebounded in the early 1970s, whilst business productivity growth remained at a low rate (see Table 2.7). For Japan the comparison is between the early 1970s and late 1960s which was the period of most rapid productivity growth.

17. Such exercises to disentangle component influences of the profit share and rate were developed by Weisskopf (1979) and elaborated in Weisskopf (1985). The

version used here differs from his in defining product wages in terms of output rather than value added prices which allow more explicit account to be taken of input costs. The Appendix to this chapter describes our decomposition more formally.

18. Looking at five periods of intensification of profit squeeze at the end of 1960s (US, Italy) or early 1970s (in the UK there were no such intensification) gives a rather different result. Productivity slowed down on average by 1.5%, real input costs deteriorated by 1.1% p.a. whilst product wages growth was unchanged (and real wage growth accelerated by 1.0% p.a.). The productivity recovery in the US in the early 1970s blurs the typical profit squeeze pattern in other countries at that time where productivity slow-down was important. Common to these various analyses is the fact that product wages did not accelerate, although real wages did. It should be noted also that the failure of product wages to slow down when real input costs were accelerating means that total real direct costs of production do rise faster in the early 1970s (line (d)).

19. Unemployment rates were generally lower after the mid 1960s (Table 2.6) but had edged up a little in the EEC and USA by 1973. Vacancy statistics however suggest that strains in the labour market may have peaked rather later than registered unemployment, in 1970 and 1973 in Germany and Japan respectively. This is confirmed by data for agricultural employment which show a maximum rate of decline in the early 1970s in France, Germany, and especially Japan.

20. Both the Chan-Lee and Sutch (1985) and Weisskopf (1985) studies of profitability find that indicators of international competition (relative unit labour costs and import penetration respectively) contributed to profit squeezes in some countries. The role of international competition in squeezing profits is a factor not analysed in the theoretical chapters in this volume.

21. Since the profit share is defined in terms of net value added it is the trend in the current price net value added to net capital stock ratio which determines the profit rate. This differs from the trend in the constant price ratio of output to gross capital stock because of: (a) changes in the price of value added relative to gross output; as already discussed the late 1960s, and 1970s saw a rise in real materials and depreciation costs which further depressed the ratio of current price value added to the capital stock; and (b) changes in the price of gross output relative to the cost of capital goods; over the 1960s and early 1970s the prices of capital goods rose on average around 1% p.a. faster than the price of manufacturing output, further reducing the output/capital ratio in current prices. There does not appear to have been any tendency for the relative price of capital goods to accelerate prior to 1973 and the calculations in Tables 2.11 and 2.12 (line (e)) suggest some deceleration after 1973. For the typical major country the average decline in the output/capital ratio was about 2% p.a. in the early 1970s. This fall was about equally comprised of a fall in the real ratio, a decline in value added prices relative to output, and of rises in relative capital goods prices (lines (7)–(9) and (e) of Table 2.11).

22. It should be noted that our profit variables are pre-tax. In the UK in particular more generous tax treatment of investment meant that the post-tax profit rate fell much less than the pre-tax rate (see Flemming *et al.* 1976). This does not seem to have happened generally.

23. Predictions, based on lagged profit rate decline, are 3.3% fall in the growth rate

of the manufacturing capital stock in the US, 1.9% for Europe, and 3.2% for Japan; actual figures were 0.9%, 2.8%, and 4.6% respectively. We are not suggesting that the fall in the accumulation rate by 1974 in Japan and Europe only reflected the direct effect of the decline in profit rate recorded up to 1973. A regression including *only* the profit rate obviously incorporates the effect of variables—such as the growth rate—which may affect both profitability and investment directly. Moreover, the accumulation rate in 1974 must have been affected to some extent by the lack of confidence flowing from the oil crisis. It is striking, however, that in the manufacturing sectors of Europe and Japan around three-quarters of the decline up to 1974 in accumulation from peak rates had occurred by *1973*.

24. It is interesting to note that the ability of Japanese management systems to obtain the commitment and co-operation of the labour force in precisely the area of maintaining smooth continuous production, has been identified as the key to the 'just-in-time' or kanban system. The economies in inventory holdings which this system yields, depend critically on the ability to keep the production system going. The Japanese success in the 1960s and 1970s in dealing with this contradiction in the Fordist pursuit of smooth, continuous production at lowest cost had the added advantage of minimizing the cost of redundant inventory when style or quality changes were introduced in final products. This reduced somewhat the emphasis on long standardized production runs. Thus the competitive challenge they could mount was based both on cost and on flexibility of product quality and design (e.g. Abernathy *et al.* 1983; Aoki, this volume). For further discussion of these issues see Marglin forthcoming and Noble (1984).

25. As argued earlier conventional growth accounting gives a relatively small weight to capital accumulation. Using our estimate of the elasticity of hourly productivity with respect to the capital/labour ratio of 0.75 (see n. 16) the decline in the rate of accumulation would explain on average half of the productivity slowdown after 1973 in six major countries, and a little more if some allowance is made for premature scrapping of capital equipment due to energy price increases (data from Maddison 1984, Tables 2.1 and 2.3).

26. Statutory controls were attempted, e.g. in the UK in the periods 1966–70 and 1972–4 and were in force throughout the 1960s in The Netherlands. In the US statutory control in 1971–4 followed government-inspired voluntary restraint in the mid 1960s (Blyth 1979).

27. Thus it has been argued that in the UK the spread of the multidivisional firm and the reorganization of industrial relations procedure following merger have been part of a management strategy to control wage costs and alter bargaining strength (Marginson 1985).

28. Rising from 3.4% to 4.5% in the US, 8.0% to 14.2% in the UK, and 10.1% to 15.8% in the rest of the EEC, with Japan recording a rise from 2.2% to 3.0% in 1973 before falling back to 2.4% in 1978 (CEPG 1979). A number of studies which adjust concentration ratios quantitatively or qualitatively for international trade and other changes in the corporate environment in this period conclude that competitive pressures were maintained or intensified, the latter especially in the case of the US and UK (EEC 1982; Marvel 1980; Utton and Morgan 1983).

29. Thus whilst unemployment compensation expenditure rose fairly rapidly from

1960 to 1975, after that the growth rate fell as more stringent eligibility criteria were introduced, and the unemployed became increasingly long term and more heavily dominated by those on the outside of the dual market especially the young and married women (OECD 1985*h*).

30. In March 1968, the US had already announced that it would no longer be prepared to convert privately held dollars into gold; nor would it support the price of gold at $35 an ounce in the free market. This led to a two-tier gold market, with official transactions at $35 an ounce and the free market allowed to reach its own level.

31. Thus the mainstream of the economics profession was overwhelmingly in favour of the floating-rate regime in the early 1970s (Llewellyn *et al.* 1985).

32. Dennison (1979) has estimated that this supply-side effect explained a fall of perhaps 0.3% p.a. in the rate of growth of US potential output after the first oil shock, out of a total decline of about 1.5% p.a.

33. Since the second oil shock affected the LDCs much more severely, the relative economic performance of these countries over the period 1974–8 is even better than suggested by the data in Table 2.22. Similarly it should be borne in mind that not all parts of the Third World did well in the inter-shock period; the economies of sub-Saharan African countries suffered a significant set-back after 1973.

34. A wide range of systematic studies have shown that Third World exports have not caused de-industrialization in the North, that the rate of growth of manufactured imports in the Southern countries was also very high, and that most non-oil LDCs remained balance-of-payments constrained. Evidence shows that the intra-Northern trade (e.g. with Japan) was far more destabilizing for Northern economies than their manufacturing trade with the South. For a full discussion of these issues, see Singh (1981), OECD (1979).

3

Macropolicy in the Rise and Fall of the Golden Age

GERALD A. EPSTEIN AND JULIET B. SCHOR

I. INTRODUCTION

The golden age was the era of demand management. Originally with monetary, and then fiscal policy, the governments of the advanced capitalist economies attempted to enhance and guide the accumulation process. The six countries which we consider in this chapter (France, Germany, Italy, Japan, United Kingdom, United States) differed in their conduct of macroeconomic policy. In the three Continental countries and Japan, policy was aimed at maximizing the rate of accumulation. Monetary and discretionary fiscal policy was therefore systematically expansionary, notwithstanding the absence of an intellectual commitment to Keynesianism in these countries. In the United States and the United Kingdom, policy was markedly less expansionary.

We will argue below that this difference can be explained by structural differences among the countries. Most important are the degree of independence of the central bank, the nature of relations between financial and non-financial corporations, the specifics of the wage-setting process, and, finally, the position of the country in the world economy. It is our view that the expansionism of France, Italy, Germany, and Japan, and the relatively more restrictive stance of the United States and the United Kingdom can be explained by reference to these factors.

As the golden age began to unravel, things changed. In all countries, the benefits from expansionary policy were reduced by structural changes in the international monetary system, the growing strength of labour, and increasing inflation. These changes also eroded the distinctions between the United States and the United Kingdom on the one hand, and France, Germany, Italy, and Japan on the other. Although some countries attempted to pursue expansionary policies throughout the 1970s, the difficulties of doing so eventually prevailed. There was a general shift to restraint, which was quite dramatic after 1979.

In the pages which follow, we explore this history. We begin with a general outline of the structural determinants of monetary policy in our six countries (Section II). Next is an account of policy during the golden age (Section III). In Section IV we discuss the effects of the erosion of the golden age on macropolicy.

II. THE POLITICAL ECONOMY OF MACROECONOMIC POLICY-MAKING

A look at the pattern of macroeconomic policy-making in the advanced capitalist countries reveals significant differences among countries. Central bankers in England, the United States, Germany, Switzerland, and Finland are given wide latitude and independence, while their counterparts in Sweden, Austria, and France are tightly bound to the government. Some countries undergo frequent cycles of inflation and exchange rate depreciation, while others maintain chronically overvalued currencies. Italy is willing to run substantial budget deficits, while Finland refuses to incur any government debt whatsoever.

In our view, these differences are to a large extent systematic, and can be explained by structural characteristics of the economies in question.[1] A few key institutions and constraints exert a highly determinant effect on policy.[2] These are the relation between financial and industrial capital, the nature of the integration of the national economy into the international economy, the relative power of capital and labour, and the relation between the policy-making apparatus and the state in general.[3]

II.1 Finance and Industry

Capitalist economies differ in the degree of integration between financial and industrial (or non-financial)[4] capital. In Table 3.1 we present one measure of the degree of integration between financial and non-financial corporations.

In the United Kingdom, which has the least integration of our six countries, banks finance virtually no long-term investment in industry, which gets funds either internally or through family connections. This has been true at least since the nineteenth century and has led

Table 3.1. Connections between finance and industry: Share of non-financial corporation liabilities held by commercial banks

	Average	Rank
France	0.10[a]	2
Germany	0.58	6
Italy	0.32	4
Japan	0.39	5
UK	0.10	2
US	0.08	1

[a] Figure for France is misleading, given other measures which indicate high levels of integration between finance and industry.

Source: OECD Financial Statistics, Part 3, various years.

banks to have little involvement with or financial stake in industry (Best and Humphries 1986; Hall 1986; JEC 1981). Policy tends to affect finance and industry quite differently; a classic example is their conflicting interests with respect to the valuation of sterling.

By contrast, Germany has the most highly integrated financial and industrial sector of the six countries (Francke 1984; Nardozzi 1983; Rybczynski 1984; Langhor 1985). Banks hold equity positions and are highly involved in the management of industry. The fortunes of industry and finance are more closely tied. This has led to a tendency, on the part of both industry and finance, to prefer exchange rate undervaluation.

Our general conclusion is that countries with more divergence between finance and industry will favour more restrictive macro-economic (and particularly monetary) policy, *ceteris paribus*. The available evidence shows that financial profitability is adversely affected by inflation, while non-financial profitability is not similarly affected (Revell 1979; Santori 1986; Federal Reserve Bank of New York 1984). Because expansionary policy is associated with inflation, and policy restrictiveness is frequently an anti-inflation measure, financial corporations are biased toward restrictiveness.

In addition, in both the United States and the United Kingdom, the financial sector has had a strong international orientation. In both cases, the domestic currency is extensively used for international transactions. Maintenance of confidence in the currency has generally entailed nominal stability. Financial interests have therefore

Table 3.2. Central bank independence[a]

	Bade and Parkin	Epstein and Schor
France	1	1
Germany	3	3
Italy	1	1 <1981
		2 >1981
Japan	2	1
UK	1	1.5
US	2	2

[a] The higher the number the more independent the bank

Sources: Bade and Parkin (1980); Authors' estimates.

opposed expansionary policy on the grounds that it jeopardizes the international role of the currency.

II.2 The Relation between the Policy-making Apparatus and the State

In the case of monetary policy, the relation between the central bank and the government is an important determinant of policy. Independent central banks pursue more restrictive policies (see Epstein and Schor 1986; Bade and Parkin 1980; Bananian 1983, 1987). In part, this is because independent banks are not statutorily required to finance budget deficits, as many non-independent banks are. But even controlling for budget deficits, independent banks are less expansionary. To some extent this is due to a traditional and often statutory function of the central bank to protect the value of the currency. But it is also because more independent banks are often closely aligned with the financial sector (e.g. United Kingdom, United States, Switzerland). By contrast, less independent banks are statistically correlated with strong labour movements and labour parties (Epstein and Schor 1986; Martin 1986 or Uusitalo 1984).[5] This creates a preference for expansionary policies, as expansion helps to fulfil labour's traditional objectives of full employment and high social expenditures.[6]

Our econometric research, as well as two case-studies of central bank movements toward independence (the Federal Reserve in 1951 and the Bank of Italy in 1981), strongly support the view that independent banks are more restrictive. In Table 3.2 we present a ranking of the degree of independence of our six central banks.

II.3 Class Struggle: Labour and Capital

We made reference above to difference between labour and capital with respect to macroeconomic policy. At the level of broad objectives, the evidence suggests that in countries where labour is stronger, policy is more expansionary (Cameron 1984; Lange and Garrett 1985).[7]

However, labour markets may exhibit particular features which necessitate a more complex analysis. Most important are the specifics of the wage-setting process and the extent of employment security. If wage-setting is Keynesian (nominal rigidity with respect to inflation), depreciation or inflation will erode the real wage and raise nonfinancial profitability (Sachs 1979; Epstein 1985). Capital may favour expansionary policy and labour may oppose it. With Marxian wage-setting (real wage protection), labour has an unambiguous interest in expansionary policy, and capital has the reverse interest.

Similarly, if there are statutory limitations on employers' ability to terminate employment, capitalists may benefit less from restrictive policy. Austerity may reduce capacity utilization and profitability without generating downward pressure on unit labour costs. Thus, one would expect to see less policy activism overall where employment security is greater.

II.4 The International Economy

The position of a nation in the international economy will have important effects on policy. As noted above, the special role of finance in the United States and the United Kingdom resulted in policy restrictiveness. Countries which have tried to follow an export-led model of industrialization (Japan, Germany, France, and Italy before 1981) often resist policy actions which appreciate their currencies. Finally, in the short term, policy may be often dictated by balance-of-payments or exchange rate crises. The more internationally integrated the economy, particularly with respect to capital markets, the more acute these crises may be.

II.5 The Effect of Policy on the Economy

Before turning to the actual macropolicy of the period, it is appropriate to ask what the influence of policy on economic outcomes actually is. Not surprisingly, there is a wide spectrum of opinion on this question, which ranges from the belief that policy has no impact on the real economy, to the view that nearly all of a country's macroeconomic performance can be attributed to its policy stance. We take an intermediate position. Both monetary and fiscal policy can affect real outcomes, we believe, but to a limited extent. The structural characteristics of an economy are also powerful determinants of macroeconomic outcomes.

Our position may be made clearer by some examples. Those who argue for policy ineffectiveness suggest that either the central bank cannot control the supply of money (because private agents are sophisticated enough to circumvent regulations) or even if it can control money, its actions can only affect prices. In regard to the latter claim, we note that it is not valid under conditions of less than full employment. For reasons discussed elsewhere in this volume, we take the view that unemployment is the norm in most capitalist economies. This is particularly true of Europe during the period we are studying, on account of war devastation and the existence of large labour reserves. On the question of whether the central bank can control private agents, our research suggests that it is an empirical issue, and the degree of effective control depends on the time-period, the political power of private agents *vis-à-vis* the state, and the degree of international integration of capital markets. Our reading of the post-war history indicates that central banks began the period with more control than they ended it with, but that during no time could they be described as completely ineffective.

Similar arguments can be applied to fiscal policy. Crowding out— the favourite mechanism of the ineffectiveness position—must be counterpoised to crowding in; particularly during the golden age the stability imparted by government policy encouraged private investment.

On balance, we believe that expansionary policy during the golden age made a positive contribution to the growth rate, through various mechanisms: easier access to credit, pegging of the interest rate, direct increases in aggregate demand, and the encouragement of investor optimism through the stabilization of activity. After the erosion of the golden age, policy was more restrictive, and certainly exacerbated the deflationary structural tendencies at work. Unfortunately, a thorough analysis of the precise mix between these two factors, and the effect of policy generally, is beyond the scope of this chapter.

III. MACROPOLICY IN THE GOLDEN AGE
(1950–1973)

Among the six countries discussed in this volume, policy did not have a uniform stance. Structural differences divide the countries into two groups. Group A (France, Italy, Japan, and Germany) is characterized by more expansionary macroeconomic policy and a more rapid rate of accumulation. Group B (the United States and the United Kingdom) exercised considerably more policy restraint. This difference was primarily due to the independence of their central banks and the international role of these two 'imperial' powers. The major qualification to this classification is Germany, which, like the United States and the United Kingdom, has an independent central bank.

III.1 Macroeconomic Policy in France, Italy, Japan, and Germany

These four countries experienced a historically unprecedented period of growth, at rates substantially exceeding those of the United States and the United Kingdom. In all four cases, policy was expansionary and accommodative. The characterization of these as 'pure credit money' economies has a firm basis in the monetary policy of the period (Aglietta 1976; Lipietz 1985; Glyn *et al.* this volume). In a credit money economy, the supply of credit adjusts to accommodate the demand for credit. In the Group A countries, the central banks did not generally exercise their powers to limit credit, but allowed the supply of credit to expand with economic growth.

The priority for macroeconomic policy during the golden age was to maximize the rate of growth in the corporate sector.[8] With the exception of Germany,[9] the central banks of these countries had little independence, either to resist the financing of fiscal deficits, or to enact a policy course significantly at odds with the government (see Table 3.2). The Bank of Japan was 'widely regarded as no more than a bureau of the Ministry of Finance' (Yamamura 1985, p. 502). The Bank of France, since its nationalization in 1936, has been similarly tied to the Treasury. The Bank of Italy was a powerful initiator and formulator of policy, but did not ultimately have the desire or ability

Table 3.3. Annual rates of growth of monetary measures, 1958–1972[a]

	Money	Quasi-money	Credit
France	9.6	12.4	12.0
Germany	8.9	11.9	12.8
Italy	14.2	13.6	13.7
Japan	16.7	16.0	16.6
UK	5.0	7.2	8.6
US	4.2	6.4	8.0
Group A	12.4	13.5	13.8
Group B	4.6	6.8	8.3

[a] All measures are in nominal values.

Source: IMF, International Financial Statistics, Data tape.

to pursue a non-accommodating monetary policy during this period.

Group A countries also shared common features with respect to capital markets, industry-finance relations, and the administrative structure of monetary policy. In all four, there was substantial integration between finance and industry. The degree of internal corporate financing was low. None of these countries had highly developed private capital markets, in the Anglo-American sense. None had more than token markets in equities or corporate bonds, so the degree of banking intermediation was quite high. In Japan and Italy (which have the highest rates of household savings in the world), the household sector was consistently in surplus, and deposited its savings in the banking system. Banks lent these surpluses to industry. Furthermore, the financial sectors in these countries were domestically orientated (Raymond 1982; Hall 1986; Epstein and Schor 1986; Suzuki 1980, 1986; JEC 1981; Langhor 1985; Rybczynski 1984).

This structure of financing gave the central bank a high degree of control over credit conditions, for a number of reasons. First, the central bank's statutory powers over banks were great, relative to the United States and the United Kingdom. Second, the central bank generally enacted interest rate ceilings, which generated an excess demand for credit from the private sector. This meant that banks were consistently desirous of borrowing from the central bank, in order to satisfy loan demand. This excess demand gave the central bank a high degree of leverage over the banking system.

These characteristics of the financial system also gave the central banks substantial influence over international capital flows. Regulations on trade financing, restrictions on capital outflows, and mandatory overseas borrowing were all potent tools used by these central banks in order to achieve balance-of-payments equilibrium or manage exchange rates.

Close integration of industry and finance also created common interests with respect to exchange rate policy. Because banks were involved in the financing of investment, they had strong interests in industry profitability. There was no independent financial sector with an interest in an overvalued exchange rate, and a low exchange rate policy was consistently the preferred policy option. Particularly in Japan and Germany, which moved into external surplus during the 1960s, the authorities were orientated towards avoiding currency revaluations. There was no important sector of business which opposed their efforts.

The final determinant of policy is the structure of capital–labor relations (see Crouch 1978; Flanagan 1983; Lange 1982; Gourevitch 1984; Sachs 1979). During the golden age the labour market institutions of Group A countries gave rise to common (accommodating) policy. Most important was the weakness of the labour movements in these four countries, as judged by historical standards. This weakness was due to a combination of labour-market conditions and political developments in the immediate post-war period.

Working-class strength in the Group A countries was inhibited by the existence of substantial labour reserves. The largest source of labour supply was an internal migration from agriculture. International migration, first from the poorer areas of Europe, and later from countries of the South, also contributed significantly to the growth of labour supply. According to EEC and OECD statistics, over 80 per cent of the total growth in EEC employment from 1955 to 1970 can be accounted for by these two sources (Bernabe 1982).

Labour was also seriously weakened by political events in the aftermath of World War II. In Japan and Germany, the combination of fascism and the policies of the American authorities during the occupation eroded the strength of militant unions.[10] In both countries, unions took a highly co-operative stance until 1970 or after.

In France and Italy, the post-war situation was quite different. The popularity of the wartime resistance translated into strong support for the Left, which appeared to be in control of the trade-union movement. Concerned about the impact this would have on American interests, US military, intelligence, and political authorities, in conjunction with representatives of the American Federation of Labor, undertook to destroy this support (Cantor and Schor 1987). Allying with conservative labour and business interests, they succeeded in dividing the union movements in both countries. In each case a three-sided trade-union movement was created, in which the unions were divided along ideological (and party) lines. In both countries, the eventual result was a weak, internally divided union movement.

The weakness of labour in all four countries meant that expansionary macropolicy would not be quickly translated into profit-threatening wage increases or discipline problems.[11]

By the end of the 1960s these conditions had changed, and workers began to exercise significant labour-market power. Labour reserves had been substantially depleted. Political developments in the three European countries (May 1968, Hot Autumn, and similar unrest in Germany) strengthened labour. The result was a transcontinental strike wave of unprecedented proportions, and a real wage explosion (see Sachs 1979; Schor 1983; Soskice 1978; Lange 1982; Gourevitch 1984; Pizzorno and Crouch 1978).

One outcome of the growth in labour strength was the transformation of European wage-setting from a process with nominal rigidity (Keynesian) to one with real wage rigidity (Marxian) (see Sachs 1979). This had predictable consequences for policy, which we take up in Section IV.

The above characterization of monetary policy is reflected in the aggregate data. Table 3.3 presents rates of growth of money, quasi-money, and credit for the each of the six countries in the study, and averages based on our typology of policy. In all categories (nominal, real, and real normalized by potential output), Group A countries had substantially higher rates of monetary expansion than Group B countries.

What about fiscal policy? As a rule, Group A countries relied much less on expansionary fiscal policy. In Japan, the government attempted to maintain a balanced budget, cutting taxes continually as growth automatically raised revenues (Yamamura 1985). In Germany, the use of counter-cyclical fiscal policy was not even statutorily permissible until the Stabilization Act of 1967, after which time the government did use traditional Keynesian policies, although

Table 3.4. General government
surplus as % of GDP, 1952–1972

France	0.7
Germany	2.2
Italy	−2.1
Japan	1.6
UK	−1.0
US	−0.8
Group A	0.6
Group B	−0.9

Source: Armstrong and Glyn (1986).

they were always conditioned by a *laissez-faire* economic orientation
(Kloten 1985). And in France, credit allocation was a far more
prominent planning tool. Of the four countries, only Italy ran a
persistent fiscal deficit. This evidence is summarized in Table 3.4.
Over the period 1952–73 the average general government surplus as
a percentage of GDP was 0.6, with only Italy showing consistent
deficits.

The actual surpluses are only partially revealing, however, as the
rapid pace of economic growth and the existence of fiscal drag contributed to growing revenues. Unfortunately, standardized high-
employment, or 'structural', budgets do not exist for the entire
period. However, we do have an estiamte for 1955–65 (see Table
3.5). This is a cyclically adjusted measure of the average stimulus
of fiscal policy to the economy, according to which fiscal policy in
Group A countries was expansionary, with an annual contribution to
GNP growth of 0.74 per cent.

The Group B countries had a much more expansionary actual
fiscal stance (average of −0.9 per cent). However, on a cyclically
adjusted basis, fiscal policy contributed almost nothing to the growth
of GNP (an average contribution of 0.125 per cent per year).[12] On
balance, it appears that fiscal policy was mildly expansionary (on a
structural basis) in the Group A countries. In Group B, the structural budget contributed little.

We have now sketched the broad outlines of macroeconomic
policy in the golden age and argued that policy was systematically
expansionary, with the aim of maximizing growth. This is not to say
that periods of restrictiveness were absent. Indeed, the very strength
of the accumulation process itself led to occasional restrictiveness. In

Table 3.5. Average annual expansionary effects, % of GNP, 1955–65[a]

	General govt. total effects	Total effects	Central Government Discretionary effects	Automatic effects
France	0.71	0.08	1.19	−1.11
Germany	0.55	−0.78		
Germany[b]	0.90	−0.28	0.92	−1.20
Italy	0.96	−0.22		
Italy[c]	1.00	−0.11	1.16	−1.27
UK	0.00	−0.58	0.19	−0.77
US	0.25	−0.05	0.36	−0.41

[a] The annual expansionary effect is a measure of the effect of the government budget on the rate of growth of GDP. It is calculated on the basis of the deviation of GNP from its trend value. See Hansen (1968) for details. General government refers to all levels of government; central government excludes lower levels. All countries include public enterprises except Germany.
[b] 1958–65.
[c] 1956–65.

Source: Estimates from Hansen (1968).

the 1950s, balance-of-payments difficulties led to a restrictive policy episode in France. In 1960s, each of these countries experienced sharp recessions (France in 1963–5, Germany in 1966–7, Italy in 1963–4, and Japan in 1965). Nevertheless, these periods of restrictiveness were exceptional, and generally quite short. The dominant thrust of policy was to encourage rapid accumulation.

III.2 Macroeconomic Policy in the US and the UK

During the golden age macropolicy in the United States and the United Kingdom was considerably more restrictive than in Group A countries. The structural features which accounted for this difference were the independence of the central banks, relations between finance and industry, and the strong economic power of labour. In the British case, we should add the influence of Keynesian economic theory.[13]

In the United States the Federal Reserve gained independence from the Treasury in the 'accord' of 1951 (Epstein and Schor 1986). Once the Fed won the ability to set interest rates independently of the Treasury's needs, it was able to pursue policies at odds with those of the Executive or Legislature.[14] However, in its fight for independence the Fed found it necessary to turn for political support to the commercial banking sector—a long-standing ally. This support, plus the traditional corruption of relations between the regulator and the regulated, resulted in a symbiotic relationship between the Fed and the commercial banking sector. Over time, the Fed came to rely on the political influence of the banking sector to protect its independence. And the banks' interests came to be represented by the Fed.

The interest of the Fed in bank profitability did not automatically translate into a concern for industrial profitability, because these two sectors are relatively separate in the US economy (see Table 3.1). Financial markets are highly developed in the United States, and firms are able to raise funds from a variety of sources.

Like London, New York was an important centre of international finance. The dollar's role in the Bretton Woods system afforded special advantage to US banks, and accelerated the growth of international banking in the United States. The central bank was accordingly devoted to maintaining the international status of the dollar. This entailed restricting the international supply of liquidity. Inflation rates comparable to the Group A countries (with the exception of Germany) would be likely to generate anxiety about the dollar and could trigger a run on the gold stock.

The situation in the United Kingdom was similar. The Bank of England was nominally nationalized in 1946, but nationalization was a 'great non-event' (Morgan 1984). The traditional relation between the City of London and the Bank continued virtually unchanged, as did Bank–Treasury relations. Through the famous City–Bank–Treasury nexus, macroeconomic policy was highly orientated towards the interests of the City.[15] Even though the Bank of England was formally obligated to accommodate fiscal deficits, the policy consensus was sufficiently pro-City to prevent consistently expansionary policy.

What were the interests of the City? The City had little involvement with British industry. Its profits lay largely in international commercial, mercantile, and financial activity—the legacy of Britain's imperial status. The constant in the macropolicy stance was the attempt to maintain the value of sterling, as it was still widely in use as an international currency.[16] Throughout the golden age both Labour and the Tories believed that the health of the City[17] depended on maintenance of the $2.80 sterling–dollar exchange rate.

This exchange rate commitment was problematic on account of underlying weakness in the economy's balance-of-payments position and the large overhang of sterling balances which remained after the war. Combined with expansionary fiscal policy aimed at full employment, the external weakness generated recurrent sterling crises. Expansionary periods were quickly aborted by balance-of-payments problems (the famous stop-go policies). Sterling crises and periods of restrictiveness occurred in 1947, 1949, 1951, 1955, 1957, 1961, throughout 1964–7. The strength of the policy consensus created by the City–Bank–Treasury nexus can be seen by the commitment to the pound throughout the 1960s, despite its adverse consequences for the economy. Proponents of expansion were unable to enact the changes (e.g. devaluation, import controls) necessary for sustained expansion. As the data on fiscal stimulus above show, the expansionary fiscal policy associated with Britain's ideological commitment to full employment was negated by the simultaneous commitment to the City.

The United States and the United Kingdom also differed from the Group A countries with respect to capital–labour relations. Both countries emerged from World War II with the power of labour enhanced. While the Cold War adversely affected the political strength of labour, in both countries workers retained significant power, particularly on the shop floor.[18] In our view, labour's asymmetric power (economic strength, political weakness) was an important reason for the relative restrictiveness of policy.

As the data on both monetary and fiscal policy show, the United States and the United Kingdom used considerably less expansionary policy than the Group A countries. They had less integrated financial and non-financial sectors, more independent central banks, more economically powerful working classes, and were both attempting to maintain an international currency. In our view, these structural differences were the major determinants of the policy variation.

IV. POLICY-MAKING IN THE AFTERMATH OF THE GOLDEN AGE (1973–1986)

By the early 1970s, the structural conditions underlying the golden age were eroding. Many policy-makers began to perceive that expansionary macroeconomic policy would harm profitability and investment rather than improve them. This perception grew over the decade, and finally resulted in a general shift towards restictive monetary and fiscal policies, even among those countries which had pursued accommodating policies in the 1950s and 1960s.

IV.1 Structural Change and the Shift to Restrictive Policy

The wage explosions and strike waves in Europe signalled a fundamental change in capital–labour relations.[19] This change can be represented as a shift from a Keynesian to a Marxian wage-setting regime, and a quite general increase in the power of labour. One result was a rise in labour's share of output, which, to varying degrees, occurred in all six countries. The labour market conditions which had facilitated expansionary policy in the Group A countries were a thing of the past.

The second structural change involved the erosion of US hegemony and the subsequent collapse of the Bretton Woods fixed exchange rate regime. While economists and policy-makers originally believed that floating rates would increase policy latitude, that hope was not fulfilled. In most countries, the freedom of flexible rates was undermined by a high level of speculative international capital flows, which drove depreciating currencies into a vicious cycle of depreciation and inflation. The 1978–9 dollar crisis revealed that even the United States was not immune from this problem of vicious cycles. By then, flexible rates and speculative capital flows may have imparted a contractionary bias to the world economy.

Ultimately, these structural changes blurred the distinction between Group A and B countries. The growth of labour strength in Group A countries made expansionary policy more threatening. For the UK and the US, the breakdown of the fixed exchange rate system created new opportunities for expansionary policy.

The oil price increases of 1973 and 1979 also undermined the possibilities for expansionary policy. By worsening the current accounts of oil-importing countries, the price increases placed pressure on governments to reduce imports. They also heightened the distributional struggle between capital and labour. This conflict led either to inflation, which harmed financial interests, or losses in industrial profitability. Where real wage bargaining (a Marxian regime) was in force, expansionary policy would harm financial profits without increasing industrial profits. Thus financial and industrial capital developed a common interest in their opposition to expansionary macroeconomic policy.[20]

Table 3.6. Monetary policy in the rise and fall of the golden age (average annual % change)

	Real money growth		Real money plus quasi-money growth	
	1958–70	1971–85	1958–70	1971–85
France	4.5	0.9	7.8	3.9
Germany	6.0	2.5	10.3	3.5
Italy	10.5	2.4	10.5	4.2
Japan	10.7	3.1	14.2	6.1
UK	−0.4	0.9	1.6	4.3
US	1.2	−0.3	4.0	2.8

[a] Real growth defined as rate of growth of monetary aggregate minus the rate of inflation of the consumer price index.

Source: IMF, International Financial Statistics.

By 1979 the policies of the Federal Reserve also contributed to the general restrictiveness, as it began a period of monetary restraint. The resulting appreciation of the dollar meant that other countries could now pursue restrictive monetary policy without fearing a loss of competitiveness from exchange rate appreciation. A reinforcing factor was the recognition that failure to pursue restrictive monetary policy could lead to inflationary over-depreciations of their currencies. Export-orientated governments, such as Germany and Japan, could now pursue their traditional goal of exchange rate undervaluation while simultaneously exercising contractionary monetary policy.

In many countries, there were alterations in the policy-making structure itself during this period, as governments attempted to reduce the use of counter-cyclical fiscal policy by subordinating fiscal to monetary policy. In Germany, Japan, Italy, and the UK, monetary targets were imposed. In France, the exchange rate was pegged to a strong currency. In Italy, where pressures for fiscal deficits were almost uncontrollable, the government pegged the lira, underwent an IMF stabilization programme, and eventually created institutional independence for the Bank of Italy.

The effects of these structural changes are most apparent with monetary policy. Table 3.6 presents data on the rate of growth of the real money supply, narrowly defined, and on the rate of growth of real money plus quasi-money. With the exception of the United Kingdom, the real rate of growth of both monetary aggregates fell dramatically between the two periods. While substantial financial innovation may account for part of the change, the large drop in the

Table 3.7. Structural budget deficits
(% of potential GNP/GDP)[a]

	1970–84	1970–2	1973–8	1979–84
France	0.0	0.7	−0.2	−0.3
Germany	−0.9	−0.1	−1.3	−0.9
Italy	−8.9	−6.8	−8.5	−10.2
Japan	−1.7	1.4	−2.0	−3.0
UK	−0.7	1.2	−3.2	0.7
US	−0.3	0.2	0.3	0.5
Memoranda:	1983	1984	1984 minus 1979	
France	−0.7	−0.1	0.7	
Germany	0.5	1.7	4.0	
Italy	−9.7	−9.4	0.3	
Japan	−2.2	−1.3	3.0	
UK	1.6	2.0	5.2	
US	−0.2	−0.5	−1.7	

[a] Average surplus or deficit. Deficit is (−)

Source: Price and Muller (1984).

rate of growth of money plus quasi-money suggests that not all of the drop can be accounted for by such changes.[21]

The picture is less clear for fiscal policy. Table 3.7 presents the OECD's calculations of structural budget balances from 1970 to 1984.[22] The data suggest that with the exception of Italy and possibly Japan, most countries' 'full-employment' budgets were close to balance in the period 1970–84. This overall balance masks some rather dramatic variations over the period, however. From 1970 to 1972, most countries' budgets were in surplus or balanced. By the middle 1970s, budgets in some countries shifted to expansion. Then, within the period 1979–84, there was a large shift towards restriction in most countries, as the last column among the memoranda makes clear. In the United Kingdom, for example, the shift towards restriction was by as much as 5 per cent of GDP. Germany and Japan were not far behind with shifts of 4 and 3 per cent respectively. Only the United States moved in an expansionary direction.

Similarly, as Table 3.8 suggests, while the overall thrust of monetary policy was more restrictive in the 1970s and 1980s, there was unevenness among the six countries. However, by 1979–82, policy was uniformly restrictive, especially when the narrow money supply is considered.

Table 3.8. Monetary growth in the fall of the golden age (average annual change)

	1970–2	1973–8	1979–2	1983–5
Real money growth				
France	5.9	0.7	−0.8	0.1
Germany	6.0	4.2	−2.4	2.7
Italy	13.5	2.7	−2.0	1.9
Japan	15.5	0.9	−0.6	1.9
UK	4.1	−0.9	−1.9	5.4
US	2.3	−1.8	−3.4	3.9
Real money plus quasi-money growth				
France	8.6	5.0	0.3	0.9
Germany	6.1	4.7	0.2	3.2
Italy	9.7	6.7	−2.4	3.4
Japan	14.9	3.8	4.5	5.1
UK	5.8	0.9	4.9	7.2
US	5.4	2.0	−2.9	8.0

[a] Real growth defined as rate of growth of monetary aggregate minus the rate of inflation of the consumer price index.

Source: IMF, *International Financial Statistics*.

Thus, while the data reveal a generalized shift towards restrictiveness, convergence was not uniform. Macroeconomic policy followed an extreme form of stop-go in virtually all these countries in the 1970s and early 1980s, with a general shift towards restrictiveness by the end of the period.

IV.2 Macroeconomic Policy on the Path to Contraction (1973–1979)

The stop-go can be partly explained by the new, adverse environment in which policy was being made. Lack of knowledge, but, more importantly, the combination of a lack of good options and high levels of political conflict led to policy instability (Boltho 1982, pp. 312–13). The extent of instability depended on the external constraints and structural differences we identified earlier. Among the external constraints facing each country, the monetary policy of the United States and international capital mobility were among the most important.

The United States abandoned the Bretton Woods system first in

1971, and then finally in 1973. Its own macropolicy combined expansionary monetary policy and tight fiscal policy. The resulting fall in interest rates and decline of the dollar limited the degree of monetary tightness which export-orientated countries, such as Japan and Germany, could pursue without risking too great a loss of competitiveness. To some extent, the policy also made monetary control more difficult for other countries, especially Germany, which were attractive havens for speculative capital flows by dollar-holders.[23] Yet while such external constraints were important, they did not completely determine domestic macroeconomic policy. Structural differences among the countries also helped to determine the timing and nature of the policies pursued.

Countries characterized by nominal wage bargaining and industry-orientated governments (or central banks) or politically strong labour and Left movements, pursued expansionary policies in response to the stagflationary conditions of the 1970s (United States before 1979, Italy before 1979, France, United Kingdom, and Japan before 1975). France pursued expansionary, or at least 'stop-go' policies in the initial aftermath of the oil price increase. These policies twice prompted France to leave the European snake and devalue.

Japan pursued expansionary policy in the early 1970s, partly in an attempt to moderate the appreciation of the yen in the face of dollar depreciation (OECD 1985*f*, p. 146). Combined with record real wage increases, the result was the 'Great Inflation' of the early 1970s (Suzuki 1986; Kagami 1984).

Of all our countries, Italy was the most expansionary, for the longest period of time. This is not surprising, given Italy's structural characteristics (non-independent central bank, close relations between industry and finance, and export-orientated development process) and the striking political developments of the period. Italy witnessed by far the most significant increase in the strength of labour, and was the only country of the six in which a left-wing electoral party (the Communist Party) posed a serious challenge. Political conflict was in part eased by large fiscal deficits, which the Bank of Italy was statutorily obligated to monetize.

As noted above, the United States and the United Kingdom gained a measure of policy latitude from the collapse of Bretton Woods and the growth of labour's power in their major trading partners. Actually, in the United Kingdom, the key structural change had come much earlier; it was the 1967 devaluation which altered the perception that sterling had to be defended at all cost (Coakley and Harris 1983, p. 23). The shift to floating rates further paved the way for the monetary accommodation of the early 1970s.

In the United States, the loss of trade competitiveness in the late 1960s and 1970s facilitated a political shift towards domestic industry. During the Nixon–Ford–Carter period policy favoured domestic, export-orientated capital. By contrast, the Kennedy–Johnson and Reagan administrations were more sensitive to the interests of multinational banks and corporations (see Ferguson and Rogers 1986). After 1971, restoration of the US trade position became a high priority. Given the apparent nominal wage rigidity for most of the early 1970s, and the advent of flexible exchange rates, expansionary policy after 1974 led to a depreciation of the dollar, a decline of real wages, and a halt to the deterioration of the trade position. One result was that the shift to flexible exchange rates created a conflict between finance capital, which was still internationally orientated and anti-inflationary, and domestic industry. This conflict was resolved in favour of expansionary monetary policy.

Eventually, however, every country that experimented with expansion reversed its policy stance in response to the accompanying profit or inflation squeeze. The timing and form of that reversal varied from country to country.

Countries with relatively independent central banks were able to tighten policy decisively as inflation accelerated or profits were squeezed, especially when elected governments either gave support or were too weak to resist (Germany in 1973, the United States in 1979). Germany applied restrictive policy well in advance of the first oil price increase, in response to wage-push pressures. With the oil price explosion the Bundesbank increased its resolve to tighten further. In a show-down with the trade unions in 1974, the Bundesbank, evidently with the support of the government, insisted on restrictive policy (Kloten 1985). Soon afterwards, Germany became the first country to announce monetary targets. As the dollar depreciated in the mid 1970s, the Bundesbank allowed the money supply to overshoot its target in order to avoid exchange rate appreciation. But once US policy tightened in 1979, the Bundesbank turned highly restrictive. By the early 1980s fiscal policy was becoming extremely tight.

Throughout the 1970s the US dollar depreciated against most

foreign currencies (Epstein 1981). This decline led to accelerating inflation and eventually to speculative attacks against the dollar. In August 1979, soon after the second oil price increase, President Carter appointed Paul Volcker to head the Federal Reserve system. By October a fully fledged crisis of confidence in the dollar led Volcker to announce a dramatic policy shift. By pledging to target monetary aggregates rather than interest rates, Volcker signalled that the central bank would allow interest rates to rise as high as would be necessary to restore the value of the dollar.

The speculative attack on the dollar in 1978–9 endangered its international role. Paul Volcker was brought in to restore confidence in the dollar and rescue the international monetary system. This entailed not only restrictive policy, but also a reassertion of the independence of the central bank, which required a strong and independent chairman, who would be welcome in the banking community. The low-dollar, inflationary policy of the mid 1970s was ultimately shown to have been an aberration, as it threatened two important structural characteristics: the political support which banks give to the Federal Reserve, and the role of the dollar in the international monetary system.

Japan had a relatively strong state apparatus, strong connections between finance and industry, and a politically weak labour movement, and was able to pursue a restrictive monetary policy even without an independent central bank. By late 1973, in the midst of the 'Great Inflation', the Bank of Japan increased its quantitative restrictions ('window guidance') and by 1975, 'price stability' became, for the first time in the post-war period, the main goal of monetary policy (OECD 1985, pp. 48–9; Suzuki 1975; Kagami 1984). Both monetary policy and fiscal policy moved in a highly contractionary position after 1979. Between 1979 and 1982, Japan reduced its structural budget deficit by 2.1 per cent of potential GDP (Muller and Price 1984). According to Suzuki (1986), the Japanese monetary authorities remained committed to fighting inflation, with most measures of the real money supply declining between 1979 and 1982.

Capitalist-orientated governments which lacked independent or powerful central banks, but which had stronger labour movements than Japan, found other mechanisms to restrict policy: IMF Stabilization programmes (United Kingdom, Italy), pegging to a hard currency (France), or creating an independent central bank (Italy).

In France, by 1976, with rising inflation and unemployment and a change of government, Prime Minister Barre pursued an orthodox stabilization plan—balancing the budget, protecting a strong franc, and maintaining a tight or neutral monetary policy (Sauter 1982, pp. 467–8; Sachs and Wyplosz 1986, p. 268). In the process, Barre led France into the European Monetary System, thereby tying its monetary policy to the mast of the Bundesbank.

Events in the United Kingdom were not dissimilar. Stagflation led to burgeoning budget deficits, and in 1976 the United Kingdom went to the IMF. One effect of the subsequent stabilization programme was the subordination of fiscal policy to monetary policy. By the end of the decade, the commitment to high employment which had characterized one pole of Britain's 'stop-go' had been abandoned (Buiter and Miller 1983). The election of Margaret Thatcher sealed this dramatic change in policy. Her government instituted a programme to reduce the public sector borrowing requirement over a number of years, making that requirement consistent with monetary targets for sterling M3 (See Buiter and Miller 1982, 1983; Kaldor 1982; Artis and Bladen-Hovell 1987).

Fiscal policy quickly became very tight, as indicated by an increase in the structural budget surplus of 6.6 per cent of potential GDP between 1979 and 1981 (Muller and Price 1984; for other estimates see Buiter and Miller 1983 and Artis and Bladen-Hovell 1987). Monetary policy has been more difficult to assess. Sterling M3 greatly overshot its targets, and most measures of monetary policy have been expansionary (see Table 3.6). Other indicators give a different picture. Interest rates, corrected for anticipated inflation and exchange rates were quite high in 1980–2.[24] The Bank of England may have allowed the money supply to exceed its targets given the other signs of financial stringency. In any case, by allowing unemployment to increase dramatically, the government made the important point: high employment would no longer be a policy concern (Buiter and Miller 1983; Kaldor 1982).

In Italy, fundamental structural changes facilitated the turn towards restraint. The Bank of Italy won the right not to finance government deficits (see Epstein and Schor 1987; Addis 1986). The Bank was also able to join the EMS and to complete its long-standing project of integrating Italian capital markets into the EEC. By 1980, with labour's loss of the FIAT strike, the power of the Left and working class had been been decisively weakened. The combination of these developments, in the context of American restrictiveness, created both the structural possibilities and the political and institutional pressures for a more restrictive monetary policy.

IV.3 Macroeconomic Policy: 1979 and beyond

After 1979, both monetary and fiscal policy became more consistently and severely contractionary.[25] Only France pursued expansionary policy, beginning after the election of Mitterrand in 1981 (see Petit 1986; Boyer 1985; Sachs and Wyplosz 1986; OECD 1985; Machin and Wright 1985; Melitz and Wyplosz 1985).

Mitterrand's policy is widely considered to have been overly expansionary and demand orientated (see Cobham 1986). In fact, fiscal policy was only mildly expansionary and quickly reversed.[26] And the monetary indicators showed only a brief expansion, because credit had to be periodically tightened to stave off periodic and severe foreign exchange crises. Mitterrand's policies were reversed within two years. The explanation for the policy failure is highly controversial. There is little doubt that the attempt to expand independently worsened the current account and contributed to a flight from the franc (Petit 1986; Sachs and Wyplosz 1986). But the currency crises which ultimately tied Mitterrand's hands were also probably induced by capital flight against the income-redistributing policies of the government (Petit 1986). Exchange controls were progressively tightened during the period but they were ultimately undermined by the decision to remain within the EMS (Sachs and Wyplosz 1986).

After 1982, some policy divergences appeared again. The United States relaxed its monetary stance in response to Mexico's suspension of debt payments. It had become clear that the viability of a number of large and medium-sized banks was contingent on the foreign debt situation. To ease that problem, a reduction in interest rates and an increase in world growth was necessary. Volcker abandoned the monetarist façade and began to act as a lender of last resort.

Among the other five countries, policy was on balance more restrictive than in the United States. One illustration of the difference is the estimated impact of monetary and fiscal policy on unemployment, holding constant other factors such as real wages and competitiveness. According to estimates by John McCallum (1986) for the years 1979–84, policy had a negative effect on employment in every country but the United States. US fiscal and monetary policy after 1982 became expansionary.

What explains the difference? For the United States, the resumption of moderately expansionary monetary policy reflects structural factors associated with its international role. Germany's restrictive policy seems to result from a perception that golden age capital–labour relations have not been restored and that expansion will only harm profits. Other European countries, having joined the EMS, are now tied to German policy.

IV.4 Alternative Explanations

There are other plausible explanations for the stance of macroeconomic policy in the last two decades. Perhaps most common is the view that by the 1980s the international integration of goods and financial markets was so great that governments could not pursue independent policies, particularly when they entailed divergence from the United States. While this view may be appealing for the period 1979–82, it cannot account for the post-1982 restraint in the European countries. It is also vulnerable to more specific criticisms.

The history of macroeconomic policy in these six countries (as well as others) is replete with examples of policies to reduce the international constraint. Italy, Japan, Germany, France, and the United Kingdom all utilized capital controls of various kinds. There is ample evidence that such controls were effective, at least in the short run, in creating policy autonomy even in a world of highly mobile capital (Argy 1982; Epstein and Schor 1988). To be sure, capital controls are problematic in the long run. Yet experience shows that they can be periodically effective in the short to medium term. The failure to use controls is a policy choice, which should be subject to the same kind of analysis as macroeconomic policy in general. Similarly, the decision to join the EMS or Snake, which *does* constrain macroeconomic policy, it itself a macroeconomic policy choice. The argument that the external constraint must be binding on policy, though it has a kernel of truth, takes as given what needn't be given at all.

V. CONCLUSION

We have by now covered a wide terrain—six countries' macroeconomic policies over a period of nearly 40 years. How can we summarize the conclusions of our inquiry? A first, obvious point is that 'golden ages' are both produced by and conducive to a permissive policy stance. By contrast, periods of slow growth and fragility result in pressures for policy restraint, which in turn reinforces an economy's poor performance.

A second point concerns the variations among countries. Our research on the structural differences among the six suggests that greater policy latitude and superior economic performance are associated with more integration between finance and industry, more state intervention, and less independent central banks. While some countries (Italy, Japan) are currently attempting to deregulate financial markets and create more international integration, our analysis counsels that this may not be a wise course.

Third, our conclusions point to the view that the external constraint may not be as binding as some observers claim. Countries have a fair degree of latitude to choose how much international integration they want, and can enact restrictions if necessary. Again, the current trends are towards more international integration, less regulation, and less domestic control over macroeconomic policy. It is not clear that these changes will benefit the citizenry in these countries.

Finally, the policy experience of 1950–87 bids us to reconsider currently fashionable views on inflation. During the golden age the most successful countries were those with expansionary policy, rapid capital accumulation, and high inflation. In the 1970s, views on inflation changed and many in the economics profession and policy-making circles came to believe that inflation impedes growth. Policy became much more restrictive, and inflation fell. Yet growth remained an illusive target. Many countries continue to pursue contractionary policies. But to what end? The poor performance of the Group B countries, with strong anti-inflation financial sectors, international currencies, and independent central banks should give us pause.

NOTES

1. We have developed this view on the basis of ongoing research, using a variety of approaches. These are: archival research, econometric modelling, interviews with policy-makers, and a reading of the institutional literature. For a more extensive discussion of our research methodology and examples of each of these approaches, see our earlier paper, 'The Political Economy of Central Banking'.

We should note also that our research to date applies only to countries in the OECD.

2. For a discussion of other theories of the determination of macroeconomic policy, see our earlier paper.

3. Lest these factors appear *ad hoc*, we should note that they are derived from a neo-Marxian theory of the state, in which state activity is determined by class struggle and structural constraints. The relations between industry, finance, and labour constitute the former. The latter are the integration of the nation in the international economy and the structural relation between the policy-making apparatus and the state. See Hall (1986) for a similar view. See also Esping-Andersen *et al.* (1976); and Black (1977, 1982).

4. Throughout, we will use the terms industrial and non-financial interchangeably.

5. Particular country examples are Sweden, Austria, and Norway.

6. The literature contains fairly strong evidence in favour of this proposition. See Cameron (1984), Lange and Garrett (1985).

7. In cyclical Marxian models, such as that of Goodwin (1967), labour's income rises with growth, as unemployment falls. This is one theoretical basis for labour's preference for expansionary policy.

8. Background literature for this section includes the following: *France*: Aftalion 1983; Raymond 1982; Bruneel 1986; Sautter 1982; Hall 1986; *Germany*: Hennings 1982; Dernburg 1975; Giersch 1973; Kloten 1985; Francke 1984; Kreile 1978; *Italy*: Rey 1982; Bank of Italy; Caranza 1983; De Vivo 1981; Fazio 1979, 1980; Nardozzi 1981, 1983; Padoa-Schioppa 1985; Jossa 1985; Monti 1979, 1983; Spaventa 1983, 1985; *Japan*: Suzuki 1980, 1986; Yamamura 1985; Presnell 1973; *Multi-country studies*: Black 1977, 1982*a*, *b*, 1984; Boltho 1982; Bruno 1985; Cowart 1978; Hodgman 1983; Hoibik 1973; Katzenstein 1978; Lindberg 1985; Thygesen 1982.

9. The German case has certain peculiarities. The experience of two hyperinflations created an unusual degree of inflation-aversion and a high sensitivity of policy to the maintenance of price stability. Partly as a result, the Bundesbank was originally created with significant independence, which it has been able to sustain.

During the golden age these differences were not especially important, because the inflation rate was low (both historically and in comparison to other European countries). The Bundesbank could accommodate demands for credit with relatively little fear of inflation. Monetary policy in Germany was as expansionary as in the other Group A countries (see Table 3.3). Indeed, the biggest problem of the Bundesbank was to manage the conflict between low inflation and an undervalued currency.

Germany's differences were more important after 1973, when inflationary pressures were strongest. Monetary policy was more restrictive than in the other Group A countries. Germany was the first country to move to monetary targeting, and 'monetarist' economic theory. Despite strong social conflict and intense pressure to accommodate, the Bundesbank was able to maintain a restrictive stance. We believe that this was largely because of its structural independence, coupled with the country's inflation aversion.

10. The American authorities attempted to destroy the remnants of a German

resistance movement. They recruited Nazis to infiltrate the labour movement in order to identify and discredit radicals and communits. In Japan, Gen. Mac-Arthur's programme of democratization was terminated by the authorities in Washington and replaced with policies which gave more power to conservative social forces. See Chomsky (1985).

11. Econometric tests (not shown) of the relationship between changes in unit labour costs and the level of economic activity in these four countries show no statistically significant relation.

12. The OECD estimates of structural budgets (Muller and Price 1984) begin in 1970. For the period 1970–3, the structural budget balance as a percentage of GDP was: France 0.7; Germany −0.1; Italy −6.8; Japan 1.4; UK 1.3; US −0.2.

13. Background literature for this section includes the following: *United Kingdom*: Wood 1983; Blackaby 1979; Dow 1964; Elbaum and Lazonick 1986; Grove 1967; Keegan 1979; Krause 1969; Pollard 1982; Tew 1978; Cooper 1968; Kareken 1968; Hall 1986; *United States*: Epstein 1982, 1984, 1986; Herman 1982; Mintz 1985.

14. Federal Reserve independence remained somewhat circumscribed as Congress always possessed the power to revoke the terms of the accord.

15. There is a significant literature on the City–Bank–Treasury nexus supporting this view: see Sayers 1976; Pollard 1982; Ingham 1984; Keegan 1979; Coakley 1983; Longstreth 1979.

16. Over one-third of all international trade was still financed in sterling in the early 1960s (Cooper 1969).

17. The considerable contribution of the City to the balance of payments was also a factor in support for the City.

18. This is in marked contrast to the situation in the Continental countries and Japan. See Arrighi and Silver (1984).

19. See Chapter 2 above.

20. In the US, where nominal wage bargaining was more the norm, a division developed between finance and industrial capital over expansionary monetary policy. See below.

21. The behaviour of the monetary aggregates for the UK is puzzling. Extraordinary financial innovation may account for some of the behaviour. Also, the dramatic reduction in the international role of sterling capped by the devaluation of the pound in the late 1960s may partly account for the freeing-up of British monetary policy. See below.

22. Unfortunately, earlier and later data are not available. These measures may be seen as lower bounds on full employment surpluses, as they are based on conservative estimates of potential output.

23. For more discussion of US policy during this period, see below.

24. Papadia (1984) estimates real interest rates at 3.26, 5.77, and 5.0% in 1980, 1981, and 1982, respectively.

25. With the exception of Mitterrand's aborted reflation. See below.

26. Muller and Price estimate that between 1980 and 1982 the structural budget deficit expanded by about 1.6% of potential GDP.

4

Profit Squeeze and Keynesian Theory

STEPHEN A. MARGLIN AND AMIT BHADURI

THIS chapter explores one aspect of the relationship between the
system of production and the macroeconomic structure, namely the
role of profitability in determining investment demand and the level
of economic activity. Within the system of production, wages are a
cost: the lower are profits per unit of production, the lower the
stimulus to investment. In a Keynesian view of the macroeconomic
structure, however, wages are a source of demand, hence a stimulus
to profits and investment. In this view, aggregate demand provides
the way out of the dilemma that high wages pose for the system of
production. If demand is high enough, the level of capacity utilization will in turn be high enough to provide for the needs of both
workers and capitalists. The *rate* of profit can be high even if the
profit margin and the share of profit in output are low and the wage
rate correspondingly high.

I. INTRODUCTION: THE UNCOMFORTABLE FACTS OF PROFIT SQUEEZE

Profit squeeze presents a problem for this Keynesian solution. How
do we reconcile the argument that profit squeeze was a major cause
of the decline in growth rates that took place in the 1970s with
Keynesian doctrine on the role of aggregate demand in reconciling
the requirements of the system of production and those of the
macroeconomic structure? That is the task of this chapter.

Our profit-squeeze story goes like this. First, profit squeeze is
itself explained by a combination of downward pressure on productivity growth and an upward pressure on wages. As a result of a long
period of high employment, productivity growth began to lag behind
wage growth in the late 1960s, and this put pressure on profits.
Pressure on profits in turn put a two-sided pressure on the growth
rate of the capital stock. On the one hand, profits were an important
source of saving, so the reduction on profits made less income

available for accumulation. On the other hand, the reduction in realized profits led business to anticipate lower profits in the future, and the fall in expected profits led to a reduction in the demand for investment. In short, high employment encouraged the growth of wages and inhibited the growth of productivity; this put pressure on profits, and the resulting pressure on profits led to a crisis of accumulation.

Basically, the Keynesian objection to this view of profit squeeze is that a higher wage should increase aggregate demand, at least under the assumption that the propensity to save out of wages is less than the propensity to save out of profits.[1] Although higher wages may diminish the profit per unit of output, business will make up the difference by an increased volume of production and sales. If investment demand increases with the rate of capacity utilization, there will be even greater aggregate demand, and both aggregate profits and the profit *rate* will be higher even as the profit *share* is lower. In this view there is no trade-off between growth and distribution. High-wage policies promote income equality, output, and growth. Policies which increase the workers' share of the pie also increase the size of the pie.[2]

This argument was a cornerstone of the 'cooperative capitalism' incorporated to a greater or lesser extent in post-World War II regimes of all the industrialized countries, and articulated in left and centre-left politics and economics until the demise of the golden age. It is rightly thought of as Keynesian in nature since aggregate demand, or more precisely deficiencies of aggregate demand, are central ingredients of the story. But a co-operative vision of capitalism based upon stagnationist or under-consumptionist ideas long antedated Keynes, as this resolution of the Leicester framework knitters, put forward in 1817, indicates:

That in proportion as the Reduction of Wages makes the great Body of the People poor and wretched, in the same proportion must the consumption of our manufactures be lessened.

That if liberal Wages were given to the Mechanics in general throughout the Country, the Home Consumption of our Manufacturers would be immediately more than doubled, and consequently every hand would soon find full employment.

That to Reduce the Wage of the Mechanic of this Country so low that he cannot live by his labour, in order to undersell Foreign Manufacturers in a Foreign Market, is to gain one customer abroad, and lose two at home. . . .
(Home Office Papers 42.160 quoted in Thompson (1963), p. 206)

At the turn of the century J. A. Hobson attempted to systematize the under-consumptionist view, as did various others in the late nineteenth and early twentieth centuries. But it took the combination of Depression and the talent of Keynes to make the stagnationist view politically and intellectually respectable. The central point of this chapter, however, is to draw a distinction between a *theory* of a capitalist economy in which aggregate demand plays a central role, and *models* built on particular assumptions about the components of aggregate demand. It is our position that while both the general theory and specific models may hold at certain times, the models are much more bound by time and place than is a theory based on the centrality of aggregate demand. In particular, we view the Keynesian insistence on aggregate demand as an important ingredient to understanding how modern capitalism works quite generally, but the stagnationist model as very much bound to particular places and times.

II. A SIMPLE MODEL

We can present the basic ideas of this chapter in terms of a reformulated aggregate demand–aggregate supply model. The reformulation consists primarily of giving a central place to income distribution in the modelling of aggregate demand. Income distribution is reflected in the sensitivity of both the demand for investment and the supply for saving to the profit share. In a second, relatively minor, modification of the usual model, we also introduce the rate of capacity utilization z as an additional state variable. The variables π and z replace the variables P and Y in the standard model. One advantage of the present model is that it is normalized in terms that permit it to be applied to the determination of equilibrium over a longer period than the conventional macro-model defined in terms of levels of prices and outputs. Here is the model in summary form:

Accounting Identity: $r = (R/K) = (R/Y)(Y/\bar{Y})(\bar{Y}/K) = \pi z \bar{a}^{-1}.$ (1)

Aggregate Demand (Investment and Saving)

Saving Function: $g^s = (S/K) = sr = s\pi z \bar{a}^{-1}$ (2)

Investment Function: $g^i = (I/K) = i(r^e(\pi, z)).$ (3)

Equilibrium Condition: $g^s = g^i$ (4)

Aggregate Supply (Producers' Equilibrium)

Flexible Mark-up $\pi = \pi_0 + b(z).$ (5)

In these equations, S, I, Y, and K have their usual meanings, R is total profits per annum, $\bar{Y}$ is potential output, r is the actual rate of profit on the aggregate capital stock, r^e is the rate of profit anticipated on new investment, π is the *share* of profits in income, z is the rate of capacity utilization ($= Y/\bar{Y}$), $\bar{a}$ is the capital/output ratio at full capacity output, and g^s and g^i are the growth rates of the capital stock desired by savers and investors respectively.

A few remarks are in order. As has been mentioned, the distinguishing feature of our model is the centrality of income distribution in the determination of aggregate demand. The saving function reflects the Classical (or Income Shares) Hypothesis, which assumes that all profit income is saved and all wage income is consumed.[3]

The investment function introduced here is somewhat unorthodox, and will be discussed and defended in some detail below. Suffice it to say here that our formulation is designed to emphasize a central element of the Keynesian view of the economy: the connection between profit expectations and the existing distribution of income between wages and profits.

Although the same class is assumed to save as well as to invest, saving and investment remain separate and distinct actions. It is *not* assumed that agents, be they households, pension funds, or corporations, necessarily save in order to invest or invest only what they individually save. Passive, or endogenous, money may be assumed to bridge the gap between desired investment and effective investment demand when the economy is in a situation of excess demand.

Lastly, we should make it clear that nothing of substance hinges on our assumptions about the supply function. As in many Keynesian analyses, we assume that firms use a mark-up over wage costs to set prices, and that the mark-up varies positively with the rate of capacity utilization ($b'(z) > 0$). The alternative of competitive profit maximization also yields a positive relationship of the mark-up (and hence the profit share) with the rate of capacity utilization, at least on fairly common assumptions about the production function and the organization of markets, specifically, an elasticity of substitution of less than one coupled with competitive product markets.[4]

Before we analyse this model, it may be useful to present its geometry. This is done in Fig. 4.1, where we use the profit share and the rate of capacity utilization z as the two state variables. The schedule IS represents goods-market equilibrium as reflected in Equation (4), in which planned expenditure equals output available

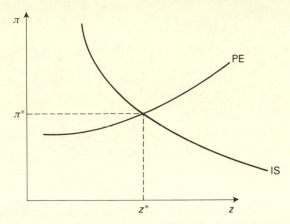

FIG. 4.1 Macroeconomic outcome jointly determined by aggregate demand (IS) and aggregate supply (PE)

and there are no unanticipated changes in inventories. PE represents the supply-side equilibrium, Equation (5), where producers are satisfied with the level of wages and prices. The upward slope of the PE schedule is evident from Equation (5). The slope of the IS schedule, however, depends on the relative magnitudes of various parameters which it is the purpose of this chapter to investigate.

The stagnationist-cooperative version of Keynesian theory turns on the IS schedule having the shape it has in Fig. 4.1. The essence of stagnationist co-operation can be seen through the simple comparative-statics exercise of changing the profit share at each point on PE, that is, by displacing this schedule. Imagine the consequences of a reduction in the mark-up, that is, an increase in the real wage, associated with each level of output. The PE schedule shifts downwards, as indicated in Fig. 4.2. As the picture shows, a higher real wage leads to a lower equilibrium profit share π' but to a higher rate of capacity utilization z'.

So far the argument says nothing about the effect on the *rate* of profit, or on the rate of growth, for that matter. The essence of stagnationist co-operation is that while π' is less than π^*, r' exceeds r^* and g' exceeds g^*, where g' and g^* both refer to goods-market equilibria at which $g^d = g^s$, that is, both are points on the IS schedule. Since

$$g^s = sr = s\pi z\bar{a}^{-1},$$

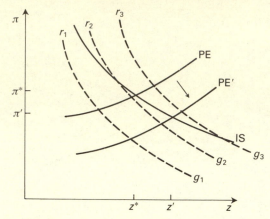

FIG. 4.2 Displacement of equilibrium by an increase in real wages

isoprofit and isogrowth contours are both rectangular hyperbolas, as indicated by the dashed lines in Fig. 4.2; they differ only by the constant factor s. Thus, the analytical essence of the argument is that the IS schedule is flatter than the dashed isoquants: in this case, movement down the IS schedule increases rates of profit and growth at the same time as it increases real wages.

Evidently this theoretical argument does not square very well with the argument that profit squeeze was implicated in the demise of the golden age, and it is difficult to reject the view that wage pressure was heavily implicated in the profit squeeze that set in during the 1960s. This appears to leave us with three choices.

First, we can throw out Keynes, that is, eliminate aggregate demand from the analysis altogether, in the fashion of the neoclassical revival that goes under various names according to time and place—rational expectations, equilibrium business cycles, monetarism, and supply-side economics. It should surprise no one that we do not take this route.

A second possibility is to follow the conventional distinction between the long and the short run and to argue that the writ of Keynes runs for the second but not for the first. In the neoclassical analysis of the long run, as in Fig. 4.3, the IS schedule simply disappears from the analysis. Equilibrium is determined by *two* supply-side considerations: one is a cleared market (CM) condition, which reflects the assumption that in the long run all markets, and in particular labour and capital markets, clear; since workers must be

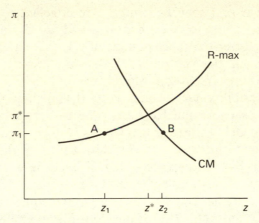

FIG. 4.3 Long-run neoclassical equilibrium

on their supply schedules for the labour market to clear, we may identify the CM schedule with a labour-*supply* schedule. The second consideration, represented by the schedule labelled R-max, is profit maximization. In equilibrium, price (or more generally, marginal revenue) and marginal cost must be equal; R-max is thus a labour-*demand* schedule. In this analysis, the wage and mark-up settle at levels consistent with full employment, which must be understood as a level of employment at which the marginal disutility of labour is equal to the marginal utility of the goods the worker can buy with his or her wages.

In the neoclassical long run, unemployment can exist only if the real wage is too high, 'too high' here having two meanings. On the one hand, the wage will be too high to make it worthwhile for capitalists to hire the number of individuals corresponding to equilibrium employment: z_1, which corresponds to π_1 on the R-max schedule (at point A), falls short of z^*. On the other hand, high wages induce a greater supply of labour than is available at a profit-maximizing, market-clearing equilibrium: z_2, which corresponds to π_1 along the market-clearing schedule (at point B), exceeds z^*.

We reject the notion that fundamentally different theories apply to the short and the long period. In our opinion, despite the short-run preoccupations of Keynes and others who worked the same street (like Michal Kalecki), Keynesian theory does far more than to offer a theory of the short run. It offers a distinctive way of viewing the capitalist economy in the long run as well. The essential novelty of this approach is precisely the central role attached to aggregate demand and particularly to investment demand as a driving force of the economy. Whatever the shortcomings of this theoretical perspective, the insistence on the centrality of demand remains an enduring contribution to understanding capitalism.[5]

A third possibility for dealing with the apparent contradiction between profit squeeze and Keynesian theory is to accept the framework of the model outlined in Equations (1)–(5), and to argue that profit squeeze is the result of outward shifts of the IS schedule against a fixed, but downward-sloping, PE schedule. Essentially this is the view of Michal Kalecki (1971) and Wesley Clair Mitchell (1913), though neither couched their arguments in terms of a model like the present one. This view is developed in the following chapter, albeit in a model that has a sufficiently different focus from that of the present one to obscure the basic similarity of the framework of analysis: both the Bowles–Boyer model and the present one are hybrids of Keynes and Kalecki or, in their terminology, Keynes and Marx. The difference is that our analysis emphasizes the role of investment, whereas the Bowles–Boyer model emphasizes the dynamics of labour extraction.

A fourth possibility is developed here. We utilize the framework summarized in Equations (1)–(5), but we do not rely on a *cyclical* squeeze of profits of the type that would be produced by an outward shift of the IS schedule against a fixed, but downward-sloping, PE schedule. Our argument is more long-run in nature, appealing to the evolution of both the IS schedule and the PE schedule in the quarter century of unprecedented prosperity that followed World War II. The focus of our analysis is on the determinants of investment demand.

III. THE THEORY OF INVESTMENT DEMAND

We begin with a formulation that does no violence to views as diverse as those of Jorgenson (1965), Tobin (1969), and Malinvaud (1980), with investment depending on expected profits and the cost of capital:

$$I = I(r^e, \sigma), \tag{6}$$

where I and r^e are defined as before and σ represents the real (inflation corrected) rate of interest. This formulation however raises more questions than it answers. First, there is the problem of normalization: if Equation (6) is supposed to hold over a period longer than the Keynesian short period, in which the capital stock is fixed, it must be normalized to reflect growth in the scale of the economy: assuming the basic structural relations remain the same, given values of r^e and σ can be expected to induce twice as much investment demand when business has doubled in size.

But how do you measure the 'size' of business? By the capital stock, or by output, or by profits? This, of course, is an unimportant issue as long as the economy is on a balanced growth path, for by definition all economic magnitudes then expand proportionately. But what if the capital/output ratio or the profit share change? In this case the choice of one normalization or another implies a theoretical assertion about the investment function, namely that for given levels of its arguments, the level of aggregate investment demand is more likely to be stable as a ratio to one magnitude rather than another.

Despite its theoretical interest, we shall elide this issue, choosing a normalization on the basis of simplicity and convention. On this basis, the capital stock is the obvious choice, and accordingly we shall assume that investment demand per unit of the capital stock is a stable function of r^e and σ. Thus in place of Equation (6) we have

$$\frac{I}{K} = i\ (r^e,\ \sigma),$$

or writing $g^i = I/K$ as the rate of growth of the capital stock desired by investors,

$$g^i = i(r^e,\ \sigma). \tag{7}$$

We shall simplify even more, by eliminating σ from the investment demand function, so that Equation (7) becomes

$$g^i = i(r^e). \tag{8}$$

We make this simplification not because we believe there is good theoretical reason for investment demand to be totally insensitive to the cost of capital, but because our focus lies elsewhere. Besides, it is a fact that over most of the period with which we are concerned, from 1945 to 1980, real interest rates exhibited very little trend, and indeed hovered near zero, despite the pronounced movement in nominal rates. Over the same period, actual profit rates, and presumably expected profit rates, showed considerable movement.

Thus, in trying to understand the behaviour of investment during the golden age and its demise, it makes empirical as well as theoretical sense to focus the analysis of investment demand on profit expectations.

The very notion of an expected rate of profit raises important conceptual problems. Although the adjective 'expected' suggests the mean of a probability distribution, the terminology of probabilities must be used very cautiously. For it is of the essence of the Keynesian view of investment that the future is *uncertain*, which is to say not only that it cannot be known precisely but that it lies beyond the grasp of a probabilistic calculus; the outcomes of investment decisions are fundamentally unlike the outcomes of roulette, to a calculus of which (following Knight 1921) the term *risk* applies.

From a Keynesian point of view, the neoclassical blurring of this distinction by means of the device of subjective probabilities is problematic, for it obscures an essential difference between investment decisions and other kinds of economic behaviour. There are of course serious problems with the very idea of subjective probability. As Ellsberg (1961) and more recently Kahneman *et al.* (1979) have demonstrated, untutored individuals stubbornly refuse to obey the axioms of probabilistic decision-making as laid down by de Finetti (1937) or Savage (1954). But with due caution the idea of subjective probability provides a useful heuristic for describing the investment-decision process. It has the great merit of emphasizing the state of mind of the investor as a crucial determinant of investment demand.

Indeed the problem with using subjective probabilities lies less in the concept itself than in its customary neoclassical bedfellow, namely the assumption that the world works as if the markets required to extend neoclassical general equilibrium theory to an uncertain world—the 'contingent commodity markets' introduced by Arrow (1953) and developed by Arrow and Debreu (1954) and Debreu (1959)—actually exist. For the existence of such markets would have the effect of eliminating the investor's state of mind from the investment-decision process. Indeed with complete markets for contingent commodities over the investment horizon, there would never be any need for an investor to hold physical capital to back his or her hunches about the future.

In fact, the inherent uncertainty that surrounds the outcome of any investment together with the absence of contingent commodity markets makes capital markets and capital accumulation fundamentally different from other economic processes. Many writers, both outside and within the mainstream of the economics profession (for example, Keynes 1936, pp. 144–5; Minsky 1986, pp. 190–2; Stiglitz and Weiss 1981) have recognized this fundamental truth and at least some of its implications, for instance in the area of adverse selection and moral hazard. But it is much less widely accepted that the imperfections inherent in capital markets require more than marginal changes in neoclassical theory, indeed, require a significantly different theory of how a capitalist economy functions in the long run as well as in the short (Marglin 1984; Gintis forthcoming).

In the Keynesian view, or at least in our 'neo-Keynesian' variant, the argument of the investment-demand function, r^e, is heavily influenced by the subjective probabilities, or state of confidence (to use an older terminology), of the capitalist class. So is the investment-demand function $i(r^e)$ itself. In the absence of contingent commodity markets, capitalists play out their intuitions about the future prospects of the economy through their willingness to add to the stock of productive capital. This assumption is key to the unique role and power that businessmen have, in the neo-Keynesian scheme of things, to shape the course of capitalist development.

In our model, the expected rate of profit depends upon the actual profit share and the rate of capacity utilization, as in Equation (3)

$$g^i = i(r^e(\pi, z)). \tag{3}$$

The first of these variables measures the return to capitalists on condition that goods can be sold; the second, an 'accelerator' variable, reflects the impact of demand conditions. The partial derivatives of expected profit with respect to each variable can plausibly be argued to be positive: a higher profit share and a higher rate of capacity utilization can each be argued to induce higher profit expectations, the first because the unit return goes up, the second because the likelihood of selling extra units of output increases.

IV. THE *IS* SCHEDULE

It should be noted at once that the shape of the IS schedule in Figs. 4.1 and 4.2 is *not* guaranteed by the formulation of investment demand summarized in Equation (3). With the saving function defined by

$$g^s = s\pi z\bar{a}^{-1} \tag{2}$$

and the IS schedule defined by Equation (4)

$$g^i = g^s, \tag{4}$$

we have

$$i(r^e(\pi,z)) = s\pi z\bar{a}^{-1} \tag{9}$$

and

$$\frac{d\pi}{dz} = \frac{s\pi\bar{a}^{-1} - i_z}{sz\bar{a}^{-1} - i_\pi}, \tag{10}$$

where

$$i_\pi = \frac{di}{dr^e}\frac{\partial r^e}{\partial \pi} \quad \text{and} \quad i_z = \frac{di}{dr^e}\frac{\partial r^e}{\partial z}.$$

The shape of the IS schedule depends on the sign and magnitude of both the numerator and the denominator of Equation (10), but the qualitative structure of the model, which tells us only that i_π and i_z are positive, provides insufficient information to determine even the sign, not to mention the magnitude, of either expression. At issue is the relative responsiveness of desired investment and desired saving to π and z.

A stagnationist regime, one in which (by definition) a lower profit share is associated with a higher level of economic activity, is characterized by a downward-sloping IS schedule: in this case, the expressions $s\pi\bar{a}^{-1} - i_z$ and $sz\bar{a}^{-1} - i_\pi$ have the same sign. In 'exhilarationist' regimes, a higher profit share goes along with a higher level of activity: the IS curve has a positive slope, which is to say the numerator and denominator on the right-hand side of Equation (10) are of opposite signs.

Under what conditions can we specify these signs? In much conventional macroeconomics the numerator is assumed to be positive for reasons of stability. The condition

$$s\pi\bar{a}^{-1} - i_z > 0 \quad \text{[Keynesian Stability]} \tag{11}$$

says that at the margin saving is more sensitive than investment to capacity utilization, and this is the standard guarantee of the stability of equilibrium in elementary versions of Keynesian theory. It is tantamount to the condition that the saving schedule be steeper than the investment schedule in a textbook diagram like Fig. 4.4. If Condition (11), which we shall refer to as the 'Keynesian Stability

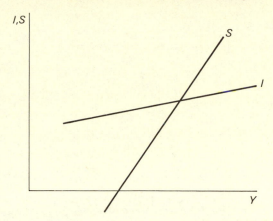

FIG. 4.4 A stable equilibrium assured by saving (S) being more responsive than investment (I) to change in output

Condition', were not to hold, changes in capacity utilization would induce more investment than saving, and any disturbance to equilibrium would set off a cumulative movement away from the initial equilibrium—the multiplier would magnify the initial excess or deficiency of aggregate demand and the process would end only at full capacity utilization or at zero output.

But the Keynesian Stability Condition, though standard in the texts, is necessary for stability only in a model which abstracts from all determinants of equilibrium but the level of output, and in particular, one which abstracts from the impact of the distribution of income between wages and profits on investment and saving.

Once the variable π enters into investment and saving functions, the Keynesian Stability Condition is not logically required to ensure that displacements from equilibrium are self-correcting. Moreover it is empirically plausible that over some portion of $z \times \pi$ space investment will be more sensitive than saving to capacity utilization, in violation of the Keynesian Stability Condition.

However even if there were adequate grounds for assuming the Keynesian Stability Condition, this would hardly clinch the issue. The slope of the IS schedule depends on the sign of the denominator of Equation (10) as well as on the numerator. If the Keynesian Stability Condition holds, then the inequality

$$sz\bar{a}^{-1} - i_\pi > 0 \quad \text{[Robinsonian Stability]} \qquad (12)$$

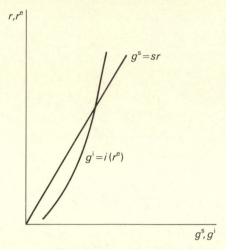

FIG. 4.5 Robinsonian equilibrium assured by saving being more responsive than investment to changes in profitability

makes $d\pi/dz$ negative and the IS schedule is stagnationist. If the inequality in (12) is reversed, the IS schedule is exhilarationist.

We shall refer to Condition (12) as the 'Robinsonian Stability Condition' because of the role this inequality, or something very much like it, plays in certain long-period formulations of Keynesian theory that drew inspiration from Joan Robinson's work (1956, 1962), particularly Harris (1978), Roemer (1980), and Marglin (1984). In these models, as in the present model, prospective profits are supposed to drive investment, but the expected rate of profit is assumed to depend on the current rate of profit alone. The model is closed by appealing to a form of rational expectations justified by the long-run context of the theory: in equilibrium the expected rate of profit r^e and the actual rate r are assumed to be equal. Robinsonian equilibrium is pictured in Fig. 4.5; in the diagram, stability of equilibrium is assured by the assumption that saving is more responsive than investment to changes in profitability (Marglin 1984, ch. 4, where the model is called 'neo-Keynesian').[6] In effect, the Robinsonian Stability Condition plays the same role in the long-run model that the Keynesian Stability Condition plays in the short-run model.

However, this line of argument is also problematic. The present model describes a longer run than the textbook short run in which capacity utilization is the sole adjusting variable, but its time frame is shorter than the Robinsonian long run in which rational expectations can be invoked to identify the expected rate of profit with the actual rate of profit. In our model there is no assumption that the rate of profit on new investment is equal to the actual rate of profit overall. Quite the contrary: in our time frame, the two rates will normally diverge. In this context, π and z play separate roles, and the single-variable Robinsonian Stability Condition cannot simply be assumed on the grounds that otherwise centrifugal forces would dominate the dynamics of the model.

We can however *derive* rather than assume the Robinsonian Stability Condition, provided we are willing to assume both the Keynesian Stability Condition and a condition we shall refer to as the 'Strong Accelerator Condition'. This last appears to be innocuous enough, requiring us to assume only that an increase in the rate of capacity utilization will, at a given *rate* of profit (as distinct from a given profit *share*), increase the expected rate of profit r^e. Write the investment demand function as

$$g^i = i(r^e(\pi,z)) = h(r^e(r,z)) \qquad (13)$$

with the functions i and h connected by the accounting identity

$$r = \pi z \bar{a}^{-1}. \qquad (1)$$

It is then straightforward to show that if the inequality

$$h_z = -i_\pi \frac{\pi}{z} + i_z > 0 \quad \text{[Strong Accelerator]} \qquad (14)$$

holds along with the Keynesian Stability Condition, the Robinsonian Stability Condition holds as well.[7]

Indeed, we can prove a stronger result, namely that the IS schedule is flatter than the iso-profit curves, so that, as in Figs. 4.1 and 4.2, the regime is *co-operative* as well as stagnationist. That is to say, a decreasing profit share goes along with a higher profit *rate* (and growth rate) as well as with a higher wage bill. The essence of a stagnationist-cooperative regime is that

$$0 > \frac{d\pi}{dz} > -\frac{\pi}{z}, \qquad (15)$$

which follows from Conditions (11) and (14).[8]

The problem with this line of argument is that it rests on a very weak premiss. It has already been noted that the Keynesian and Robinsonian Stability Conditions cannot be carried over to the present model from the single-variable models in which only capacity utilization or the profit share vary. With respect to the Strong Accelerator Condition, the issue is more complicated. Despite its incorporation into many neo-Keynesian formulations of investment demand (e.g. Rowthorn 1982; Taylor 1985), it is by no means certain or even especially likely to be the case that an increase in the rate of capacity utilization will induce additional investment when the profit rate is held constant. The reason is a simple one: if the rate of capacity utilization increases while the rate of profit remains constant, it *must* be the case that the profit margin and share fall. So the effect on investment is the resultant of two forces: the positive impact of higher capacity utilization and the negative impact of lower unit profits. Mathematically h_z is the difference between i_z and $i_\pi(\pi/z)$, and the qualitative structure of the model gives us no grounds for asserting anything about the relative magnitude of the two terms. This is to say that in a linear approximation of the form

$$g^i = \alpha r + \beta z = \alpha \pi z \bar{a}^{-1} + \beta z \qquad (16)$$

the sign of β, where $\beta = h_z$, is indeterminate. It requires a belief in rather strong capacity utilization effects to argue that β is positive.

This belief would be justified if the prime concern of capitalists is whether or not they can sell additional output. In this case the capacity utilization effect may be expected to dominate, and the partial derivative h_z will be positive. If, however, capitalists are confident of their ability to sell extra output, and are concerned rather with their profit margin, the negative, profit share, effect will dominate, and h_z will be negative. One might 'rationally' except the capacity utilization effect to be stronger at low levels of capacity utilization, but the subjective aspect of expectations makes it possible that some or even a large number of capitalists will be confident about their ability to sell their output even when the overall rate of capacity utilization is relatively low. In short, the sign of h_z is an empirical matter about which we are not in a position to make *any* categorical assertion.

As a consequence of the lack of conditions which allow us to attach definite signs to the numerator and denominator of Equation (10), both stagnationist and exhilarationist regimes—downward and up-

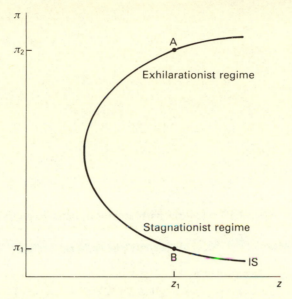

FIG. 4.6 A 'C'-shaped IS schedule with stagnationist and exhilarationist branches

ward sloping IS schedules—are possible. Indeed the slope of the IS schedule can change signs in various ways. For instance, it is possible that the IS schedule will have the shape of a 'C', as in Fig. 4.6. Observe that in such a case there are two routes to high capacity utilization: one follows the stagnationist logic of higher wage shares, while the other follows the exhilarationist logic of higher profit shares. As Fig. 4.6 is drawn, neither stagnationist nor exhilarationist policy is 'wrong'. Either a policy of a high wage share or one of a high profit share, pursued consistently and aggressively, will provide sufficient aggregate demand for high employment and high capacity utilization. In this situation the fatal error is moderation: a compromise of middling wages and profits will provide the worst of possible worlds, in which low capacity utilization and low growth become the order of the day.

However, if high wage and high profit shares are each consistent with high capacity utilization, the implications for growth and distribution of the two strategies are very different. An exhilarationist outcome like A, representing the pair $<z_1, \pi_2>$ is more favourable for capitalists and less favourable for workers (at least in its immediate consequences) than a stagnationist outcome like B, which repre-

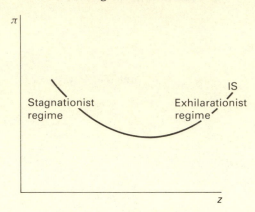

FIG. 4.7 A 'U'-shaped IS schedule with stagnation and exhilaration dependent on capacity utilization

sents $<z_1, \pi_1>$: the point is that π_2 exceeds π_1. And not only does a higher profit share map to a higher profit rate for a given z; since investment and saving are both positive functions of the profit share, the exhilarationist outcome is more favourable for growth as well as for profit. (Thus the long-term consequences for workers are more favourable than the short-term ones.)

The coexistence of exhilarationist and stagnationist branches sharpens the point made at the outset of this chapter, that to reject the policies inspired by a stagnationist reading of Keynes does not require one to reject the Keynesian framework of analysis. One need not reject the theory, as critics from Viner (1936, see especially pp. 162–3) to modern monetarists, supply-siders, and enthusiasts of rational expectations and equilibrium business cycles have done, or limit its applicability to the short period, as the mainstream has done, in order to reach neoclassical conclusions about the relationship between wages, profitability growth, and the level of economic activity. The programme of a Margaret Thatcher, which is usually justified in terms of one version or another of neoclassical theory, also makes logical sense as an attempt to move the British economy from a stagnationist regime to an exhilarationist one. One may agree or disagree with the implicit assumptions about the energy of the British capitalist class, but this justification of Thatcherism is more plausible than one based on the presuppositions of monetarism and supply-side economics.

An alternative to Fig. 4.6 is the 'U'-shaped IS schedule presented in Fig. 4.7, in which stagnationist logic governs at low levels of capacity utilization and exhilarationist logic at high levels of capacity utilization. In the situation described by Fig. 4.7, high wages would be appropriate to combat a severe depression, for in this case it is plausible that private investment demand would be weak. But continuation of high-wage policies may be inappropriate at higher levels of capacity utilization, as profit prospects stimulate capitalists to high levels of investment demand. Economists whose imaginations were formed and limited by the background of depression from which Keynesian theory emerged might easily fail to see that the theory transcends its background. Temperamentally, economists as well as generals are better equipped to fight the last war than the next one.

V. CO-OPERATION AND CONFLICT

So far we have emphasized the distinction between stagnationist and exhilarationist regimes, but we have also had occasion to distinguish between co-operative and conflictual regimes, regimes in which workers and capitalists have a common interest in expansion and regimes in which one class or the other loses from an increase in the level of capacity utilization. If the class interest of workers is identified with the size of the wage bill and the class interest of capitalists with the profit rate (or equivalently—since the capital stock is fixed in the short run—with aggregate profits),[9] then the exhilarationist as well as the stagnationist regime is a co-operative one provided the IS schedule is sufficiently flat. That is, a flat IS schedule, whether upward or downward sloping, will exhibit a positive relationship between capacity utilization and *both* the wage bill and the profit rate.

For the stagnationist regime, this result has already been demonstrated: the wage rate and employment, as well as the profit rate, increase as capacity utilization increases—provided the IS schedule is flatter than the isoprofit curve described by rectangular hyperbolae of the general form $r = s\pi z\bar{a}^{-1}$, in other words, provided the elasticity restriction described by Condition (15) is met. Condition (15), we have seen, is guaranteed by Keynesian and Robinsonian Stability Conditions, or by the first of these conditions along with the Strong Accelerator Condition. In other words, sufficient conditions for a co-operative *and* stagnationist regime are the 'standard' stability condition that saving responds more strongly to changes in capacity utilization than does investment and the 'innocuous' assumption that the response of investment to capacity utilization, holding the rate of profits constant, is positive.

A similar elasticity restriction applies to the exhilarationist regime. By the very definition of exhilaration, the profit share increases with capacity utilization, so it only remains to establish the conditions under which the wage bill does too. Denote the wage bill by Ω and write

$$\Omega = (1 - \pi)\, z\bar{a}^{-1}\, K.$$

Then we have

$$\frac{\partial \Omega}{\partial z} = \left[-z\bar{a}^{-1}\, \frac{\mathrm{d}\pi}{\mathrm{d}z} + (1-\pi)\, \bar{a}^{-1} \right] K$$

$$= \left(1 - \pi - z\, \frac{\mathrm{d}\pi}{\mathrm{d}z} \right) \bar{a}^{-1}\, K.$$

For positive $\mathrm{d}\pi/\mathrm{d}z$, $\partial\Omega/\partial z$ is also positive provided

$$\frac{1-\pi}{z} > \frac{\mathrm{d}\pi}{\mathrm{d}z}. \tag{17}$$

In short, the distinction between co-operative and conflictual regimes refers to the *elasticity* of the IS schedule. By contrast, the distinction between stagnationist and exhilarationist regimes refers to the *slope* of the IS schedule.

Together these two characteristics of the IS schedule characterize wage-led and profit-led growth regimes. A flat and downward-sloping schedule—the intersection of co-operative and stagnationist regimes—describes a wage-led growth regime, a result which follows immediately from the definition of wage-led growth as one in which a higher wage share is associated with a higher rate of accumulation. In a world where accumulation depends on profits, this requires a higher rate of profit. Such a conjuncture is at once *stagnationist* (since under present assumptions the only way a higher wage share can induce a higher rate of profit is by increasing the rate of capacity utilization) and *co-operative* (since the wage share and the profit rate move together). Every other combination of elasticity and slope corresponds to profit-led growth. The stagnationist-conflictual regime is exceptional in that higher growth and profit rates are achieved at lower rates of capacity utilization. The other two profit-led regimes, which correspond to an exhilarationist IS schedule, are like the stagnationist-cooperative regime in that higher profit and growth rates go along with higher capacity utilization rates.

Enough of taxonomy: it must be recognized that all discussion of the shape of the IS schedule is necessarily hypothetical. The truth is that we know relatively little about its shape even in the neighbourhood in which the economy has actually been operating and even less about its global shape; it is a matter of pure conjecture what investment and saving propensities would be at levels of profit and capacity utilization far removed from those that have obtained in recent history. Nevertheless, we believe that the historical experience of the golden age suggests some general conclusions about the shape of the investment function at least during the 1960s and early 1970s. The key is that wage pressure squeezed profit rates as well as profit margins, a fact inconsistent with a wage-led growth regime. To explain profit squeeze within our framework compels the conclusion that the IS schedule was highly inelastic or upward sloping (or both), that is, either that the economy was in a conflictual-stagnationist regime, as in Fig. 4.8*a*, or in an exhilarationist regime, as in Fig. 4.8*b*. The first possibility seems the more likely if we assume that the immediate post-war period was a time in which the assumptions of wage-led growth held, for the IS schedule need only have shifted from being relatively flat to being relatively steep in order to bring about the conditions of profit squeeze.

VI. PROFIT SQUEEZE IN A KEYNESIAN PERSPECTIVE: FROM CO-OPERATION TO CONFLICT

Here, we believe, is how investment demand evolved over the period 1945–80. In our formulation of $i(r^e(\pi, z))$, there are two steps in the mapping from $<z, \pi>$ to I/K; investment demand depends on r^e, and r^e depends on z and π. To recapitulate, the step from $<z, \pi>$ to r^e reflects the idea that expected profitability depends both on the likelihood of additional capacity being justified by demand conditions, and, assuming the output can be sold, on the profit margin. The step from r^e to I/K reflects pure 'animal spirits', which according to Keynes, 'urge to action rather than inaction' (see Keynes 1936, ch. 12).

It is difficult if not impossible to make a strict separation between the factors which influence one component or the other of the overall mapping from $<\pi, z>$ to I^d/K. Some variables, like the cost of capital, the fiscal structure (particularly profit taxes and depreciation

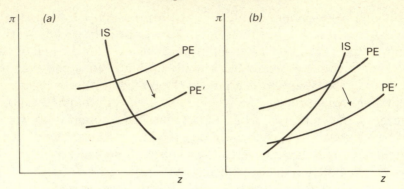

FIG. 4.8 High-employment profit squeeze: (*a*) a steep, downward-sloping IS schedule; (*b*) an upward-sloping IS schedule

allowances), and perhaps the full capacity capital/output ratio, may be analysed more in terms of their effect on the mapping from $<\pi, z>$ to r^e than in terms of their effect on the mapping from r^e to I^d/K. But factors of a more political, social, and cultural character, like the state of class relations or the state of confidence in the international financial system, cannot be neatly compartmentalized.

All these and other considerations were important to the evolution of investment demand over the post-war period. As has been oberved, those who embraced Keynes and saw aggregate demand as the key to prosperity were deeply influenced by the depression of the 1930s. Many Keynesians saw the Great Depression as the direct consequence of the unevenness of prosperity in the 1920s. In the United States, for example, profits grew much more rapidly than wages over the 1920s, and even Keynesians not completely given over to the gospel of wage-led growth believed that the decline in the wage share had led to a shortfall of demand, which in turn led to the pre-war crisis.

In general Keynesians thought it extremely unlikely that private investment demand would play a very active role in the post-war economy. Even if prosperity were 'artificially' maintained by deficit spending, as Keynesians urged, the memory of the Depression and the fear of another would inhibit business from responding to a high profit share with heavy spending on plant and equipment, at least in the short run. Once burned, twice shy. The remedy for the post-war period was seen as lying in a distributional balance tilted towards wages. In short, stagnationist and co-operative logic were coupled to produce a policy of wage-led growth, particularly in the United States.

This may have been a correct diagnosis of the situation immediately after World War II. Profit margins were high practically everywhere in the capitalist world, higher than before the war broke out (Japan being an exception). In the United States the productivity gains of the better part of a decade had yet to be translated into higher real wages, and in war-torn Europe and Japan real wages had declined by more than had productivity. Profit margins improved well into the 1950s.

But lacking confidence in the future, fearing that depression, which was widely predicted as the 'natural' aftermath of war, would make additonal capacity redundant, capitalists were initially reluctant to commit themselves to new plant and equipment. Investment, in short, was not very responsive to the current profit margin; in our terminology pre-war history had an adverse impact on the mapping from the *current* level of the profit share to the anticipated profitability of investment. Under these circumstances, the IS schedule may well have sloped downwards and been relatively flat; the strategy of wage-led growth may have been the best—indeed, the only—game in town.

Wage-led growth would have benefited capital as well as labour. The same history that made the prospective rate of profit and hence investment demand unresponsive to π would increase responsiveness to z, the more so if a high level of capacity utilization could be maintained for a substantial period of time. At the very least, increasing wages would allow capitalists to earn the same rate of profit—if the increase in volume only made up for the reduction in unit profits.

It is a plausible conjecture that the gospel of co-operative capitalism was a sensible one for the particular circumstances of the immediate post-war period. But as time passed, profit margins remained high and even improved; more important, the anticipated depression never materialized. The consequence was that prospective profits increased even more than actual profits: the mapping from $<z, \pi>$ to r^e shifted outwards. And the derivative i_π increased more than did the derivative i_z. Finally, even if the Strong Accelerator Condition held initially, it need not have continued to hold. And once the prospective rate of profit became sufficiently responsive to

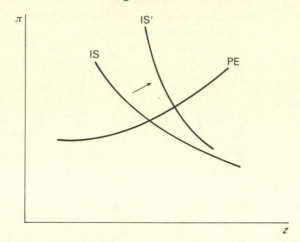

FIG. 4.9 Movement of the IS schedule over the 1950s and 1960s

the profit share to reverse the inequality of the Strong Accelerator Condition, that is, once

$$i_\pi \pi > i_z z,$$

the IS schedule no longer was consistent with a co-operative regime, even if stagnation remained the order of the day.[10]

That is what we believe happened over the first phase of the golden age, over the 1950s and into the early 1960s. The shift in the IS schedule is pictured in Fig. 4.9. The 1960s were by and large a period of great prosperity, but beginning in the late 1960s, when the productivity-growth slow-down and wage acceleration began to displace the PE schedule downwards, the equilibrium moved down the new, conflictual IS schedule, as in Fig. 4.10. The result was a modest increase in the rate of a capacity utilization, but a fall rather than a rise in the rate of profit. Table 4.1 documents this fall in profits.

If this were all that happened, the rate of growth of the capital stock should have fallen as well; given our formulation of saving, capital-stock growth is directly proportional to the profit rate. In fact, the growth rate continued high well into the 1970s, as Table 4.2 shows. Apparently the share of profit devoted to saving rose after the golden age began to tarnish (see below, Section VII). This in turn suggests that investment demand continued to increase, because the IS schedule appears to have moved relatively little at this time.

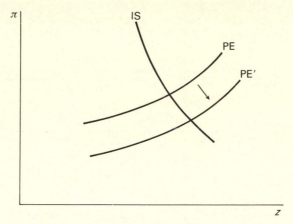

FIG. 4.10 A crisis in two parts: movement of the PE schedule in the late 1960s and early 1970s

(If investment demand had not increased, the IS curve would have shifted downwards and to the left.)

This characterizes the situation into the 1970s. But then new elements enter the picture. First, the cost of energy increases dramatically and the full capacity capital/output ratio increases. Second, aggregate demand management is pursued less aggressively. Finally, towards the end of the 1970s, the very integrity of the international financial system begins to play an increasingly important role. The shift in the position of the PE schedule against a steep IS schedule no longer summarizes the demise of the golden age; the part of the story that deals with the capital/output ratio, demand management, and the international financial system must be told in terms of a downward shift in the IS schedule and a decline in the rate of growth associated with a given equilibrium. This is the part of the story represented in Fig. 4.11.

VII. PROFIT SQUEEZE AND INVESTMENT RESILIENCE

Observe that the share of investment in *output* fell very little over the period we have been considering, except in Japan, as Table 4.3 demonstrates. Indeed given that the profit share fell markedly (see Table 4.4), the propensity to save out of profits must have risen if we assume capitalist economies were operating on or near their IS

Table 4.1. Corporate business net profit rate, 1951–1983 %[a]

Year	ACC[b]	ACC-US	Europe[c]	Canada	France	Germany	Italy	Japan	UK	US
1951	17.5	14.6	14.8	12.4	10.3	21.7	15.0	15.2	12.9	20.2
1952	15.9	14.8	15.1	12.6	9.0	24.8	13.7	14.2	12.6	17.0
1953	15.4	14.9	15.0	11.5	8.6	24.0	13.2	18.9	13.0	15.9
1954	14.7	15.0	15.3	9.4	9.0	23.3	14.3	19.9	13.6	14.5
1955	14.4	16.0	16.2	12.9	9.3	25.8	14.2	18.3	13.9	13.0
1956	15.6	15.6	15.8	13.2	9.5	24.9	14.3	18.3	12.7	15.5
1957	14.7	15.7	15.8	10.6	10.8	24.4	13.8	22.5	12.3	13.8
1958	13.1	14.8	15.1	9.1	10.5	22.5	14.3	20.3	11.6	11.6
1959	15.0	15.3	15.7	9.4	9.8	23.2	15.5	20.4	12.3	14.7
1960	14.9	16.3	16.5	8.8	11.2	22.9	16.6	25.7	13.5	13.5
1961	14.4	15.2	14.9	8.9	11.0	20.2	16.2	26.4	11.2	13.6
1962	14.9	14.1	13.6	9.3	10.2	18.0	14.8	24.3	10.4	15.7
1963	15.2	13.7	13.0	9.9	10.4	16.2	12.6	23.3	11.4	16.9
1964	16.0	14.1	13.3	10.7	11.4	17.0	10.4	123.3	11.8	18.2
1965	16.7	13.8	13.2	10.0	11.6	16.5	11.9	121.4	11.2	20.0
1966	16.4	13.5	12.6	9.7	11.9	15.1	12.8	23.0	9.8	19.8
1967	15.6	13.8	12.5	9.6	12.6	14.3	13.4	26.3	9.5	17.6
1968	16.2	15.4	13.4	10.2	13.2	15.9	14.9	31.6	9.6	17.2
1969	15.4	15.6	13.8	9.7	14.8	15.8	15.8	30.5	9.3	15.1
1970	13.5	15.0	12.6	8.6	14.3	14.5	15.0	32.0	7.5	11.8
1971	12.9	13.4	11.7	8.2	14.6	13.3	11.7	24.8	7.4	12.4
1972	13.1	13.2	11.7	8.9	14.7	12.8	12.0	22.7	7.7	13.0
1973	12.9	12.7	11.3	10.7	14.2	12.2	11.0	19.6	8.0	13.1
1974	10.4	10.5	9.3	10.7	12.2	10.4	10.2	15.2	4.6	10.2
1975	9.5	8.3	6.9	8.3	9.4	9.2	4.1	13.5	3.3	10.9
1976	10.2	9.1	7.7	8.1	7.9	10.7	6.6	14.5	4.0	11.6
1977	10.8	9.6	8.5	7.7	9.2	11.0	5.3	14.4	6.3	12.4
1978	11.0	10.2	8.9	8.0	9.3	11.7	5.6	15.8	6.5	12.2
1979	10.6	10.5	9.4	9.4	9.5	12.2	9.2	14.7	5.4	10.7
1980	9.9	10.3	8.8	9.6	8.5	10.5	11.4	15.4	4.9	9.3
1981	9.6	9.3	7.8	8.5	7.2	9.6	8.3	14.4	5.5	10.0
1982	8.7	9.1	8.0	6.8	6.8	9.6	7.7	13.7	6.9	8.1
1983	9.5	9.2	8.4	6.9	7.1	10.7	4.5	12.9	8.6	9.8

[a] Net profits divided by net fixed capital stock (mid-year) of private sector and public enterprises. Series for Canada, Germany, and Italy are approximations to non-agricultural, non-financial business including imputed profits of self-employed. Series for UK includes North Sea Oil.
[b] ACC (Advanced Capitalist Countries) is an unweighted average of the seven countries in the table.
[c] Europe is an average of the four European countries.

Table 4.2. Business gross fixed capital stock, 1952–1983 (annual % growth rates)

Year	ACC	ACC-US	Europe	Canada	France	Germany	Italy	Japan	UK	US
1952	3.6	3.0	2.8	4.3	1.6	4.1	4.1	4.0	2.1	4.0
1953	3.5	3.5	2.9	6.9	1.5	4.5	4.3	4.4	2.3	3.5
1954	3.7	3.7	3.3	5.7	1.5	5.5	4.7	4.4	2.4	3.8
1955	3.6	4.0	3.9	5.3	2.2	6.1	5.4	3.6	2.8	3.3
1956	4.1	4.5	4.3	5.6	2.3	7.7	5.9	4.6	2.3	3.7
1957	4.3	5.0	4.6	6.4	2.7	8.0	6.2	6.2	2.4	3.6
1958	4.3	5.2	4.7	6.3	3.1	7.2	6.2	8.0	2.7	3.5
1959	3.6	4.9	4.6	5.4	3.3	7.0	6.0	6.4	2.7	2.4
1960	3.9	5.2	5.0	4.9	3.3	7.4	6.3	7.5	3.1	2.7
1961	4.2	5.7	5.3	4.6	3.6	7.3	7.1	9.8	3.7	2.9
1962	4.4	6.2	5.8	4.2	4.3	7.5	8.4	12.4	3.7	2.6
1963	4.5	6.0	5.6	4.0	4.6	7.1	8.7	11.6	3.1	3.0
1964	4.5	5.8	5.5	4.2	4.7	6.5	8.6	10.3	3.2	3.1
1965	4.9	6.1	5.5	4.7	5.0	6.7	6.0	11.6	4.3	3.6
1966	5.2	5.6	5.2	5.4	4.8	6.5	4.5	9.1	4.2	4.6
1967	5.4	5.6	5.1	5.8	5.1	5.9	4.8	8.9	4.1	5.1
1968	5.1	5.6	4.7	5.6	5.1	4.7	5.3	11.0	4.2	4.6
1969	5.3	5.8	4.7	5.3	5.2	4.6	5.6	12.9	4.0	4.6
1970	5.6	6.3	5.1	5.1	5.9	5.3	5.7	13.7	3.9	4.9
1971	5.5	6.6	5.3	5.2	6.1	6.0	5.4	14.4	3.9	4.2
1972	5.2	6.5	5.3	5.1	6.1	6.1	5.2	13.1	3.7	3.7
1973	5.3	6.2	4.9	5.2	6.4	5.4	4.8	12.6	3.3	4.1
1974	5.5	6.1	4.8	5.4	5.7	5.0	5.1	11.6	3.5	4.8
1975	5.0	5.5	4.5	5.7	6.5	3.8	5.0	9.0	3.5	4.4
1976	3.9	4.6	3.6	5.6	4.7	3.3	3.6	7.4	3.0	3.0
1977	3.8	4.3	3.7	5.4	4.9	3.4	3.8	6.1	2.9	3.1
1978	4.0	4.2	3.6	4.9	4.6	3.4	3.5	6.0	3.0	3.6
1979	4.2	4.1	3.5	4.7	4.5	3.6	3.1	5.9	3.0	4.3
1980	4.4	4.4	3.6	4.8	4.3	3.9	3.1	6.6	3.0	4.4
1981	4.3	4.5	3.7	5.3	4.3	3.8	3.5	6.7	3.0	3.9
1982	4.2	4.3	3.3	5.2	4.3	3.3	3.0	6.6	2.6	4.0
1983	3.6	4.0	3.2	4.5	3.9	3.3	2.5	6.8	2.7	3.2

Source: Armstrong and Glyn (1986).

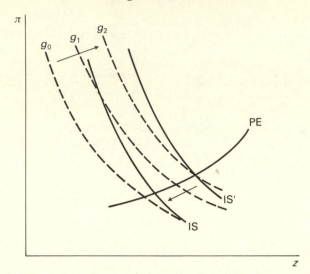

FIG. 4.11 Crisis, part two: both the IS schedule and the growth isoquants shift adversely

schedules. But this resilience of the investment share to the fall in profitability should not suggest that profits are irrelevant for accumulation. If the profit margins of the 1950s and early 1960s had been maintained in the 1970s and 1980s, then investment demand might have continued to increase, perhaps by enough to offset the decline in the full-capacity capital/output ratio caused by the increase in the price of energy. Moreover, to the extent that restrictive demand-management policies were themselves a response to profit squeeze and an attempt to restore profit margins, the case for restrictive policies would have been weakened considerably. In short, no accumulation crisis need have occurred.

This argument does not however imply that a restoration of profit margins would, in the current business climate, produce immediate benefits in terms of growth. It is one thing to maintain the momentum of a long period of high profits and high growth. It is quite another to *restore* that momentum after a long interlude of desultory performance. If the relatively robust performance of investment over the post-war period is traceable ultimately to a gradual diminution of depressionary fears, then the resurgence of such fears—at present focusing on the weakness of the international financial system—may inhibit the responsiveness of prospective profitability to actual pro-

Year	ACC	ACC-US	Europe	Canada	France	Germany	Italy	Japan	UK	US
1952	10.0	10.8	9.9	13.8	12.1	11.9	13.1	13.3	5.3	9.5
1953	10.3	10.8	9.7	14.7	11.3	12.2	12.7	13.7	5.1	10.0
1954	10.4	11.0	10.1	14.1	10.9	12.8	12.4	13.7	6.2	9.9
1955	10.8	11.8	11.3	14.4	11.6	14.6	12.5	12.7	7.3	10.1
1956	11.8	12.9	11.7	16.7	12.0	14.9	12.6	16.4	7.9	11.0
1957	12.2	13.6	12.0	17.8	12.7	13.9	13.2	19.0	8.8	11.0
1958	11.2	13.2	12.0	15.5	12.6	14.0	12.3	17.3	9.2	9.5
1959	11.3	13.3	12.0	14.7	12.2	14.1	12.6	18.0	9.2	9.6
1960	12.1	14.2	12.4	14.3	12.2	14.2	13.9	21.2	9.7	10.2
1961	12.6	15.2	13.1	12.2	13.4	14.6	14.3	24.0	10.5	10.1
1962	12.5	14.9	13.0	11.8	13.3	14.7	14.3	23.3	9.9	10.1
1963	12.3	14.6	12.8	12.1	13.5	14.1	14.4	21.9	9.5	10.1
1964	12.4	14.4	12.3	13.5	12.9	14.2	11.9	21.7	9.9	10.5
1965	12.6	13.9	12.0	14.5	12.6	14.3	10.2	19.5	10.1	11.4
1966	12.9	14.0	11.9	15.8	13.1	13.7	10.2	19.8	9.8	11.8
1967	12.8	14.2	11.6	14.6	13.2	12.2	11.2	21.5	9.7	11.3
1968	12.8	14.3	11.4	12.9	12.4	11.8	11.4	22.3	9.9	11.3
1969	13.3	15.0	11.9	12.8	12.8	13.0	11.5	23.4	9.8	11.6
1970	13.7	15.8	12.5	13.1	12.8	14.3	11.8	24.1	10.4	11.3
1971	13.2	15.4	12.7	12.8	13.1	14.5	11.9	22.4	10.6	10.7
1972	13.1	14.8	12.3	12.5	13.1	13.5	11.4	21.2	10.4	11.1
1973	13.6	15.3	12.3	13.0	13.3	12.5	12.5	22.4	10.8	11.7
1974	13.6	15.0	12.1	13.4	13.3	11.2	13.3	21.8	11.1	12.0
1975	12.7	14.0	11.3	14.7	12.2	10.9	11.5	19.5	10.7	11.2
1976	12.5	13.7	11.6	13.5	13.0	11.1	11.5	18.3	10.8	11.1
1977	12.6	13.5	11.6	13.4	12.6	11.3	11.1	17.4	11.3	11.6
1978	13.0	13.5	11.7	13.3	12.3	11.6	10.5	17.2	12.0	12.5
1979	13.6	14.1	11.9	14.4	12.1	12.2	10.7	18.3	12.3	13.0
1980	13.7	14.5	12.2	15.3	12.7	12.5	11.1	18.9	12.0	12.7
1981	13.6	14.3	11.8	16.1	12.3	12.1	10.9	18.6	11.4	12.7
1982	13.0	13.8	11.3	15.0	12.0	11.7	9.7	18.0	11.5	12.0
1983	12.3	13.2	10.9	12.6	11.4	11.9	8.6	17.4	10.9	11.3

^a Total fixed investment less government investment less housebuilding. It is therefore understated by extent (substantial in UK for example) of government house-building.

Source: Armstrong and Glyn (1986).

Table 4.4. Corporate business net profit share, 1951–1983 (%)[a]

Year	ACC	ACC-US	Europe	Canada	France	Germany	Italy	Japan	UK	US
1951	24.7	26.0	25.5	23.2	27.5	26.9	27.3	30.6	22.2	23.8
1952	23.0	25.8	25.5	23.4	25.4	29.7	24.5	28.6	22.7	21.0
1953	21.9	25.1	24.3	22.3	22.9	28.2	22.4	31.3	22.9	19.6
1954	21.5	24.5	24.2	19.3	22.5	27.8	22.9	28.7	23.1	19.2
1955	23.8	25.5	24.9	25.7	21.8	29.6	21.7	28.2	24.4	22.4
1956	22.2	25.3	24.0	26.3	20.9	29.2	21.6	30.4	22.7	19.9
1957	22.2	26.1	24.4	23.2	22.2	29.6	21.2	35.7	22.5	18.9
1958	20.9	25.0	23.6	22.3	21.0	28.5	21.4	33.1	21.7	17.4
1959	22.8	26.0	24.3	22.9	20.1	29.7	22.4	35.0	22.9	20.1
1960	22.8	27.6	25.2	22.4	21.7	29.4	23.1	40.0	24.5	18.4
1961	22.5	26.6	23.3	23.0	20.9	27.3	22.3	40.5	21.5	18.6
1962	22.4	24.9	21.9	24.0	19.4	25.7	20.2	36.3	20.6	20.0
1963	22.7	24.6	21.3	25.0	19.0	24.5	17.0	35.8	22.5	21.0
1964	23.3	24.9	21.7	26.3	20.0	25.7	14.8	34.5	23.2	21.3
1965	23.6	24.2	21.8	24.8	20.1	25.2	17.3	31.8	22.3	23.0
1966	23.3	24.0	21.1	24.0	20.6	23.8	18.4	32.9	20.2	22.5
1967	22.9	24.9	21.3	24.7	21.3	23.8	18.4	35.2	20.5	21.0
1968	23.5	26.6	22.0	25.8	21.4	24.6	19.3	38.9	20.8	20.5
1969	22.4	26.2	22.2	25.0	22.4	22.6	20.1	36.4	20.6	18.4
1970	20.8	25.6	20.4	23.5	21.6		18.7	38.4	17.5	15.5
1971	20.4	23.8	19.6	23.1	21.6	21.5	15.8	33.6	18.1	16.6
1972	20.7	24.0	19.9	24.7	21.8	21.0	16.4	32.8	19.0	17.0
1973	20.0	23.0	18.9	27.4	21.1	19.8	14.8	30.4	18.8	16.7
1974	17.3	20.0	16.1	27.8	18.8	17.6	14.3	26.2	12.6	14.3
1975	17.0	17.2	12.7	23.8	15.7	16.5	6.5	25.0	9.3	16.7
1976	17.7	18.1	13.9	23.0	13.7	18.3	10.0	25.6	11.5	17.3
1977	18.6	19.1	15.4	22.4	15.3	18.6	8.3	25.6	17.3	18.0
1978	19.0	20.2	16.0	24.4	15.2	19.8	8.7	27.7	17.8	17.5
1979	18.4	20.7	16.7	29.2	15.5	20.8	13.2	26.6	15.3	15.7
1980	18.0	21.1	16.0	30.4	14.3	18.7	15.6	28.6	14.5	14.4
1981	18.0	20.0	14.9	26.7	12.4	17.9	12.0	27.6	16.5	15.7
1982	17.0	19.7	15.5	22.2	11.8	18.4	11.4	26.7	19.7	13.7
1983	18.2	20.1	16.3	24.3	12.4	20.3	7.1	25.8	23.5	16.0

[a] Net profits divided by net value added of private sector and public enterprises. Series for Canada. Germany and Italy are approximations to non-agricultural, non-financial business including imputed profits of self-employed. Series for UK includes North See Oil.

Source: Armstrong and Glyn (1986).

fit margins. Even a substantial improvement in actual profitability might fail to stimulate an investment boom because of fears that the improvement is only temporary. As at the beginning of the golden age, the stagnationist game of wage-led growth could turn out to be the only game in town!

VIII. BY WAY OF SUMMARY

The primary purpose of this chapter has been to release the Keynesian theory of the capitalist economy both from the stagnationist-cooperative straitjacket that has dominated Left Keynesian thought and from the marginal role that the mainstream has accorded Keynesian theory as a theory of no relevance to understanding the functioning of the capitalist economy apart from the short period. In our view neo-Keynesians at Oxford and Cambridge like Roy Harrod and Joan Robinson were developing an important insight of Keynes and Kalecki when they argued that aggregate demand plays a central role in the capitalist economy, in the long run as well as in the short. Furthermore, at least for a large country like the United States or for a large unit like the European Economic Community, for which the small open economy model is of little relevance, investment demand is the centrepiece of the story, both because it is likely to be the most variable and elusive element of aggregate demand, and because of its direct role in the accumulation of capital.

More specifically, this chapter has focused on the dual role of profits in a capitalist economy. Today's profits are, on the one hand, a primary source of saving for the accumulation of business capital. Tomorrow's profits, on the other hand, are the lure which attracts the investor. Under existing institutions, capital accumulation requires high profits, and a squeeze on profits generally leads to a squeeze on capital-stock growth.

Wages also have a dual character under capitalism. On the one hand, wages are costs to the capitalist. On the other hand, wages, or more precisely, the wages of the employees of *other* businesses, are a source of demand. High wages are bad for the capitalist as *producer* but good for the capitalist as *seller*, especially when demand from other sources is weak.

The social democrats and their academic allies, the Left Keynesians, put forward the political and intellectual case for the view that high capacity utilization would resolve the contradiction between high wages and high profits. Emphasizing the demand side, neglecting the cost side, they believed that high wages would contribute not only to high levels of output and employment but also to high levels of profits and accumulation. Capitalists would make up in larger volume what they lost on each unit because of higher wage costs.

The illusion that a new era of 'co-operative capitalism' had replaced the antagonistic class relations of an earlier period persisted until a profit squeeze developed in the late 1960s. At this point, the co-operative interpretation of Keynes became increasingly inconsistent with the facts. One could of course deny the facts. Or deny the theory. Or, as a compromise, relegate the theory to the short period, perhaps a period in which economic agents are surprised by government actions.

Our approach has been different. We believe that the problem has been the way a basically sensible *conception* of the economy was cast into a misleading *model* of the economy. Our purpose here has been to recast the model so that it retains the sense and the insight of Keynesian theory—particularly its insight on profit as the engine of capitalist accumulation.

But the present malaise is not a problem of profits alone. Restoration of profit margins would probably not, at least not very quickly, restore the high levels of investment demand that obtained throughout the golden age and even after its demise. As Schumpeter is reputed to have remarked, one no more restores economic health by simply reversing bad economic policies than one restores the health of someone who has been run over by a truck by simply backing the truck off. A healthy capitalism requires profitability, but in circumstances like the present profitability may follow from wage-led rather than from profit-led growth policies. Over the longer run profit-led growth may once again be feasible, but the transition will surely require active demand management, presumably a possibility only after a successful reform of the international financial system.

The alternative is a much more radical break with the past, a new institutional structure that would decouple accumulation from profitability altogether, as was presumably the ultimate intention of the Meidner plan (Meidner 1978) of a decade ago. We question the timeliness of such a radical rupture, but we would hasten to add that the two alternatives, restoring profitability and freeing accumulation from dependence on profitability, need not be altogether disjoint. In fact, in our view the essential elements of any left alternative to mainstream policies for restoring growth are (*a*) to recognize the present need for profitability, (*b*) to recognize the ultimate desirability of making accumulation independent of profitability, and (*c*) to provide a bridge from here to there.

NOTES

1. Proponents of life-cycle and permanent income hypotheses will object at once. And it is the case that the available empirical evidence does not suggest important differences between the propensities to save out of wage and property income across households, at least not for the United States. This is partly due to shortcomings of the data, but more due to the unimportance of household saving, properly defined, in the accumulation of plant and equipment. The bulk of saving for the business sector is done by corporations and pension funds. A contemporary specification of the Kaldor–Robinson–Pasinetti two-class model would distinguish corporations, pension funds, and households, rather than capitalists and workers. See Chapter 1 above, and Marglin (1984, chs. 17–18).

2. A positive relationship between wages and profits can hold only up to full capacity utilization, at which point higher wages will induce higher prices rather than higher output. In the full capacity case, there can be no squeeze on profit margins at all.

3. The assumption that capital formation is financial entirely out of profits is not necessary to the argument of this chapter, but it simplifies the exposition. It *is* necessary to assume that the propensity to save out of profits exceeds the propensity to save out of wages. If the propensity to save is assumed to be uniform across income classes, as is standard in elementary texts, it is difficult to produce the downward-sloping IS schedule on which the stagnationist model relies.

4. It is by no means necessary to assume the PE schedule slopes upwards. A labour extraction model of the kind developed in ch. 5, for example, will generally lead to the conclusion that the PE schedule turns downwards at high levels of capacity utilization. Within limits, nothing in our argument hinges on the slope of the PE schedule, and in any case our attention here will focus elsewhere.

   For the record, we note that competitive profit maximization was Keynes's own way of modelling the supply side in the *General Theory*. Realism apart, the difficulty with this approach for present purposes is that it makes the real wage depend exclusively on the level of capacity utilization. Within the strict confines of the *General Theory*, one simply cannot examine the consequences of a change in the distribution of income. Distribution is itself a consequence of demand and output rather than a cause, a thermometer rather than a thermostat.

5. Marglin (1984, ch. 4) presents a long-run version of Keynesian theory in a comparative framework. Ch. 19 suggests some problems with the theory (pp. 473–9), and ch. 20 attempts to synthesize Keynesian and Marxian perspectives.

6. One aspect of the Robinsonian model which has gone generally unnoticed is that it implies a stagnationist-cooperative view of capitalism. Since investment

demand is a function of r alone, the derivative h_z vanishes and the IS schedule in $\pi \times z$ space is a rectangular hyperbola. Since in this model it is the *rate* of profit that is determined by saving and investment, the profit share and the volume of output are inversely proportional.

7. By assumption, we have

$$h_z = -i_\pi \frac{\pi}{z} + i_z > 0 \quad \text{and} \quad s\pi\bar{a}^{-1} - i_z > 0.$$

Combining these two inequalities gives $s\pi\bar{a}^{-1} - i_\pi \dfrac{\pi}{z} > 0$, from which the Robinsonian Stability Condition follows directly.

8. From Condition (14), we have

$$-i_\pi \frac{\pi}{z} + i_z > 0$$

and from Conditions (11) and (12)

$$0 > \frac{d\pi}{dz} = -\frac{s\pi\bar{a}^{-1} - i_z}{sz\bar{a}^{-1} - i_\pi}.$$

Hence, combining these two inequalities give us

$$0 > \frac{d\pi}{dz} > -\frac{s\pi\bar{a}^{-1} - i_\pi \dfrac{\pi}{z}}{sz\bar{a}^{-1} - i_\pi} = -\left(\frac{sz\bar{a}^{-1} - i_\pi}{sz\bar{a}^{-1} - i_\pi}\right)\left(\frac{\pi}{z}\right) = -\frac{\pi}{z}.$$

9. There is an element of arbitrariness in identifying the class interest of workers with the wage *bill*, as against the wage *rate*. In effect, we are attaching no social utility to the involuntary unemployment that accompanies excess capacity. But there is, or may be, an important 'insider' vs. 'outsider' problem here: the gains of expansion accrue to the newly employed workers, the losses to the already-employed.

   The case for identifying the interests of the capitalist class with the profit rate rather than the profit share is less problematic: we need only assume that idle capacity depreciates as rapidly as utilized capacity.

10. Diminution of the fear of depression could produce not only a shift in the IS schedule, but a change in the sign of its slope as well. If anticipated profitability becomes sufficiently responsive either to the actual profit margin or to the actual rate of capacity utilization, the regime can change from stagnationist to exhilarationist.

5

A Wage-led Employment Regime: Income Distribution, Labour Discipline, and Aggregate Demand in Welfare Capitalism

SAMUEL BOWLES AND ROBERT BOYER

THIS chapter addresses the relationship between wages and unemployment, on the one hand, and labour effort, productivity, profits, and aggregate demand on the other. It thus complements the previous chapter's emphasis on the relationship between profitability and investment. Emphasizing different aspects of a common theoretical vision, these two chapters together formalize central features of a common approach to understanding capitalist development.

I. INTRODUCTION: THE KEYNES–MARX HIATUS AND AN ALTERNATIVE

The historically unprecedented post-World War II long boom in the world capitalist economy has baffled economists; why did output per capita grow three times faster during the period 1950–73 than the average of the previous 130 years?[1] No less baffling is the unravelling of this golden age during the late 1960s and the enduring global economic instability, stagnation of living standards, and high unemployment during the 1970s and 1980s.

Attempts to understand this epoch, and to fashion policy alternatives to continuing economic insecurity are hampered by an unwarranted hiatus between two major theoretical perspectives addressed to the problem of instability and crisis in the capitalist economy: those focusing respectively on aggregate demand and on class conflict. The Keynesian tradition focuses on product markets and on the macroeconomic problems associated with the failure of these markets to clear at full employment levels. Models in the Marxian tradition emphasizing class conflict focus on the labour market, and the debilitating consequences for capital precisely when this market *does* clear.

Thus, according to these views, the accumulation process may falter in response to two quite distinct types of difficulties: insufficient aggregate demand or a high-employment profit squeeze. The former aspect has been amply investigated in what we will term the Keynes–Kalecki tradition, while the latter has been studied primarily by economists of what has been called the labour process school working in the Marxian tradition. While Marx's theory of capitalist dynamics took account of both sources of instability and stagnation—crises of realization of surplus value and crises of production of surplus value—most recent theoretical work has pursued one or the other strand in isolation.[2]

The unfortunate consequences of the mutual separation of the labour process school and the Keynes–Kalecki tradition are nowhere more evident than in the interpretation of the post-war boom and its demise in the advanced capitalist countries.[3] For if the high-employment profit squeeze interpretation favoured by the labour process school provides a convincing explanation of the productivity slow-down, the wage explosion, and the decline in the profit rate in at least some of the major countries in the 1960s and early 1970s, it surely cannot explain why the low employment which has characterized these economies since 1973 did not provide the basis for another sustained boom. And if the low levels of capacity utilization of the late 1970s and early 1980s provide a compelling Keynesian explanation of deceleration of capital accumulation during this period, a similar explanation fails to explain the reversal of the long post-war acceleration in the rate of accumulation which occurred under conditions of high capacity utilization and buoyant aggregate demand during the late 1960s and early 1970s.

In this chapter we integrate the two approaches—Keynesian and Marxian—by means of a model in which the income distribution is at once a key determinant of aggregate demand, as in the Keynes–Kalecki tradition, and the endogenous result of the level of employment and economic activity, as in the neo-Marxian class conflict view. In the resulting model the wage rate will play a triple role: a source of consumption demand, a component of unit labour costs and hence a deduction from profits, and as an instrument in capital's labour-disciplining strategies (and hence a determinant of output per hour of labour employed). From the standpoint of capital these roles are contradictory; depending on the relative importance of each, profits may either rise or fall with the wage rate. Similarly, as we will see, taking account of the effect of the wage on both aggregate demand and the endogenous determination of output per labour hour, the level of employment may respond either positively or negatively to changes in the wage rate giving rise to what we term a wage-led or classical employment regime, respectively.[4]

The Keynes–Kalecki approach and the labour process school share a conception of the wage rate as a key to understanding both stability and crisis; but for both approaches, the wage plays a dual rather than triple role in the economy. For those who focus on aggregate demand, the wage is both a cost to the employer and a source of demand for consumer goods; an 'appropriate income distribution' is one which reconciles these two aspects of the wage in such a way as to permit stable accumulation.[5] The labour process school, on the other hand, focuses on labour discipline and the endogenous determination of output per hour of labour employed, where the wage is both a cost to the employer and an employers' instrument in the system of control of the labour process: under conditions of less than full employment, high wages enhance what may be termed the worker's employment rent—the difference between the employed worker's income and his or her next best alternative—and hence constitute both the carrot and the stick of labour discipline. The 'profit-maximizing wage rate' is that which balances the costs of the wage against the cost of worker surveillance or alternative means of eliciting hard work (and good work) from workers.

By contrast to both the Keynesian and Marxian approaches, the triple role of the wage rate may be elucidated in a model which simultaneously determines the real wage and the equilibrium level of employment (along with the level of labour productivity and hence the profit share) through the joint effects of two relationships. The first, based on a model of capital–labour conflict over the real wage and the intensity of labour, expresses the equilibrium real wage as a positive function of the level of employment, $w^* = w^*(h)$. The second basic relationship of our model is an aggregate demand for labour function based on an income equal to expenditure condition similar to the Keynesian labour-demand function in that it treats the level of employment as a function, *inter alia*, of the real wage, $h^* = h^*(w)$.

The first relationship is derived jointly from the first order conditions for cost minimization by firms (*firm equilibrium*) and the condition that while each firm takes the wage as an instrument in its labour control strategy, equivalent labour must be paid equally throughout the economy in equilibrium (*wage uniformity*).[6] The joint satisfaction of both wage uniformity and firm equilibrium conditions results in the *general labour-extraction equilibrium* (GLEE) condition underlying the relationship $w^* = w^*(h)$. The second relationship, $h^* = h^*(w)$, is the *aggregate demand equilibrium condition* (ADE); it is a condition for the stationarity of h requiring the absence of excess supply or demand on product markets. It is derived from the endogenously generated level of labour productivity and the components of aggregate demand, on the assumption that firms are always demand-constrained and hence will vary their employment positively with the level of excess demand.

The joint equilibrium (JE) of this system is one in which product markets clear but labour markets do not clear. The failure of labour markets to clear even under conditions of atomistic competition and flexible prices and wages, as we shall see, results from the fact that workers do not deliver their labour costlessly to their employer upon the signing of the labour contract; rather the intensity of labour continues to be an object of class conflict. In this conflict it will always be in the interest of capital to pay labour more than its next-best opportunity; workers who know they could find equivalent work at equivalent pay have little reason to heed management's directives when these conflict with the workers' own work-time projects, such as conviviality, safety, or simply on-the-job leisure. The resulting employment rent earned by the employed worker is both a critical part of the employer's labour discipline strategy and axiomatic evidence of the existence of involuntary unemployment, which is to say, non-clearing labour markets. We will see why competition among workers will not eliminate this employment rent.

To assert, as we do, that employers select an optimal level of the employment rent is not to suggest that they can determine the level of employment, much less that they deliberately generate unemployment through their hiring policies so as to maintain labour discipline. Thus, the microeconomic reasoning which demonstrates the equilibrium nature of non-clearing labour markets does not by itself provide a theory of employment and unemployment. The level of employment and unemployment is not determined by capital's labour control strategy alone but by the interaction of this structure of labour control with the aggregate demand for goods and services.

Our more important results may be briefly summarized. First, under quite general conditions, our model exhibits a high-employment profit squeeze. As a consequence, full employment equilibrium is impossible except under highly restrictive conditions. Beyond a limiting level of employment, aggregate demand expansion policies will be ineffective in the absence of institutional changes in the organization of the labour process and the determination of wages and work intensity.

Second, we show that combining the Keynesian and Marxian approaches generates a series of what we term employment regimes —configurations of labour control systems, state spending, and aggregate demand. Some of these employment regimes may be characterized as wage-led in that the equilibrium-level of employment and the real wage are positively related. The possibility of a wage-led employment regime is hardly surprising given the complementary logic of the Keynesian aggregate demand and Marxian labour process approaches: according to both (and in sharp contrast to the neoclassical model), the wage may be either too high or *too low* from the standpoint of profitability, accumulation, and employment. However even if we adopt assumptions which would appear quite favourable to a wage-led employment regime—exogenous investment demand and no savings out of wage income—a wage-led employment regime is not guaranteed.

Third, increases in the employment level, however produced, will eventually transform a wage-led employment regime into its opposite. This result does not depend in any way on non-linearities in the investment or savings functions; it is generated endogenously via the effect of the employment level on real wages and thence on profitability.[7]

Fourth, if expansion of the welfare state takes the form of reducing the difference between the wage and the social wage, the result will tend to generate wage-led employment regimes. Thus there may be a symbiotic quality to the social democratic programme which has insisted that wage increases and an adequate welfare state may enhance employment. However, it is also clear from our model that increases in unemployment insurance benefit and other income-replacing social payments characteristic of the welfare state may promote a profit squeeze and thus possibly jeopardize the long-run accumulation process. This 'social-wage-based profit squeeze' occurs because unemployment insurance buffers workers from the threat of joblessness and strengthens labour's bargaining power in its conflict with capital over work and pay; it will thus obtain even if welfare state payments are not financed by taxes on capital.

In the next section we will model the endogenous determination of the real wage and labour intensity, and then in Section III use these results to explore labour costs and profitability. A product-market-clearing condition and the aggregate demand for labour is introduced in Section IV, and the resulting macroeconomic equilibrium and corresponding employment regimes are described. In the concluding section we offer some speculations on the extent to which this model can illuminate the post-war boom and its end.

Throughout, we adopt what may be termed highly competitive but short-run assumptions. We assume full information optimizing behaviour by all agents; but labour supply, production technology, and the capital stock are assumed constant. Because general issues of investment and capacity utilization are addressed in the previous chapter, we will model the generation of aggregate demand and the conditions for product market-clearing on the assumption that the demand for investment goods and net exports is exogenously determined, allowing us to focus with greater simplicity on the endogenous generation of savings, government borrowing, and demands for consumer goods financed by both the wage and the social wage. We turn first to the determination of the wage rate and the intensity of labour.[8]

II. WORK DISCIPLINE, THE OPTIMAL WAGE, AND EQUILIBRIUM UNEMPLOYMENT

The standard Walrasian model of the economy represents the production process as two equations: a production function and a cost function. This, along with a behavioural axiom of cost minimization, provides the fundamentals of the supply side of most neoclassical and Keynesian macroeconomic models. But if the extent and quality of labour input per hour of labour employed varies endogenously, this approach is nonsensical, for the labour argument of the production function—the amount of work actually done—is not the same as the labour argument in cost function—hours of labour hired. A third equation is required, one which relates the hours of labour hired to the amount of work done. This third relationship—which we term the *labour-extraction function*—is central to our approach, for as we will presently see it provides the basis for making labour intensity and the wage rate a function of the level of employment and hence endogenous.

Because labour intensity—the amount of work done per hour—is endogenously determined, we must distinguish between work effort—labour—and labour time. The former is measured in effort units, the latter in hours.[9] Consider the production function of a representative firm, one of a large number which make up the economy:

$$Q = Q(L) = qeH, \tag{1}$$

where Q = level of output per period of time,
L = amount of labour (work) addressed to production over this period,
H = hours of labour hired by the firm over the period,
e = amount of work effort performed per hour of labour hired,
q = output per unit of work effort, a constant.

The intensity of labour, e, is influenced by workers and employers acting both individually and collectively through unions, employers' associations, and the state. These forms of collective interaction, and the resulting collective bargaining agreements, health and safety regulations, work norms, and worker resistance and commitment to the work process provide the institutional environment in which e is determined.

The amount of work done per hour by each worker, e, is—in a proximate sense—selected by each worker or work group in response to the above environment and the employer's labour-extraction strategy, along with external labour market and unemployment insurance conditions. For simplicity we assume that people work harder the larger is the expected cost (to the worker) of working at effort levels below management expectations.[10] We further assume that labour is homogeneous, and that there are no hiring, training, or termination costs. Thus, the intensity of labour is determined on the basis of the labour-extraction function

$$e = e(w_c), \text{ with } e' > 0, e'' < 0 \text{ and } e(0) = \underline{e}, \tag{2}$$

where w_c = the expected cost to the worker should his or her job be terminated; and
$\underline{e}$ = the intensity of labour performed voluntarily by the worker when $w_c = 0$.

The expected cost of job-loss w_c is the difference between the worker's current income and a weighted average of income prospects should the worker lose his or her job. Thus w_c depends on the current wage, the probability of re-employment, the expected re-employment wage, and the extent of unemployment insurance or similar means-tested social payments.[11] In highly simplified form,

$$w_c = w - (hw_a + (1 - h)w_u), \tag{3}$$

where $w =$ the worker's current wage,
   $w_a =$ the worker's expected wage in alternative employment should the worker's job be terminated and an alternative job be secured,
   $w_u =$ unemployment insurance and other income-replacing government payments which an unemployed worker may expect to receive,
   $h =$ the probability of securing an alternative job should the worker lose the current job.

The re-employment probability, h, may be plausibly equated to the ratio of labour demand to labour supply or the employment rate. For simplicity we assume that the wage, the alternative wage, and the income replacing 'social wage' are all paid in units of the produced good. We assume that all social wage costs are financed by government borrowing, thus setting aside the issue of taxes on profits or wages. It is clear from its construction that we may interpret w_c as an employment rent, that is, an income associated with having a job above and beyond the worker's next best alternative.

As the microeconomic logic of the extraction function has been explored in a series of other papers (see Bowles 1985 and references therein), suffice it to say that *ceteris paribus* and for w_u less than w_a, the worker's level of work effort is a negative function of h, the probability of finding new employment and, correspondingly, work effort is a positive function of the wage rate.[12] Further, in the range of actually implemented employer strategies, the effectiveness of a change in the cost of job-loss in inducing labour effort (the derivative of e with respect to w_c, or e') is a declining function of the level of w_c or $e'' < 0$.

The firm's problem is to select H and w so as to maximize the rate of profit, r. Setting the capital stock arbitrarily equal to unity the profit rate is equal to total profits, and

$$r = (qe - w)H. \tag{4}$$

The firm hires enough labour hours to produce its desired sales, Q_d, and firm employment is thus

$$H = Q_d/qe \text{ and} \tag{5}$$

$$r = (qe - w)Q_d/qe, \text{ or} \tag{6}$$

$$r = (1 - w/qe)Q_d. \tag{7}$$

Letting $w/e = c$, the ratio of the hourly wage to the hourly amount of work done, or the cost of an effective unit of work,

$$r = (1 - c/q)Q_d. \tag{8}$$

The expression w/qe (or c/q) is the cost in output units of a unit of output, or equivalently, the wage share of output. Given that the capital stock is unity, the profit rate is thus the profit share (one minus w/qe, which is the wage share of output) times output. To maximize profits, then, the firm must minimize w/e.

Assuming that the level of the firm's output does not alter the labour-extraction process, the firm may proceed sequentially: first determine the cost-minimizing w, and then determine the level of output.[13]

Given a particular extraction function, the firm may not be able to impose its optimal wage, w^o, of course, if it is faced with a labour union capable of making the firm a take-it-or-leave-it offer.[14] The optimal wage itself will depend on the structure of competition among employers as buyers of labour and on the level of the social wage, w_u. We will focus here on this last institutional determinant of the firm's strategy.[15]

In order to minimize c the firm will seek to set w so as to equate the marginal effectiveness of the extraction strategy with its average effectiveness: differentiating the cost of a unit of labour with respect to the wage and setting the result equal to zero yields:

$$e_w - e/w = 0, \tag{9}$$

where e_w is the derivative of e with respect to w or

$$e_w = (e') (dw_c/dw). \tag{10}$$

As all the terms in w_c are exogenous to the firm except w, the worker's alternative income stream, $hw_a + (1 - h)w_u$, is an exogenous quantity, $\underline{w}$, thus $w_c = w - \underline{w}$, and dw_c/dw is unity, a unit increase in the firm's wage increasing w_c by one.[16] In this case the firm's first-order conditions for a cost minimum are simply

$$e' = e/w \tag{11}$$

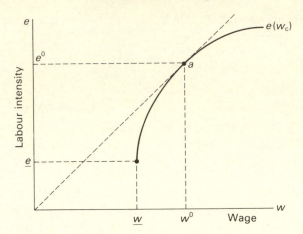

FIG. 5.1 The optimal wage in firm equilibrium with endogenous labour intensity

which allows us to define the optimal wage as

$$w^o = e(w)/e'(w) \tag{12}$$

The firm's cost-minimization problem is illustrated in Fig. 5.1.

The comparative static analysis of the firm equilibrium reveals, not surprisingly, that an increase in the employment rate, h, or the social wage, w_u, will raise w^o. Thus

$$dw^o/dh = (d\underline{w}/dh)(dw^o/d\underline{w}) \tag{13}$$
$$= (w_a - w_u)(we'' - e')/we''$$

and

$$dw^o/dw_u = (d\underline{w}/dw_u)(dw^o/d\underline{w}) \tag{14}$$
$$= (1 - h)(we'' - e')/we''.$$

The first term on the right-hand side of both expressions is the effect of an increase in the employment rate or the social wage payment, respectively on the worker's alternative income stream, in both cases positive. The remainder of the numerator and the denominator are both unambiguously negative by the second-order conditions for a cost minimum. Thus

$$dw^o/dh > 0, \text{ and} \tag{15}$$
$$dw^o/dw_u > 0. \tag{16}$$

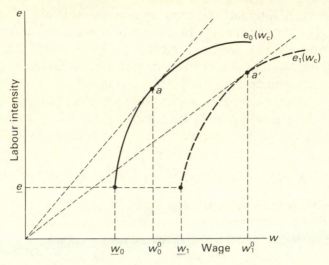

FIG. 5.2 An increase in employment or unemployment insurance increases the optimal wage

In Fig. 5.2 it can be seen that an increase in either the employment rate or the unemployment insurance benefit shifts the extraction function horizontally to the right, leading to a higher optimal wage and a higher average cost of an effective labour unit. A change in h will generally alter the optimal extraction strategy. This is because a higher level of h lowers e/w and raises its inverse, the cost of a unit of effort, thus disturbing the first-order conditions (11).[17]

III. GENERAL LABOUR-EXTRACTION EQUILIBRIUM: THE HIGH-EMPLOYMENT PROFIT SQUEEZE

Firm equilibrium requires only that the firm's first-order conditions be satisfied; general labour-extraction equilibrium entails wage uniformity, or $w = w_a$, as well. The firm continues to adopt a strategy based on the first-order conditions (11) and the exogeneity of the alternative wage; the wage-uniformity condition does not imply that the firm may alter the alternative wage as an instrument in its labour control strategy. But the resulting wage must be such that both $w = w_a$ and $e' = e/w$ obtain.

An increase in h, for example, will generate an increase in each firm's workers' alternative income stream, $\underline{w}$, which will induce each firm to raise its wage (as the firm equilibrium analysis shows), which will in turn raise $\underline{w}$, inducing another round of wage increases, and so on. Thus we may decompose the effect of an increase in employment on the general labour-extraction equilibrium wage rate, w^*, as the direct effect—dw°/dh—and an indirect effect associated with the effect of the generalization of successive rounds of the wage increases and its impact on the worker's alternative wage, and hence on $\underline{w}$. Thus

$$dw^*/dh = (dw^\circ/dh)\{1 - (d\underline{w}/dw_a)(dw^\circ/d\underline{w})\}^{-1}. \qquad (17)$$

The 'multiplier' term on the right of (17) reflects the indirect effects of an employment increase through the competitive upward bidding of the wage. At low levels of employment, the cumulative effect of successive rounds of wage increases converge, leading to a positive finite effect. But what may be termed 'the wage-explosion multiplier' becomes infinitely large when

$$(d\underline{w}/dw_a)(dw^\circ/dw) = 1, \qquad (18)$$

or using (14), when

$$h(we'' - e')/we'' = h(1 - e'/we'') = 1, \qquad (19)$$

from which it is clear that w^* rises with h to a $h_{\lim} < 1$ at which dw^*/dh and w^* become infinite. Using (19) the limiting level of employment may be defined as

$$h_{\lim} = \lim(1 - e'/we'')^{-1}, \qquad (20)$$

which is clearly less than one as e' and w are positive and e'' is negative.

The economic basis for this high-employment wage explosion is that as h approaches unity each increase in the firm equilibrium wage is reflected in subsequent rounds as other firms pursue similar wage policies in response to the same labour-market conditions, in the workers' alternative income stream, provoking a further increase in wages as firms vainly attempt to execute their optimal labour control strategy.[18]

Before turning to the question of aggregate demand, two results remain to be demonstrated: first, that the equilibrium real cost of an effective labour unit, c^*, $(= w^*/e^*)$ will be a positive function of the employment rate, h, and second, that the labour-extraction model precludes full employment as an equilibrium.

The first proposition, that dc^*/dh is positive—that labour costs rise with the employment level—follows from the comparative static analysis of the firm's first-order conditions (11). The result is intuitively obvious, for it is clear that an increase in the employment level represents an exogenous shift in the capital–labour bargaining environment which is favourable to workers. Indeed as effort has a maximum and as the cost-minimizing real wage goes to infinity at an employment rate less than one, the profit squeeze will be such that profit disappears altogether at high levels of employment.[19]

In considering the full-employment profit squeeze it will be useful to note that when the wage-uniformity condition holds we can express the cost of job-loss as

$$w_c = (1 - h)(w - w_u). \qquad (21)$$

Considering a given wage rate, two effects will determine the movement of the total profits, r (which—given a particular level of capital stock normalized at unity—is also the profit rate), as the employment rate rises: increasing h will tend to raise r if profit per hour of labour is positive but will tend to lower r through the negative effect of increased labour-market tightness on the cost of job loss $(-(w - w_u))$ and hence on labour intensity. Thus

$$r = h(eq - w) \quad \text{and} \quad dr/dh = eq - w - he'q(w - w_u) \qquad (22)$$

indicating that for positive profits as h rises r will first rise and then fall, describing a high-employment profit squeeze. Correspondingly, the effect on total profits of a wage increase (for a constant h) reflects a positive labour-intensity effect operating via the impact of the wage increase on cost of job-loss $(1 - h)$, offset by a negative wage effect. It will be unambiguously negative in the neighbourhood of the firm's optimum:

$$dr/dw = h\{e'q(1 - h) - 1\} < 0 \quad \text{for} \quad w > w_{rmax}. \qquad (23)$$

(The bracketed expression $e'q(1 - h)-1$ will be zero at the wage, w_{rmax}, which maximizes total profits for a given level of employment. This is the wage which would be set by a single profit-maximizing cartel.)[20]

We should restrict our analysis to reproducible states in which

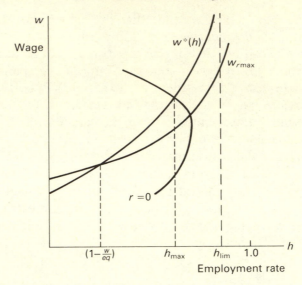

FIG. 5.3 Employment limits: the wage explosion and reproducibility

profit is non-negative. This *reproducibility condition* may be written simply as net output per hour must exceed the wage

$$qe - w \geq 0. \tag{24}$$

The reproducibility condition defines a feasible set of outcomes in wh space. Its limit, defined by (24) has the slope

$$\mathrm{d}w/\mathrm{d}h = \frac{qe'(\mathrm{d}w_c/\mathrm{d}h)}{1 - qe'\ (\mathrm{d}w_c/\mathrm{d}w)} \tag{25}$$

which, given wage uniformity, is equal to

$$\mathrm{d}w/\mathrm{d}h = qe'(w_u - w)/\{1 - qe'(1 - h)\}. \tag{26}$$

Thus the reproducibility frontier is horizontal for $w_u = w$ and vertical for $1 - qe'(1 - h) = 0$. This last equality is obtained under the hypothetical condition that for each level of employment the capitalist class as a whole sets the wage to maximize profits.[21] In Fig. 5.3 we present the reproducibility condition, labelled $r = 0$, along with the schedule w_{rmax}, and w^*, and the employment limits h_{lim} and h_{max}.

Our first result, that the cost of an effective labour unit rises with the employment rate motivates the second proposition: that $h = 1$ cannot be an equilibrium state. This is apparent by combining the reproducibility constraint with the wage-determination function, $w^*(h)$. Because w^* goes to infinity as h goes to $h_{lim} < 1$, even arbitrarily large increases in efficiency, q, will not maintain a positive rate of profit.

The same result may be demonstrated on the basis of the extraction model itself. We know that the firm will set a wage such that w_c is positive except in the improbable case of a work process in which there is no conflict of interest between employer and worker. In this limiting case the optimal labour strategy for the employer is to pay the worker the lowest wage consistent with labour supply conditions and then let the workers do whatever they want to on the job. Note that were this the case it would never be rational for the firm to hire surveillance personnel or equipment. The fact that they do, as well as common sense, suggests the artificiality of the case.[22]

Because each worker faces a non-zero w_c and (abstracting from more complex representations of the worker's utility) is hence not indifferent between working or losing his or her job, it follows that the unemployed workers (who are, by assumption, identical to the employed workers) are involuntarily unemployed. Though involuntary, this unemployment is consistent with equilibrium, for should the unemployed offer their services to the employer at a wage less than that currently offered, it would be refused, for the wage selected by the employer is that which already minimizes costs.[23]

Thus there is no way in which the unemployed workers can compete away the employment rents of the employed workers and thus eliminate involuntary unemployment. The resulting non-clearing labour market is in equilibrium in the conventional sense: none of the actors with an interest in recontracting or altering the terms of exchange has the ability to do so, and none of those with the ability to do so has an interest in any changes. The conventional axiomatic identification of market clearing and equilibrium is thus misplaced.

Our analysis thus far has been throughly microeconomic, inferring equilibrium wages, labour intensity, labour costs, and profits from a given level of h. However, equilibrium in the labour market, or in the macroeconomy as a whole, requires an endogenous determination of the employment rate, h, as a function of the wage rate, w. We will see that the equilibrium level of employment may vary positively or negatively with the wage rate depending on the level of employment, the intensity of the high-employment profit squeeze, and the level of the unemployment benefit.

IV. THE DEMAND FOR LABOUR:
WAGE-LED AND CLASSICAL REGIMES

The demand for labour is simply the total demand for goods and services divided by the average product of labour, or what is equivalent, the level of employment at which excess demand for goods is zero. In order to model the aggregate demand for labour in the simplest possible way, we will assume that capitalists save all of their income (profits) and workers consume all of theirs irrespective of whether they are employed or not. Thus consumption demand is just the wage bill, wh, plus total unemployment insurance expenditures, $(1 - h)w_u$. For simplicity we abstract from net exports, take intended investment as exogenous, i, and assume that the level of government borrowing is just autonomous borrowing to cover expenditures unrelated to unemployment, b, plus total transfers to the unemployed. Thus we may express the equality of total output and total demand or the aggregate demand equilibrium condition (ADE) as: total supply equals privately financed consumption plus socially financed consumption plus autonomous government borrowing and investment, or

$$qeh = wh + (1 - h)w_u + b + i \qquad (27)$$

on which basis we may write labour demand as an implicit function:

$$h = \{wh + (1 - h)w_u + b + i\}/qe, \qquad (28)$$

or the more familiar

$$h(qe - w) - \{b + (1 - h)w_u\} = i, \qquad (29)$$

which is simply a restatement of the ADE condition as private savings minus government borrowing equals investment.[24]

Does the equilibrium level of employment rise or fall with the real wage? The answer to this question is given by the slope of the labour-demand function, which by total differentiation of the ADE condition is

$$dh^*/dw = \frac{\{1 - qe'(1 - h)\}h}{qe - w + w_u - qhe'\,(w - w_u)}. \qquad (30)$$

Because investment and export demand are exogenously determined, the slope of the labour-demand function may also be determined from the condition that along the labour-demand function, net savings (s) must be constant, or:

$$s_w dw + s_h dh^* = 0, \tag{31}$$

where s_w and s_h respectively are the partial derivatives of net savings with respect to the wage rate and the employment rate.[25] From (31) it is clear that

$$dh^*/dw = -s_w/s_h. \tag{32}$$

The numerator of dh^*/dw is recognizable: because all profits are saved it is simply the negative of the effect of a wage change on total profits, as can be determined from (23). Where the wage rate is that which maximizes profits for a given level of h, s_w will by definition be zero. Hence the ADE function will be vertical where it intersects the w_{rmax} function. Above w_{rmax} the effect of wage increases on profits and hence on savings is negative and the numerator is positive. Because the firms' wage-determination function $w^*(h)$ lies above w_{rmax} except at implausibly low levels of employment (h less than the profit share) we may regard the numerator as positive over the observable range of variation of h.

The slope of the ADE function thus depends on the denominator, which is the derivative of net savings with respect to employment. As one can see, this is made up of the effect of variations in h on government borrowing and on profits (which in turn depends on the level of employment and the intensity of the high-employment profit squeeze).

The slope of the ADE function, and hence the possibility of a wage-led employment regime thus depends critically on the labour-extraction process. If the labour-intensity effect, e', is small, and if h is low and w_u is large, the ADE function will be upward sloping: an increase in the wage will reduce savings, and in order to restore balance between income and expenditure an increase in employment (which under these conditions will increase savings) is required.

However, if the labour-intensity effect is large and if employment is high and the social wage small, an increase in employment may reduce rather than increase savings (because of the full-employment profit squeeze). In this case, the reduction in savings occasioned by a small increase in the wage can be offset only by an employment contraction (which will induce an increase in savings). Thus dh^*/dw will be negative; a profit-led employment regime will obtain.

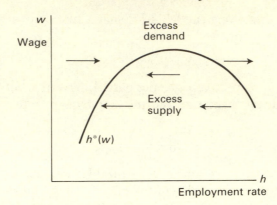

FIG. 5.4 Product market-clearing and the demand for labour. *Note*: The arrows indicate the direction of dynamic adjustment of the employment rate in response to the pressure of excess demand or excess supply.

The slope of the ADE schedule, and hence the nature of the employment regime, depends not only on the strength of the intensity effect relative to the hourly profit effect but on the level of employment as well. Indeed as h rises the hourly profit effect ($qe - w$) goes to zero (as the reproducibility frontier is approached) and the intensity effect $\{-qhe'(w - w_u)\}$ must predominate. As a result, high employment levels necessarily preclude a wage-led employment regime whatever the form of the extraction function as long as e' and ($w - w_u$) are both positive.[26] Thus the increase in the level of employment will itself undermine a wage-led employment regime.

We may summarize our results thus far by using (24) and (28) to divide (h, w) space into regions of excess demand and excess supply. Considering only the economically relevant regions above w_{rmax} the result is Fig. 5.4. In the neighbourhood of firm equilibrium a wage increase will lower profits and hence diminish savings and generate excess demand.[27] Thus all points above $h^*(w)$ are characterized by excess demand, and conversely. The arrows indicate the direction of employment adjustment in each region.

We have identified the characteristics of distinct employment regimes, but have explored neither the stability of the resulting equilibria nor the closely related question of the effectivenss of demand management and employment policies. To these we now turn.

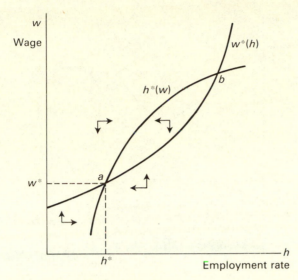

FIG. 5.5 A wage-led employment regime

V. JOINT EQUILIBRIUM: THE CONTRADICTIONS OF WAGE-LED EMPLOYMENT POLICY

Joint equilibrium requires both aggregate demand and general labour extraction equilibrium. Rearranging the market-clearing function to arrive at an expression for w, and equating that to $w^*(h)$,

$$\underbrace{w^*(h) = w^*}_{\text{GLEE}} = \underbrace{qe^* - (i + b)/h^* - w_u(1 - h^*)/h^*}_{\text{ADE}}, \qquad (33)$$

which may be interpreted as requiring that the firm's cost-minimizing wage must be equal to that portion of hourly output which is not demanded in the form of consumption demand by the unemployed plus autonomous investment and autonomous government borrowing.

Fig. 5.5 presents the joint equilibrium of a wage-led employment regime. The arrows indicate directions of adjustment based on our dynamic assumptions: employment increases in the case of excess demand on product markets and wage increases for wage rates below $w^*(h)$. Thus a is a stable equilibrium.[28]

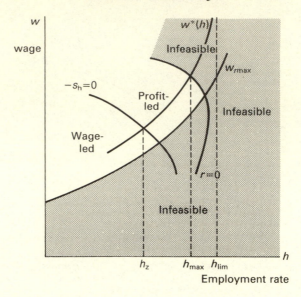

FIG. 5.6 Wage-led, classical, and infeasible regimes

Consider, now, the contrary case of a classical employment regime illustrated in Fig. 5.6. Because, as we have seen, an increase in the wage will increase excess demand, a small displacement of the wage above its equilibrium value will induce employment increases. But we know from the sign of the numerator of (32) in the case of classical employment that employment increases will reduce savings, further augmenting excess demand. The equilibrium, b, is evidently unstable.

Under the savings and investment assumptions we have made, the boundary between wage-led and classical regimes is the point at which the denominator of dh^*/dw, $-s_h$, changes sign. We may write a locus of points for which $-s_h = 0$; the hourly profit effect, labour-intensity effect, and the government borrowing effect just offsetting one another so that changes in employment do not affect savings. We may refer to this as the regime shift locus. In the economically relevant region above w_{rmax}, the regime shift locus can be shown to slope downwards, for the transparent reason that the lower the wage the larger will be the hourly profit effect and hence the more likely will it be that employment increases raise savings.

As can be seen in Fig. 5.6, the $s_h = 0$ locus along with the reproducibility constraint and the w_{rmax} function divide w, h space into four segments: a stable wage-led employment regime, an unstable classic-al employment regime, and two regimes which are infeasible as competitive firms would not choose to set wages low enough to operate in this region. We will ignore the infeasible regimes in what follows.

The limit between wage-led and classical employment equilibria, h_z, is the intersection of the regime shift locus with the wage-determination function. The regime·shift locus and the three employment limits—the regime shift limit (h_z), the reproducibility limit (h_{max}), and the wage-explosion limit (h_{lim})—are illustrated in Fig. 5.6.

We are now in a position to investigate the effect of shifts in economic policy, bargaining power, and investment on the wage-led employment equilibria depicted in Fig 5.5. An autonomous upward shift in the wage function—the result of a strengthening of labour's bargaining position—will clearly raise both equilibrium employment and wages, as is shown in Fig. 5.7a.

It is clear in this model that government demand management—in this case simply expenditure financed by borrowing—can regulate the equilibrium level of employment, h^*. Total differentiation of the equilibrium condition (28) confirms what is obvious: that in the neighbourhood of the stable equilibrium a, $dh^*/db > 0$. Thus an increase in autonomous borrowing shifts the aggregate demand function to the right, again raising the equilibrium values of both wages and employment, as shown in Fig. 5.7b.

We know from the reproducibility condition and the wage-explosion limit that this demand expansion cannot produce full employment, but it confronts two other limits as well. First, the economy may move from a stable wage-led employment regime to an unstable classical regime, the stability limit being the level of employment h_z for which $s_h = 0$ at the equilibrium wage rate. Or, secondly, demand expansion beyond h_E in Fig. 5.7 may render $h(w)$ and $w(h)$ non-intersecting and hence may generate a configuration of labour relations and aggregate demand for which no equilibrium exists.

Now consider the effects of varying the level of unemployment insurance, w_u. Interestingly, as ($w - w_u$) falls the labour-intensity effect vanishes, ensuring that as long as profits per hour is positive ($eq > w$), employment increases will increase savings and hence that the employment regime will be wage-led. Indeed, if the

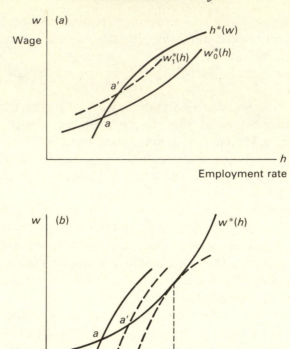

FIG. 5.7 Two properties of a stable, wage-led employment regime: (*a*) an upward shift in the wage function for a given aggregate demand raises the equilibrium levels of both wages and employment; (*b*) an increase in autonomous expenditure raises the equilibrium levels of both wages and employment

unemployment insurance replacement rate (w_u/w) were unity, the numerator of dh^*/dw is simply hourly output, qe. In this case employment increases necessarily raise net savings, as consumption is simply a constant, w, and as employment rises, every increase in privately financed consumption is exactly offset by a decrease in consumption financed by government borrowing. Thus for $w_u = w$, the employment regime is necessarily wage-led at any level of employment though the corresponding demand for labour function may lie wholly in the non-reproducible range of values of w and h. Thus while the successful pursuit of high employment levels militates against the survival of a wage-led employment regime, the expansion of the welfare state has the opposite effect in so far as it does not propel the economy into the non-reproducible region.

An increase in the social wage will increase the employment level generated by each wage if the economy is at a stable wage-led employment equilibrium, and conversely. This may be seen from totally differentiating the ADE function with respect to h and w_u:

$$dh^*/dw_u = \frac{(1 - h)(1 + hqe')}{qe - w + w_u - hqe'(w - w_u)}. \tag{35}$$

In the numerator, $(1 - h)$ is simply the effect of an increase of the social wage on government borrowing. Recalling that $dw_c/dw_u = (1 - h)$, it can be seen that $(1 - h)(hqe')$ is the effect (negative) of an increase in w_u on total output (and hence on savings) via the effect of the social wage on w_c. Thus, as would be expected, the numerator is the negative of the effect of a change in w_u on net savings. Because as the social wage increases government borrowing increases and total output (and hence private savings) falls, the numerator is unambiguously positive.

As in the case of dh^*/dw, the denominator determines the sign of dh^*/dw_u. It is clear, and not too surprising, that wage-led employment regimes are also social-wage-led employment regimes; correspondingly when the denominator is negative (implying a profit-led employment regime) an increase in the social wage will reduce employment.

Because of the critical role of the social wage in the determination of the cost of job-loss, an increase in unemployment insurance will shift both the labour-demand function and the wage-determination function. As we have seen, an increase in the social wage will raise w^*. If the economy is characterized by a stable wage-led employment equilibrium, the result is an unambiguous increase in both equilibrium employment and the equilibrium real wage.

VI. CONCLUSION

The main analytical contributions of this provisional synthesis of aggregate demand and labour process analysis would appear to be the following.

The model provides a coherent basis for the high-employment profit squeeze and for the notion of a limit to the level of employment below the level at which there is a job for every worker. The limit in an employment level bears the interesting implication that, in the absence of changes in the organization of the labour process and wage determination, full employment will be unattainable even under the most apparently favourable savings and investment assumptions. While we do not model the collective determination of wages and work intensity by workers, it is clear from the slope of our reproducibility condition that more collective action on the side of employers and workers—wage restraint in return for investment guarantees, for example—may allow higher levels of employment.[29]

Using the model we are able to distinguish between wage-led and classical employment regimes, and to analyse the endogenous generation of regime shifts. Social-wage-led employment regimes are also possible.

One important result is that taking account of labour-intensity effects yields classical results—lower wages going along with higher levels of activity—even under rather extreme 'Keynesian' assumptions concerning savings, investment, exports, and the effects of government borrowing. Indeed, high levels of employment preclude wage-led employment regimes except under very high social insurance levels, suggesting the intrinsically contradictory nature of the social democratic full-employment programme. Conversely we have shown that increases in the social wage tend to produce a wage-led employment regime, indicating a strong symbiotic relationship among elements in the social democratic programme when the employment level is low. But when combined with high employment levels, increases in the social wage will drive the profit rate to zero, inducing a crisis of accumulation in so far as investment remains determined by the profit expectations of capitalists.

Four quite drastic simplifications adopted in the preceding pages suggest caution in interpreting these results. First, we have assumed a form of wage bargaining and labour extraction in which the social nature of the labour process is given scant attention. Reasonable alternative formulations would surely generate different results. Particularly interesting would be to model the wage-formation and labour-intensity determination under more collective assumptions: let workers not only vary effort on the job, but exercise the threat of withdrawing their labour altogether through strikes; and let their employers recognize that while formally autonomous, each wage settlement affects others.[30] It would be fruitful to explore the possibility that distinct labour-extraction regimes may coexist, perhaps in the context of segmented labour markets. (see Zylberberg and Perrot-Dormont 1986).

Second, taxes have been set aside, so as to allow the analysis of the effects of changes in the social wage on labour intensity and product market-clearing without having simultaneously to account for tax effects on worker's incomes and the cost of job-loss. While the resulting covariation of endogenous government borrowing with the unemployment rate is no doubt an important feature of real capitalist economies, the integration of taxes into the model would generate a richer set of results. For example, if all social wage costs were financed by taxes on workers' incomes rather than by government borrowing, the effects of this aspect of the expansion of the welfare state would appear entirely in the labour-extraction process rather than in the generation of aggregate demand. This result suggests a considerable rethinking of the public finance literature on the relationship between the welfare state and the accumulation process: the welfare state might affect employment and growth not primarily through the generation of aggregate demand (as its advocates claim) nor through its effects on labour supply (as its detractors suggest), but through its effect on class bargaining over pay and work.

Third, both investment and export demand have been exogenously determined; but they are clearly endogenously generated in part by the very movements in labour costs upon which we have focused. Our reproducibility condition is motivated in part by the implausibility of positive investment with negative profits, but this is hardly an adequate treatment. Were we to have expressed investment and export demand as highly responsive functions of the profit share and possibly of the level of activity of the economy our results concerning wage-led and classical employment regimes would certainly be altered, though the viability of both types of regimes and the endogenous generation of regime shifts would most likely remain.

Fourth, we have adopted an extreme form of the classical (or income shares) hypothesis—capitalists only save and workers only consume. A polar opposite savings hypothesis—savings proportional to income, for example—would significantly alter our results: as savings would then be determined solely by income level rather than by income level and distribution, wage increases would operate via labour-intensity effects necessarily to raise rather than lower savings, dramatically altering the analysis of the critical slope of the ADE.[31]

While we believe that this model—even in the radically simple form presented here—may cast light on the post-war boom and its unravelling, it would be premature to make any strong claims until the above suggested extensions and a substantial amount of empirical work have been completed. None the less, restricting ourselves to the terms of our model and therefore abstracting from the crucial issue of investment, the following may be presented as a working hypothesis concerning one aspect of the boom and its demise. Let us distinguish three phases.

Starting from relatively low levels of employment in the 1950s, wage-led growth regimes obtained, allowing for the successful pursuit of high wage strategies by labour. Growing labour-union strength in the 1960s and an expansion of the welfare state led to a long-term upward shift in the wage function. Because the employment regime was wage-led, the wage and social wage share of net output rose with the employment rate over the whole period, but most markedly in the 1960s.[32] Thus class conflict in an economy with an aggregate-demand-driven accumulation process appeared as a non-zero-sum game just as the Keynesian model suggested. Substantial gains in workers' living standards were compatible with continued rapid growth and high employment.

In the second phase, the resulting increases in the demand for labour during the course of the 1960s drove down the profit share and pushed the employment level towards the regime switch or instability limits. This in turn may have fostered high-employment macroeconomic instability and fuelled the ideological shift from expansionary demand-side policies to anti-labour supply-side policies, and contractionary demand policies.

Restrictive fiscal and monetary policies in the 1970s and 1980s and the success of the anti-labour anti-welfare state agenda ushered in the third macroeconomic phase. These policies dampened the demand for labour, reduced the wage-determination function, and shifted the regime shift limit to the right. The resulting higher levels of unemployment halted and in some cases reversed the rise in the wage share and possibly recreated wage-led employment regimes.

This narrative is consistent with the empirical chapters of this book; with the account of the post-war boom presented by Glyn *et al.*; with the analysis of macroeconomic policy presented by Epstein and Schor; and with the insights concerning the institutional basis of high-employment economies presented by Glyn and Rowthorn. Demonstrating that this is indeed what happened, and that this is why it happened, would carry us far beyond the boundaries of this essentially theoretical exercise.

Notwithstanding the radically incomplete nature of the project, a number of significant provisional results may be noted. Most broadly, we have found that endogenizing the labour-extraction and wage-determination process makes a significant difference in the analytical structure of macroeconomic models. Moreover the resulting model, suitably expanded as suggested above, might provide the basis for a plausible historical and theoretical account of the post-war boom and its demise. Finally, the model demonstrates that the organization of work and the determination of pay are key elements in a full-employment strategy; labour control systems based on the threat of dismissal and wage-determination systems based on competition among workers effectively preclude full employment.

NOTES

1. Averaging 12 now advanced capitalist countries, Maddison estimates that per capita gross domestic product grew at 3.8% p.a. between 1950 and 1973, and at 1.19% p.a. between 1820 and 1950 (Maddison 1982, Table 4.7).
2. An exception is Thomas Weisskopf's illuminating accounting framework, which integrates the two aspects of capitalist crisis (along with a third, the tendency of the profit rate to fall due to a rise in the organic composition of capital) and assesses the ability of each to illuminate movements in the profit rate in the US since the end of World War II. Weisskopf (1979). In many respects disequilibrium employment theory addresses this issue when opposing Keynesian to classical unemployment. See Benassy (1982).
3. A number of accounts—especially those working within the social structure of accumulation or regulation framework have attempted to integrate the concerns of both traditions. See Armstrong *et al.* (1984). See also Aglietta (1976); Lipietz (1983); Boyer and Mistral (1983); and Bowles *et al.* (1983*a*).
4. These two regimes may be compared with the stagnationist–exhilarationist distinction proposed in ch. 4. Note, however, this difference: here the real wage is the key variable since we determine productivity endogenously, while the Marglin–Bhaduri formulation is concerned with the consequences of income distribution for aggregate demand and so takes income shares as the starting-point of the argument. Observe that a 'classical' employment regime is not the same as 'profit-led' growth, as that term was used in the previous chapter. In ch. 4, 'profit-led' indicated a positive relationship between unit profit and *output*; here a classical regime is one in which the relationship between wages and employment is negative. As long as productivity is variable, the connection between profits and output need not be opposite to the relationship between

wages and employment. Output and employment need not move in the same direction when productivity varies with employment.

5. The term appropriate income distribution is from Malinvaud (1980).

6. If firms' technologies differ in ways which affect the extraction function, the wage uniformity assumption will generally be violated, as firms will find it optimal to pay equivalent labour differently. As we have assumed that firms use identical technologies and that the prodution process and the extraction process are formally separable this possiblity does not arise in our model.

7. This result may be compared to the analogous finding of Marglin and Bhaduri concerning the possibility of an IS schedule with stagnationist and exhilaration-ist segments. The two results are complementary, as our finding based on the high employment profit squeeze makes no use of non-linearities in the invest-ment function.

8. The dependence of investment on profitability and hence labour costs, may readily be introduced. See Bowles and Boyer (1988).

9. The difficulty of measurement of work effort is paradoxically what makes it so important to the economic theory of the production process—if it were costless-ly observable the firm could buy effort rather than labour time—and at the same time so difficult to study empirically. The only study of the production process in a macroeconomic setting using actual measures of work intensity to our knowledge is Schor (1988). However there is a considerable amount of indirect evidence that the variability of effort is a product of both labour relations and macroeconomic conditions: see Naples (1986); Schor and Bowles (1987); Weisskopf *et al.* (1983); and Rebitzer (1987).

10. A more complete model would take account of the employer's worker monitoring or surveillance system, and a variable probability of job termination for workers working below management demands, as in Bowles (1985). We lose nothing in this case by assuming that the probability that the errant worker will be detected by the employer is exogenously determined, and making the no doubt extreme assumption that the worker found working at levels unsatisfactory to the manage-ment will always have his or her job terminated. It is perhaps paradoxical that while we have assumed a conflictual labour process, we have not explicitly modelled the role of bosses in commanding labour. Were we to take explicit account of surveillance labour we could enrich our model considerably. Of particular importance, if as seems reasonable surveillance labour were considered not to vary with the employment rate—bosses are overhead labour—a more realistic picture not only of the labour process but of cyclical behaviour of output per hour (including the fixed hours of the supervisors) and labour costs would result: at low levels of employment labour productivity would vary positively with employment and at high levels of employment inversely.

11. Time-series measures of w_c have been estimated for the US and the UK. See Schor and Bowles (1987) and Schor (1988).

12. The microeconomic logic of the class conflict theory of production is developed in Bowles (1985) where it is distinguished from what are generally termed 'efficiency wage' models.

13. Strictly speaking the assumption that the extraction function and the production function are separable and hence the firm may proceed sequentially is unrealis-

tic: larger firms may have labour control problems different from smaller firms, and in a more extended model with other inputs, the choice of technology will generally alter the cost of monitoring the labour process and the difficulty of extracting labour from labour power. On the relationship between technology and labour extraction, see Marglin (1974) and Bowles, 'Social Institutions and Technical Change', in Goodwin *et al.* (1988).

14. We use the superscript o to denote the firm's optimal wage offer corresponding to our concept of firm equilibrium; the superscript * denotes the wage in general labour-extraction equilibrium, that is when both firm equilibrium and wage uniformity obtain.

15. A collectively bargained wage model yields similar results.

16. Firms may of course recognize that their wage-setting will influence the wage-setting patterns of other firms, either through a wage-setting leadership pattern or through collective-bargaining agreements. Assuming, for example that firms take dw_a/dw to be unity rather than zero yields an interesting alternative set of first-order conditions, which would require a more extended discussion than we can provide here. National economies differ considerably in which extraction strategy and wage-setting patterns—including a collectively bargained wage rate not analysed here—are more applicable. In a more extensive treatment, distinct sectors of the capitalist economy might be represented by distinct labour-extraction and wage-setting strategies; primary labour markets being characterized by collective bargaining, recognition by employers of their mutual interdependence, and perhaps other features such as long-term employment, while the secondary sectors conforming more closely to the atomistic case above. Alternatives to dismissal-based labour-discipline systems such as long-term employment arrangements and co-operative monitoring by labour may entail high wages as a cost of ensuring co-operation or for other reasons.

17. With a higher average cost of effort, it will generally be optimal for the firm (if it continues to hire labour at all) to engage in more intensive labour extraction, extending the cost of job-loss until the marginal return is depressed to the now lower average level of effort per dollar of wage, e/w, and thus restoring the first-order conditions (11).

Thus the firm will—if it adjusts fully to a change in h—adopt a higher w_c at higher levels of h. The same result holds for increases in the social wage. This somewhat unexpected result was first pointed out by Herbert Gintis and Tsuneo Ishikawa. This result can be confirmed by inspection of the term

$$dw_c/dw = dw^o/dw - 1,$$

which from (14) above is

$$= (we'' - e')/we'' - 1$$
$$= 1 - e'/we'' - 1$$
$$= - e'/we'',$$

which from the first- and second-order conditions for the firm's cost-minimization must be positive. Firms appear not to fully adjust their labour-extraction strategies cyclically in a manner predicted; the strongly *counter-cyclical* movement of an empirical estimate of w_c suggests that firms do not adopt an optimal extraction strategy at all points over the cycle. If firms adjusted their extraction strategies fully at all points in the cycle we would find a pro-cyclical movement of w_c (and correspondingly of e as well) (see Schor and Bowles (1987)). Rebitzer (1987) develops a more sophisticated treatment of short-run variations in extraction strategies under the more realistic assumptions of long-term employment arrangements.

18. It may be seen from the firm's first-order conditions that an increase in employment induces an increase in the optimal level of w_c. It is this increase in w_c which accounts for w^* going to infinity at $h < 1$. If, by contrast, the firm adopted a constant extraction strategy over all h so that $dw_c/dh = 0$, it would then be the case that $h_{lim} = 1$.

19. The most comprehensive study of the high-employment profit squeeze to date is Weisskopf (1979). On real wages, see Schor (1985*b*) and Kahn (1980). The pro- or counter-cyclical nature of real wages is a matter of debate, and there is considerable evidence that real wages move counter-cyclically—as the Keynesian model suggests and contrary to the model presented here—during periods of generalized economic crisis and instability such as the 1930s, 1890s, and possibly 1970s. See Schor (1985*b*) and T. Weisskopf *et al.* (1982).

20. From (11) and (2) it can be shown that the atomistically competitive wage, w^* exceeds w_{rmax} for reasonable values of h, i.e. for $h > (1 - w/qe)$, or for all employment rates in excess of the profit share.

21. This is evident from the fact that $qe'(1 - h)$ is simply the effect of a wage increase on output per hour, given that under conditions of wage uniformity dw_c/dw is just $(1 - h)$.

22. The lowest wage the firm can pay is the social wage, at which under the condition of wage uniformity, $w_c = 0$ and hence $e = \underline{e}$. Thus as long as $\underline{e}q < w_u$, profits will be negative for $w_c = 0$. The argument that $w_c = 0$ cannot be an equilibrium does not rely on any particular values of these variables, however.

23. Essentially the employer would not believe the unemployed worker's promise to work as hard for less, and with good reason in this model, given that workers are identical.

24. The schedule defined by this condition is identical to the IS function in ch. 4, except of course that in the present formulation the focus is on the endogenous determination of labour productivity rather than investment. In addition, but less central, our formulation includes endogenous government borrowing and expenditures.

25. The same result may be derived simply by totally differentiating the ADE function (27) with respect to w and h, taking account of the effects of variations in each on w_c.

26. The transformation of a wage-led to a classical regime may, however, take place at levels of h for which the reproducibility condition is violated.

27. This may be confirmed at levels of employment exceeding the profit share by the relationship in Fig. 5.3 of $w^*(h)$ and w_{rmax}.

28. As is clear from Fig. 5.5, an unstable wage-led employment equilibrium, b, can also exist, depending on the relative slopes of $h^*(w)$ and $w^*(h)$. A more elaborate technical discussion of the stability properties of the model would serve little purpose here.

29. One thinks in this respect of the contrast drawn in ch. 6 between the social democratic high-employment economies and the capitalist high-employment case—Japan.
30. This would involve integrating a model of strike activity along the lines developed in Schor and Bowles (1987) with an interdependent wage-determination function, and then combining this wage- and intensity-determination function with a model of aggregate demand generation.
31. These four simplifying assumptions are hardly exhaustive, of course. Our total abstraction from the financial side of the economy is difficult to justify, particularly if the endogenously generated government borrowing has effects on the cost of borrowing facing potential investors and consumers. Equally, our assumption that labour supply is exogenously determined is at best an artificial convenience: movements in w, e, h, and w_u provide the basis for endogenizing labour supply and thus enhancing the model.
32. An account of the political and institutional basis of this underlying macroeconomic model, and a shift to a profit-led employment regime is Bowles (1982).

6

The Diversity of Unemployment Experience since 1973

BOB ROWTHORN AND ANDREW GLYN

I. AN OVERVIEW

The year 1973 is widely considered to be a decisive turning-point in the post-war history of the OECD economies. Since that date, virtually all OECD countries have experienced a reduction in the growth of industrial production; this, in turn, has induced a considerable, though less dramatic, fall in the growth of service output. In some countries, the growth of agricultural production has also slowed since 1973, but the deceleration is by no means universal, and is largely unrelated to the industrial slow-down. The scale of what has happened can be gauged from Table 6.1.

The reduction in output growth has been accompanied by a considerable reduction in productivity growth. As a result, its impact on employment has been relatively small. In the OECD as a whole, the growth rate of total employment has fallen from 1.1 per cent p.a. before 1973 to 0.9 per cent p.a. since then. This represents a fall of only 0.2 percentage points, which is really very small compared to the fall in output growth. Of the fall in output growth since 1973, nearly nine-tenths is statistically accounted for by slower productivity growth and only one-tenth by slower employment growth (see Table 6.1). The picture is rather different if we look at individual sectors.

In the industrial sector (manufacturing, construction, mining, and energy), there has been a marked reversal in employment trends. After rising quite fast prior to 1973, industrial employment has been falling over the past decade. In 1985 there were 104 million people employed in the industrial sector of the OECD countries. If industrial employment had continued to rise at the pre-1973 rate, this figure would have been 129 million. Thus, the reversal of the pre-1973 trend in industrial employment represents a loss of around 25 million potential jobs in the OECD as a whole. This loss is probably

Table 6.1. Output, productivity, and employment in the OECD, 1960–1983 (average annual % growth rates)

	1960–73	1973–85	Change
Output (real value-added)			
Agriculture	1.6	1.6	0.0
Industry	5.3	1.8	−3.5
Services	5.0	3.0	−2.0
total	4.9	2.4	−2.5
Output per worker			
Agriculture	5.2	3.3	−1.9
Industry	3.9	2.3	−1.6
Services	2.6	0.8	−1.8
total	3.8	1.6	−2.2
Employment			
Agriculture	−3.4	−1.7	1.7
Industry	1.3	−0.5	−1.8
Services	2.5	2.2	−0.3
total	1.1	0.9	−0.2

Sources: OECD *Historical Statistics 1960–85*; OECD *Labour Force Statistics*.

the largest single factor behind the observed increase in unemployment since 1973. If industrial employment had continued rising at its pre-1973 rate there would have been no increase at all in unemployment. Official statistics indicate that the number of people unemployed in the OECD area rose by 20 million over the period 1973–85 (from 11 million to 31 million), as compared to the loss of 25 million potential industrial jobs caused by the reversal of the pre-1973 trend.

I.1 Labour Supply

So far we have been talking almost exclusively about the demand for labour. To explain what has happened to unemployment, we must also look at the supply of labour. To measure the supply of labour is not easy and raises a host of conceptual and practical problems, some of which are considered below. The conventional approach is to regard certain activities as non-economic and to classify all people who perform them as 'economically inactive'. As a result, many students, housewives, and others potentially available for paid work are excluded from the supply of labour as conventionally measured. So, too, are the majority of retired persons, irrespective of whether or not they are potentially available for paid work. When all of these various categories are excluded, the result is the narrow definition of labour supply which appears in official statistics under the heading 'labour force'. This measure of labour supply varies either because the underlying population of working age alters in size, or else because persons previously in the category 'inactive' become economically active. The latter phenomenon is recorded as a change in the 'participation rate'. The growth rate of the labour force is equal to the growth rate of the population plus the growth rate of the participation rate. As explained in the Appendix, the growth of unemployment depends on the difference between labour-force growth and employment growth.

Table 6.2 shows how these factors have contributed to the growth of unemployment since 1973. Information is given separately for males and females because the experience of these two groups has been so radically different.

From Table 6.2 it can be seen that, in the OECD as a whole, employment and labour force grew roughly in step during the period 1960–73. As a result, the measured unemployment rate remained virtually constant during this period, fluctuating in a narrow band between 3 and 4 per cent. Since 1973, however, the situation has changed radically. As previously mentioned, employment growth has slowed (from 1.1 per cent p.a. to 0.8 per cent p.a.), whilst labourforce growth has accelerated (from 1.1 per cent p.a. to 1.3 per cent p.a.).[1]

The recent acceleration in labour-force growth is not a demographic phenomenon, but has been caused by variations in the participation rate. After falling in the 1960s, the overall participation rate (i.e. men and women combined) began to rise in the 1970s. The growth rate of working-age population has not accelerated during this period and in most countries it has grown somewhat more slowly. Thus, the huge rise in OECD unemployment since 1973 is not in general the result of increased demographic pressures.

I.2 Male and Female Unemployment

Of the rise in total unemployment since 1973—male and female combined—about two-fifths is statistically 'explained' by faster growth in the labour force, and three-fifths by the slower growth rate of employment. However, as can be seen from Table 6.2, the relative

Table 6.2. Employment and labour force: OECD countries, 1960–1985[a] (average annual % growth rates)

	1960–73	1973–85	Change
Male and Female			
Population aged 15–64	1.2	1.0	−0.2
Participation rate[b]	−0.1	0.2	0.3
Labour force	1.1	1.3	0.2
Employment	1.1	0.8	−0.3
Employment/labour force[c]	0.0	−0.5	−0.5
Employment/population 15–64	−0.1	−0.2	−0.1
Male			
Population aged 15–64	1.3	1.1	−0.2
Participation rate[b]	−0.5	−0.4	0.1
Labour force	0.8	0.7	−0.1
Employment	0.8	0.3	−0.5
Employment/labour force[c]	0.0	−0.4	−0.4
Employment/population 15–64	−0.5	−0.8	−0.3
Industrial employment	1.3[d]	−0.5	−1.8
Services employment	2.1[d]	1.6	−0.5
Female			
Population aged 15–64	1.1	1.0	−0.1
Participation rate[b]	0.6	1.2	0.6
Labour force	1.7	2.2	0.5
Employment	1.7	1.8	0.1
Employment/labour force[c]	0.0	−0.4	−0.4
Employment/population 15–64	0.6	0.8	0.2
Industrial employment	1.6[d]	0.1	−1.5
Services employment	3.3[d]	3.0	−0.3

[a] For 19 countries, except for industrial and services employment for which data is available only for 9 countries.

[b] Participation rate $= \dfrac{\text{labour force}}{\text{population aged 15–64 years}}$.

[c] Note that employment/labour force $= 1 - $ unemployment rate.
[d] 1964–73.

Source: OECD *Labour Force Statistics.*

importance of these factors is quite different for men and women. For men, it is the growth rate of employment which is the crucial factor. This has fallen from 0.8 per cent p.a. before 1973 to 0.3 per cent p.a. afterwards. For women, on the other hand, the crucial factor is labour-force growth. Female employment has grown more rapidly since 1973 than before, but the increase has not been sufficient to keep pace with the even greater increase in labour-force

Table 6.3. Accounting for increased unemployment in 19 OECD countries, 1973–1985 (millions)

| | Unemployment | | Change in unemployment 1973–85 | | | | |
| | | | | due to change in growth rate[a] of: | | | |
	1973	1985	Total	employment	participation	population	residual
Male	5.1	15.8	10.7	13.2	1.4	−3.9	0.0
Female	4.2	11.9	7.7	−1.8	10.2	−2.3	1.6
TOTAL	9.3	27.7	18.4	11.4	11.6	−6.2	1.6

[a] as compared to the period 1960–73.

Source: OECD *Labour Force Statistics.*

growth (from 1.7 per cent p.a. to 2.2 per cent p.a.). The latter, in turn, is the result of a much faster growth in the female participation rate (from 0.6 per cent p.a. to 1.2 per cent p.a.).

The calculations in Table 6.3 highlight this contrast. Between 1973 and 1985 male unemployment in the OECD countries increased by 10.7 million. This increase is entirely the result of slower employment growth as compared to the preceding period 1960–73. Between 1973 and 1983 female unemployment rose by 7.7 million. This rise is entirely explained by the faster growth in female participation rates; it has occurred despite the fact that female employment has risen faster since 1973 than before.

Thus, rising male unemployment is primarily a demand-side phenomenon, reflecting the slower growth of male employment since 1973. This in turn reflects the decline in industrial employment. Meanwhile the growth rate of service employment for men has fallen. Between them, these developments explain why total employment for men in the OECD has risen very slowly in recent years, and this accounts for the steep rise in male unemployment.

The situation faced by women is more complex.[2] Employment opportunities for women have increased rapidly since 1973 in most OECD countries. Indeed the female 'employment rate' (i.e. the ratio of employment to population of working age) has grown faster since 1973 than before. However, this development has been accompanied by important structural shifts in the sectoral composition of female employment and in the type of women employed. On the one hand women, like men, have experienced a shrinkage of employment opportunities in the industrial sector. After substantial growth in the 1960s, industrial employment for women—especially in traditional areas such as textiles and clothing—has stagnated. On the other

hand, there has been an extremely fast growth of employment opportunities for women in the service sector with hardly any slow-down
since the pre-1973 period. This explains why, depsite the stagnation
of industrial jobs, total employment for women has continued to
grow rapidly since 1973. However, such employment growth has
been swamped by an even more rapid increase in the female labour
force, caused mainly by the growing tendency for women to continue
in paid employment after marriage and to return sooner to the paid
labour force after childbirth. As a result, there has been a considerable rise in female unemployment, as measured by official statistics,
despite the growth in employment opportunities for women.

The qualification 'as measured by official statistics' is important
here. Official statistics are notoriously inadequate in their treatment
of female unemployment and consistently understate its true magnitude. However, the degree of understatement has almost certainly
declined in recent years and so the true increase in female unemployment is less than indicated by official statistics.[3]

Finally, we would mention that unemployment among single,
especially young, women has increased despite the growth of female
employment in general. This is partly due to the fact that employers
often prefer married women, sometimes because they are willing
to work part-time, often for very low rates of pay, and sometimes
because they are more experienced. Whatever the reason, the growing reliance on married women may have also reduced employment
opportunities for single women, thereby contributing to unemployment amongst the latter. In some countries it may have also helped
to increase male unemployment because married women have been
hired in jobs which had traditionally been reserved for men.

II. DIVERSITY OF UNEMPLOYMENT
EXPERIENCE

II.1 Unemployment Rate Diversity

We turn now to the main task of this paper: to examine the diversity
of experience within our sample of OECD countries.[4]

The data in Table 6.4 show this diversity in 1985, ranging from
Switzerland with an official rate of 0.9 per cent to Spain with a rate
of 22.1 per cent.[5] Because unemployment rates were mostly low in
1973, the correlation between levels of unemployment in 1985 and

Table 6.4. Unemployment and employment indicators: 1985 levels

	Unemployment rates (%)			Employment rates (%)		
	Total	Female	Male	Total	Female	Male
Switzerland	0.9	1.1	0.8	70.7	52.7	88.6
Norway	2.5	3.0	2.1	75.4	66.3	84.2
Japan	2.6	2.7	2.6	70.6	55.7	85.5
Sweden	2.8	2.9	2.7	79.7	75.9	83.4
Austria	4.2	3.6	4.6	63.0	48.8	77.7
New Zealand	4.2	7.5	2.3	62.2	44.1	80.2
Finland	4.9	4.4	5.4	72.7	70.3	75.1
US	7.2	7.4	7.0	67.5	58.9	76.3
Denmark	7.3	8.2	6.6	74.2	68.4	79.9
Australia	8.2	8.7	7.9	64.0	49.9	77.8
Germany	8.4	9.5	7.8	58.5	45.6	71.5
Italy	10.2	16.2	6.8	52.2	34.2	71.7
France	10.4	12.8	8.6	57.5	47.9	67.2
Canada	10.5	10.7	10.3	65.5	55.6	75.4
UK	11.7	8.8	13.6	64.8	54.7	74.9
Belgium	12.3	16.5	9.4	54.4	42.1	66.6
Netherlands	13.0	12.2	13.4	51.2	36.2	65.9
Ireland	17.6	13.5	19.7	49.9	31.7	67.5
Spain	22.1	25.6	20.5	42.5	25.0	60.1
Europe	10.7	11.7	10.5	57.5	44.4	70.8
OECD	8.0	8.5	7.9	63.3	51.5	75.4

	Participation rates (%)			Part-time (% employment)		
	Total	Female	Male	Total	Female	Male
Switzerland	71.4	53.2	89.4	na		
Norway	77.3	68.3	86.1	30.0	54.8	11.7
Japan	72.5	57.2	87.8	10.5	21.1	4.8
Sweden	82.0	78.2	85.8	25.4	46.2	7.3
Austria	65.8	50.6	81.5	8.3	19.8	1.5
New Zealand	65.0	47.6	82.0	14.6	28.3	5.2
Finland	76.4	73.5	79.3	8.3	12.5	4.5
US	72.7	63.6	82.0	14.4	23.3	7.6
Denmark	80.1	74.5	85.5	23.7	44.7	6.6
Australia	69.8	54.7	84.5	17.2	35.9	6.1
Germany	63.9	50.4	77.4	12.6	30.0	1.7
Italy	58.1	40.8	76.4	4.6	9.4	2.4
France	64.2	54.9	73.5	9.7	20.1	2.6
Canada	73.2	62.3	84.1	15.4	26.2	7.6
UK	73.4	60.0	86.7	19.1	42.4	3.3
Belgium	62.0	50.4	73.5	8.1	19.7	2.0
Netherlands	58.9	41.2	76.1	21.2	50.3	6.9
Ireland	60.6	36.6	84.1	6.7	15.7	2.7
Spain	54.6	33.6	75.7	na		
Europe	64.4	50.2	78.6	na		
OECD	68.8	56.2	81.6	na		

Note: The employment rate is the ratio of employment to population of working age (15–64 years).

Source: OECD *Labour Force Statistics, Employment Outlook.*

changes since 1973 (Table 6.5) is inevitably high; however, it is by no means perfect (0.89) as there were a few countries which already had substantial unemployment in 1973 (Canada, US, and Italy). Throughout the present section our analysis will be mainly concerned with *changes* in the unemployment rate since 1973, as we are mainly concerned with the extent to which countries have held down unemployment growth in the less favourable economic circumstances after 1973.

Intertemporal changes in participation rates have an important influence on unemployment performance. These changes vary greatly from country to country. For example, over the period 1973–85 the overall participation rate fell by more than 8 per cent in Spain and Switzerland, and rose by more than 10 per cent in Canada and Norway (Table 6.5).[6] As a result, changes in *unemployment* do not fully capture the extent to which the economies have provided additional jobs for the population.[7] For example the Netherlands has performed better than Germany in terms of employment but worse in relation to unemployment, because participation rates have risen in the Netherlands and fallen in Germany.

II.2 Population, Participation, and Employment

The first panel in Table 6.6 shows how the increase in each country's unemployment can be decomposed into three key variables: growth in population, growth in participation rates, and growth in employment. The second panel repeats this analysis using *changes* in growth rates between 1960–73 and 1973–85. The latter approach is of interest, since *changes* in the growth rate of certain variables may be of more importance in explaining unemployment performance than is the absolute level of these growth rates. Tables 6.A3–6.A5 showing decompositions for the non-agricultural sector and for men and women separately, are given in the Appendix.

A glance at the tables shows a rather bewildering diversity of experience. What follows, therefore, is an attempt to discern systematic patterns through regression analysis. We start with the 'supply-side' of the labour market—the growth of population and participation rates—before examining the impact of changes in employment and its structure.

On a bivariate basis, there is no systematic relation over the period 1973–85 between the extent to which unemployment increased with-

Table 6.5. Unemployment and employment indicators: Changes 1973–85

	Unemployment rate (%)			Employment rates (%)		
	Total	Female	Male	Total	Female	Male
Switzerland	0.9	1.1	0.8	−8.9	−2.7	−11.9
Norway	1.0	0.6	1.1	12.9	34.3	0.4
Japan	1.4	1.5	1.3	−0.4	4.2	−3.7
Sweden	0.4	0.2	0.5	8.2	24.7	−3.1
Austria	3.2	2.0	4.0	−6.8	−4.5	−9.0
New Zealand	3.9	7.2	2.0	−2.3	12.6	−8.6
Finland	2.7	2.2	3.1	−0.1	12.9	−10.2
US	2.3	1.4	2.9	6.5	22.8	−3.8
Denmark	6.5	7.1	5.9	0.4	5.6	−3.7
Australia	5.9	5.4	6.1	−5.2	8.2	−11.8
Germany	7.4	8.3	6.9	−12.5	−6.8	−16.6
Italy	3.8	4.8	2.5	−2.4	14.1	−8.2
France	7.7	8.3	7.0	−10.4	0.5	−16.6
Canada	5.0	4.1	5.4	4.8	26.2	−6.7
UK	9.5	8.0	10.6	−7.8	4.1	−15.1
Belgium	9.9	13.2	7.5	−10.2	2.4	−16.8
Netherlands	10.7	10.4	11.0	−6.9	26.1	−18.6
Ireland	11.9	9.9	13.3	−16.0	−3.4	−20.8
Spain	19.5	23.1	17.9	−26.6	−20.9	−29.4
Europe	8.1	8.3	8.2	−9.6	1.2	−15.5
OECD	4.9	4.6	5.1	−2.3	9.9	−9.5

	Participation rates (%)			Part-time (% employment)		
	Total	Female	Male	Total	Female	Male
Switzerland	−8.1	−1.6	−11.2	na		
Norway	14.0	35.1	1.6	6.5	7.2	3.0
Japan	1.0	5.8	−2.5	2.6	6.4	0.2
Sweden	8.6	24.9	−2.7	7.4	7.2	3.0
Austria	−3.7	−2.5	−5.1	1.9	4.2	0.1
New Zealand	1.7	21.4	−6.7	3.8	6.3	0.5
Finland	2.8	15.6	−7.2	1.6	2.0	1.2
US	9.1	24.7	−0.9	0.4	−0.5	0.4
Denmark	7.4	13.8	2.4	2.5	−0.4	0.9
Australia	0.9	14.7	−5.9	5.8	8.6	2.7
Germany	−5.4	1.7	−10.4	2.5	5.6	−0.1
Italy	1.8	20.7	−6.3	−1.8	−4.6	−1.3
France	−2.7	10.0	−10.2	2.5	5.4	0.0
Canada	10.7	32.0	−1.1	4.8	5.9	2.5
UK	2.0	13.2	−4.7	3.1	3.3	1.0
Belgium	−0.1	18.6	−10.0	4.3	9.5	1.0
Netherlands	4.6	41.1	−8.3	na		
Ireland	−3.8	7.6	−7.7	0	−1.1	0
Spain	−8.3	3.6	−13.5	na		
Europe	−1.5	10.7	−8.4	na		
OECD	2.8	15.3	−4.8	na		

Note: The employment rate is the ratio of employment to population of working age.

Sources: OECD *Labour Force Statistics, Employment Outlook.*

Table 6.6. Decomposition of unemployment changes 1973–1985[a] (average annual % growth rates)

	U	LF	Emp.	Resid.	Pop.	Particip.
Whole economy 1973–85						
Japan	0.11	0.95	0.83	0.00	0.86	0.08
Canada	0.41	2.61	2.15	−0.05	1.75	0.85
US	0.19	2.15	1.94	−0.02	1.41	0.73
Australia	0.49	1.76	1.23	−0.04	1.68	0.08
New Zealand	0.33	1.61	1.27	−0.01	1.47	0.14
Austria	0.26	0.41	0.14	−0.01	0.73	−0.31
Belgium	0.83	0.60	−0.30	−0.07	0.60	0.00
Denmark	0.54	1.03	0.47	−0.03	0.44	0.59
Finland	0.23	0.76	0.53	−0.01	0.53	0.23
France	0.64	0.70	0.01	−0.05	0.93	−0.23
Germany	0.62	0.19	−0.45	−0.03	0.66	−0.46
Ireland	0.99	1.12	−0.01	−0.14	1.45	−0.32
Italy	0.31	0.98	0.64	−0.03	0.84	0.14
Netherlands	0.89	1.69	0.71	−0.09	1.31	0.37
Norway	0.08	1.73	1.65	0.00	0.62	1.10
Sweden	0.03	0.89	0.86	0.00	0.20	0.69
Switzerland	0.08	−0.20	−0.27	0.00	0.51	−0.70
UK	0.79	0.64	−0.21	−0.06	0.47	0.17
Spain	1.62	0.43	−1.42	−0.23	1.16	−0.72
Whole economy 1973–85 less 1960–73						
Japan	0.14	−0.34	−0.49	0.00	−0.85	0.50
Canada	0.48	−0.21	−0.75	−0.05	−0.51	0.30
US	0.24	0.21	−0.06	−0.02	−0.28	0.48
Australia	0.42	−0.96	−1.42	−0.03	−0.61	−0.34
New Zealand	0.32	−0.57	−0.90	−0.01	−0.51	−0.06
Austria	0.37	0.61	0.22	−0.01	0.66	−0.05
Belgium	0.90	−0.15	−1.12	−0.07	0.25	−0.41
Denmark	0.62	−0.22	−0.87	−0.03	−0.28	0.06
Finland	0.16	0.42	0.25	−0.01	−0.45	0.86
France	0.52	−0.31	−0.88	−0.04	−0.13	−0.17
Germany	0.61	0.06	−0.58	−0.03	0.30	−0.23
Ireland	0.99	1.04	−0.09	−0.14	0.92	0.13
Italy	0.26	1.41	1.13	−0.03	0.28	1.12
Netherlands	0.77	0.67	−0.18	−0.08	−0.17	0.83
Norway	0.05	0.38	0.33	0.00	−0.06	0.45
Sweden	−0.03	0.25	0.28	0.00	−0.32	0.57
Switzerland	0.08	−1.65	−1.73	0.00	−0.72	−0.92
UK	0.72	0.25	−0.54	−0.06	0.23	0.02
Spain	1.61	−0.39	−2.23	−0.23	0.33	−0.71

[a] The basis for this decomposition is explained in the Appendix.
U = unemployment rate (% point change p.a.); LF = labour force; Emp. = employment;
Pop. = population of working age; Particip. = participation rate.

Source: as Table 6.5.

in a country and the growth rate of population of working age (Equation 1 of the bivariate regressions reported in Table 6.A4). Amongst the group of countries with relatively small increases in unemployment were the US with rapid population growth and Sweden with the slowest (Table 6.6).

For most of the countries concerned, a rapidly growing population after 1973 represented a mere continuation of the pre-1973 trend, and so these economies were already geared up to providing a rapidly growing number of jobs. It is not surprising that their unemployment after 1973 was on average no worse than in those countries with a slower growth of working age population throughout. However, an *acceleration* in population growth after 1973 might be expected to put countries at a disadvantage as compared to those where population growth slowed down. Indeed, *changes* in population growth of working age after 1973 are significantly correlated with *changes* in unemployment (Equation 2). The R^2 implies that nearly one-third of the variance of unemployment increases over the period 1973–85 as a whole can be accounted for by changes in the growth of working-age population. Whilst population of working age can be manipulated by immigration policies (see section IV for the cases of Austria and Switzerland), other changes in population growth (such as occurred in Japan), are entirely fortuitous. Any effect they may have had on unemployment since 1973 is exogenous. In the preceding section, we showed that demographic factors do not explain why total unemployment has risen in the OECD as a whole. However, the evidence presented here suggests that such factors do help to explain why certain countries have been worse hit by unemployment than others. Extreme examples are Japan, which had the biggest slow-down in population growth (−0.8 per year), and Ireland with the biggest acceleration (0.9 per cent per year).

In a few countries, a faster release of people out of agriculture after 1973 seems to have exacerbated unemployment problems, Ireland and Spain being the obvious examples. In most other countries, however, the worsening unemployment situation has reduced the exodus from agriculture (often substantially), and thus helped to keep down the rise in measured unemployment. Not surprisingly, given this complex pattern, non-agricultural population growth is only a little better as an explanatory variable than total population growth in accounting for the diversity of unemployment experience (Equation 3).[8]

A rise in the participation rate adds to the growth of the labour force. If such movements were independent of employment opportunities reflecting only underlying social developments (extension of education, changes in provision of child care, and so forth), then rising participation rates would tend to be associated with rising unemployment. Over the years since 1973 the reverse pattern occurred (Equation 4), with unemployment changes being inversely correlated with changes in participation.

We anticipated that this negative relationship between unemployment and participation rates would be stronger for women than for men, in line with the conventional wisdom that women are more likely to move in and out of the recorded labour force in response to economic conditions. In fact, the negative relationship between unemployment and participation rates applies only to men (Equations 5 and 6). Presumably, men who lost their jobs were more able than women to leave the labour force via the less financially painful route of early retirement.

Despite the absence of a cross-sectional relationship between changes in female participation and *un*employment rates, the female labour force does seem to respond to *employment* opportunities. Regressing participation rate changes on changes in the employment rate (Equation 35), shows a strong positive relationship. The coefficient of nearly 0.7 implies that for every 10 extra women's jobs created after 1973 (over and above those necessary to keep pace with population growth) registered unemployment was, on average, held down by only 3. It is interesting to note that female participation has frequently outstripped job opportunities, so that female unemployment has risen despite a rapid increase in jobs for women. The most striking example is the Netherlands which has experienced the biggest percentage rise in female participation and the second biggest rise in the female employment rate combined with the third biggest increase in female unemployment (Table 6.5). A possible explanation of this phenomenon is that much of the additional female employment consists of part-time jobs taken by married women. So a rapid expansion of employment in this category does not preclude rising unemployment amongst women seeking full-time jobs.

Whilst the picture on the supply side of the labour market is complex, and our analysis leaves a number of intriguing loose ends, some basic conclusions are clear. There is a tendency for unemployment to rise less in those countries where growth of population of working age has slowed down after 1973. In addition, reduced employment opportunities have a depressing effect on participation rates. This makes the growth of the labour force partially endogenous. These two effects work in opposite directions and over the period 1973–85 have statistically counterbalanced each other. As a result, there is no cross-sectional relationship between labour-force growth and unemployment changes over this period (Equation 7).

II.3 Employment Patterns

The growth of unemployment is simply the difference between the growth of the labour force and the growth of employment. There were very large differences between countries in the rate of employment growth, and these did not simply mirror differences in labour-force growth. As a result, the trend of unemployment was significantly affected by employment growth (Equations 8–10). The coefficient of 0.2 for the period as a whole implies that every 1 per cent faster growth of employment was associated with 0.2 per cent per year slower rise in unemployment—the remainder being accounted for by a faster growth of the labour force.[9]

Labour can, in principle, move between sectors of the economy. It would therefore be natural to expect that unemployment would be more closely correlated with total employment than with employment in any particular sector. The most striking result of our statistical analysis is that this is not so. The change in the growth rate of *industrial* employment is a much better predictor of relative unemployment performance since 1973 than is total employment (Equations 17–19). Furthermore, the correlation between unemployment changes and the growth of sectoral employment is a good deal stronger in the case of industry than services (Equations 23–6).

Thus the rise in unemployment after 1973 has a strongly structural character. This seems particularly true of the years since 1979, during which some three-quarters of unemployment diversity is statistically explained by variations in the reduction of industrial employment (Fig. 6.1) The much weaker correlation over the period 1973–9 is partly accounted for by the extreme case of Switzerland which took special efforts to preserve a low rate of measured unemployment despite a big fall in industrial jobs. But even omitting Switzerland the correlation is much weaker than after 1979 (see Equations 20–2).

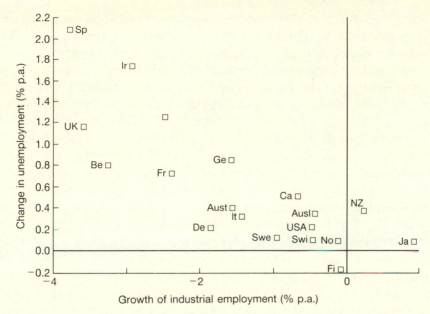

FIG. 6.1 Unemployment and industrial employment, changes 1973–1985 (% p.a.)

After discovering this relationship, we anticipated that industrial employment would prove a stronger predictor of male unemployment than female unemployment; after all, around three-quarters of industrial jobs are held by men, and women also have greater access to service jobs. This expectation was confounded by Equations 27–32, which show that total industrial employment was as closely correlated with female as with male unemployment.[10]

To summarize with Equation A1 in Table 6.A5 (total unemployment, whole period), the coefficient indicates that a 1 per cent a year speed-up in population growth contributed about 0.4 per cent per year to unemployment, whilst a 1 per cent a year slow-down in the rate of provision of industrial jobs raised unemployment by 0.23 percentage points per year (about twice the statistically insignificant coefficient for services employment). Since industrial employment was about one-third of the total, the latter coefficient implies that most of the slow-down in industrial employment was reflected in rising unemployment rather than in more people working in services. Differences between the coefficients for men and women are generally rather small. The variables shown in these equations 'account for' about two-thirds to three-quarters of the overall variance in unemployment growth. The degree of explanation is much the same for each sub-period and when employment is split up by gender.

The greater importance of industrial jobs in determining measured unemployment may be explained as follows. Amongst industrial workers the vast majority are full-time (around 95 per cent in the UK and Germany in 1983—Schoer 1987). Their skills are often specific to industrial work and of little use elsewhere in the economy. Moreover, industrial employment is often geographically concentrated in particular areas. When there is a major decline in industrial employment this cannot be achieved through natural wastage, but only through wholesale redundancies in which large numbers of middle-aged workers are laid off. As a result, the local labour market in the industrial areas may be flooded with relatively immobile middle-aged workers, without the skills for immediate redeployment elsewhere in the economy. Even when the decline in industrial employment is achieved by natural wastage the result is a drying-up of job opportunities for the children of the many industrial workers living in the area.

In principle a decline in industrial employment can be offset by increasing employment in services. However, if the industrial decline is severe, this is unlikely to be sufficient. Most service employment, such as health, education, local administration, and distribution is population-based and spread relatively uniformly around the economy. Such population-based employment has limited potential as a device for combating severe regional unemployment. Some service activities (for example, producer services) are more geographically mobile, but they often require different skills from those available in the old industrial areas. Moreover, many of the new service jobs created nowadays are part-time and do not provide adequate replacement for full-time industrial jobs. As a result, they are frequently occupied by married women drawn back into the labour force, rather than displaced industrial workers. Thus the growth of service employment may have only a limited impact on the unemployment created by the loss of industrial jobs.

The rise in unemployment, especially after 1979, has substantially the character of an industrial crisis. A number of countries (Spain, UK, Belgium, Ireland, Netherlands, France) lost industrial jobs at a very rapid rate (2.4 to 3.8 per cent per year), and unemployment increased sharply despite the fact that in some of these countries

(UK and Netherlands) service employment continued to grow as fast or faster than before 1973. In some other countries (Japan and Canada), where the growth rate of industrial employment also slowed down a great deal, the situation was eased by a very substantial slow-down in the growth rate of the population.

A substantial part of the female labour force consists of women who require full-time work. Most industrial employment is full-time, so a reduction in this type of employment directly reduces the number of full-time jobs available for women. Moreover, if the decline in industrial employment is geographically concentrated it may have a knock-on effect in certain types of local service employment through its effect on local incomes (for example, distribution), thereby reducing still further the amount of full-time employment available for women. The increase in *measured* unemployment refers mainly to a section of the female labour force directly or indirectly affected by the decline in industrial employment, whilst the simultaneous creation of new service employment may provide jobs for women not previously in the official labour force and not, therefore, officially classified as unemployed.

II.4 General Economic Performance

At this point it may be helpful to round out the picture by considering the relationship between production and unemployment. Has the ability to keep unemployment down flowed directly from success in maintaining growth rates of output, for example?

In fact, the relationship between unemployment and GDP growth, far from being very close, is barely if at all significant (Equations 37–40). Those countries which have maintained low unemployment rates have done so with widely differing rates of GDP growth and of GDP slow-down (Fig. 6.2 illustrates this rather striking result). This does not, of course, imply that *ceteris paribus* an individual country would not have achieved lower unemployment by faster output growth.

The relationship with industrial output is a little bit stronger (Equations 51–3), but is much weaker than with industrial employment. This suggests that the maintenance of industrial output growth was neither a necessary nor sufficient condition for maintaining industrial jobs. It was only in the second sub-period (1979–85) that GDP and industrial growth (and slow-downs) bore a significant

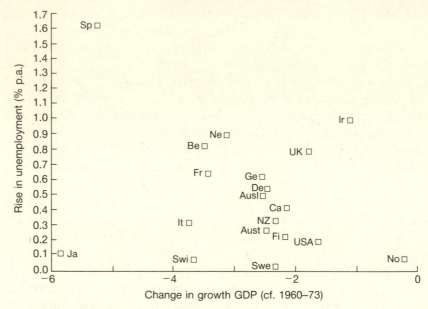

FIG. 6.2 Unemployment and GDP, 1973–1985

relationship to unemployment; this could perhaps be explained by the reduced importance of employment protection policies by governments (and resistance to lay-offs by unions) which had attenuated the relationship between output and unemployment after the first oil shock.[11]

Investment plays a complex role in unemployment determination—driving up output through direct demand effects and through enhanced competitiveness but reducing the employment requirements per unit of output through the incorporation of labour-saving technology. The relationship between investment and unemployment increase is a bit more significant than GDP (Equations 41–3). Since it is also more significant than industrial output it cannot simply reflect the fact that investment demand is an important component of industrial output. Moreover, since productivity growth is if anything positively related to unemployment increase (Equations 44 and 45), it cannot be because high investment has maintained productivity growth and competitiveness.[12] A possible explanation could be that the ability to maintain investment growth is an indication of the degree of employer confidence which is simultaneously reflected in the maintenance of employment.

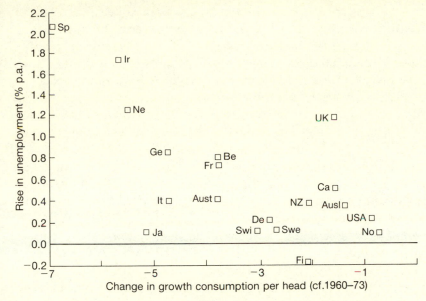

FIG. 6.3 Unemployment and consumption per head, 1979–1985

The years since the late 1960s have seen a pronounced slow-down in productivity growth and deterioration in the terms of trade in the OECD countries (see Chapter 2). The failure of real wages to respond flexibly to these conditions is a popular explanation for the subsequent increase in unemployment.[13] On a cross-section basis over the period 1973–9 there was a tendency for those countries with faster product wage growth (or less of a slow-down) to exhibit a bigger increase in unemployment. About one-quarter of the variance in unemployment changes is statistically explained by the behaviour of product wages during this period (Equations 54–8). After 1979, however, the relationship is not significant at all. It seems likely that the industrial crises which provoked the big increases in unemployment after 1979 reflected far more deep-seated problems than a temporary rise in product wages.

Finally (Equations 46–50), increased unemployment was strongly correlated with the growth of real consumption per head of population over the final sub-period 1979–85 (Fig. 6.3); but not at all during the years 1973–9. This underlines again the different character of the two sub-periods. During the first period, it appears that the ability to contain unemployment was largely independent of the extent to which economic circumstances were squeezing what was available for consumption (via slower growth, terms of trade effects, and so forth). In the harsher climate after 1979 economic 'realities' reasserted themselves and slow growth of consumable resources was frequently, although not universally, off-loaded on to one section of the population—the unemployed—who took a major cut in consumption. Impressive, therefore, was the performance of those countries (Japan and Italy stand out) which held down unemployment after 1979 despite a much slower growth of consumption per head than prior to 1973. Conversely the performance of the UK since 1979 was particularly poor in that there was a very large rise in unemployment despite a relatively small fall in the growth of consumption.

Table 6.A6 shows the results of a multivariate analysis relating the growth of unemployment to the slow-down of population of working age and changes in the growth rates of GDP and product wages. A little over one-third of the variance in unemployment increases is accounted for by these variables.[14] Population slow-down is always of significance in reducing a rise in unemployment, GDP more or less significant and product wages only in the first sub-period. The lack of significance of the product wage rate in the second sub-period is probably misleading. The wage measure used here is pre-tax and includes such items as employers' contributions to social security. Later on, when discussing the so-called 'star performers', we shall suggest that a more appropriate variable, especially in recent years, may be the post-tax real wage. Unfortunately, international statistics on this latter variable are not readily available.

II.5 Conclusion

It is clear that economic growth is only loosely correlated with unemployment; countries with similar economic growth rates have widely differing rates of unemployment. The impact of population growth on unemployment, which has generally been neglected, clearly deserves stress. Some countries, notably Japan, benefited substantially from a fortuitous slow-down in population growth of working age at the time economic conditions deteriorated. Most significantly the role of structural change, and in particular of industrial employment, is of central importance in understanding the variation in unemployment performance. The massive rise in unemployment, which is concentrated in a number of European economies—France,

Germany, UK, Netherlands, and Belgium with Ireland and Spain on
the fringes suffering even more severely—has substantially the character of an industrial crisis. The countries which have succeeded in
keeping unemployment down have in some way or other escaped
from or contained this crisis.

Our analysis suggests, therefore, that two conditions are required
for a country to maintain a low level of unemployment:

(i) *Industrial Employment.* Wholesale redundancies must be avoided
and any decline in industrial employment must be gradual. If
this condition is not satisfied, the result will be structural unemployment which cannot easily be eliminated through the creation
of additional service employment.

(ii) *Service Employment.* Sufficient service employment must be created to absorb new entrants to the labour market (be they young
people or married women) plus transfers from the industrial
sector (on the modest scale assumed under condition (i)). If
condition (ii) is not satisfied the result will be an increase in
measured unemployment even if industrial employment holds up
reasonably well.

The final sections of the chapter will examine the extent to which,
and more importantly how, the so-called 'star performers' have met
these conditions and thereby held down employment.[15]

III. LABOUR MARKET PERFORMANCE COMPARED

From the preceding discussion, it is clear that various indices can be
used to measure the labour-market performance of a country. In
Table 6.7 the countries of our sample are ranked according to a
number of such indices. Two of these indices are concerned with
unemployment, as officially measured, and the remainder with employment. There is a well-defined correlation between the various
rankings; however, it is by no means perfect. Only Norway does well
according to all of the indices shown in the table, although the
performance of Sweden is also very impressive. At the opposite end
of the spectrum are Belgium, France, and Spain whose performance
is uniformly bad. These countries have all experienced a dramatic
reversal of fortunes since 1973. The table also reveals examples of
inconsistency among the various indices. For example, Switzerland

Table 6.7. Ranking of employment performance[a]

	Level in 1985		Growth rate 1973–85				Change in growth rate 1960–73 to 1973–85		
	U/L	E/P	U/L[b]	E/P	E	E_n	E/P	E	E_n
Switzerland	1	5	3	16	16	16	17	18	18
Norway	2	2	2	1	3	2	4	2	2
Japan	3	6	4	7	7	7	5	9	17
Sweden	4	1	1	2	6	9	3	3	3
Austria	5	11	7	12	12	13	10	5	6
New Zealand	6	12	9	9	4	6	9	15	11
Finland	7	4	6	6	10	8	2	4	10
US	8	7	5	3	2	3	6	6	4
Denmark	9	3	12	5	11	12	11	13	13
Australia	10	10	11	10	5	5	14	17	16
Germany	11	13	13	17	18	18	15	11	9
Italy	12	16	8	8	9	4	1	1	1
France	13	14	14	15	13	14	12	14	15
Canada	14	8	10	4	1	1	8	12	12
UK	15	9	15	13	15	15	13	10	7
Belgium	16	15	16	14	17	17	18	16	14
Netherlands	17	17	17	11	8	11	7	8	5
Ireland	18	18	18	18	14	10	16	7	8
Spain	19	19	19	19	19	19	19	19	19

[a] Rankings are based on fastest employment growth (highest level) and slowest unemployment growth (lowest level).

[b] Refers to absolute change in U/L; all other ratings refer to percentage growth rates.

Note: U/L = unemployment as percentage of labour force (national definitions); E = civil employment; E_n = non-agricultural employment (= industry and services); P = population aged 15–64 years.

Source: Tables 6.4, 6.5, 6.A1.

has maintained a low level of measured unemployment, yet its record on employment growth during this period is amongst the worst. The reason for this anomaly is a reduction in the labour force since 1973, which is unique to the sample (see Table 6.6). The opposite case is Canada, which has experienced the highest rate of employment growth in our sample, yet also has a very high rate of unemployment (more than 10 per cent), due to a 36 per cent increase in the labour force. In this respect the US is similar to Canada.

A final interesting case is Italy. It is one of the few in our sample where employment growth has accelerated since 1973 (see Table

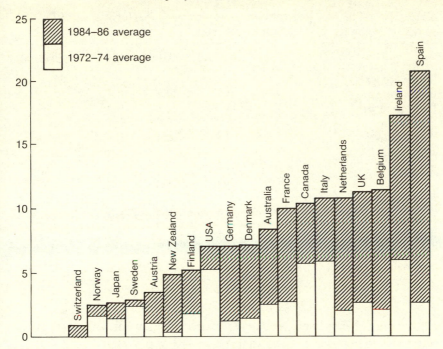

FIG. 6.4 Percentage unemployment in OECD countries[a]
[a]OECD standardized unemployment rate. *Source*: OECD *Labour Statistics*, plus authors' estimates

6.6). Moreover, Italy is the *only* country where non-agricultural employment (i.e. industry and services combined) has grown faster since 1973 than before. However, because of a steep rise in female participation rates, Italy's unemployment rate has actually risen.

III.1 The 'Star Performers'

The above examples illustrate the difficulties involved in choosing an index of labour-market performance. In the discussion which follows we shall focus our assessment of performance on unemployment rates as standardized by the OECD (where available). To avoid the distortion involved in choosing a single year, we shall take as our index a three-year average of unemployment rates for the period 1984–6. From Fig. 6.4 we can identify only five 'star performers' which have kept measured unemployment really low since 1973; Switzerland, where the unemployment rate was still only 1 per cent

Table 6.8. The star performers: employment performance 1973–1985 compared (average annual % growth rates)

	Norway	Sweden	Japan	Austria	Switzerland
Whole economy					
Employment	1.7	0.9	0.8	0.1	−0.3
Labour force	1.7	0.9	1.0	0.4	−0.2
Population	0.6	0.2	0.9	0.7	0.5
Participation rate	1.1	0.7	0.1	−0.3	−0.7
Employment by sector					
Industry	0.0	−0.9	0.3	−1.2	−1.7
Services	3.1	2.1	1.9	1.8	1.0
Participation rates					
Male	0.1	−0.2	−0.2	−0.4	−1.0
Female	2.5	1.9	0.5	−0.2	−0.1
Share of part-time employment	0.5	0.6	0.2	0.2	na

Source: Tables 6.5, 6.6, 6.A2, 6.A3, and OECD *Labour Force Statistics.*

in the mid 1980s; then Norway, Japan, Sweden, and Austria where unemployment was in the range of 2½–3½ per cent.[16]

III.2 Common Features

Let us now consider what features, if any, our star performers (Switzerland, Norway, Japan, Sweden, and Austria) have in common (see Tables 6.8 and 6.9). We shall consider three types of features structural change; industrial production; wages and consumption.

III.3 Structural Change

Earlier we argued that for a country to maintain a low rate of measured unemployment: (i) any decline in industrial employment must be gradual, and (ii) service employment must grow sufficiently fast to absorb new entrants to the labour market plus transfers from the industrial sector. Of our star performers, Norway and Japan conform to this pattern well, and Sweden moderately well. All three have experienced a fairly slow decline in industrial employment over the period 1973–85 as a whole, and also within both sub-periods 1973–9 and 1979–85. Moreover, all three have had a sufficient increase in service employment. As a result, all three have experi-

Table 6.9. The star performers: output and consumption compared 1973–1985[a] (average annual % growth rates)

	1973–9	1979–85	1973–85
GDP (per head)			
Switzerland	−0.4	0.9	0.3
Norway	4.3	2.5	3.4
Japan	2.8	3.1	3.0
Sweden	1.7	1.5	1.6
Austria	2.5	0.8	1.7
OECD	1.4	1.0	1.2
Industrial production (per head)[b]			
Switzerland	−0.7	0.4	−0.2
Norway	6.8	3.2	5.0
Japan	2.3	4.5	3.4
Sweden	0.7	1.5	1.1
Austria	2.0	0.4	1.2
OECD	0.5	0.6	0.6
Manufacturing output (per head)[b]			
Switzerland	−1.0	0.2	−0.4
Norway	−0.4	−0.6	−0.5
Japan	2.6	7.0	4.8
Sweden	0.4	1.3	0.9
Austria	2.3	1.2	1.8
OECD	0.9	1.2	1.1
Personal consumption (per head)			
Switzerland	0.7	0.2	0.5
Norway	3.3	2.2	2.8
Japan	3.3	1.7	2.4
Sweden	1.7	0.1	0.9
Austria	2.8	0.7	1.7
OECD	1.9	0.8	1.4

[a] Per head of population aged 15–64.
[b] Real value added, except Switzerland where figures refer to gross product.
Source: OECD *Historical Statistics, Main Economic Indicators, National Accounts.*

enced only a very small increase in measured unemployment since 1973.

Austria fits the pattern less well. Industrial employment in Austria has fallen quite fast, especially since 1979, whilst the growth rate of service employment has been equal to the OECD average. Such a combination would normally lead to a noticeable rise in measured unemployment. This has been largely avoided in Austria because many of those who have lost their jobs are foreigners who are not included in the official statistics on Austrian unemployment. The increase in such hidden unemployment is reflected in the overall participation rate which has fallen noticeably since 1973 (Table 6.6).

Even more anomalous is the case of Switzerland, where service employment has stagnated whilst industrial unemployment has fallen dramatically. Yet measured unemployment remains negligible. As in the case of Austria, the reason is that unemployment in Switzerland has been either exported to other countries or simply ignored by official statistics.

III.4 Industrial Production

As we have seen earlier, there is a degree of inverse correlation between industrial growth and unemployment. Countries which have experienced the greatest increase in industrial production per capita, have in general experienced the smallest rise in unemployment. The reasons are obvious. Rapid growth in industrial production makes it easier to maintain industrial employment, and hence avoid some of the structural problems which contribute to unemployment. It also provides in a painless fashion the material resources required to support expanding employment in the service sector. Of our star performers, Norway and Japan conform unambiguously to this general pattern, and Austria fits it quite well. Sweden is a striking exception. Over the period 1973–85 as a whole, industrial production in Sweden has risen very slowly indeed (Table 6.9). Yet the country created a massive number of new jobs and experienced virtually no rise in measured unemployment. The Swedish example is important. It proves that rapid industrial growth, although helpful, is not absolutely essential for large-scale job creation and full employment. Under the right social conditions, both objectives can be achieved without rapid growth. Switzerland is another exception. Industrial production has stagnated but for reasons mentioned above, and discussed at length below, measured unemployment has remained negligible.

III.5 Wages and Consumption

Consumption per capita is strongly influenced by pre-tax real wages, the share of wages absorbed by taxes, the proportion of wages saved, and finally, the proportion of the adult population in employment.

The behaviour of these variables during the period 1973–85 shows considerable variation within the group of star performers. In Austria and Japan, both pre-tax wage rates and per capita personal consumption rose more or less continuously. In Switzerland, real wage rates also rose continuously. However, total employment fell and the population rose, so wages per head of population remained almost stationary. This explains why per capita personal consumption in Switzerland hardly changed over the period 1973–85 despite a fairly rapid growth in real wage rates. In Sweden the situation was reversed. Real wage rates fell noticeably from 1977 onwards (see Fig. 6.5). However, this was accompanied by a large increase in female employment, mainly in the public services. As a result, total family income and average personal consumption were maintained.

Interestingly, Switzerland and Sweden have had much the same growth of personal consumption per head. However, in Switzerland an increasing fraction of the population is without employment, whilst in the Swedish model a growing fraction of the population is employed. Thus, in terms of personal consumption of a typical family, the two models are similar. However, the Swedish model involves a much faster growth of public services and is, thus, superior both in terms of overall living standards and opportunities to participate in paid employment, especially for women.

The case of Norway is interesting because during the years of its oil boom the country combined Swedish-style social policy with Japanese-style industrial growth. Real wages were kept down whilst industrial productivity increased because of oil production. The resulting oil profits were taxed to finance an increase in public sector employment for women, together with a large rise in incomes for farmers. Despite the virtual freeze on real wages, many families received a substantial increase in total income and personal consumption.

IV. THE EXPERIENCE OF INDIVIDUAL COUNTRIES

IV.1 Switzerland

Switzerland is frequently praised as a shining example of how to combine stable prices with full employment—a model of labour-market 'flexibility'. In fact, its economic performance since 1973 has been very poor. Whilst it is true that Switzerland has experi-

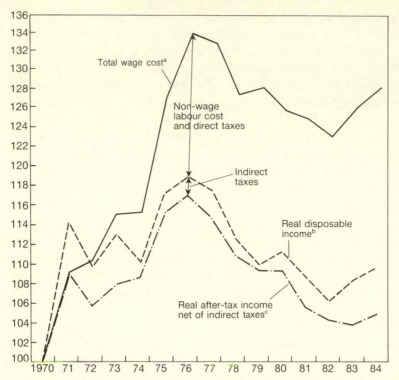

FIG. 6.5 Real wages in Sweden. a = Total labour cost deflated by net price index. b = Compensation after tax deflated by net price index. c = Compensation after tax deflated by consumer price index. *Note*: Calculations are based on yearly income for a single industrial worker, engineering. *Source*: *OECD Economic Survey of Sweden*, May 1984

enced one of the lowest inflation rates in the OECD since 1973, this has been purchased at enormous cost in terms of output and employment. The result has been a massive, but hidden, rise in unemployment.

Over the period 1973–85 Switzerland experienced the slowest GDP growth of any country in our sample (0.3 per cent p.a.). The fall in manufacturing output was second only to the UK. This performance on the output side was accompanied by a large fall in total employment. In almost any other country, such a fall in employment would have led to a massive rise in measured unemployment. However, this did not happen in Switzerland. Many of the workers who lost their jobs were foreigners with temporary residence permits. By agreement between the unions and employers, such people are the first to be fired when jobs are eliminated and the last to be hired when new jobs become available. On being fired, unless they can find a new job quickly, they must leave the country. This mechanism provides a safety-value which permits a considerable reduction in employment to occur without having Swiss nationals unemployed. It also allows the Swiss to export their unemployment to surrounding countries. This mechanism was particularly import-ant after the first oil shock. Over the period 1973–7 total employ-ment fell by 280,000 (8.7 per cent), and the number of foreign workers in the labour force was reduced by 251,000. There was virtually no increase at all in unemployment as officially measured, which rose by a mere 12,000. Of course, Switzerland has not been the only country to behave in such a fashion. Germany and Austria have also kept down their unemployment rates by excluding fore-igners, but neither has done so on quite the scale practised by Switzerland.

The large-scale exclusion of foreigners is no longer a viable option in Switzerland. The country's ability to maintain near-full employ-ment more recently is due to trends in participation rates. Women's participation rate has remained virtually stationary since 1977 (in most other OECD countries it has risen strongly). For men the participation rate has been falling in virtually all OECD countries, but in Switzerland the decline has been amongst the fastest (see Table 6.5).

A simple calculation will illustrate the combined importance of these two factors. Assume that both the number of foreign workers and the overall participation rate had remained constant since 1973. By 1983 there would have been an additional 504,000 people in the Swiss labour force. Given the number of jobs actually available in 1983, this addition to the labour force would have meant a twenty-fold increase in unemployment (from 26,000 to 530,000). Instead of an unemployment rate of 1 per cent the figure would have been 15 per cent, which is higher than in any OECD country in our sample with the exceptions of Ireland and Spain. This is, of course, only an illustrative calculation. Even so, it does indicate the orders of magni-tude of the exported and hidden unemployment.

Despite its supposed commitment to free trade and 'labour-market

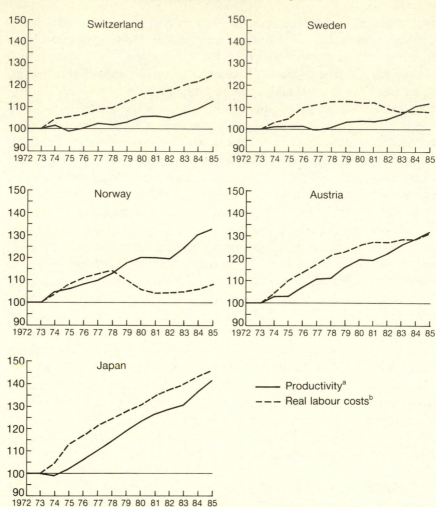

FIG. 6.6 a = Productivity = GDP per person in civil employment at 1980 prices. b = Real labour costs = compensation per employee (including employer's contributions to social security and the like), deflated by GDP deflator. *Source*: OECD *National Accounts* and *Labour Force Statistics*.

flexibility', Switzerland is really a good example of so-called 'Euro-sclerosis'.[17] Indeed, the country has been strongly criticized by the OECD for its failure to restructure its industry by developing new products or shifting into new activities with long-term market potential (see OECD 1984, p. 40). Switzerland has restructured by cutting back and rationalizing old sectors, but has not yet developed sufficient new activities. This explains why total industrial output has stagnated since 1973.

Another striking feature of the Swiss economy is the relatively fast growth of labour costs, which have risen by around 25 per cent in real terms since 1973 (Fig. 6.6). Given the weak state of the Swiss economy and its lack of dynamism, this rise in labour costs may well have been a factor behind the stagnation of output and the collapse of employment. Those who have managed to keep their jobs in Switzerland have done quite will since 1973, but this may have been at the expense of others who have lost their actual or potential jobs during this period. The Swiss economy is sometimes praised because of its apparent ability to combine a commitment to free market economics with a decentralized system of consensual labour relations. In terms of output and employment, this combination has been a clear failure since 1973. Contrary to the common perception, the Swiss achievement has been to provide the core labour force with a rising standard of living at the expense of marginal groups excluded from this charmed circle.

IV.2 Japan

Both manufacturing output and industrial production as a whole have grown rapidly in Japan (Table 6.9). This growth is almost certainly of greater importance in explaining Japan's low unemployment than the 'lifetime' employment policies of large industrial companies. Such policies have helped to keep unemployment down in the short run, but this has been against a background of continued growth. It is questionable how far these policies could withstand prolonged economic stagnation of the kind experienced in much of Europe. Besides, lifetime employment policies cover only a part of the industrial work-force and do not explain why industrial employment has held up so well in many smaller companies.

Labour-hoarding during recessions is a well-established feature of the Japanese economy (OECD 1986; Hamouda and Kurosaka, 1986; Aoki, Chapter 7 below). However, the importance of this factor should not be exaggerated. During the industrial crisis following the 1973 oil shock, employment fell sharply—by 10 per cent for males and 13 per cent for females.[19] Some of this reduction occurred through lay-offs, often by small firms not operating lifetime employment policies, and some through lower recruitment by firms of all kinds. In most countries, such a large reduction in manufacturing employment would soon be reflected in official unemployment statistics. However, in Japan many of those who became unemployed were officially classified as economically inactive, and thus excluded from the unemployment statistics. This is especially true for women in the age group 25–54 years, whose labour-force participation declined by about 4 per cent between 1973 and 1975. With the exception of Switzerland no other country experienced anything like such a fall in female participation during these years.

Over the period 1973–85 employment growth in Japan has been about average for the OECD (Table 6.7). However, it has been much slower than in the preceding period 1960–73. The difference is most striking for non-agricultural employment (i.e. industry and services combined), where the growth rate has fallen from 3.0 per cent p.a. in the first period to 1.3 per cent p.a. in the second. Only Belgium and Switzerland have experienced a comparable decline in employment growth (Table 6.7). Why has this not led to mass unemployment in Japan? In purely statistical terms the answer is as follows. As employment growth has slowed in the non-agricultural sector, there has been a virtually identical slow-down in labour-force growth in this sector of the economy. Prior to 1973, employment and labour force in the non-agricultural sector both grew extremely fast at about the same rate; since that year they have both grown far more slowly, though again at about the same rate. As a result, measured unemployment has not altered very much.[19] Of the 1.6 per cent reduction in non-agricultural labour-force growth after 1973, about half is due to slower population growth and half to the reduced outflow of population from agriculture.

To illustrate the orders of magnitude, suppose that population growth had continued after 1973 at its previous rate. Then, *ceteris paribus*, given the actual growth in non-agricultural employment, the measured unemployment rate by 1985 would have been around 12 per cent. Moreover, if in addition the outflow of population from agriculture had continued on the pre-1973 scale, then by 1985 measured unemployment in Japan would have been around 20 per cent of the labour force. Of course, faster growth in the non-agricultural labour force would probably have spontaneously induced some additional employment in the non-agricultural sector, so the rise in unemployment would have been less than the figures above suggest.

Table 6.10. Non-agricultural employment and labour force: Japan, 1960–1985 (% p.a.)

	1960–73	1973–85	Change[a]
Contributions to labour force growth			
Total population[b]	1.7	0.9	−0.9
Shift from agriculture[c]	1.2	0.3	−0.9
Non-agric. population (= (1) + (2))	2.9	1.2	−1.8
Non-agric. participation rate	0.0	0.2	0.2
Non-agric. labour force (= (3) + (4))	2.9	1.4	−1.6
Employment growth			
Industrial employment	3.4	0.3	−3.1
Service employment	2.7	1.9	−0.8
Non-agric. employment	3.0	1.3	−1.7

  [a] note rounding errors.
  [b] aged 15–64 years.
  [c] $= g_{P_n} - g_P$, where P_n and P are, respectively, non-agricultural and total population aged 15–64 years; for the definition of non-agricultural population see note 8.

Source: OECD *Labour Force Statistics.*

However, one should not exaggerate the ability of the Japanese economy to generate employment under the harsher world economy conditions of the past 15 years. The lifetime employment system of large companies is reasonably good at preserving employment for existing workers, but it is not designed for the creation of jobs for people not already in employment.[20] To have achieved this objective would have required a deliberate government policy, either to promote much faster growth of output, or else to reduce the rate of productivity growth and thereby encourage firms to employ additional labour.

IV.3 Norway[21]

Like Japan, Norway has experienced a large increase in industrial production since 1973. This is mainly due to the growth of oil production; in the manufacturing sector output has remained virtually constant since 1973. In most countries, such a prolonged stagnation in manufacturing output would have been accompanied by large-scale redundancies and considerable unemployment (OECD 1985*b*). In Norway oil revenue has been used to subsidize ailing firms and slow the fall in manufacturing employment. As a result manufacturing employment fell by only 6 per cent during the period 1973–85.

Norway has also used oil revenues to finance government employment, which has risen by more than 40 per cent since 1973. The deliberate use of oil revenues to preserve and create employment stands in stark contrast to the use of oil revenues in the UK under the Thatcher government. The Thatcher government has encouraged private firms to lay off workers, whilst at the same time reducing government employment. As a result, total employment has fallen and there has been a spectacular rise in unemployment. The cost of supporting the unemployed is considerable and absorbs much of the UK's oil revenues.

The difference between Norway and the UK is not an accident, nor is it the result of 'mistakes' in UK policy. It is due to profound political differences between the two countries. In Norway, there is a durable compromise between social classes, under which the maintenance of full employment is one of the main objectives of government policy. Such a compromise is feasible because both workers and employers are centrally organized, and each organization can bargain on behalf of its members and ensure they largely abide by the terms of the agreement. On the union side, a condition for cooperation is that the government pursue a full employment policy. In return they contain their wage demands within limits consistent with this objective. Such behaviour is typical of what Mancur Olson (1982) calls 'encompassing' organizations which represent a broad social interest rather than the sectional interest of some narrow subgroup. By their very nature, encompassing organizations take a comprehensive view of events and take into account the macroeconomic consequences of their action. When society is dominated by a few such organizations a durable compromise is feasible, indeed likely, because each side has a powerful material interest in a compromise which helps to stabilize the economy, and will be willing to pay a considerable price to make such a compromise work.

This is, of course, a familiar theme in the literature on 'corporatism' and we shall not explore it further.[22] Suffice it to say that the existence of strong, centralized organizations for capital and labour is a major element in Norway's success in preserving full employment. Of these, a strong, centralized trade-union movement is the most important, for it allows the working class to act coherently as a class and impose full employment policies which might otherwise be rejected. The existence of a strong, centralized employers organization is a useful bonus but is probably not the vital ingredient in explaining why Norway has so resolutely pursued the goal of full employment.

Norway provides an extraordinary example of social solidarity. Between 1977, when oil and gas production began to build up, and 1985, total industrial production rose by 44 per cent. Yet there was no increase at all in real wages for the bulk of employed workers. Instead, the revenues from oil and gas were used to achieve general social objectives—to repay the country's foreign debt; to raise farm incomes by around 50 per cent so as to stem the outflow of population from the countryside; to expand employment in the public services, especially for women; and finally, to maintain employment in the geographically scattered manufacturing industry. With the exception of Sweden, no other OECD country has displayed anything like this degree of solidarity. In recent times the Norwegian economy has suffered a severe blow from the fall in oil prices. As a result, the country is now facing a prolonged period of austerity and retrenchment. However, given the degree of internal solidarity in the country this burden should be widely shared amongst the population and, it is hoped, there should be no major increase in unemployment.

IV.4 Austria

Austria has had a larger than average increase in both manufacturing output and industrial production since 1973 (Table 6.9). Even so, its growth rate has not been all that impressive and the country has suffered from a marked acceleration in the growth rate of working-age population since 1973. We would therefore have expected to see a much larger rise in unemployment than has actually occurred. There are several reasons why unemployment has been kept in check. In the industrial sector, much of which is nationalized, deliberate efforts have been made to maintain employment (OECD 1985a). Moreover, many of the workers who have lost their jobs in this sector are foreigners who do not appear in Austria's unemployment statistics. Both the policy of maintaining industrial employment and reducing the number of foreign workers are a concession to Austria's powerful labour movement (Katzenstein 1984). In Austria, as in Norway, there is a social compromise between well-organized groups. The exact nature of this compromise and the character of the organized groups is somewhat different in the two countries. But in

both cases, the labour movement is powerful and centrally organized. The protection of employment for Austrians is one of the
central goals of Austrian unions, and in large measure they have been
able to impose this goal in return for co-operation in broader economic policy. Furthermore, because of increased production Austria
has been able to combine a fairly high degree of employment protection with rising real wages. However, there are signs that the
social compromise is beginning to fragment. The political balance
has shifted against the traditional labour movement in recent years
and employment protection is no longer such a central plank of
government policy. The massive subsidies to nationalized industries
are to be phased out and heavy redundancies are expected. The
result will almost certainly be a significant rise in unemployment
(*Guardian*, 24 July 1987).

IV.5 Sweden

This brings us to Sweden. As can be seen from Table 6.9, Swedish
manufacturing output and industrial production per capita were
almost stationary over the period 1973–85. Yet during this period
industrial employment declined slowly and a vast number of service
jobs, many of them part-time, were created. Both of these developments were the result of government policy. In the industrial sector a
massive programme of job protection was implemented following the
1973 oil shock. The idea was to preserve employment in the older
sectors of the economy, such as shipbuilding and steel, whilst re-
training workers and developing new industries. This policy was
very effective, as even the previously sceptical OECD reports (1985c)
now admit. The Swedish economy has now successfully restructured
and has been growing quite fast in recent years. All this was achieved
without the wholesale shake-out which occurred in many other European economies faced with similar difficulties, such as Belgium or
the UK. As far as service employment is concerned, the crucial
factor behind the expansion was government employment which rose
by well over a third during the period 1973–85. One of the objectives of this expansion in government employment was to provide
jobs for displaced industrial workers, together with new entries to
the labour market such as young people and married women.

As in Norway, the conscious pursuit of full employment was the
fruit of a social compromise in which a strongly organized and

centralized labour movement could impose such an objective as the price of its co-operation in wider economic policies.[23] However, there is one crucial difference between the two countries. In Norway, the huge increase in the tax revenues from oil provided a ready means to finance the protection of old jobs in manufacturing and the creation of new jobs in government services. In Sweden, there were no oil revenues. On the contrary, the country is a large importer of oil and its energy bill was greatly increased by higher oil prices. Moreover, total industrial production was virtually stagnant. The full employment programme was therefore financed through a combination of wage restraint and higher taxes. This meant a considerable fall in real take-home pay for the average worker (Fig. 6.5). There were, of course, compensations. Public services were greatly improved and family pay was often boosted through the provision of additional work for married women. Even so, the policy required enormous restraint on the part of well-organized workers in the more secure areas of the economy. Of all the OECD countries, Sweden exhibits the highest degree of social solidarity in the face of adversity over the past 15 years. The basis of this solidarity is a well-organized, disciplined, and politically conscious working class. The Swedish trade unions are not as centralized as in Austria or Norway, being divided into two major confederations which are sometimes in dispute with each other.[24] Even so, Swedish workers have displayed an impressive degree of unity in pursuing the objective of full employment. Moreover, until now at least, they have been willing to make the sacrifices required to achieve this objective.

IV.6 Concluding Remarks

The first conclusion of this chapter is unsurprising. It is that there is no single factor, either demographic or economic, which accounts for the major differences in unemployment performance amongst the OECD countries. There is a wide dispersion of patterns of population growth, labour force growth, and economic growth within which unemployment has been less successfully or more successfully contained. Fortuitous changes in population growth have played an important and neglected role. Relatively high growth rates of industrial production have clearly helped to keep down unemployment. So too has the ability of economies to adapt their employment policies to whatever industrial performance they have achieved and to avoid wholesale industrial redundancies. However, these general findings do not in themselves explain the mechanisms which lie behind success or failure. A closer look at the success stories is required.

Our list of 'star performers' is short: Switzerland, Norway, Japan, Sweden, and Austria. Of these, Switzerland is really a failure, and its low unemployment rate is extremely misleading. Although there are differences, especially between Japan and the European countries, all of the genuinely successful countries have had one thing in common. They have pursued highly interventionist economic policies, and their governments have played a vigorous role in guiding the economy and moulding its future. All of them have rejected the *laissez-faire* ideas of the New Right, with its emphasis on deregulation and market forces. Yet their performance, in general, has been impressive by international standards and their unemployment record good. Even Sweden, whose industrial growth rate was for a time very low, is now experiencing an industrial renaissance.

Our second point concerns the European countries. Three of the European star performers—Norway, Sweden, and Austria—are examples of what has been called '*social* corporatism'. In all of them, the working class is powerful and possesses a high degree of organizational unity. This strength and unity allows the working class to develop coherent objectives and strike an advantageous bargain with other social groups. In particular, it allows this class to establish full employment as a major national priority. Not only is such a priority accepted by the other social groups, but the working class in return honours its own side of the bargain and accepts the sacrifices required to achieve its employment objectives. Norway, Sweden, and Austria are not the only countries which might be classified under the heading 'social corporatism'. Both Denmark and Finland are often classified under this heading: in each of them social compromise is a pervasive phenomenon, and in each of them the labour movement is quite strongly organized. However, in neither of them is the working class as powerful as in the three former countries, nor does it display the same internal coherence and unity of purpose (see Fig. 6.7). This may help to explain, perhaps, why full employment has not been such a priority in Denmark and Finland, and why these countries have higher unemployment rates than do our star performers, Norway, Sweden, and Austria.[25] This is only a hypothesis, but a plausible one.

It seems that there are three routes to full employment under current conditions in Western capitalist economies. There is the

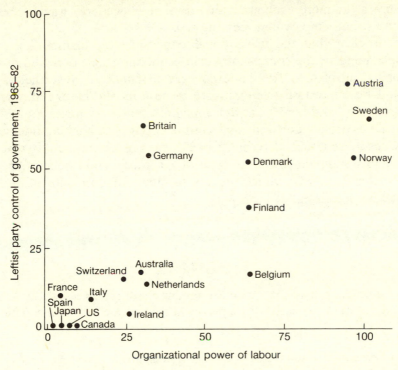

FIG. 6.7 Labour movement strength in various countries. *Source*: Cameron (1984).

Swiss model in which the unemployed are pushed out of the country or simply excluded from the official statistics. There is the Japanese model in which a powerful, centralized bourgeoisie formulates a coherent strategy for industrial development which it imposes on a weak and fragmented working class. This is sometimes called 'concertation with labour excluded' (see Lehmbruch 1984). The third model is *social* corporatism, in which a powerful, unified working class strikes a bargain with the bourgeoisie and other social groups. Under the terms of this bargain, the working class co-operates in capitalist development in return for policies which ensure the maintenance of a high level of employment. Both routes to genuine full employment, it should be noted, involve a highly interventionist state. But in political terms, they are at opposite ends of the spectrum. Under the Japanese model the working class is politically marginalized and economically fragmented, whilst under social corporatism this class is a major political actor and uses its power to ensure a far more egalitarian distribution of welfare (wages, social services, and employment conditions).

It is clear that the institutional conditions for maintaining full employment in the context of world economic stagnation cannot be simply transplanted from one country to another. Nevertheless it would be interesting to investigate more fully the nature of 'social corporatism' and how it has developed in various countries, how this model has broken down in some countries (e.g. the Netherlands) and has been strengthened recently in others (e.g. Australia). It would also be useful to analyse the type of macroeconomic policies, both internal and external, which seem to facilitate full employment under social corporatism.

APPENDIX

This appendix explains the formulae linking the variables shown in Table 6.2. As officially measured, unemployment satisfies the following equation:

$$U = L - E, \tag{1}$$

where L is the labour force and E is employment. Dividing by L, we obtain the unemployment rate:

$$\frac{U}{L} = 1 - \frac{E}{L}. \tag{2}$$

Differentiating:

$$\frac{\mathrm{d}}{\mathrm{d}t}\left[\frac{U}{L}\right] = -\frac{\mathrm{d}}{\mathrm{d}t}\left[\frac{E}{L}\right]$$

$$= \frac{E}{L}\left[\frac{1}{L}\cdot\frac{\mathrm{d}L}{\mathrm{d}t} - \frac{1}{E}\frac{\mathrm{d}L}{\mathrm{d}t}\right]$$

$$= \frac{E}{L}\left[g_L - g_E\right], \tag{3}$$

where the g's are logarithmic growth rates. Thus, the unemployment rate increases when the labour force grows more rapidly than employment, and falls when the opposite is the case.

The participation rate is defined as follows:

$$P = \frac{L}{N}, \tag{4}$$

where N is the underlying population, which following the OECD convention, we shall take as all persons aged 15–64. Thus:

$$L = PN \tag{5}$$

and

$$g_L = g_P + g_N. \tag{6}$$

Substituting in (3), we obtain the following approximate expression for changes in the unemployment rate:

$$\frac{d}{dt}\left[\frac{U}{L}\right] = \frac{E}{L}\left[g_N + g_P - g_E\right]. \tag{7}$$

This equation shows how the measured unemployment rate is affected by variations in population, labour-force participation, and employment.

NOTES

1. Hereafter 'OECD' refers to the sample of 19 countries (representing 93% of OECD employment in 1985) analysed in Section II below (see n 4).
2. For a good general discussion of female unemployment in the OECD countries see Paukert (1984).
3. The explanation for this is as follows. At one time there was a vast amount of hidden unemployment among married women. Millions of married women without jobs were excluded from official statistics on unemployment, even though they were potentially available for paid work. The extent of such hidden unemployment has declined for two reasons. First, most countries have witnessed a massive increase in employment opportunities for married women over the past 10 or 15 years. As a result, the true level of unemployment among such women has almost certainly fallen. Second, unemployment insurance schemes have become more comprehensive in their coverage of women so that a woman without employment is nowadays more likely to be officially classified as unemployed than used to be the case.
4. Of the 24 countries for which OECD assembles comprehensive labour force data, we have excluded Iceland and Luxembourg because they are so small, having a population of well under half a million. Greece and Turkey are excluded because of their highly agrarian employment structure (agriculture accounted for 29% and 57% respectively of total employment in these two countries in 1985). Portugal is excluded because reliable intertemporal comparisons are made impossible by the severe disruptions caused by the 1974 revolution (it was also the only other country with over 20% of employment in agriculture).
5. In this section we use the official definitions of unemployment used by each country to calculate unemployment rates as a percentage of the civilian labour force. The OECD's standardized series for unemployment are not available for

Appendix 6.A1. Decomposition of unemployment changes: non-agriculture 1973–1985 (% p.a. growth rate)

	U	LF	Emp.	Resid.	Pop.	Particip.
1973–85 Non-agricultural sector						
Japan	0.12	1.39	1.27	0.00	1.16	0.23
Canada	0.43	2.75	2.27	−0.05	1.81	0.92
US	0.19	2.25	2.04	−0.02	1.46	0.78
Australia	0.52	1.89	1.33	−0.04	1.77	0.12
New Zealand	0.37	1.66	1.28	−0.01	1.48	0.17
Austria	0.28	0.77	0.48	−0.01	0.98	−0.21
Belgium	0.84	0.70	−0.22	−0.07	0.66	0.04
Denmark	0.57	1.33	0.72	−0.03	0.62	0.70
Finland	0.24	1.33	1.07	−0.01	0.91	0.41
France	0.68	1.08	0.35	−0.06	1.19	−0.10
Germany	0.65	0.38	−0.30	−0.03	0.80	−0.41
Ireland	1.08	2.11	0.84	−0.19	2.06	0.06
Italy	0.30	1.68	1.34	−0.04	1.20	0.47
Netherlands	0.93	1.82	0.79	−0.10	1.37	0.44
Norway	0.08	2.13	2.05	0.00	0.82	1.29
Sweden	0.03	1.09	1.06	0.00	0.32	0.77
Switzerland	0.08	−0.11	−0.19	0.00	0.61	−0.71
UK	0.81	0.69	−0.18	−0.06	0.51	0.18
Spain	1.85	1.47	−0.71	−0.33	1.79	−0.31
1973–85 less 1960–73 Non-agricultural sector						
Japan	0.19	−1.55	−1.74	−0.01	−1.77	0.22
Canada	0.54	−0.61	−1.21	−0.06	−0.75	0.14
US	0.27	−0.03	−0.32	−0.02	−0.44	0.40
Australia	0.45	−1.15	−1.64	−0.04	−0.71	−0.43
New Zealand	0.35	−0.83	−1.20	−0.01	−0.66	−0.17
Austria	0.43	0.00	−0.45	−0.01	0.25	−0.24
Belgium	0.93	−0.43	−1.44	−0.08	0.11	−0.54
Denmark	0.68	−0.69	−1.41	−0.04	−0.56	−0.13
Finland	0.20	−0.91	−1.12	−0.01	−1.60	0.68
France	0.56	−0.99	−1.60	−0.05	−0.54	−0.44
Germany	0.65	−0.32	−1.00	−0.03	0.04	−0.36
Ireland	1.18	0.67	−0.71	−0.20	0.65	0.03
Italy	0.33	0.72	0.35	−0.04	−0.29	0.99
Netherlands	0.80	0.46	−0.43	−0.09	−0.32	0.77
Norway	0.06	−0.16	−0.23	0.00	−0.35	0.20
Sweden	−0.02	−0.29	−0.26	0.00	−0.72	0.44
Switzerland	0.08	−2.17	−2.25	0.00	−1.05	−1.11
UK	0.74	0.15	−0.65	−0.06	0.17	−0.01
Spain	1.88	−0.94	−3.16	−0.34	0.16	−1.08

Notes and *Sources:* as for Table 6.6.

Appendix 6.A2. Decomposition of unemployment changes 1973–1985: women (% p.a. growth rate)

	U	LF	Emp.	Resid.	Pop.	Particip.
Women 1973–85						
Japan	0.12	1.22	1.09	0.00	0.74	0.47
Canada	0.34	4.15	3.77	−0.05	1.77	2.34
US	0.12	3.24	3.11	−0.01	1.37	1.85
Australia	0.45	2.89	2.40	−0.04	1.73	1.15
New Zealand	0.60	3.15	2.51	−0.04	1.50	1.63
Austria	0.17	0.36	0.19	0.00	0.57	−0.21
Belgium	1.10	1.99	0.75	−0.14	0.56	1.43
Denmark	0.59	1.49	0.86	−0.04	0.41	1.08
Finland	0.19	1.59	1.39	−0.01	0.37	1.21
France	0.69	1.79	1.02	−0.08	0.99	0.80
Germany	0.69	0.60	−0.13	−0.04	0.46	0.14
Ireland	0.82	2.11	1.19	−0.09	1.49	0.61
Italy	0.40	2.38	1.90	−0.07	0.78	1.58
Netherlands	0.87	4.23	3.26	−0.10	1.28	2.91
Norway	0.05	3.14	3.08	0.00	0.58	2.54
Sweden	0.01	2.07	2.06	0.00	0.20	1.87
Switzerland	0.09	0.43	0.34	0.00	0.57	−0.13
UK	0.66	1.46	0.76	−0.04	0.42	−1.04
Spain	1.92	1.35	−0.91	−0.33	1.05	0.30
Women 1973–85 less 1960–73						
Japan	0.16	0.39	0.22	0.00	−0.91	1.28
Canada	0.27	−1.18	−1.49	−0.04	−0.56	−0.59
US	0.11	0.09	−0.03	−0.01	−0.36	0.44
Australia	0.45	−2.12	−2.60	−0.04	−0.61	−1.47
New Zealand	0.58	−0.51	−1.13	−0.04	−0.55	0.04
Austria	0.29	0.58	0.29	−0.01	0.74	−0.16
Belgium	1.03	0.51	−0.66	−0.14	0.26	0.25
Denmark	0.61	−2.32	−2.96	−0.04	−0.18	−2.12
Finland	0.10	1.43	1.31	−0.01	−0.45	1.87
France	0.49	0.26	−0.30	−0.07	0.02	0.23
Germany	0.66	0.49	−0.21	−0.04	0.39	0.10
Ireland	0.81	1.79	0.89	−0.09	0.97	0.81
Italy	0.09	3.11	2.97	−0.05	0.28	2.81
Netherlands	0.77	2.02	1.15	−0.10	−0.06	2.06
Norway	−0.10	−0.16	−0.05	0.00	−0.04	−0.11
Sweden	0.00	−0.11	−0.10	0.00	−0.25	0.14
Switzerland	0.09	−0.96	−1.05	0.00	−0.37	−0.58
UK	0.68	0.25	−0.48	−0.04	0.27	−0.03
Spain	1.84	−0.88	−3.05	−0.33	0.33	−1.20

Notes and Sources: as for Table 6.6.

Table 6.A3. Decomposition of unemployment changes: men 1973–1985

	U	LF	Emp.	Resid.	Pop.	Particip.
Men 1973–85						
Japan	0.11	0.77	0.66	0.00	0.98	−0.21
Canada	0.45	1.64	1.14	−0.04	1.73	−0.09
US	0.24	1.38	1.13	−0.02	1.46	−0.07
Australia	0.51	1.12	0.58	−0.03	1.63	−0.51
New Zealand	0.17	0.85	0.68	0.00	1.44	−0.58
Austria	0.33	0.44	0.10	−0.01	0.89	−0.44
Belgium	0.62	−0.23	−0.89	−0.03	0.64	−0.87
Denmark	0.50	0.66	0.15	−0.02	0.47	0.20
Finland	0.26	0.07	−0.20	−0.01	0.70	−0.62
France	0.58	−0.03	−0.63	−0.02	0.88	−0.90
Germany	0.57	−0.06	−0.65	−0.02	0.86	−0.91
Ireland	1.11	0.74	−0.54	−0.17	1.42	−0.67
Italy	0.22	0.30	0.13	0.04	0.85	−0.54
Netherlands	0.91	0.62	−0.38	−0.08	1.35	−0.72
Norway	0.09	0.80	0.70	0.00	0.67	0.13
Sweden	0.04	−0.02	−0.07	0.00	0.20	−0.23
Switzerland	0.07	−0.54	−0.61	0.00	0.44	−0.98
UK	0.88	0.12	−0.84	−0.08	0.53	−0.40
Spain	1.49	0.06	−1.62	−0.19	1.28	−1.20
Men 1973–85 less 1960–73						
Japan	0.13	−0.81	−0.95	0.00	−0.79	−0.02
Canada	0.59	−0.10	−0.74	−0.06	−0.47	0.36
US	0.33	0.12	−0.23	−0.02	−0.21	0.32
Australia	0.43	−0.66	−1.12	−0.03	−0.62	−0.04
New Zealand	0.16	−0.77	−0.93	0.00	−0.48	−0.29
Austria	0.43	0.62	0.18	−0.01	0.56	0.07
Belgium	0.77	−0.62	−1.43	−0.04	0.25	−0.87
Denmark	0.61	0.91	0.27	−0.02	−0.41	1.30
Finland	0.22	−0.41	−0.64	−0.01	−0.45	0.04
France	0.52	−0.74	−1.28	−0.02	−0.29	−0.44
Germany	0.58	−0.21	−0.80	−0.02	0.18	−0.38
Ireland	1.11	0.74	−0.54	−0.17	0.87	−0.12
Italy	0.26	0.60	0.38	0.04	0.25	0.35
Netherlands	0.78	−0.02	−0.88	−0.08	−0.27	0.24
Norway	0.13	0.39	0.26	0.00	−0.08	0.47
Sweden	−0.03	0.24	0.27	0.00	−0.38	0.62
Switzerland	0.07	−2.03	−2.10	0.00	−1.08	−0.94
UK	0.77	0.17	−0.67	−0.08	0.19	−0.02
Spain	1.50	−0.29	−1.98	−0.19	0.32	−0.61

Notes and *Sources:* as for Table 6.6.

Table 6.A4. Unemployment regressions

	Period	Indep. variable	Const.	Coeff.	t-value	R̄ squared
1	1973–85	Pop.	0.280	0.235	1.2	0.020
2	1973–85	D % p.a. Pop.	0.556	0.432	2.9	0.297
3	1973–85	D % p.a. Non-ag. pop.	0.719	0.433	3.0	0.316
4	1973–85	Part. rate	0.419	−0.583	2.1	0.162
5	1973–85	Fem. U on Partic. Rate	0.634	−0.094	0.7	−0.027
6	1973–85	Male U on Partic. Rate	0.246	−0.472	2.2	0.182
7	1973–85	D% p.a. Lab. force	0.490	0.030	0.2	−0.056
8	1973–85	Civil Employment	0.639	−0.233	3.3	0.352
9	1973–9	"	0.497	−0.146	2.3	0.192
10	1979–85	"	0.767	−0.491	4.9	0.564
11	1973–85	D % p.a. Civ. emp.	0.396	−0.247	2.7	0.263
12	1973–9	"	0.339	−0.172	2.6	0.248
13	1979–85	"	0.330	−0.398	2.8	0.268
14	1973–85	Industrial Employment	0.254	−0.244	3.5	0.382
15	1973–9	"	0.353	−0.077	1.3	0.036
16	1979–85	"	0.094	−0.354	5.9	0.648
17	1973–85	D % p.a. Ind. emp.	−0.080	−0.274	4.2	0.472
18	1973–9	"	0.259	−0.082	1.3	0.036
19	1979–85	"	−0.361	−0.378	7.3	0.740
20	1973–85	" " " " (ex. Switz.)	−0.101	−0.301	5.2	0.602
21	1973–9	" " " " "	0.187	−0.151	2.5	0.241
22	1979–85	" " " " "	−0.345	−0.374	6.8	0.727
23	1973–85	Services Employment	1.068	−0.295	2.4	0.214
24	1973–9	"	0.837	−0.204	2.8	0.267
25	1979–85	"	1.227	−0.369	2.2	0.174
26	1973–85	D % p.a. Serv. emp.	0.478	−0.034	0.3	−0.052
27	1973–85	Male U on Ind. Emp.	0.275	−0.200	3.0	0.300
28	1973–9	" " " " "	0.296	−0.047	1.0	0.002
29	1979–85	" " " " "	0.130	−0.347	6.0	0.656
30	1973–85	Female U on Ind. Emp.	0.227	−0.297	3.8	0.425

Table 6.A4. (*cont.*)

Period	Indep. variable	Const.	Coeff.	t-value	R̄ squared
31 1973–9	Female U on Ind. Emp.	0.436	−0.127	1.5	0.071
32 1979–85	" " " "	0.061	−0.336	4.8	0.552
33 1973–85	Fem. U on Serv. emp.	1.240	−0.373	2.8	0.268
34 1973–85	Male U " "	0.985	−0.260	2.2	0.166
35 1973–85	Fem. Part. on Emp/Pop	0.787	0.688	7.8	0.749
36 1973–85	Male Part. on Emp/Pop	−0.067	0.447	5.8	0.645
37 1979–85	GDP	0.682	−0.083	0.8	−0.023
38 1973–85	D % p.a. GDP	0.285	−0.077	1.1	0.010
39 1973–9	" "	0.301	−0.039	0.8	−0.022
40 1979–85	" "	0.078	−0.171	1.9	0.121
41 1973–85	Investment	0.597	−0.147	1.9	0.133
42 1973–85	D % p.a. Investment	0.130	−0.065	2.0	0.152
43 1979–85	" " "	0.089	−0.095	3.0	0.308
44 1973–85	Productivity	0.166	0.195	2.1	0.154
45 1973–85	D % p.a. Productivity	0.536	0.017	0.2	−0.056
46 1973–85	Cons/head	0.695	−0.176	1.7	0.099
47 1973–9	"	0.412	−0.009	0.1	−0.058
48 1979–85	"	0.767	−0.376	4.3	0.490
49 1973–85	D % p.a. Cons/head	0.077	−0.158	2.6	0.243
50 1979–85	" "	−0.119	−0.216	3.5	0.394
51 1973–85	Industrial output	0.691	−0.098	1.4	0.058
52 1973–85	D % p.a. Ind. out.	0.192	−0.077	1.8	0.124
53 1979–85	" " "	−0.180	−0.175	3.0	0.316
54 1973–85	Product wages	0.295	0.129	1.3	0.041
55 1973–9	"	0.084	0.139	2.6	0.233
56 1979–85	"	0.610	−0.012	0.1	−0.058
57 1973–85	D % p.a. Product wages	0.436	−0.024	0.3	−0.054
58 1973–9	" " " "	0.681	0.152	2.1	0.162

Notes: Dependent variable is average annual change in total unemployment rate for 19 countries (% points), unless specified by, for example, 'Male U on'. Independent variables are measured as average annual % growth rate unless specified as D % p.a. which means change in annual growth rate between period specified and 1960–73. Pop. = population of working age; Non-ag. pop. = non-agricultural population of working age; Partic. rate = participation rate; Fem. U = female unemployment; Male U = male unemployment; Lab. force = labour force; Emp/Pop = ratio of employment to population of working age (employment rate); Investment = total gross fixed capital formation; Productivity = GDP per person employed; Cons/head

Table 6.A5. Unemployment and structural change

	Dep. var.	Const.	Pop.	Ind. emp.	Serv. emp.	$\bar{R}2$
[A1] 1973–85	Unemp.	0.018	0.428 (2.9)	−0.23 (3.8)	−0.112 (1.3)	0.726
[A2] 1973–85	Male U	0.039	0.412 (2.6)	−0.221 (3.6)	−0.076 (0.8)	0.674
[A3] 1973–85	Female U	−0.033	0.477 (2.6)	−0.249 (3.4)	−0.190 (1.9)	0.689
[A4] 1973–9	Unemp.	0.298	0.420 (5.3)	−0.05 (1.5)	−0.301 (7.0)	0.822
[A5] 1979–85	Unemp.	−0.241	0.258 (1.6)	−0.349 (6.3)	0.032 (0.3)	0.762

Notes. Dependent variable is average annual change in unemployment rate (% points), total, or male, or female for 18 countries (Switzerland is excluded). Independent variables are measured as changes in average annual growth rates between period specified and 1960–73. Unemp. = total unemployment; Male U = male unemployment; Female U = female unemployment; Pop = population of working age; Ind. emp. = industrial employment; Serv. emp. = services employment; bracket figures ( ) are *t* values.

Tables 6.A6 Unemployment and economic performance

	Const.	Pop	GDP	PW	$\bar{R}^2$
[B1] 1973–85	0.305	0.541	−0.157	0.074	0.353
		(3.3)	(2.2)	(1.0)	
[B2] 1973–9	0.468	0.286	−0.137	0.198	0.390
		(2.1)	(2.8)	(3.0)	
[B3] 1979–85	0.199	0.483	−0.165	0.022	0.356
		(2.0)	(1.4)	(0.2)	

Notes: Dependent variable is average annual change in unemployment rate (% points) for 19 countries. Independent variables are measured as changes in average annual growth rates between period specified and 1960–73. Pop=population of working age; PW=product wages; bracketed figures are *t* values.

all our 19 countries. The correlation between the national and standardized rates of unemployment, and between changes in the two measures, is very high (0.99 for changes in the rate between 1973 and 1983).

6. For women, participation rates rose everywhere except Switzerland and Austria, and by more than one-third in Norway and Netherlands. Male participation rates fell everywhere except Norway and Denmark, and by 10% or more in a nudmber of European countries.

7. The R^2 between changes in employment rates and changes in unemployment rates between 1973 and 1985 is 0.69 (0.36 for women and 0.78 for men).

8. Non-agricultural population is estimated as total population (aged 15–64 years) less agricultural employment. This crude method of estimation assumes that participation and employment rates amongst the agricultural population are 100%. For most countries (including Spain and Italy) there are far less women officially recorded as employed in agriculture than men, whereas in a few countries (Germany and Japan) the recorded numbers of men and women are practically the same. In the former countries female participation in agriculture is probably underestimated. One simple method for correcting this defect is to assume that the true number of men and women employed in agriculture is the same. Under this assumption, total employment in agriculture can then be estimated simply by doubling the official figure for male employment in agriculture. The effect of such a correction is, of course, to alter our estimates of non-agricultural population and its growth rate. For example, in the case of Spain, the growth rate of non-agricultural population over the period 1973–85 is raised from 1.8% a year to 2.2% a year; for Italy the corresponding figures are 1.2% and 1.4%.

9. Except for 1973–9, the absolute growth rate of employment is more closely correlated with unemployment changes than is the *change* in employment growth as compared to 1960–73 (Equations 22–4). This is a little surprising since it might be anticipated that deteriorations in the rate of growth of jobs, rather than slow growth in employment, would be more closely related to unemployment.

10. This picture is confirmed when changes in unemployment rates for men and

women are further regressed separately on industrial employment growth of men and women. (Data are only available for 13 out of the 19 countries and for the period after 1973.)

11. Not surprisingly there is no relationship between unemployment and the growth of individual components of demand such as exports or government spending.

12. We noted in Section I that most of the reduction in output for OECD as a whole had been reflected in lower productivity rather than slower employment growth. It is interesting that this 'beneficial' effect of productivity slow-down on unemployment is also reflected on a cross-sectional basis and over a substantial time period.

13. This is usually explained in neoclassical terms of declining marginal productivity. It is important to note that the NAIRU approach (Rowthorn 1977; Layard and Nickell 1986) does not necessarily include such a relationship since real wages are determined by companies' mark-up on costs which may be insensitive to the cycle. In this approach a deterioration of the terms of trade or a productivity slow-down would result in a higher level of unemployment if wage bargainers could not be induced to accept lower real wages (or smaller increases).

14. The degree of explanation may appear to be very low in comparison with the results of unemployment equations estimated by Bruno (1986) and McCallum (1986). It should be noted, however, that their results are for pooled time series and cross-section data and it may very well be that a disproportionate amount of the variance being explained is in fact of a time-series nature. The pattern of unemployment change over time within countries may be well explained by variables with little or no explanatory power in explaining unemployment differences between countries (budget balances or world trade performance, for example). Where the focus of interest is on inter-country differences it seems preferable to estimate simple cross-section equations of the type used in this chapter. It may also be noted that McCallum uses in his explanatory variables 'Okun coefficients' which measure the response within a country of unemployment to output changes. Since the diversity of such responses is amongst the main features to be explained, it is an unfortunate procedure and makes the R^2 quite misleading as an indicate of what is really being explained.

15. The relation of our analysis to the NAIRU approach is discussed in Glyn and Rowthorn (1988).

16. Two other countries with fairly low unemployment are New Zealand and Finland, with a rate of approximately 5% in the mid 1980s. Finland is a borderline case. The country was hit hard by the world recession in the mid 1970s and unemployment rose noticeably, but in more recent years its performance has been outstanding. Indeed, Finland is the only OECD country where the unemployment rate actually fell over the period 1979–85. However, an unemployment rate of 5% is too high to justify inclusion in our list of star performers. The same observation applies to New Zealand. Although its unemployment rate of 5% is still moderate by international standards, it represents a marked deterioration as compared to the early 1970s when measured unemployment was virtually zero.

17. The term 'Eurosclerosis' has been popularized by Giersch (1985) who criticizes

European countries for the supposed slowness in adapting their productive structures in line with new economic realities. On a purely descriptive level there is something in this criticism. However, for what seem to be largely ideological reasons, Giersch ascribes this slowness to market 'imperfections', and his remedy is extensive deregulation and free rein for market forces. The experience of Switzerland suggests that the analysis of Giersch is, to say the least, simplistic. Indeed, some of the most successful economic restructuring in recent years has occurred in corporatist economies, such as Finland and Sweden, where state intervention and labour market 'imperfections', in the sense of Giersch, are legion.

18. The timing of this fall was different for males and females; the figure for males refers to 1974–8, that for females to 1973–5.
19. Note that we are ignoring hidden unemployment in the agricultural sector and elsewhere.
20. On this point see ch. 7 below.
21. Our discussion of Norway draws heavily on the following works: Flanagan *et al.* (1983), Gustavsen and Hunnius (1981), OECD (1982*a*), and Olsen (1983).
22. There is now an immense and confusing literature on corporatism. For a useful survey of the theoretical aspects of this topic see Williamson (1985). Amongst the writings on corporatism which have most influenced us are Bruno and Sachs (1985), Cameron (1984), and Stephens (1979). As this chapter was being revised we came across an interesting article by Schmidt (1987), whose approach is very similar to our own. Therborn (1986) also has a similar approach, although for reasons which are not entirely clear he is dismissive of corporatism as a useful theory.
23. For a discussion of the so-called Swedish model see Korpi (1978), Lundberg (1985), and Morgan (1986).
24. For a description of the stresses in this relationship see Lash (1985) and Peterson (1987).
25. For the case of Denmark see Flanagan *et al.* (1983).

7

A New Paradigm of Work Organization and Co-ordination? Lessons from Japanese Experience

MASAHIKO AOKI

I. INTRODUCTION

In Chapter 2 we have seen that Japan exhibited superior performance in the period of the golden age as well as in the aftermath of the first oil shock in terms of growth, the rate of unemployment, the inflation rate, etc. Now it is clear that Japan's good record has extended well into the mid 1980s. At that time Japan's share in the gross global product exceeded 10 per cent. As of 1986 Japan's net foreign assets were the largest ever achieved. Japan, once regarded as a shrewd technological follower, seems to be gathering her industrial strength effectively to become a formidable technological leader in a number of global markets. The presence of Japanese companies is visible all over the world, meeting ambivalent reactions as both unwelcome invaders in the market and as creators of jobs.

What is the key to the continued developmental capability of the Japanese economy and its flexible adaptability to changing environments? Is there any specific Japanese way of running the economy at all? If so, is it culturally unique, or can it be emulated in the Western context? Alternatively, does the Japanese economy have to adapt its economic structure more in conformity with the Western norm in order to cure the international imbalance and crisis caused by its persistent trade surplus? Social scientists' views on these questions are diverse and inconclusive.

Within the scope of this chapter, all these problems cannot be dealt with in a satisfactory manner. Therefore I shall focus on an aspect of Japanese competitive strength: the efficient and flexible work organization and co-ordination in manufacturing industry. In Sections II and III, I discuss the nature and performance characteristics of Japanese work organization and co-ordination structure in comparison with the conventional Western model of hierarchy. The Japanese model relies very heavily upon the information-processing capacity of the worker and this makes the body of employees a viable and indispensable element of the firm. Section III discusses its implications for micro-behaviour of the firm and suggests some macro-economic implications as well. Normally as the bargaining power of employees is strengthened, the firm tends to restrain the growth of employment creating a distinction between 'insiders' and outsiders'. This version of the classic insider vs. outsider problem I call the 'dilemma of industrial democracy'. Section IV discusses how this dilemma is dealt with in the Japanese economy without mass unemployment. Section V concludes with a brief discussion of whether the Japanese model is unique to Japanese culture and whether there is anything to be learnt and emulated in the Western context.[1]

II. THE TRADITIONAL PARADIGM OF HIERARCHY

In order to make a comparative assessment of the Western and Japanese work organizations and intra-firm co-ordination mechanisms from the decision-making perspective, let us first distinguish *strategic* decision-making and *operational* decision-making. The former is concerned with those decisions of the firm (corporate organization) which structure the basic framework of its operations. Decisions regarding investments in new equipment and buildings, the direction of research and development, diversification, acquisition and divestiture, etc. fall into this category. Given these strategic decisions, the firm needs to adapt its operating tasks to evolving technical and human problems (the malfunction of machines, defective products, absenteeism of workers, etc.) and changing market circumstances. Such adaptation involves the assignment of specific tasks to each member of the work organization, operational co-ordination among functional work units (such as teams, shops, etc.), piecemeal improvements in the work process, and so on. I will subsume this type of decision-making under the heading of operational decision-making. In this and the following sections, I assume strategic decision-making as given and focus attention on the operating and adaptive attributes of highly stylized 'Western' and 'Japanese' firms. In Section IV, I will consider the interactions between relations between the operating and strategic attributes of the two.

The stylized nature of operational co-ordination in the Western unionized firm may be captured by a simple traditional model of hierarchy characterized by the following three basic attributes: (i) every constituent unit is crystallized around a well-defined *specialized* function; (ii) each constituent unit has one and only one immediate superordinate to which it reports and co-ordination between any two (or more than two) constituent units is performed by the lowest superordinate common to them; and (iii) there is only one unit (the central office) which is superordinate to every other unit. In particular, the manufacturing department may be conceived as being composed of several operating units, which I will call the shop for simplicity's sake. The shop is further comprised of a group of workers, each of whom is assigned to a specific job according to an articulated job classification scheme as stipulated in the collective agreement with the union (assuming that the shop is unionized). Within the limit set forth in the collective agreement, the foreman of a shop has a discretionary power to specify concrete operating tasks for each job and direct co-ordination among different jobs in response to *local shocks*, or unusual events within the shop, such as work stoppage due to machine malfunction, absenteeism, an unusual increase in defective outputs, etc. There is a clear demarcation between operating jobs and jobs dealing with such local problems. The latter are performed by specialists such as repairmen, reliefmen, product inspectors, and the like. The remuneration to workers on the shop-floor is made in accordance with job titles.

For simplicity's sake, let us imagine that the adjustment of output levels of various final outputs in response to *system shocks* (e.g. changing market demands or supply shocks)—as well as accommodating adjustments in the flow of intermediate products, materials, parts, etc. between shops and the amounts of buffer inventories to be held at each shop—are directed from the centralized office of production planning (possibly through an intermediate administrative office).

O. E. Williamson has advanced a most comprehensive argument in defence of hierarchy on the grounds of efficiency (Williamson 1985, ch. 19). According to him, the hierarchical organization of work and co-ordination saves transaction costs for the following reasons:

1. *Saving of transaction costs:* Hierarchy economizes on buffer inventories and expenses involved in inter-shop transportation through

centralized planning and co-ordination of material requirements.

2. *Economies of specialization:* The talents of employees are most effectively utilized by the specialized assignment of different operating tasks as well as the separation between managerial and operating tasks.

3. *Economies of centralized handling of shocks:* Hierarchies have the best responsiveness to system shocks because of the centralization of market and other environmental information and decision-making. Also the capacity to recognize and implement system innovations is high because of specialized contributions of engineers.

However, he admits that hierarchy may have a certain negative incentive attribute:

4. *Lack of responsiveness to local shocks:* Employees working under hierarchies may not be motivated to work intensively because the link between reward and effort is not direct (the payment to employees is normally made according to job titles). They may be also less responsive to local shocks because they are not authorized to deal with them under the job classification scheme.

But this disadvantage (4) may be outweighed by gains from the specialization of jobs and the centralization (hierarchical ordering) of decision-making listed under (1)–(3) above. Opposing a radical view (e.g. Marglin 1974) that hierarchies emerged in the capitalist economy not because of their efficiency, but out of capitalists' desire to control work processes, Williamson concludes: 'Hostility to hierarchy thus lacks a comparative institutional foundation' (Williamson 1985, p. 231).

His comparative analysis may appear reasonable at first sight. However, alternatives in his analysis are primitive production organizations, such as the putting-out system and inside contracting, historically preceding and replaced by hierarchical systems. The alternative to a hierarchical system is an idealized utopian system, such as communes, in which workers rotate among various jobs on the basis of common ownership of capital. Such utopian organization have never grown beyond minuscule size. Implicit in his comparative analysis seems to be the assumption of market and technological environments in which economies of scale loom large. Suppose that production is for mass markets in which relatively standardized commodities are demanded by numerous anonymous consumers. In order to exploit economies of scale, the production process may be subdivided into a multiplicity of tasks, each of which may be performed with the aid of special-purpose machines (the attribute (2) is relevant here). Also demands in these markets are more or less predictable thanks to the law of large numbers, and adaptation to changing market circumstances may be adequately made by regularly revised centralized production planning. Interim adaptation may be achieved through the adjustment of buffer inventories without overall production rescheduling (the attributes (1) and (3) are relevant here).

However, if economies of scale are not so important and if flexible and quick adaptation to local and systematic shocks becomes imperative for competitive efficiency, the efficiency of hierarchical decision-making and co-ordination may become problematical. This point may be illustrated by an example. Modern car assembly-lines, specifically designed for the production of a particular model, are increasingly turning out literally tens of thousands of varieties of cars, distinguished by different combinations of engine and transmission, colour, body type, optional extras, etc. This kind of intensive product diversification is becoming an important feature of modern factories producing goods ranging from consumer products, such as automotive and home-entertainment electronics, to steel products. Through intensifying global competition among producers from different countries national markets are becoming more integrated into a single global market, and in order to capture a larger market share each producer is forced to treat these markets more like 'fashion markets', where product life-cycles are short, shifting demand from one type of product to another is volatile, the batch of production is small, and therefore the shortening of lead time from order to delivery becomes imperative. The apparent result of this trend is that economies of scale, so effective in mass production, are losing ground. It also seems to cast doubt on economies available from the hierarchical integration of specialized jobs for the following reasons.

1. As product diversification within a single manufacturing department is intensified, the number of parts, materials, and half products to be integrated may soar, causing production co-ordination through buffer inventories to become very costly (high inventory costs).
2. In adapting work organization to meet diverse and volatile market demand quickly and flexibly, rigid specialization based on an

articulated job classification scheme may not be conducive to the efficient utilization of the work-force. It may become necessary to assign diverse tasks to workers in response to evolving circumstances. It may also become necessary to deal with local shocks (such as the malfunction of machines and absenteeism) quickly without calling in specialized help (such as engineers, servicemen, or reliefmen) from outside the shop. But doing so will require workers with more versatile skills (the rigidity of specialization).

3. The centralization of information and decision-making may be subject to noise disturbance in the process of communication and time-lag from the perception of shocks to the implementation of operational response. (Information concerning volatile market conditions is first screened by the marketing department, and then transmitted to and transformed into a production plan by the centralized office of planning. The production plan is then communicated to each constituent unit.) Also, if intermediate product flow is controlled centrally, valuable on-the-spot information available at interfaces of constituent units, such as on the quality of intermediate products and emergent events affecting timing of delivery, etc. may remain unutilized (communication costs in the hierarchy).

4. The negative incentive attribute of hierarchy referred to may be aggravated in the increasing needs of flexible adaptation. The cooperative participation in problem-identification and problem-solving by workers may be motivated only if they participate in the sharing of rewards as well (the lack of incentive to respond to local shocks).

Thus hierarchical decision-making and co-ordination based on the separation of control and specialized tasks may no longer have the efficient characteristics attributed to them by Williamson in the emerging market conditions. But are there any alternative modes of work organization and co-ordination mechanism which can respond to increasingly volatile market conditions and complex technological conditions more effectively?

III. A NEW PARADIGM? THE JAPANESE MODEL

The Japanese firm has a legal corporate structure and a formal internal organization similar to that of a Western firm. However, the operating and adaptive decision-making structure is somewhat different from the stylized model of the Western system as described in Section II. Let us illustrate this point by describing the essential characteristics of the well-known 'kanban' system which is used to adapt the production process to changing market demand at Japanese automobile manufacturers.

The structure of the automobile production process may be compared with that of a river. The final assembly line is analogous to the mouth of a river through which the stream of final output runs to the ocean of the 'market'. If one goes upstream, the river (production process) divides itself into many streams (parts of the production process), each of which is in turn formed by still smaller brooks. Let us imagine that flow-controlling stations (shops) are set up at every point of confluence. One way of controlling the flow of streams at the mouth of the river is to set up a central office which monitors the difference between the desired and actual levels of the final flow and, depending on the difference, dispatches periodic instructions with regard to water control to each station. Meanwhile the need for the fine tuning of water control at each station to respond to unexpected local emergencies may be dealt with by means of reservoirs (inventories), the levels of which are adjusted as required.

Needless to say, controlling the production flow of automobiles is much more complicated than controlling the regular flow of water, as the former involves the production of a thousand varieties of final outputs distinguished by specific combinations of thousands of parts. But the crude analogy of water control along the river suffices for our immediate purpose. It is to be noted, however, that in the centralized control system, production of final outputs is made according to the centralized plan and that the demand and supply of each variety within a certain planning period may be matched by the use of the price mechanism (i.e. by the use of devices such as rebates, discounts, and undesired options).

The essence of the 'kanban' system may be characterized as one in which all the communications needed for the control of water-flow emanate from the station at the mouth of the river and flow in exactly the reverse direction (upstream) to the water-flow throughout the entire system. More concretely, it runs as follows: a tentative production schedule may be worked out by the central planning office at regular intervals, say once every two weeks, just as in the hierarchical system. But this centralized schedule only provides for each shop a general guide-line of production for that period. Information regarding actual demand for types of car monitored by the marketing department is utilized to fine-tune the production schedule in a shorter period and this schedule is directly fed into the final assembly line a few days before actual production takes place. In implementing the production schedule, the final assembly-line dispatches a 'kanban' (an order form placed in a vinyl envelope) to each shop located at an immediately upstream location specifying the amount and timing of delivery of each type of part or in-process goods (as engine, transmission, body, etc.) to be supplied. A 'kanban' is dispatched normally a few times a day to each upstream shop and is returned to the final assembly-line together with the parts specified. Thus the 'kanban' plays the dual role of order form and delivery notice. The shop which receives a 'kanban' from the final assembly-line, in turn dispatches its own 'kanban' to each shop located at an immediate upstream position at a similar interval, and the chain of this bilateral order–delivery link between immediately neighbouring shops, intermediated by the circular flow of 'kanban', extends as far as outside suppliers who have long-term relations with the final assembly manufacturer.

This 'kanban' system appears to be rather a crude information system, but it turns out to be effective in reducing the amount of inventory when the assembly of a multitude of parts is involved in producing final outputs. The upstream shops are supposed to adapt their production according to the order of downstream shops specified in the 'kanban' and not to respond by the adjustment of inventories. In fact, the 'kanban' system is also called a 'zero inventory' method or 'just-in-time' method to capture this attribute. In contrast to the vertical hierarchical control, let us conceptualize the essential feature of the 'kanban' system as 'semi-horizontal operational co-ordination', where 'semi' refers to the fact that preliminary centralized planning needs to proceed in providing a general framework for horizontal informational flow. We assert that: *Semi-horizontal operational co-ordination is effective in reducing the amount of inventories, when the production process involves the flow of a multitude of intermediate goods.*

As already stated, the essence of the semi-horizontal operational co-ordination is to feed information concerning the changing market demands directly to the production system and distribute it throughout constituent bodies, as required, without the mediation of the centralized office. In this way, the entire production system may be able to respond to diverse market demands quickly and precisely.

When a multitude of intermediate products (parts) are involved, this adaptation of the production system may require a considerable degree of flexibility and speed on the part of each constituent shop in adjusting the amount, kinds, and timing of production of its in-process products. Also the 'zero-inventory' requirement necessitates the effective control of local emergencies, such as the malfunction of machines, absenteeism of workers, quality defects, and so on in order to minimize their effects on the smooth operation of semi-horizontal co-ordination.

Another important element of the Japanese system which meets these needs is the work organization in which job demarcation is ambiguous and fluid. The widely prevailing shop-floor practice at Japanese factories is the regular rotation of workers. The team of workers led by the subforeman is assigned to a cluster of interconnected jobs on the shop-floor and they rotate jobs among themselves in an egalitarian way. The size of the team and the frequency of rotation normally depends on the nature of the work involved as well as the shop convention. In typical cases the size may range from 7 to 15 workers and the rotation may be made as frequently as every few hours. Even the most inexperienced workers may be assigned a very difficult job, in which case the most experienced workers assist by working side by side with them.

This rotation scheme seems to sacrifice economies of specialization, but such possible short-term inefficiency may be compensated in the following ways. First, through rotation, workers become skilled in a relatively wider range of jobs. The multi-functionality of workers may enable each shop to adapt its work organization flexibly to the requirements of the changing composition and urgency of its products specified in the 'kanban' sent in from the downstream shop. The assignment of a worker to a set of different kinds of machine— say lathe, drilling, and milling machines laid out in a linear sequence, instead of multiple machines of a single type arranged around the operator—can save time necessary for the transport and loading of in-process products, as well as the amont of in-shop inventories. Also multi-functional workers are more effective in operating multi-purpose machines which are beginning to take over single-purpose machines as the emphasis shifts from economies of scale to economies of timing in producing varieties of products. This follows Adam Smith's dictum: 'the extent of specialization is limited by the size of the market'. When demand from the downstream shop slackens, idle workers may be deployed in the maintenance of machines and the cleaning of the shop.

A more subtle, yet probably even more significant, reason for the dynamic efficiency of a rotational scheme is the one emphasized by Kazuo Koike (1984, pp. 44–75). According to him, the rotation scheme is effective in making workers familiar with the whole work process involved in the shop and this is not readily acquired when work organization is based on clear and unambiguous job demarcation. This familiarity or knowledge may be tacit and not readily transferable through formal language, but useful in identifying on-the-spot—and in solving semi-autonomously—local emergencies, such as breakdown of machines and product defects, and in improving on quality control. Those workers trained in a wide range of skills may be able to understand, for instance, why defective products have increased, and to devise and implement measures to deal with the situation, and prevent the recurrence of the problem without much, if any, help from 'outside' services. It is important for the smooth operation of semi-horizontal operational co-ordination that product defects should be spotted not at the final inspection station, but at the very place where the problem occurs and that remedial measures be taken immediately. Thus the semi-horizontal co-ordination mechanism crucially depends on the skills, judgement, and co-operation of a versatile and autonomous work-force on the shop-floor. Koike has called such a system an 'integrative system', in that operating tasks and tasks dealing with emergencies are integrated and not specialized.

Not only the job demarcation among workers on the shop-floor is flexible, the extent of workers' participation in local problem-solving and responses to local shocks may also entail a certain degree of blurring of job territoriality between workers on the one hand and foreman, engineers, programmers, etc., on the other. This blurring of function is also reflected in the status differentiation of employees within the firm. The foreman is regarded more as the leader of the work group, and the position often represents the most advanced career opportunity for blue-collar workers rather than the lowest end of the managerial hierarchy which exercises the control over workers. It is taken for granted that foremen belong to the same enterprise union as workers whom they they lead and their legitimacy is never questioned. Blue-collar workers are also paid by monthly salaries not by hourly wages, and fringe benefits available to blue- and white-collar employees are not qualitatively different.

To summarize: *the fluid job demarcation and the job rotation system on the shop level may sacrifice static efficiency available in the specialization scheme, but contributes to dynamic efficiency of semi-horizontal operational co-ordination by fostering collective learning by workers and encouraging semi-autonomous problem-solving and adaptation to local shocks by the versatility of workers on the shop-floor.*

Relative costs of sacrificing static inefficiency available in the specialization scheme *vis-à-vis* gains from dynamic efficiency obtained in the rotation scheme depend on various parameters, such as the speed of learning relative to the rate of obsolescence of technology instituted, the nature of stochastic elements, and interdependence of jobs involved in shop technology. In a recent paper I constructed a formal comparative model to analyse the relative efficiency of the two systems (see Aoki 1987). One of the interesting conclusions drawn from the analysis was that for the system relying on collective learning to be relatively efficient, learning alone is not sufficient, but the initial level of workers' knowledge about the nature of technology involved and their capacity to identify and solve local problems seems to be essential as well. In fact, Japanese firms have come to emphasize, along with the importance of learning-by-doing at the shop level, the importance of the formal education of workers in relevant engineering and technology, in a classroom environment at regular intervals during their work career Koike 1987).

An essential element of semi-horizontal operational co-ordination is the institutionalization of effective learning-by-doing. In Japan, this institutionalization is facilitated by 'seniority' and 'lifetime' employment aspects of the production system and the rules of coordination. Indeed, both seniority and tenure may be seen as incentives to foster learning-by-doing. Seniority means that the salary of a worker is determined not by his job (what his job is may not be clear), but by his grade relative to his number of years' service with the firm, as well as to the degree of his skills more or less generally conceived. There is no formal contractual agreement for life-time employment, but there is a general understanding between employer and employee that the employment relationship will continue up to the time of mandatory retirement unless an unexpected emergency on either side necessitates its termination. In fact employment turn-over is by no means negligible (particularly at early stages of working life) even in the Japanese labour market. But leaving a job in mid-career penalizes a worker financially, as the mandatory retirement carries a substantial lump-sum payment of *taishokukin* (retirement compensation).

The theory of human capital has made it clear that a rising age-profile of earnings is related to having workers bear some of the cost of on-the-job training at the early stage of an employee's working life and preserving acquired firm-specific skills by discouraging departure from a firm in mid-career. Also the recent development of contract theory suggests that rank-ordering of workers by the amount of learning acquired provides an incentive for a worker to maximize his learning potentiality throughout his working life.[2] Further the independence of the level of individual compensation from specific job category may facilitate, or at least not hinder, the acquisition of wide-ranging skills through the rotation scheme, while the seniority aspects of the compensation scheme may promote inter-generational transmission of skills through the teaching of junior workers by senior workers in the group.

As already indicated, semi-horizontal operational co-ordination is a way of adapting quickly to changing market circumstances without accumulating costly buffer inventories where many types of output involving a large number of parts are produced. On the other hand, it is observed that hierarchical control of the production system performs adequately, and there is relatively little to be gained from the point of view of operational efficiency by introducing semi-horizontal co-ordination, when the system produces a relatively small number of homogeneous outputs involving a relatively small number of parts at a relatively steady rate (see Abbeglen and Stalk 1986). Moreover, the reduction of buffer inventories may make the system vulnerable to 'large' or drastic change. The 'kanban' system connects not only shops within a factory, but also the prime manufacturer and many geographically dispersed suppliers. If the transportation of materials and parts from a supplier to the prime manufacturer is disrupted by a major shock, such as natural disaster, then the smooth operation of the whole system operated on minimal inventories may fail. Also the capacity of workers to deal with changes in the composition of products, as well as with local emergencies, may be specific to the global framework set out in the strategic decision-making of the firm. Such capacities may be effective in dealing with continual and incremental changes within that framework, but not with drastic changes in the market and other environmental factors. Therefore: *Semi-horizontal operational co-ordination may be effective in response to continual and incremental changes in the system environment, but not to drastic shocks in the system nor to a very stable environment.*

Finally let us turn to an incentive aspect of the Japanese system. My starting hypothesis is that a worker's life-time earnings involve an element of sharing of quasi-rents that are made possible through the efficient operation of semi-horizontal operational co-ordination. As is clear by now, the efficient operation of the entire co-ordination crucially depends on workers' collective capacity to identify and solve emergent local problems and, in the sense that such capacity can be only nurtured through collective learning on the shop-floor, it becomes truly firm-specific and therefore not individually market-able. But the workers as a collectivity may exercise effective bargain-ing power over the disposition of rents.

If workers have a reasonable ground to expect, from repeated bargaining with management, that a fair share in forthcoming rents is assured for them, it would be rational for them to make efforts to contribute to the maximization of those rents. In a situation where delay in response to system and local shocks makes it possible for competitors to snatch away potential rents, workers may be moti-vated to find an efficient solution to such shocks without delay and in co-operation with management. Putting aside discussion of a possible free-rider problem (shirking by workers at the expense of the efforts of others) and other related questions, we may summarize the above argument as follows: *Workers are likely to participate in the sharing of rents available from the efficient working of semi-horizontal operational co-ordination and thus be motivated to contribute to and be responsible for local problem-solving and quick responses to local as well as system shocks which would enhance the amount of rents.*

IV. THE SHARING SYSTEM

As we have seen, in the Japanese firm employees are given incentives to develop skills relevant to the effective working of semi-horizontal operational co-ordination through learning-by-doing over time. If their career development is suspended because of lay-offs, or dis-charges necessitated by the loss of competitiveness of the employ-ing firm, the cost would be great in terms of sacrifice of otherwise available future returns to learning in the form of seniority premiums and retirement compensation. On the other hand, if the firm keeps expanding, better career prospects are opened for its employees in the form of better chances for future promotion and the increased earnings accompanying such promotion. Thus the utility function of the representative worker includes not only the conventional variable of the current level of earnings but also such strategic variables as employment, growth rate of the firm, etc. If that is the case, it is not internally efficient from the viewpoint of the profit-earners (stockholder) and the employees that only workers' earnings are determined jointly by the two parties (possibly through collective bargaining) and that decisions on other strategic variables relevant to the well-being of employees are unilaterally made by management which strives to maximize profits, taking the wage as given. In this decision-making procedure, the outcome would always be off the contract curve, on which efficient bargaining should settle. Both the level of earnings, and those strategic variables need to be determined conjointly.

Suppose that both parties are 'time-impatient' in the sense that they are fully aware that potential rents may be lost if an efficient adjustment of the firm's strategic market variables *and* mutual co-operation in their implementation is delayed. Then both parties may be motivated to reach an agreement, implicit or explicit, both on strategic market decisions and distribution without delay. A recent contribution to game theory shows that if bargaining on these matters can take place in a 'time-efficient' manner (in the technical sense that the time-interval between proposals and counter-proposals becomes infinitesimally small), an outcome known as the 'Nash bargaining solution' is likely to emerge as the 'perfect equilibrium' in which neither party can expect to do better (Binmore *et al*. 1986). At this equilibrium, the percentage utility gain from marginal change in any variable (distributional or strategic) relative to the total utility gain from co-operation is equalized for both parties.

In an analysis of the Nash bargaining solution involving the strategic variables of the firm, I concluded that under a certain regularity condition, the shares which determine the distribution of rents between two parties may be fixed once and for all, independent of changing market conditions, reflecting their relative bargaining power *and* the equilibrium choice of strategic variables can be made, responding to changing market conditions, by weighting the optimal choices of this by their respective shares. One may call this the *dual parametric rule*.[3] In other words, the equilibrium policy of the firm would be the weighted average of the optimal policy of the stockholder-controlled firm (the profit-maximizing firm) and the worker-controlled firm *à la* Ward and Domar. According to this theory, if the Japanese firm chooses a lower lay-off rate than the one which the neoclassical paradigm of profit-maximization under the hourly wage system would predict, it is not because management can unilaterally reduce worker's compensation to expand the employment level, but because the worker's preference for job security and worksharing is duly reflected in managerial policy-making, possibly in exchange for a lower wage-level.

The equilibrium property of the dual parametric rule suggests that strategic managerial variables need not be subject to explicit bargaining as market conditions change once a proper share parameter is specified (as long as the relative bargaining power between stockholders and workers is stable). Adjustments in managerial policy may be delegated and entrusted to management, provided management follows the weighting rule in formulating and adjusting strategic managerial variables, in which case the principle of sharing in decision-making is not lost. I regard the role of management as that of a referee in a bargaining game (Aoki 1984*c*) rather than that of sole agent of the stockholders as in neoclassical theory, or the maximizer of its own utility as in managerialist theory.

There are two important macroeconomic implications of micro-behaviour derived from the dual parametric rule. The first concerns a comparison of behaviour between that derived from the dual parametric rule and that derived from the neoclassical rule of profit-maximization. The second concerns how the microeconomic behaviour of the firm changes when share parameters change to reflect the strengthening of the relative bargaining power of the workers.

First, suppose an equilibrium configuration of internal distribution and strategic decision-making, such as about lay-offs or the rate of expansion of the firm, derived by the application of the dual parametric rule. Then fix only the internal distribution at the equilibrium value and make managerial strategic variables changeable. Let us choose the profit-maximizing strategic variables and compare them with the equilibrium values chosen under the dual parametric rule. If the increased value of strategic variables enhances the well-being of the worker, other conditions being constant, then the profit-maximizing value is generally lower than the equilibrium value chosen under the dual parametric rule. This is because when the profit-maximizing rule is applied it is equivalent to the weighting rule in which zero weight is allotted to the worker (the worker is excluded from sharing in decision-making), while the weight allotted to the profit-earners remains less than one, as used in the dual parametric rule.

Therefore, even though the relative bargaining powers of profit-earners and employees remains constant, whether the workers' preference is duly reflected in strategic decision-making is important for the micro-behaviour of the firm. In general, if the collective preference of workers, as represented by the enterprise-based union, is such that the marginal rate of substitution between additional job-security (or promotional opportunities) and the current level of earnings is positive, one can expect that management, which would take account of such workers' preference, would set the level of employment (or the rate of growth of the firm) higher than the profit-maximizing level. The neoclassical view that management should always maximize profit is based on the assumption that workers' preferences can be dealt with in wage-bargaining. But this assumption is erroneous in the modern context in which the emergence of internal organization and the associated long-term attachment of workers to the firm makes their well-being dependent on a wider range of strategic decision-making than the current earning level, unless the scope of bargaining covers issues concerned with the firm's strategic decision-making.

Secondly, consider the relative change in internal bargaining power between profit-earners and workers as reflected in a change in share parameters. The dual parametric rule suggests that, since the equilibrium strategic decision is the weighted average of optimal strategic decisions for the two bargaining parties, the result of parametric changes can be easily predicted by examining qualitative and quantitative differences in strategic decision-making.

Let us compare first the preference for the growth of the firm by both constituents. Even if the workers can benefit from the growth of the firm through better chances of promotion, their preference for that growth may not be as strong as that of the profit-earners. This can be seen from the following: First, assume the firm to be controlled by stockholders. The stockholders may, if they wish, opt to monopolize gains from growth in the form of capital gains while they bear all the cost of growth among themselves in the form of forgone dividends. (When they opt to make new members bear a part of the costs of growth in the form of new equity shares, capital gains accruing to them are reduced by an amount equal to the value of the new equity issue, assuming a perfectly competitive financial market and no taxation.)

Imagine next a twin firm controlled fully by the workers, but otherwise identical. Suppose that, in order to finance growth, the workers have to sacrifice their current earnings, such earnings being retained by the firm. Growth would normally entail the expansion of the work-force, unless labour-saving technological progress made that unecessary. Even if status differentiation is created concurrently between the senior workers and new employees, the ongoing organization would normally sustain the basic features of the firm's structure so that at least some of the incoming workers would eventually participate in the sharing of benefits from growth in the form of promotion, etc. In other words, incumbent workers cannot monopolize the benefits from growth, as the stockholders do, even if they bear the cost of growth. The possibility of external debt-financing would mitigate this effect to some extent as it would shift some portion of the cost of growth to incoming workers.

From this, one can predict that the firm would choose slower growth, or more labour-saving technology if the relative bargaining power is tilted in favour of workers. Also when a future risk of lay-off is involved, the firm would choose the lower level of employment so that the probability of lay-off would be reduced (see Miyazaki 1984). Thus the increasing power of workers within the firm may have an adverse effect on the demand for new employment. I have called this conflict between outsiders and insiders the 'dilemma of industrial democracy' (Aoki 1984c).

Evidence suggests that the Japanese firm has not escaped this dilemma. Since the 1973–4 depression in the aftermath of the oil shocks, Japanese large firms have considerably limited the expansion of their work-forces through limiting new employment, the increasing use of 'part-time workers', the acceleration of labour-saving technology, and organizational innovation through the promotion of efficient semi-horizontal operational co-ordination, etc. Also the simplification of hierarchical layers and the reduction of blue-collar workers have been achieved through increased hiving-off of subsidiaries. In my estimation, the subsidiarization alone contributed to a 3.5–4.5 per cent reduction in the employment/sales ratio (in real terms) in the electric machinery and electronics industry over the period 1973–82, controlling for the effect of labour-saving technological and organizational innovation and the scale effect. The autonomous rate of labour saving per sales due to internal organizational and technological innovation is estimated to be as high as about 10.0 per cent per annum (Aoki 1984*a*).

If Japanese firms limit new employment relative to sales, why does the dilemma of industrial democracy not manifest itself at the macro-level as a conspicuous phenomenon of unemployment? Unemployment in Japan was fairly constant at a rather low level of around 3 per cent up to the mid 1980s. One reason why restrictions on the level of employment at large firms has not led to massive unemployment is the relative increase in the number of 'part-time' workers. Second, the employment policies of large firms are facilitated by the hiving-off of subsidiaries, increased use of sub-contractors, and the transfer of employees to relatively smaller, satellite companies at inferior conditions of employment. In the next section, I focus on the latter mechanism.

V. THE DUAL STRUCTURE RE-EMERGING?

As already mentioned, it is a conspicuous phenomenon since the mid 1970s that large Japanese firms have been getting rid of many fully owned or partially owned subsidiaries as well as relying on the extensive use of sub-contractors in which prime manufacturers often have a minority holding (see Aoki 1984*b*). These firms are frequently related to prime manufacturers in long-term business relations in a more or less systematic manner. For example, in the automobile industry, where such relations are most systematized, prime manufacturers normally maintain direct first-tier relations with a hundred-odd suppliers, who are frequently organized into exclusive associations of firms co-operating with the prime manufacturers, and in turn have second-tier relations with still smaller sub-contractors. According to a survey by the Agency for Small and Medium-sized Enterprises conducted in 1977, a leading auto manufacturer had direct relations with 122 first-tier suppliers, and indirect relations with 5,437 second-tier suppliers, and 41,703 third tier suppliers. Adjusting for double-counting, this manufacturer stood at the apex of a corporate grouping, supported by hierarchical transactional relations, numbering some 35,768 enterprises (Japanese Agency for Small and medium-sized Enterprises 1977).

Long-standing folklore dictates that large firms in Japan use such relatively small, related firms as a business-cycle buffer to maintain permanent employment in larger firms. However, such relationships are much more subtle nowadays. For example, in the automotive industry many first-tier firms supply essential components, such as electronic parts, and brakes, for the manufacture of which the prime manufacturer does not have comparable technological expertise, or are sub-contracted to assemble particular models of final products. Contracts between the prime manufacturer and these first-tier suppliers normally extend through the life-cycle of a particular model and are renewable unless the suppliers fail to meet the quality and cost standards of the prime manufacturer in the contractual period. For example, between 1973 and 1984, only three firms left the Association of Toyota Co-operating Firms composed of first-tier suppliers, and 21 firms joined it. (see Sakamoto 1985).

Prime manufacturers thus do not use their first-tier supplier firms to buffer business-cycle conditions. The semi-exclusive reliance of the prime manufacturer on first-tier firms for the supply of certain parts and components, and the clear demarcation of work between the prime and first-tier suppliers make it imperative for the prime manufacturers to maintain permanent transactional relations with the latter. A recent econometric study on sub-contracting groups indicates that fluctuations in income are shared between contracting firms and sub-contracting suppliers, normally with the former taking a larger share of business risks than the later (Kawasaki and Macmillan, 1987). Since the prime contracting firm is usually in a better position to assume such risks than the smaller subcontracting supplier, through diversification in its product portfolio and the accumulation of financial assets, it is an efficient arrangement that the former absorbs more risk in exchange for its monopsonistic gain (Aoki 1984*b*).

The terms of transaction are negotiated between the prime manufacturers and each member of the first-tier group, usually twice a year and at the same time as collective bargaining with the union regarding biannual bonuses. Prime manufacturers guarantee amortization charges for the specific equipment and tools required by suppliers, and in addition the division of the rents enjoyed by the group is negotiated (Asanuma 1985).

Because of these transactional and distributional arrangements, first-tier firms relate to the prime manufacturer in much the same way as in-house divisions of an integrated firm. Indeed, workers of the first-tier firms are sometimes organized into a single 'enterprise-group' union with workers of the prime manufacturer. On the other hand, in spite of minority holdings in first-tier suppliers by the prime manufacturer, the former retain considerable autonomy in operational control. Moreover, many first-tier supplier firms are very active in pursuing their own research and development, because the development of new technology endows them with considerable bargaining power *vis-à-vis* the prime manufacturer over the disposition of group rents. It is also not unusual for technologically advanced suppliers to have simultaneous transactional relations with a number of prime manufacturers.[4]

Economies of quasi-disintegration in the form of semi-autonomous groupings come partly from the efficiency of the operational coordination mechanism. This is very similar in its functioning to the semi-horizontal operational co-ordination among in-house shops we discussed in Section III. In fact, the 'kanban' system normally applies to communications between the prime manufacturer and first-tier suppliers, and may extend even to transactions between first-tier suppliers and second-tier suppliers. Response to system shocks, such as fluctuating final demand, is initiated by the final assembly-lines of the prime manufacturer and distributed beyond the corporate boundary of the prime manufacturer throughout the whole group through the medium of 'kanban' and without the intervention of a single higher controlling power, although responsibility to respond to local shocks, such as quality defects and machine malfunction, is placed firmly on each supplier. This semi-horizontal operational co-ordination beyond corporate boundaries which dispenses with a single corporate control may be regarded as saving transaction costs of the same order as are attributable to the intra-firm mechanism. This saving manifests itself dramatically in that the management hierarchy of the prime manufacturer in Japan is much flatter than that of large American integrated firms. In American auto manufacturers, the chief executive officers are normally six or seven management-layers away from a typical plant manager, whereas in Japanese auto manufacturers' main plant managers are often appointed to the companies' boards of directors (which are overwhelmingly 'inside' boards) and, at most, are two levels below the chief executive officer.

Employees of first-tier suppliers usually enjoy benefits comparable with those of workers at prime manufacturers. Thus, although there is strong pressure on first-tier suppliers and their workers to ensure

Table 7.1. The rates of increase in wages and value added productivity by establishment size and period (%)

	500 or more	100–499	30–99	5–29
Wages				
1960–5	8.1	11.0	12.2	15.0
1965–70	14.7	14.9	14.4	14.2
1970–5	18.1	18.2	17.3	17.3
1975–83	7.5	6.9	6.7	6.7
Value added productivity				
1960–5	6.9	10.0	11.9	14.5
1965–70	17.2	16.8	16.5	16.3
1970–5	10.8	13.8	13.1	13.8
1975–83	11.6	9.2	8.6	8.2

Source: Japanese Ministry of Labour, *Monthly Labour Survey*; Ministry of International Trade and Industry, *Industrial Statistics*.

the efficient functioning of operational co-ordination, one of the primary economic reasons for the existence of first-tier, semi-autonomous suppliers stems from the informational efficiency made possible by avoiding a high degree of integration.

But it seems true that quasi-disintegration is also a way of securing benefits for workers at prime manufacturers and strong first-tier suppliers by limiting the number of employees at those levels. In this way, prime manufacturers and strong first-tier suppliers can hive off the potential problem of securing jobs and other benefits for workers to smaller satellite firms. As one goes down the hierarchy in the supplier group, the technological expertise of lower-tier suppliers becomes less and less indispensable. The fact that these suppliers can easily be replaced by other competitors makes their bargaining power over the participation in rents enjoyed by the group extremely weak.

A look at Table 7.1 reveals that after 1975 the difference in the rate of increase in value-added productivity began to favour larger establishments, although some portion of slower productivity growth at small establishments was offset by relatively lower wage increases. However, when one compares the wages of workers in the same age group and with the same job tenure, differentials according to estab-lishment size are not so large. For instance, regularly paid wages to male workers of establishments with 10–99 employees in manufac-turing industries in the age groups 20–24 and 25–29 were 98.6 per

Table 7.2. Size differential in welfare-related labour costs[a]

	Welfare costs legally required	Welfare costs legally not-required	Costs for retirement compensation
1973–75	76.1	44.8	32.2
1976–79	70.1	34.8	33.9
1980–82	72.0	29.4	29.2

[a] Relative ratio for establishments with 30–99 employees; establishments with 1,000 or more employees = 100.

Source: Japanese Ministry of Labour, *Analysis of Labour Economy*, 1983.

cent and 94.5 per cent respectively, of those paid to workers of establishments with 1,000 or more in 1983 (Japanese Ministry of Labour 1960–83).

Such equalization of standard wages probably accounts for the fact that the widening of wage differential between firms of different size did not mirror the difference in value-added productivity. However, if one compares benefits paid in the form of non-standard wages, such as bonuses, pensions, and lump-sum payment, on retirement, there is evidence of a widening of differentials between larger and smaller firms (see Table 7.2). It is also at these smaller firms that one finds a bigger proportion of 'part-timers' who are underpaid and deprived of various benefits such as job-security, bonuses, and pensions.

One may provisionally assume therefore that larger firms in the corporate group gained increasingly larger shares in group rents, with the workers' share of these rents taking the form of non-standard wage benefits; the bargaining power of smaller firms within the group was adversely affected, with workers there gaining only near-competitive wages. This appears reminiscent of the dual labour-market hypothesis, but the present structure is characterized more by fine gradation from the co-operative game that characterizes large firms at the apex of the group through relatively well-off supplier firms at the upper tier of the supplier hierarchy to the competitive system at the lowest tier. In the early 1960s, there was also a differential in regularly paid wages (standard wages) according to size of firm, but this differential was narrowed and almost disappeared in the period of high growth, and does not appear to have re-emerged since. Scale differentials appear in the form of non-standard wage benefits, a part of which may be understood as participation in rent.

This gradational structure seems to be facing a turning-point, however. Since the realignment of exchange rates starting from the intervention of G-5 and accelerated by the fall in the price of oil, lower-tier suppliers are losing ground to lower-cost supplies from abroad. Thus the prime manufacturer has begun to consider the merits of foreign sources, either from their own subsidiaries and/or foreign suppliers. At the same time most large first-tier suppliers are looking for foreign bases of operation. Thus the substitution of foreign suppliers (or Japanese subsidiaries in foreign countries) for Japanese suppliers may not affect first-tier suppliers immediately to spoil the efficiency of close networking of semi-horizontal co-ordination, but it may well have the effect of hitting employment opportunities hard at the lower end of the hierarchy.

VI. CONCLUSION: IS THE JAPANESE MODEL CULTURALLY UNIQUE?

In Section III, I have suggested that semi-horizontal operational co-ordination, coupled with the integrative approach to operating and problem-solving on the shop-floor, may contribute to the dynamic efficiency of firms in certain industries and surpass that of a combination of specialism and hierarchical co-ordination. Those industries for which the Japanese methods may operate more efficiently would be the ones in which market conditions are characterized by continual and incremental changes and in which production involves many processes. But it may not be dynamically efficient in industries where market conditions are relatively stable and/or the production process is comparatively straightforward. The mass-production method, utilizing economies of specialization and centralized co-ordination, may operate more efficiently for such industries.

In Section IV, I have also hinted that it is extremely costly to develop the integrative skills of workers to cope with drastically changing market or technological environments. Further, in such an environment, entrepreneurial leadership to seize on market and engineering possibilities and initiate new designs may be more crucial to the viability of the firm than a capacity to respond quickly to demands for existing products.

Therefore one may expect that the 'Japanese-type', less hierarchical and less specialized system, would be found more frequently in industries characterized by medium-batch production of many varieties, while the more hierarchical and more specialized system may be found in industries characterized by continuous or mass-production methods. The latter may be also found in industries characterized by customized production or responding to drastically changing market environments. Such is indeed what the 'contingency' paradigm of organization predicts and in the US there seems to be empirical support for this hypothesis. In Japan, however, this theory does not seem to hold. For example, in a recent statistical study of 50-odd companies in central Indiana and the Atsugi region in the vicinity of Tokyo, it was found that the Japanese companies had less specialized job classifications and that *de facto*, decision-making took place at lower levels, regardless of their industrial characteristics (Lincoln *et al.* 1986, pp. 338–64). This finding is consistent with often-made claims in business economics that Japan is comparatively stronger in industries characterized by medium-range market volatility and multi-step manufacturing processes, such as in the automobile, electrical, and precision-machinery industries, but weak in industries characterized by stable markets or continuous manufacturing processes such as food-processing, paper, and petro-chemicals (e.g. Abbeglen and Stalk 1986; Kagone *et al.* 1985).

One may conjecture that, if the less specialized *and* less-hierarchical (in the sense that *de facto* the decision-making level is comparatively lower) method is consistently chosen in Japan, regardless of its economic efficiency, it must be rooted in Japanese culture. One may continue to argue further that if the Japanese system is cultural, then it is unique to Japan and not exportable. But we ought to be careful about drawing such conclusions.

First of all, it may be agreed that the less clear demarcation of jobs within a small work-group is a distinctive characteristic of the Japanese and that this organizational orientation may be culturally conditioned by the collective memory of agrarian village life, where the nature of rice production required co-operative working involving the rotation of tasks, and *ad hoc* and flexible collective responses to continual and incremental environmental changes. But the team approach to work does not automatically ensure an efficient work system in the context of the large organizations characteristic of our own times. If the task of a functional unit is carried out by a relatively egalitarian and cohesive work-team, the latter may tend to become autonomous and assert its own localized interests by taking advantage of its monopolistic position within the organization. Co-ordination between functional units then becomes problematical.

This problem was not indeed unusual in the pre-industrial age. Villages in the Edo period, organized as coherent, *relatively* homogeneous user-units of the irrigation system and, except for tax obligations, free of the control of castle-towns, often engaged in fierce disputes among themselves over the distribution of water resources. These disputes, known as *mizu-arasoi* (water-disputes), sometimes led to bloody clashes between neighbouring villages in times of water scarcity. Elaborate arbitration schemes along the irrigation system had to be developed in this period to cope with such social conflict. Famous agrarian leaders at that time, like Ninomiya Kinjiro and Mutsugawa Chiyozaburo, were associated with the organization and effective management of their arbitration schemes.

The need for inter-group co-ordination and conflict resolution is no less important for modern Japanese firms. In a criticism of Chie Nakane, who emphasizes the cultural uniqueness of Japanese organization relying on small-group values (Nakane 1979), Rohlen comments:

The total company situation is more complicated. While the nature of work groups is best approached from the question of their fundamental conceptualization, it is less likely that an ideology emphasizing small-group values will have the same significance for large organizations. Company leaders may be devoted to such values, but they are not in a position to unite the personnel of a company in the same immediate way group leaders are, and the best they can accomplish is to make success of the directors' and other high level small groups. Companies have been able to elaborate a wide manner of activities of symbolic participation (such as ceremonies, gatherings of representatives, company-wide outings, and civic and charitable programs), but none of this will be sufficient to secure the sense of connectedness of individuals to the whole, a crucial matter to Japanese companies (Rohlen 1975, pp. 208–9).

From this perspective, it is not too difficult to see that some elements of 'semi-horizontal' operational co-ordination in the context of the modern firm are the product of conscious management design. For example, the 'kanban' system was developed by the ingenious effort of industrial engineers at an automobile manufacturing firm who imported the method of replenishing on-shelf stocks of the American supermarket system and adapted it to the requirements of co-ordinating manufacturing and inventory control.

The practice of rotating personnel *beyond functional units* is also a device to facilitate communications between units and restrain the development of unit-specific interests. Such rotation is found, for example, among engineers in the manufacturing division, who may be transferred to the central research laboratory to participate in the development of a new product, or the production site for supervising the setting-up of a new manufacturing process. It may facilitate the formation of feedback loops between the downstream and upstream phases of design as well as between the manufacturing process and the preceding design process (see Aoki 1988, ch. 6.3).

Inter-functional unit rotation may be considered as a magnified version of job rotation within the small group. But while job rotation on the shop-floor began spontaneously through the initiative of foremen and sub-foremen (see Koike 1984, p. 163), the practice of inter-unit rotation was cultivated by management and centrally administered by the personnel department of the firm. Although the Japanese firm has come to rely on less hierarchical control over operating tasks, in order to ensure that the functional units, and members of each work-group therein, comply with the organizational goal, the personnel administration of the Japanese firm has become much more centralized than the Western firm. Decentralization in one dimension seems to be compensated by centralization in another.

Even though the development of semi-horizontal co-ordination in Japan is a rational management response to the 'culture' of small-group values, if it turns out to be more responsive to market and other environmental changes of an incremental nature and thus can avoid the rigidity of hierarchical co-ordination, it may be worth considering its adoption elsewhere as an alternative to hierarchical co-ordination. But it is to be remembered that semi-horizontal operational co-ordination in Japanese firms, which has developed as a response to small-group values, in turn relies on the problem-solving capacity of each functional unit (shop). This localized approach aims at the effective utilization of on-the-spot information that may be implied, subtle, unprogrammable, yet economically valuable for problem-solving.[5] And such utilization is made possible by enhancing the job experiences of workers, sharing knowledge among them, and cross-jurisdictional communications at the operating level. But is a less rigid, flexible job demarcation, which would facilitate the formation of the integrative skills of workers, possible in the cultural tradition of specialization?[6] This question may be answered only after painstaking efforts in that direction on the part both of labour and management rather than by the intellectual exercise of scholars. Once the efficient and humanistic aspects of the integrative approach are understood, however, such effort would seem to be worth while.[7]

NOTES

1. A more extensive discussion of these and other issues mentioned above is to be found in Aoki (1988).
2. This assertion is based on the reinterpretation of McLeod and Malcomson (1986). See also Aoki (1988), ch. 2.2.
3. Aoki (1984), ch. 5. There I call the second part of the dual rule the *weighting rule* (pp. 74–80).
4. For an example, Toyota corporate group owns about 28% of the stock of Nihon Denso which supplies car electronic equipment, but the latter is also a member of the Association of Co-operating Firms for Mitsubishi Auto Industry Ltd., Fuji Heavy Industry Co., and Isuzu Motor Co.
5. The emphasis on the integrative approach is also exactly the point that Swedish management and labour unions have agreed in the Development Contract as a key to productivity growth and improvement of the quality of work.
6. See Cole (1979) for the cultural aspect of the development of specialization in the US.
7. There are many stories of experiments of more flexible schemes of job classification in the US, but a true hybrid of two Japanese and American giant firms— New United Motor Manufacturing Inc. (NUMMI) founded in 1983 at Fremont, California—provides a particularly interesting example in showing that the Japanese rotation scheme may be a viable alternative even in the US union setting.

References

Abbeglen, J., and Stalk, G., jun. (1986). *Kaisha: The Japanese Corporation* (New York: Basic Books).

Abernathy, W. J., Clark, K. B., and Kantrow, A. M. (1983). *Industrial Renaissance: Producing for a Competitive Future for America* (New York: Basic Books).

Addis, E. (1987). 'Il Cambiamento dei Canali di Trasmissione della Politica Monetaria e la Riallocazione di Potere tra Stato, Mercato e Banca Centrale in Italia', *Stato e Mercato*, 19.

Aftalion, F. (1983). 'The Political Economy of French Monetray Policy', in D. Hodgman (1983), pp. 7–25.

Aglietta, M. (1976). *Regulations et crises du capitalisme: les expériences des États-Unis* (Paris: Calmann-Levy). English trans., *Theory of Capitalist Regulation* (London: New Left Books).

—— and Orléan, A. (1982). *La Violence de la monnaie* (Paris: PUF).

—— and Brender, A. (1984). *Métamorphoses de la société salariale* (Paris: Calmann-Levy).

Aliber, R. Z. (1979). *The International Money Game* (3rd. edn., New York: Basic Books).

Aoki, M. (1984a). 'Innovative Adaptation through Quasi-Tree Structure: An Emerging Aspect of Japanese Entrepreneurship', *Zeitschrift für Nationaloekonomie*, supplement, pp. 177–98.

—— (ed.) (1984b). *The Economic Analysis of the Japanese Firm* (Amsterdam: North-Holland).

—— (1984c). *The Cooperative Game Theory of the Firm* (Oxford: OUP).

—— (1987). 'Horizontal vs. Vertical Structures of the Firm', *American Economic Review* 77 (Dec.).

—— (1988). *Information, Incentives and Bargaining in the Japanese Economy* (Cambridge: CUP).

Argy, V. (1981). *Post-War International Monetary Crisis: An Analysis* (London: Allen & Unwin).

—— (1982). 'Exchange Rate Management in Theory and Practice,' *Princeton Studies in International Finance*, no. 50 (Oct.).

Armstrong, P., and Glyn, A. (1986). *Accumulation, Profits, State Spending 1952–83* (Oxford: *mimeo*).

—— Glyn, A., and Harrison, J. (1984). *Capitalism since World War II* (London: Fontana).

Arrighi, G., and Beverly Silver, J. (1984). 'Labor Movements and Capital Migration: The United States and Western Europe in World-Historical Perspective', in C. Berquist, *Labor in the Capitalist World-Economy* (Beverly Hills: Sage Publications), pp. 183–216.

Arrow, K. (1953). 'Le rôle des valeurs boursières pour la répartition la meilleure des risques', *Econometrie*, pp 41–8.' English trans., 'The Role of Securities in the Optimal Allocation of Risk', *Review of Economic Studies* (1964), 31, pp. 91–6.

Arrow, K. J., and Debreu, G. (1954). 'Existence of an equilibrium for a competitive economy', *Econometrica*, 22, pp. 265–90.

Artis, M., and Bladen-Hovell, R. (1987). 'The U.K.'s Monetarist Experiment, 1979–1984', *International Review of Applied Economics*, 1/1, pp. 23–47.

Artus, J. (1977). 'Measures of Potential Output in Manufacturing', *IMF Staff Papers* (Mar.).

Asanuma, B. (1985). 'The Organization of Parts Purchases in the Japanese Automotive Industry', *Japanese Economic Studies* (Summer), pp. 32–53.

Avramovitch (1982). 'The International Debt Problem' (Geneva: *mimeo*).

Azouvi, A. (1979). *Emploi, qualifications et croissance dans l'industrie 1. Les industries d'équipments* (Collections d'INSEE, serie E., no. 58).

Bade, R., and Parkin, M. (1980). 'Central Bank Laws and Monetary Policy' (University of Western Ontario: *mimeo*).

Ball, R. J. (1982). *Money and Employment* (London: Macmillan).

Bananian, K. (1988). 'Making the Fed More Politically Responsible Isn't Likely to Reduce Inflation: A Comparative Study of Central Banking Arrangements and Inflation in the Industrial Countries', in T. Willett (1987).

—— Laney, L., and Willett, T. (1983). 'Central Bank Independence: An International Comparison', *Federal Reserve Bank of Dallas Economic Review* (Nov.), pp. 1–13.

Bank for International Settlements, *Annual Report*, various years (Basle: Bank for International Settlements).

Bank of Italy, *Annual Report*, abridged version, various years.

Baran, P., and Sweezy, P. (1968). *Monopoly Capital* (Harmondsworth: Penguin).

Barou, P. (1979). 'La Croissance japonaise', *Statistiques et études financières*, 39.

Batchelor, R., Major, R., and Morgan, A. (1980). *Industrialisation and the Basis for Trade* (Cambridge: CUP).

Bean, C. R., Layard, P. R. G., and Nickel, S. J. (1986). 'The Rise in Unemployment: A Multi-country Study', *Economica*, 53, supplement.

Beckerman, W. (1962). 'Projecting Europe's Growth', *Economic Journal* 72/288.

Benassy, J. P. (1982) *The Economics of Market Disequilibrium* (New York: Academic).

Bernade, F. (1982). 'The Labour Market and Unemployment', in A. Boltho (1982), pp. 159–88.

Berry, M. (1985). 'Des robots au concret: les réalités cachées derrière les mythes', *Annales des Mines*, Série *Gérer et comprendre*, no. 1.

Best, M., and Humphries, J. (1986). 'The City and Industrial Decline', in B. Elbaum and W. Lazonick (1986), pp. 223–39.

Binmore, K., Rubinstein, A., and Wolinsky, A. (1986). 'The Nash Solution in Economic Modeling', *Rand Journal of Economics*, 17/2.

Black, S. W. (1977). *Floating Exchange Rates and National Economic Policy* (New Haven: Yale Univ. Press).

—— (1982*a*). *Politics versus Markets: International Differences in Macroeconomic Policies* (Washington, DC: American Enterprise Institute).

—— (1982*b*). 'Strategic Aspects of the Political Assignment Problem in Open Economies', in R. E. Lombra and W. E. Witte, *The Political Economy of Domestic and International Monetary Relations* (Ames: Iowa State Univ. Press).

—— (1984). 'The Use of Monetary Policy for Internal and External Balance in Ten Industrial Countries', in J. Frenkel, *Exchange Rates and International Macroeconomics* (Chicago: Univ. of Chicago Press).

Blackaby, F. T. (ed.) (1979). *British Economic Policy 1960–74* (London: CUP).

Blair, J. M. (1972). *Economic Concentration: Structure, Behavior and Public Policy* (New York: Harcourt Brace Jovanovich).

Block, F. L. (1977). *The Origins of International Economic Disorder* (Berkeley: Univ. of California Press).

Blyth, C. A. (1979). 'The Interaction Between Collective Bargaining and Government Policies in Selected Member Countries', in *Collective Bargaining and Government Policies* (Paris: OECD).

Boltho, A. (1975). *Japan: An Economic Survey 1953–73* (Oxford: OUP).

—— (1982*a*). *The European Economy: Growth and Crisis* (New York: OUP).

—— (1982*b*). 'Course and Causes of Collective Consumption Trends in the West', in R. C. O. Matthews and G. B. Stafford, *The Grants Economy and Collective Consumption* (London: Macmillan).

—— and Keating, M. (1973). 'The Measurement of Domestic Cyclical Fluctuations', *OECD Economic Outlook*, Occasional Studies (July).

Bowles, S. (1982). 'The Post-Keynesian Capital Labour Stalemate,' *Socialist Review*, 65.

—— (1985). 'The Production Process in a Competitive Economy: Walrasian, Marxian and neo-Hobbesian Models,' *American Economic Review*, 75/1, pp. 16–36.

—— and Edwards, R. (1985). *Understanding Capitalism: Competition, Command, and Change in the U.S. Economy* (New York: Harper & Row).

—— and Boyer, R. (1988). 'Labor Discipline and Aggregate Demand: A Macroeconomic Model', *American Economic Review*, 78/2, pp. 395–400.

—— and Gintis, H. (1986). *Democracy and Capitalism: Property, Community, and the Contradictions of Modern Social Thought* (New York: Basic Books).

—— and Gordon, D., and Weisskopf, T. (1983*a*). *Beyond the Wasteland*

(New York: Anchor Press).

—— and Gordon, D., and Weisskopf, T. (1983*b*). 'Power and Profits: The Social Structure of Accumulation and the Profitability of the Post-war US Economy', *Review of Radical Political Economics*, 18/1 & 2, pp. 132–67.

—— (1989). 'Social Institutions and Technical Change', in Massimo Di Matteo, Richard Goodwin, and Alessandro Vercelli (eds.), *Technological and Social Factors in Long Term Fluctuations: Proceedings of an International Workshop Held in Siena, Italy, December 16–18, 1986*. New York: Springer-Verlag.

Boyer, R. (1985). 'The Influence of Keynes on French Economic Policy: Past and Present,' CEPREMAP Discussion Paper, no. 159.

—— (ed.) (1986). *La Flexibilité du travail en Europe* (Paris: La Découverte).

—— and Mistral, J. (1978). *Accumulation, Inflation, Crises* (Paris: PUF; enlarged edn., 1983).

—— and Petit, P. (1981). 'Progrès technique, croissance et emploi: un modèle d'inspiration Kaldorienne pour six industries Européenes', *Revue Économique*, 32/6.

Braverman, H. (1974). *Labor and Monopoly Capital* (New York: Monthly Review Press).

Brown, A. J. (1984). *World Inflation Since 1950* (NIER, Cambridge: CUP).

Brown, W. A., and Opie, R. (1953). *American Foreign Assistance* (Washington, DC: Brookings Institution).

Bruneel, D. (1986). 'Recent Evolution of Financial Structures and Monetary Policy in France' (Banque de France: *mimeo*).

Bruno, M. (1986). 'Aggregate Supply and Demand Factors in OECD Unemployment: An Update', *Economica*, 53, supplement.

—— and Sachs, J. (1985). *Economics of Worldwide Stagflation* (Cambridge, Mass: Harvard Univ. Press).

Buiter, W. (1983). 'Changing the Rules: Economic Consequences of the Thatcher Regime', *Brookings Papers on Economic Activity* (Washington, DC: Brookings Institution), 2, pp. 305–80.

—— and Miller, M. (1981). 'The Thatcher Experiment: The First Two Years', *Brookings Papers on Economic Activity*, 2, pp. 315–79.

Calvo, G. (1979). 'Quasi-Walrasian Theories of Unemployment', *American Economic Review*, 69/2, pp. 102–7.

Cambridge Economic Policy Group (1979). *Economic Policy Review* (Farnborough: Gower Press), no. 5 (Apr.).

Cameron, D. R. (1984). 'Social Democracy, Corporatism, Labour Quiescence and the Representation of Economic Interests in Advanced Capitalist Society', in J. H. Goldthorpe (1984).

Camps, M. (1966). *European Unification in the Sixties* (New York: McGraw-Hill).

Cantor, D., and Schor, J. (1987). *Tunnel Vision: Labour, the World Eco-*

nomy, and Central America (Boston, Mass.: South End Press).

Caranza, C., and Fazio, A. (1983). 'Methods of Monetary Control in Italy', in D. Hodgman (1983).

Caves, R., and associates (1968). *Britain's Economic Prospects* (Washington, DC: Brookings Institution).

—— and Uekusa, M. (1976). *Industrial Organization in Japan* (Washington, DC: Brookings Institution).

Cette, G. (1981). 'L'Efficacité du capital fixe dans 17 industries, 1959–79', *Economie et Prévision*, no. 5.

—— and Jolly, P. (1984). 'La Productivité industrielle en crise: une interprétation', *Economie et Statistique*, no. 166 (May).

Chandler, A. D. (1977). *The Visible Hand: The Managerial Revolution in American Business* (Cambridge, Mass.: Harvard Univ. Press).

—— (1986). 'The Evolution of Modern Global Competition', in M. E. Porter. *Competition in Global Industries* (Boston, Mass.: Harvard Business School).

Chan-Lee, J., and Sutch, H. (1984). 'Profits and Rates of Return' (OECD: *mimeo*).

Comsky, N. (1986). *On Power and Ideology* (Boston, Mass.: South End Press).

Chouraqui, J.-C., and Price, R. W. R. (1984). 'Medium Term Financial Strategy: The Co-ordination of Fiscal and Monetary Policies', *OECD Economic Studies*, no. 2 (Spring), pp. 7–49.

Clarke, W. (1967). *The City in the World Economy* (London: Penguin).

Cline, W. (1984). *International Debt: Systemic Debt and Policy Responses* (Washington, DC: Institute for International Economics).

Coakley, J., and Harris, L. (1983). *The City of Capital* (Oxford: Blackwell).

Cobham, D. (1986). 'French Macro-Economic Policy Under President Mitterrand: An Assessment', *National Westminster Bank Review*, pp. 41–51.

Cole, R. (1979). *Work, Mobility and Participation: A Comparative Study of American and Japanese Industry* (Berkeley: Univ. of California Press).

Cooper, R. (1968). 'The Balance of Trade', in R. Caves and associates (1968), pp. 147–97.

Corden, W. M. (1977). *Inflation, Exchange Rates and the World Economy* (Oxford: Clarendon Press).

Coriat, B. (1978). *L'Atelier et le chronomètre* (Paris: Christian Bourgeois).

—— (1984). 'Crise et électronisation de la production: robotisation d'atelier et modèle fordien d'accumulation du capital', *Critiques de l'économie politique*, nos. 26–7 (Jan.–June), pp. 71–94.

Cornwall, J. (1977). *Modern Capitalism: Its Growth and Transformation* (Oxford: Martin Robertson).

Council of Economic Advisers (1988). *Economic Report of the President* (Washington, DC: GPO).

Cowart, A. (1978). 'The Economic Policies of European Governments, Part I: Monetary Policy', *British Journal of Political Science*, 8 (July), pp. 285–311.

Crouch, C., and Pizzorno, A. (1978). *The Resurgence of Class Conflict in Western Europe Since 1968* (London: Holmes & Meier).

Debreu, G. (1959). *Theory of Value* (New York: Wiley)

de Finetti, B. (1937). 'La Prévision: ses lois logiques, ses sources subjectives', *Annales de l'institut Henri Poincaré*, 7, pp. 1–68. English trans. in H. E. Kyburg and H. E. Smokker, *Studies in Subjective Probability* (2nd. edn., New York: Krieger), pp. 53–118.

Delorme, R., and André, C. (1982) *L'État et l'économie* (Paris: Seuil).

De Montmollin, M., and Pastre, O. (eds.) (1984). *Le Taylorisme* (Paris: La Découverte).

Denison, E., and Chung, W. (1976). *How Japan's Economy Grew So Fast* (Washington, DC: Brookings Institution).

Dennison, E. F. (1979). *Accounting for Slower Economic Growth: the U.S. in the 1970's* (Washington, DC: Brookings Institution).

Dernburg, T. F. (1975). 'Fiscal Analysis in the Federal Republic of Germany: The Cyclically Neutral Budget', *International Monetary Fund Staff Papers*, 22/3, pp. 825–57.

Despres, E. (1973). *International Economic Reform* (New York: OUP).

De Vivo, G., and Pivetti, M. (1980). 'International Integration and the Balance of Payments Constraint: The Case of Italy', *Cambridge Journal of Economics*, 4/1, pp. 1–22.

Doeringer, P., and Piore, M. J. (1971). *Internal Labour Markets and Manpower Analysis* (Lexington: D. C. Heath Co.).

Dow, J. C. R. (1964). *The Management of the British Economy 1945–60* (Cambridge: CUP).

Dubois, P. (1985). 'Ruptures de croissance et progrès techniques', *Economie et Statistique* (Oct.).

Eatwell, J., Llewelyn, J., and Tarling, R. (1974). 'Money Wage Inflation in Industrial Countries', *Review of Economic Studies*, 41/4.

Edgren, G., Faxen, K. O., and Odhner, C. E. (1973). *Wage Formation and the Economy* (London: Allen & Unwin).

Edwards, C. D. (1967). *Control of Cartels and Monopolies: An International Comparison* (Dobbs Ferry, NY: Oceana Publications Inc.).

Edwards, R. (1979). *Contested Terrain* (New York: Basic Books).

European Economic Community (1982). *Eleventh Report on Competition Policy* (Brussels/Luxembourg Commission of the European Communities).

Elbaum, B., and Lazonick, W. (eds.) (1986). *The Decline of the British Economy* (Oxford: OUP).

Ellsberg, D. (1961). 'Risk, Ambiguity, and the Savage Axioms', *Quarterly Journal of Economics*, 75/4.

Epstein, G. (1982). 'Federal Reserve Politics and Monetary Instability', in A. Stone and E. Harpham, *The Political Economy of Public Policy* (Beverly Hills: Sage Publications).

—— (1985). 'The Triple Debt Crisis', *World Policy Journal*, 2/3, pp. 625–57.

—— and Ferguson, T. (1984). 'Monetary Policy, Loan Liquidation and Industrial Conflict: The Federal Reserve and the Open Market Operations of 1932', *Journal of Economic History*, 64/4, pp. 957–83.

—— and Schor, J. (1986). 'The Political Economy of Central Banking', *Harvard Institute for Economic Research*, Discussion Paper, no. 1281 (Nov.).

—— and Schor, J. (1989). 'The Divorce of the Banca d'Italia and the Italian Treasury: A Case Study of Central Bank Independence', in P. Lange and M. Regini, *The State and Social Regulation: New Perspectives* (Cambridge: CUP), forthcoming.

—— and Schor, J. (1988). 'The Structural Determinants and Economic Effects of Capital Controls in the OECD' (Harvard University: *mimeo*).

Esping-Andersen, G., Friedland, R., and Wright, E. O. (1976). 'Modes of Class Struggle and the Capitalist State', *Kapitalistate*, 4, 5.

—— and Korpi, W. (1984). 'Social Policy as Class Politics in Post-War Capitalism: Scandinavia, Austria, and Germany', in J. H. Goldthorpe (1984).

Faxen, K. O. (1980). 'Incomes Policy and Centralized Wage Formation', in A. Boltho (1982).

Fazio, A. (1979). 'Monetary Policy in Italy', *Kredit und Kapital*, no. 2, pp. 145–80.

—— and Lo Faso, S. (1980). 'The Control of Credit and Financial Intermediation in Italy', *Review of Economic Conditions in Italy*, no. 3, pp. 459–79.

Federal Reserve Bank of New York (1986). *Recent Trends in Commercial Bank Profitability: A Staff Study* (New York: Federal Reserve Bank of New York).

Federal Reserve Bulletin (1984). (Washington, DC: GPO), 70.

Feinstein, C. H., and Reddaway, W. B. (1983). 'OPEC Surpluses, the World Recession and the U.K. Economy', in R. O. C. Mathews and J. R. Sargent, *Contemporary Problems of Economic Policy* (London: Methuen).

Feldstein, M. (1973). 'Tax Incentives, Corporate Saving, and Capital Accumulation in the United States', *Journal of Public Economics*, 2, pp. 159–71.

Ferguson, T., and Rogers, J. (1986). *Right Turn: The Decline of the Democrats and the Future of American Politics* (New York: Hill & Wang).

Flanagan, R. J., Soskice, D. W., and Ulman, L. (1983). *Unionism, Econo-*

mic Stabilisation and Incomes Policies: European Experience (Washington, DC: Brookings Institution).

Flemming, J. S., Price, L. D. D., and Imgram, D. H. A. (1976). 'Trends in Company Profitability', *Bank of England Quarterly Bulletin* (Mar.).

Flora, P., and Heidenheimer, A. J. (eds.) (1981). *The Development of Welfare States in Europe and America* (New Brunswick and London: Transaction Books).

—— and Alber, J. (1981). 'Modernization, Democratization and the Development of Welfare States in Western Europe', in P. Flora and A. J. Heidenheimer (1981).

Fodor, G. (1986). 'Why did Europe need the Marshall Plan in 1947?', *Political Economy*, 2/1, pp. 73–104.

Francke, H.-H., and Hudson, M. (1984). *Banking and Finance in West Germany* (New York: St Martin's Press).

Franko, L. G. (1978). 'Multinationals: The End of US Dominance', *Harvard Business Review* (Nov.-Dec.).

Freeman, C., Clark, J., and Soete, L. (1982). *Unemployment and Technical Innovation* (London: Francis Pinter).

Friedman, A. (1977). *Industry and Labour* (London: Macmillan).

Friedman, M. (1951). 'The Case for Flexible Exchange Rates', *Essays in Positive Economics* (Chicago: Univ. of Chicago Press), pp. 157–203.

—— (1957). *A Theory of the Consumption Function* (Princeton: Princeton Univ. Press).

Gardner, R. (1969). *Sterling-Dollar Diplomacy* (New York and Maidenhead: McGraw-Hill).

Giersch, H. (ed.) (1973). *Fiscal Policy and Demand Management* (Tübingen, W. Germany: JCB Mohr).

—— (1985). *Eurosclerosis*, Kiel Discussion Papers, no. 112 (Kiel University).

Gintis, H. (forthcoming). 'Financial Markets and the Political Structure of the Enterprise', *Journal of Economic Behavior and Organization*.

Glyn, A., and Rowthorn, B. (1988). 'West European Unemployment—Corporatism and Structural Change', *American Economic Review*, Papers and Proceedings, 78/2, pp. 194–99.

Godley, W. A. H., and Cripps, F. (1983). *Macroeconomics* (London: Fontana).

Gold, D. A., Lo, C. Y., and Wright, E. O. (1975). 'Recent Developments in Marxist Theories of the Capitalist State', *Monthly Review Press*, 27/5, pp. 29–43; 27/6, pp. 36–51.

Goldthorpe, J. H. (ed.) (1984). *Order and Conflict in Contemporary Capitalism* (Oxford: Clarendon Press).

Goodwin, R. (1967). 'A Growth Cycle', in C. H. Feinstein, *Capitalism and Economic Growth* (Cambridge: CUP).

Gordon, D. M., Edwards, R., and Reich, E. (1982). *Segmented Work, Divided Workers: The Historical Transformation of Labour in the U.S.* (Cambridge: CUP).

Gourevitch, P., Markovits, A., Martin, A., and Ross, G. (1984). *Unions, Change and Crisis* (London: Allen & Unwin).

Grove, J. W. (1967) *Government and Industry in Britain* (London: Longmans).

Guinchard, J. (1984). 'Productivité' et compétition comparées des grands pays industriels', *Economie et Statistique*, no. 162 (Jan.).

Gustavsen, B., and Hunnius, G. (1981). *New Patterns of Work Reform—The Case of Norway* (Oslo: Universitetsforlaget).

Hall, P. A. (1986). *Governing the Economy: The Politics of State Intervention in Britain and France* (Oxford: OUP).

Hall, R. L., and Hitch, C. J. (1939). 'Price Theory and Business Behavior', *Oxford Economic Papers*, 2 (May).

Halm, G. N. (1968). *International Financial Intermediation: Deficits Benign and Malignant* (Princeton Univ.: Princeton Essays in International Finance).

Hamada, K., and Kurosaka, Y. (1986). 'Trends in Unemployment, Wages and Productivity: The Case of Japan', *Economica*, 53, supplement.

Hansen, B. (1968). *Fiscal Policy in Seven Countries 1955–1965* (Paris: OECD).

Harris, D. (1978). *Capital Accumulation and Income Distribution* (Stanford: Stanford Univ. Press).

Harris, S. F. (ed.) (1950). *Foreign Economic Policy of the United States* (New York).

Harrod, R. F. (1951). *Life of John Maynard Keynes* (London: Macmillan).

Helliwell, J. F. (ed.) (1976). *Aggregate Investment: Selected Readings* (Harmondsworth: Penguin Books).

Hennings, K. H. (1980). 'West Germany', in A. Boltho (1982), pp. 472–501.

Herman, E. (1982). *Corporate Power, Corporate Control* (Cambridge: CUP).

Hodgman, D. (ed.) (1983). *The Political Economy of Monetary Policy: National and International Aspects*, Conference Series, no. 26 (Boston, Mass.: Federal Reserve Bank of Boston).

Hoibik, K. (ed.) (1973). *Monetary Policy in Twelve Industrial Countries* (Boston, Mass.: Federal Reserve Bank of Boston).

Horsefield, J. K. (1969). *The International Monetary Fund 1945–65* (Washington DC: IMF).

Hughes, A., and Singh, A. (1980). 'Mergers, Concentration and Competition in Advanced Capitalist Economies: An International Perspective', in D. C. Mueller, *The Determinants and Effects of Mergers* (Cambridge, Mass.: OG and H Publishers).

Hultgren, T. (1965). *Costs, Prices and Profits, Their Cyclical Relations* (New York: National Bureau of Economic Research).

Hutchison, M. M. (1986). 'Japan's "Money Focused" Monetary Policy', *Economic Review* (Federal Reserve Bank of San Francisco), no. 3, pp. 33–46.

Ingham, G. (1984). *Capitalism Divided? The City and Industry in British Social Development* (London: Macmillan).

International Monetary Fund (1983). *World Economic Outlook* (Washington, DC: IMF).

—— (1986). *World Economic Outlook* (Washington, DC: IMF).

—— *International Financial Statistics*, data tape (Washington, DC: IMF).

Itoh, M. (1980). *Value and Crisis* (London: Pluto Press).

Japanese Agency for Small and Medium-Sized Enterprises (1977). *A Survey of Division of Labour Structure (Automobile)*.

Japanese Ministry of Labour (1960–83). *Basic Survey of Wage Structure*.

Johannsen, L. (1982). 'The Possibility of an International Equilibium with Low Levels of Activity', *Journal of International Economics*, 4/1.

Joint Economic Committee, US Congress (1981). *Monetary Policy, Economic Growth and Industry in France, Germany, Sweden and the United Kingdom* (Washington, DC: US Govt. Printing Office).

Jorgenson, D. (1965). 'Anticipations and Investment Behavior', in J. S. Duesenberry, G. Fromm, L. R. Klein, and E. Kuh, *The Brookings Quarterly Econometric Model of the United States* (Chicago: Rand Mc-Nally), pp. 35–92.

Jossa, B., and Panico, C. (1985). 'Banking Intermediation during the Italian Economic Crisis (1964–1984)' (University of Naples: *mimeo*).

Kagami, N. (1984). 'Japan', in E. Solomon (1984), pp. 70–97.

Kagone, T., Nonaka, Y., Sakakibara, K., and Okumura, A. (1985). *Strategic vs. Evolutionary Managements: A U.S.–Japan Comparison of Strategy and Organization* (Amsterdam: North-Holland).

Kahn, L. (1980). 'Bargaining Power, Search Theory, and the Phillips Curve', *Cambridge Journal of Economics*, 4, pp. 233–44.

Kahn, R. (1950). 'The Dollar Shortage and Devaluation', *Economica Internazionale*, 3/1.

Kahneman, D., Slovic, P., and Tversky, A. (1982). *Judgement under Uncertainty* (Cambridge: CUP).

Kaldor, N. (1967). *Strategic Factors in Economic Development* (Ithaca: Cornell Univ. Press).

—— (1982). *The Scourge of Monetarism* (Oxford: OUP).

Kalecki, M. (1943). 'Costs and Prices', *Selected Essays on the Dynamics of the Capitalist Economy* (Cambridge: CUP).

—— (1971), 'Class Struggle and Distribution of National Income', *Selected Essays on the Dynamics of the Capitalist Economy* (Cambridge: CUP).

Kareken, J. (1968). 'Monetary Policy', in R. Caves *et al.* (1968), pp. 68–103.

Katzenstein, P. J. (ed.) (1978). *Between Power and Plenty: Foreign Economic Policies of Advanced Industrial States* (Madison: Univ. of Wisconsin Press)

—— (1983). 'The Small European States in the International Economy: Economic Dependence and Corporatist Politics', in J. G. Ruggie, *The Antinomies of Interdependence* (New York: Columbia Univ. Press).

—— (1984). *Corporatism and Change: Austria, Switzerland and the Politics of Industry* (Ithaca: Cornell Univ. Press).

—— (1985). *Small States in World Markets: Industrial Policy in Europe* (Ithaca: Cornell Univ. Press).

Kawasaki, S., and Macmillan, J. (1987). 'The Design of Contracts: Evidence from Japanese Subcontracting', *Journal of the Japanese and International Economies*.

Keegan, W., and Pennant-Rae, R. (1979). *Who Runs the Economy?* (London: Temple Smith).

Kendrick, J., and Grossman, E. (1980). *Productivity in the United States: Trends and Cycles* (Baltimore: Johns Hopkins).

Keohane, R. O. (1984). 'The World Political Economy and the Crisis of Embedded Liberalism', in J. H. Goldthorpe (1984).

Keynes, J. (1936). *The General Theory of Employment, Interest and Money* (London: Macmillan).

Kindleberger, C. P. (1965). *Balance of Payments Deficits and the International Market for Liquidity* (Princeton Univ.: Princeton Essays in International Finance), 46 (May).

—— (1967). *Europe's Post War Growth: The Role of the Labour Supply* (Oxford: OUP).

—— (1986). 'International Public Goods without International Government', *American Economic Review* 76/1

—— (1987). *Marshall Plan Days* (Boston, Mass and London: Allen & Unwin).

Kloten, N., Ketterer, K.-H., and Vollmer, R. (1985). 'West Germany's Stabilization Performance', in L. Lindberg and C. Maier (1985), pp. 353–402.

Knight, F. H. (1921). *Risk, Uncertainty and Profit* (Boston, Mass. and New York: Houghton Mifflin Co.).

Koike, K. (1984). 'Skill Formation System in the U.S. and Japan', in M. Aoki (1984*b*).

—— (1987). 'Human Resource Development in the Japanese Industry', in K. Yamamura and Y. Yasuba, *The Japanese Political Economy*, 1 (Stanford: Stanford Univ. Press).

Korpi, W. (1978). *The Working Class in Welfare Capitalism* (London: Routledge & Kegan Paul).

Krause, L. (1969). 'Britain's Trade Performance', in R. Caves *et al.* (1968), pp. 192–228.

—— (1970). 'A Passive Balance of Payments Strategy for the United States', *Brookings Papers on Economic Activity*, 3, pp. 339–68.

Kreile, M. (1978). 'West Germany: The Dynamics of Expansion', in P. Katzenstein (1978), pp. 191–224.

Kudrle, R. T., and Marmor, T. R. (1981). 'The Development of Welfare States in North America', in P. Flora and A. J. Heidenheimer (1981).

Lacci, L. (1976). 'The Changes in the Compensation of Employees and in the Returns Paid to Other Factors of Production in Italy During the Period of Rapid Inflation Registered in the First Half of the 1970s', *Review of Economic Conditions in Italy*, 5, pp. 414–34.

Lange, P., and Garrett, G. (1985). 'The Politics of Growth: Strategic Interaction and Economic Performance in the Advanced Industrial Democracies, 1974–1980', *Journal of Politics*, 47/3, pp. 792–827.

—— Ross, G., and Vannicelli, M. (1982). *Unions, Change and Crisis: French and Italian Union Strategy and the Political Economy, 1945–1980* (London: Allen & Unwin).

Langhor, H., and Santomero, A. M. (1985). 'The Extent of Equity Investment by European Banks', *Journal of Money, Credit and Banking*, 17 (May), pp. 243–52.

Lash, S. (1985). 'The End of Neo-Corporatism?: The Breakdown of Centralised Bargaining in Sweden', *British Journal of Industrial Relations* 23/2.

Lawson, T., Tarling, R., and Wilkinson, F. (1982). 'Changes in the Inter-industry Structure of Wages in the Post-war Period', *Cambridge Journal of Economics* 6/3.

Layard, P. R. G., and Nickell, S. J. (1986) 'Unemployment in Britain', *Economica*, 53, supplement.

Lehmbruch, G. (1984). 'Concertation and the Structure of Corporatist Networks', in J. H. Goldthorpe (1984).

Lewis, W. A. (1954). 'Economic Development with Unlimited Supplies of Labour', *Manchester School*, 22, pp. 139–91.

Leyland, N. H. (1952). 'Productivity', in G. D. N. Worswick and P. H. Ady, *The British Economy 1945–1950* (Oxford: OUP).

Lieberman, S. (1977). *The Growth of European Mixed Economies 1945–70* (New York: Wiley).

Lincoln, J., Hanada, M., and McBride, K. (1986). 'Organizational Structure in Japanese and U.S. Manufacturing', *Administrative Science Quarterly*.

Lindbeck, A. (1983). 'The Recent Slowdown of Productivity Growth', *Economic Journal*, 93/1.

Lindberg, L., and Maier, C. (1985). *The Politics of Inflation and Global*

Stagnation (Washington, DC: Brookings Institution).

Lindberg, L., and Maier, C. (1986). *The Politics and Sociology of Global Inflation* (Washington, DC: Brookings Institution).

Linhart, D., and Linhart, R. (1985). 'Naissance d'un consensus', *CEPRE-MAP Couverture Orange*, no. 8515.

Lipietz, A. (1978). 'La Dimension régionale du développement du tertiaire', *Travaux et Recherches de Prospective*, no. 75. English shorter version in 'Interregional Polarization and the Tertiarization of Society', *Papers of the Regional Science Association*, no. 44 (1980).

—— (1979). *Crise et inflation: pourquoi?* (Paris: F. Maspero).

—— (1983). *Le Monde enchanté: De la valeur à l'envol inflationniste* (Paris: La Découverte). English trans., *The Enchanted World: Inflation Credit, and the World Crisis* (London: Verso, 1987).

—— (1985). *Mirages et miracles—problèmes de l'industrialisation dans le tiers monde* (Paris: La Découverte). English trans., *Mirages and Miracles: The Crisis in Global Fordism* (London: Verso, 1987).

—— (1986). 'Behind the Crisis: The Tendency of the Rate of Profit to Fall. Considerations about Some Empirical French Works', *Review of Radical Political Economics*, 18/1 & 2.

Llewellyn, J. (1983). 'Resource Prices and Macroeconomic Policies: Lessons from Two Oil Shocks', *OECD Economic Studies*, 1/1, pp. 197–212.

—— Potter, S., and Samuelson, L. (1985). *Economic Forecasting and Policy, the International Dimension* (London: Routledge & Kegan Paul).

Longstreth, F. (1979). 'The City, Industry and the State', in C. Crouch, *State and Economy in Contemporary Capitalism* (London: Croom Helm).

Lundberg, E. (1985). 'The Rise and Fall of the Swedish Model', *Journal of Economic Literature*, 23 (Mar.).

McCallum, J. (1986). 'Unemployment in OECD Countries in the 1980s', *Economic Journal*, 96, pp. 942–60.

Machin, H., and Wright, V. (1985). *Economic Policy Making under the Mitterrand Presidency, 1981–84* (New York: St Martin's Press).

McCracken, P., and associates (1977). *Towards Full Employment and Price Stability* (Paris: OECD).

McKersie, R. B., and Hunter, L. C. (1973). *Pay, Productivity and Collective Bargaining* (London: Macmillan).

McLeod, W. B., and Malcomson, J. M. (1986). 'Reputation and Hierarchy in Dynamic Models of Employment' *(mimeo)*.

Maddison, A. (1982). *Phases of Capitalist Development* (Oxford: OUP).

—— (1984). 'Comparative Analysis of the Productivity Situation in the Advanced Capitalist Countries', in J. Kendrick, *International Comparisons of Productivity and Causes of the Slowdown* (Cambridge, Mass.: Ballinger Publishing Co.).

Maier, C. P. (1978). 'The Politics of Productivity: Foundations of American Economic Policy after World War II', in P. J. Katzenstein (1978).

Maizels, A. (1963). *Growth and Trade* (Cambridge: CUP).

Malinvaud, E. (1980). *Profitability and Unemployment* (Cambridge: CUP).

Marginson, P. (1987). 'The Multidivisional Firm and Control over the Work Process', *International Journal of Industrial Organization* 3 (Mar.), pp. 37–56.

Marglin, S. A. (1974). 'What Do Bosses Do?', *Review of Radical Political Economics*, 6/2, pp. 60–112.

—— (1984). *Growth, Distribution, and Prices* (Cambridge, Mass.: Harvard Univ. Press).

—— (1987*a*). 'Investment and Accumulation', in J. Eatwell, M. Milgate, and P. Newman, *The New Palgrave* (London: Macmillan).

—— (forthcoming). 'Losing Touch: The Cultural Conditions of Worker Accommodation and Resistance' (Harvard University: *mimeo*).

Markovits, A. S. (1986). *The Politics of the West German Trade Unions* (Cambridge: CUP).

Martin, A. (1986). 'The Politics of Employment and Welfare in Advanced Capitalist Societies: National Policies and International Independence', in K. Banting, *The State and Economic Interests* (Toronto: Univ. of Toronto Press).

Martin, W. E. (ed.) (1981). *The Economics of the Profits Crisis* (London: HMSO).

Marvel, H. P. (1980). 'Foreign Trade and Domestic Competition', *Economic Inquiry*, 18/1.

Matthews, R. C. O. (1968). 'Why has Britain had Full Employment since the War', *Economic Journal*, 78/3.

—— (ed.) (1982). *Slower Growth in the Western World* (London: Heinemann).

—— Feinstein, C. H., and Odling-Smee, J. C. (1982). *British Economic Growth 1856–1973* (Stanford: Stanford Univ. Press).

Means, G. C. (1935). *Industrial Prices and their Relative Inflexibility*, 74th Congress, 1st Session, Senate Doc. 13.

—— (1940). 'Big Business, Administered Prices and the Problems of Full Employment', *Journal of Marketing* (Apr.).

Meek, P. (1982). *Central Bank Views on Monetary Targeting* (New York: Federal Reserve Bank).

Meidner, R. (1978). *Employment Investment Funds: An Approach to Collective Capital Formation* (London: Allen & Unwin).

Meir, G. M. (1974). *Problems of a World Monetary Order* (New York: OUP).

Melitz, J., and Wyplosz, C. (1985). *The French Economy: Theory and Policy* (Boulder: Westview Press).

Milward, A. S. (1984). *The Reconstruction of Western Europe 1945–51* (London: Methuen).

Minsky, H. P. (1986). *Stabilizing an Unstable Economy* (New Haven and

London: Yale Univ. Press).

Mintz, B., and Schwartz, M. (1985). *The Power Structure of American Business* (Chicago: Univ. of Chicago Press).

Mistral, J. (1986). 'Régime internal et trajectoires nationales', in R. Boyer, *Capitalisme, fin de siècle* (Paris: PUF).

Mitchell, W. C. (1913). *Business Cycles.* (Berkeley: Univ. of California Press).

Miyazaki, H. (1984). 'Internal Bargaining, Labor Contracts, and a Marshallian Theory of the Firm', *American Economic Review*, 74/3.

Modigliani, F., and Brumberg, R. (1954). 'Utility Analysis and the Consumption Function: An Interpretation of Cross-Section Data', in K. Kurihara, *Post Keynesian Economics* (New Brunswick: Rutgers Univ. Press).

Monti, M., and Siracusano, B. (1979). 'The Public Sector's Financial Intermediation, the Composition of Credit and the Allocation of Resources', *Review of Economic Conditions in Italy*, no. 2, pp. 223–53.

—— Cesarini, F., and Scognamiglio, C. (1983). *Report on the Italian Credit and Financial System*, special issue of *Banca Nazionale del Lavoro Quarterly*.

Morgan, B. (1986). *Can the UK be as Abnormal as Sweden*, paper presented to the SER/ECSTRA Conf. (Nov.).

Morgan, E. V. (1966). 'Is Inflation Inevitable?', *Economic Journal*, 76 (Mar.).

Morgan, K. (1984). *Labour in Power 1945–1951* (New York: OUP).

Morishima, M. (1982). *Why has Japan 'Succeeded'?: Western Technology and Japanese Ethos* (Cambridge: CUP).

Muller, P., and Price, R. (1984). 'Structural Budget Deficits and Fiscal Stance', OECD Economics and Statistics Dept., Working Papers (Paris: OECD).

Nakagawa, K. (ed.) (1979). *Labor and Management: Proceedings of the Fourth Fuji Conference*, International Conference on Business History, Fuji (Tokyo: Univ. of Tokyo Press).

Nakane, C. (1979). *Japanese Society* (Berkeley: Univ. of California Press).

Naples, M. (1986). 'The unraveling of the Union-Capital Truce and the U.S. Industrial Productivity Crisis', *Review of Radical Political Economics*, 18/1 & 2, pp. 110–31.

Nardozzi, G. (1981). 'Accumulazione di Capitale e Politica Monetaria', in G. Lunghini, *Scelte Politiche e Teori Economiche in Italia* (Turin: Einaudi).

—— (1983). 'Structural Trends of Financial Systems and Capital Accumulation: France, Germany, Italy', *Economic Papers*, 14 (Brussels: Commission of the European Communities).

Newell, A., and Symons, J. (1987). *Corporatism, the Laissez-Faire and the*

Rise in Unemployment, Discussion Papers in Economics, no. 87–05 (London: Univ. College).

Noble, D. F. (1984). *Forces of Production* (New York: OUP).

Nordhaus, W. (1983). 'Chaos and Confusion: The International Economy Today', in J. Tobin. *Macroeconomics, Prices and Quantities* (Oxford: Blackwell).

OECD (1961). *The Problem of Rising Prices* (Paris: OECD).

—— (1978). *Public Expenditure Trends*, Studies in Resource Allocation, no. 5 (Paris: OECD).

—— (1979). *Collective Bargaining and Government Policies* (Paris: OECD).

—— (1981). *International Investment and Multinational Enterprises: Recent International Direct Investment Trends* (Paris: OECD).

—— (1982*a*). *Economic Survey of Norway* (Paris: OECD).

—— (1982*b*). *Women in Public Employment* (Paris: OECD).

—— (1984*a*). *Economic Survey of Switzerland* (Paris: OECD).

—— (1984*b*). *Merger Policies and Recent Trends in Mergers* (Paris: OECD).

—— (1985*a*). *Economic Survey of Austria* (Paris: OECD).

—— (1985*b*). *Economic Survey of Norway* (Paris: OECD).

—— (1985*c*). *Economic Survey of Sweden* (Paris: OECD).

—— (1985*d*). *Economic Survey of Switzerland* (Paris: OECD).

—— (1985*e*). *Employment Outlook* (Paris: OECD).

—— (various years). *Economic Outlook* (Paris: OECD).

—— (1985*f*). *Exchange Rate Management and the Conduct of Monetary Policy* (Paris: OECD).

—— (1985*g*). *OECD Historical Statistics 1960–83* (Paris: OECD).

—— (1985*h*). *Social Expenditure 1960–1990: Problems of Growth and Control*, OECD Social Policy Studies (Paris: OECD).

—— (1986). *Economic Survey of Japan* (Paris: OECD).

—— (1987). *Economic Survey of Japan* (Paris: OECD).

—— (various years). *OECD Financial Statistics* (Paris: OECD).

Olsen. J. P. (1983). *Organised Democracy: Political Institutions in a Welfare State—The Case of Norway* (Bergen: Universitetsforlaget).

Olson, M. (1982*a*). *The Rise and Decline of Nations* (London: Yale Univ. Press).

—— (1982*b*). 'Capital Accumulation and Productivity Growth', in R. C. O. Matthews, *Slower Growth in the Western World* (London: Heinemann).

Oppenheimer, P., and Posner, M. V. (1983). 'World Economic Expansion Amidst Monetary Turbulence', in R. C. O. Matthews and J. R. Sargent, *Contemporary Problems of Economic Policy* (London: Methuen).

—— and Reddaway, W. B. (1985). 'The United States' Economy: An Overview', *Midland Bank Review*.

Padoa-Schioppa, T. (1985). 'Qualitative Policy and Monetary Control: The Italian Experience' (*mimeo*).

Papadia, F. (1984). 'Estimates of *Ex-Ante* Real Rates of Interest in the EEC Countries and in the United States, 1973–1982', *Journal of Money, Credit and Banking*, 16/3, pp. 335–44.

Paukert, L. (1984). *The Employment and Unemployment of Women in OECD Countries* (Paris: OECD).

Penrose, E. F. (1953). *Economic Planning for the Peace* (Princeton: Princeton Univ. Press).

Perez, C. (1983). 'Structural Changes and Assimilation of New Technologies in the Economic and Social Systems', *Future* (Oct.).

Peterson, R. B. (1987). 'Swedish Collective Bargaining—A Changing Scene', *British Journal of Industrial Relations*, 25/1.

Petit, P. (1986). 'Full-Employment Policies in Stagnation: France in the 1980s', *Cambridge Journal of Economics*, 10/4, pp. 393–406.

Piore, M. J., and Sabel, C. F. (1984). *The Second Industrial Divide: Possibilities of Prosperity* (New York: Basic Books).

Pollard, S. (1982). *The Wasting of the British Economy* (London: Croom Helm).

Prais, S. (1981). *Productivity and Industrial Structure* (Cambridge: CUP).

Pressnell, L. S. (ed.) (1973). *Money and Banking in Japan*, Bank of Japan Economic Research Dept., trans. by S. Nishimura (London: Macmillan).

Price, R., and Muller, P. (1984). 'Structural Budget Indicators and the Interpretation of Fiscal Policy Stance in OECD Economies', *OECD Economic Studies* (Autumn), pp. 28–71.

Raymond, R. (1982). 'The Formulation and Implementation of Monetary Policy in France', in P. Meek (1982), pp. 105–17.

Rebitzer, J. (1987). 'Unemployment, Long-term Employment Relations, and Productivity Growth', *Review of Economics and Statistics*, LXII, 4.

Revell, J. (1979). *Inflation and Financial Institutions* (London: Financial Times).

Rey, G. M. (1982). 'Italy', in A. Boltho (1982), pp. 502–27.

Robinson, J. (1956). *The Accumulation of Capital* (3rd edn., 1969, London: Macmillian).

—— (1962). *Essays in the Theory of Economic Growth* (London: Macmillan).

Roemer, J. E. (1978). 'Marxian Models of Reproduction and Accumulation', *Cambridge Journal of Economics*, 2/1.

Rohlen, T. (1975). 'The Company Work Group', in E. Vogel, *Modern Japanese Organization and Decision-making* (Berkeley: Univ. of California Press).

Rowthorn, R. E. (1977). 'Conflict, Inflation and Money', *Cambridge Journal of Economics* 1/3.

—— (1980). *Capitalism, Conflict, and Inflation: Essays in Political Economy* (London: Lawrence & Wishart).

—— (1982). 'Demand, Real Wages, and Economic Growth', *Studi Economici*, 18, pp. 3–53.

—— and Hymer, S. (1971). *International Big Business, 1957–67* (Cambridge: CUP).

—— and Wells, J. (1987). *Deindustrialisation and Foreign Trade* (Cambridge: CUP).

Rybczynski, T. M. (1984). 'Industrial Finance System in Europe, U.S. and Japan', *Journal of Economic Behavior and Organization*, 5, pp. 275–86.

Sabel, C. (1982). *Work and Politics* (Cambridge: CUP).

Sachs, J. (1979). 'Wages, Profits, and Macroeconomic Adjustment: A Comparative Study', *Brookings Papers on Economic Activity*, 2, pp. 269–332.

—— and Wyplosz, C. (1986). 'The Economic Consequences of President Mitterrand', *Economic Policy*, 1/2, pp. 261–322.

Sakamoto, K. (1985). *Technological Innovation and the Structure of the Firm* (in Japanese) (Kyoto: Minerva).

Salop, S. C. (1979). 'A Model of the Natural Rate of Unemployment', *American Economic Review*, 69/1, pp. 117–25.

Salter, W. G. (1959). *Productivity and Technical Change* (Cambridge: CUP).

Salvati, M. (1981). 'May 1968 and the Hot Autumn of 1969: The Responses of Two Ruling Classes', in S. D. Berger, *Organizing Interests in Western Europe* (Cambridge: CUP).

—— (1985). 'The Italian Inflation', in L. Lindberg and C. Maier (1985), pp. 509–63.

Santilli, G. (1985). 'L'automatisation comme forme de contrôle social', *Travail*, no. 8 (June).

Santori, G. J. (1986). 'The Effects of Inflation on Commercial Banks', *Federal Reserve of St. Louis Review* (Mar.), pp. 15–86.

Sargent, J. R. (1982). 'Capital Accumulation and Productivity Growth', in R. C. O. Matthews, *Slower Growth in Western World* (London: Heinemann).

Sautter, C. (1982). 'France', in A. Boltho (1982), pp. 449–71.

Savage, L. (1954). *The Foundations of Statistics* (New York: Wiley).

Sawyer, M. (1982). 'Income Distribution and the Welfare State', in A. Boltho (1982).

Sayer, A. (1985). 'New Developments in Manufacturing and their Spatial Implication: From Flexible Manufacturing to Just-in-Time', Lesbos (Greece) Conference, *Spatial Structure and Social Process* (Aug.).

Sayers, R. S. (1976). *The Bank of England 1891–1944* (London: OUP).

Scammell, W. M. (1983). *The International Economy since 1945* (2nd edn., London: Macmillian).

Schmidt, M. G. (1985). 'The Politics of Labour Market Policy', paper prepared for World Congress of the International Political Science Association.

Schoer, K. (1987). 'Part-time Employment: Britain and West Germany', *Cambridge Journal of Economics* 11/1.

Schor, J. (1983). 'Social Welfare Benefits and the Rise of Labour Militance: Reinterpreting the Strike Waves of 1968–1970', paper presented at Annual Meeting of Council for European Studies, Washington, DC.

—— (1985*a*). 'Wage Flexibility, Social Welfare Expenditures and Monetary Restrictiveness', in M. Jarsulic, *Money and Macro Policy* (Boston, Mass.: Kluwer-Nijhoff).

—— (1985*b*). 'Changes in the Cyclical Pattern of Real Wages: Evidence from Nine Countries, 1955–1980', *Economic Journal*, 95, pp. 452–68.

—— (1988). 'Does Work Intensity Respond to Macroeconomic Variables?: Evidence from British Manufacturing, 1970–1986', *Harvard Institute for Economic Research*, Discussion Paper #1379.

—— and Bowles, S. (1987). 'Employment Rents and the Incidence of Strikes', *Review of Economics and Statistics*, LXII, 4, pp. 584–92.

Servan-Schreiber, J. J. (1967). *Le Défi américain* (Paris: Fayard).

Shapiro, C., and Stiglitz, J. E. (1984). 'Equilibrium Unemployment as a Worker Discipline Device', *American Economic Review*, 74/3, pp. 433–44.

Shonfield, A. (1968). *Modern Capitalism* (Oxford: OUP).

Singh, A. (1977). 'The U.K. Industry and the World Economy: A Case of De-industrialisation?' *Cambridge Journal of Economics*, 1/2.

—— (1981). 'Third World Industrialisation and the Structure of the World Economy', in D. Currie and associates, *Microeconomic Analysis: Essays in Microeconomics and Development* (London: Croom Helm).

—— (1984). 'The Interrupted Industrial Revolution of the Third World Problems and Prospects for Resumption', *Industry and Development*, 12, pp. 43–68.

—— (1986). 'The World Economic Crisis, Stabilisation and Structural Adjustment: An Overview', *Labour and Society*.

—— (1987). 'Manufacturing and Deindustrialisation', in J. Eatwell, M. Milgate, and P. Newman, *The New Palgrave* (London: Macmillan).

Solomon, E. (1984). *International Patterns of Inflation: A Study in Contrasts* (New York: The Conference Board), Report no. 853.

Soskice, D. (1978). 'Strike Waves and Wage Explosions, 1968–1970: An Economic Interpretation', in C. Crouch and A. Pizzorno (1978).

Spaventa, L. (1983). 'Two Letters of Intent: External Crises and Stabilization Policy, Italy, 1973–77', in J. Williamson, *IMF Conditionality* (Washington, DC: Institute for International Economics).

—— (1985). 'Adjustment Plans, Fiscal Policy and Monetary Policy', *Review of Economic Conditions in Italy*, no. 1, pp. 9–35.

Spero, J. E. (1977). *The Politics of International Economic Relations* (London: Allen & Unwin).

Stephens, J. D. (1979). *The Transition from Capitalism to Socialism* (London: Macmillan).

Stiglitz, J. E., and Weiss, A. (1981). 'Credit Rationing in Markets with Imperfect Information', *American Economic Review*, 71/3, pp. 393–410.

Stokman, F., Zeigler R., and Scott, J. (eds.) (1984). *Corporations and Corporate Power* (Oxford: Polity Press).

Streeten, P. (1962). 'Wages, Prices and Productivity', *Kyklos*, 15, pp. 723–31.

Surrey, M. (1982). 'United Kingdom', in A. Boltho (1987), pp. 528–53.

Suzuki, Y. (1980). *Money and Banking in Contemporary Japan* (New Haven: Yale Univ. Press).

—— (1986). *Money, Finance, and Macroeconomic Performance in Japan* (New Haven: Yale Univ. Press).

Sweezy, P. M. (1939). 'Demand under Conditions of Oligopoly', *Journal of Political Economy*, 74/4.

Tarling, R., and Wilkinson, F. (1985). 'Mark-up Pricing, Inflation and Distributional Shares: a Note', *Cambridge Journal of Economics*, 9/2, pp. 179–86.

Taylor, L. (1985). 'A Stagnationist Model of Economic Growth', *Cambridge Journal of Economics*, 9/4, pp. 383–403.

Tew, J. H. B. (1979). 'Policies Aimed at Improving the Balance of Payments', in F. Blackaby (1979).

Therborn, G. (1986). *Why Some Peoples are More Unemployed than Others* (London: Verso).

Thompson, E. P. (1963). *The Making of the English Working Class* (New York: Vintage Books).

Thygesen, N. (1982). 'Monetary Policy', in A. Boltho (1982), pp. 329–64.

Tobin, J. (1969). 'A General Equilibrium Approach to Monetary Theory', *Journal of Money, Credit, and Banking*, 1, pp. 15–29.

Triffin, R. (1961). *Gold and the Dollar Crisis* (New Haven: Yale Univ. Press).

Turner, H. A. T., and Jackson, D. A. S. (1970). 'On the Determination of the General Wage Level—A World Analysis; or "Unlimited Labour Forever"', *Economic Journal*, 80/4, pp. 827–49.

Tylecote, A. (1981). *The Causes of the Present Inflation* (London: Macmillan).

Ulman, L., and Flanagan, R. J. (1971). *Wage Restraint: A Study of Incomes Policies in Western Europe* (Berkeley: Univ. of California Press).

UNCTAD (1981). *Trade and Development Report 1981* (New York: United Nations).

UNECE (1955). *Economic Survey of Europe* (Geneva: United Nations).

UNIDO (1985). *Industry in the 1980s* (New York: United Nations).

United Nations (1972). *Economic Survey of Europe in 1971, Part 1: The European Economy from the 1950s to the 1970s* (New York: United Nations).

—— (1978). *Transnational Corporations in the World Development: A Re-*

examination (New York: United Nations).

Ure, A. (1835). *The Philosophy of Manufactures* (London: Charles Knight).

Utton, M. A., and Morgan, A. D. (1983). *Concentration and Foreign Trade* (Cambridge: CUP).

Uusitalo, P. (1984). 'Monetarism, Keynesianism and the Institutional Status of Central Banks', *Acta Sociologica*, 27, pp. 31–50.

Van der Beugel, E. H. (1966). *From Marhshall Aid to Atlantic Partnership* (Amsterdam: Elsevier).

Van Dormel, A. (1978). *Bretton Woods: Birth of a Monetary System* (New York: Holmes & Meier).

Vernon, R. (1977). *Storm over the Multinationals: The Real Issues* (Cambridge, Mass.: Harvard Univ. Press).

Viner, J. (1936). 'Mr. Keynes on the Causes of Unemployment. A Review', *Quarterly Journal of Economics*, 51/1, pp. 147–67.

Wallraf, G. (1985). *Ganz Unten* (Cologne: Tiepenhauser & Witsch).

Walsh, K. (1983). *Strikes in Europe and the United States* (New York: St Martin's Press).

Walton, R. E. (1985). 'From Control to Commitment in the Workplace', *Harvard Business Review* (Mar./Apr.).

Weisskopf, T. (1979). 'Marxian Crisis Theory and the Falling Rate of Profit'. *Cambridge Journal of Economics*, 3/4, pp. 341–78.

—— (1985). 'Sources of Profit Rate Decline in the Advanced Capitalist Economies' (Ann Arbor: *mimeo*).

—— (1987). 'The Effect of Unemployment on Labour Productivity: An International Comparison', *International Review of Applied Economics*, 1.

—— and Gordon, D. and Bowles, S. (1982). 'Long Swings and the Non-reproductive Cycle', *American Economic Review*, 73/2, pp. 151–7.

—— and Gordon, D. and Bowles, S. (1983). 'Hearts and Minds: A Social Model of U.S. Productivity Growth', *Brookings Papers on Economic Activity*, 2, pp. 381–450.

Weitzman, M. (1984). *The Share Economy* (Cambridge, Mass.: Harvard Univ. Press).

Willett, T. (ed.) (1987). *Political Business Cycles: The Political Economy of Money, Inflation, and Unemployment* (Durham, NC: Duke Univ. Press).

Williamson, O. E. (1975) *Markets and Hierarchies: Analysis and Anti-Trust Implication* (New York: Free Press).

—— (1985). *The Economic Institutions of Capitalism* (New York: Free Press).

Williamson, P. J. (1985). *Varieties of Corporatism—A Conceptual Discussion* (Cambridge: CUP).

Wood, G. E. (1983). 'The Monetary Policy Decision Process in the United Kingdom', in D. Hodgman (1983), pp. 93–113.

World Bank (1981). *World Development Report* (Washington, DC: World Bank).

—— (1985). *World Development Report* (Washington, DC: World Bank).

—— (1978). *World Development Report* (Oxford: OUP).

Yamamura, K. (1985). 'The Cost of Rapid Growth and Capitalist Democracy in Japan', in L. Lindberg and C. Maier (1985), pp. 467–508.

Yellen, J. L. (1984), 'Efficiency Wage Models of Unemployment', *American Economic Review* 74 (May), pp. 200–5.

Zylberberg, A. and Perrot-Dormont, P. (1986). 'Flexibilité du marche du travail: analyses en termes de salarie d'efficience', *colloque AFSE*, 22–23 September.

Index

Index compiled by Peva Keane